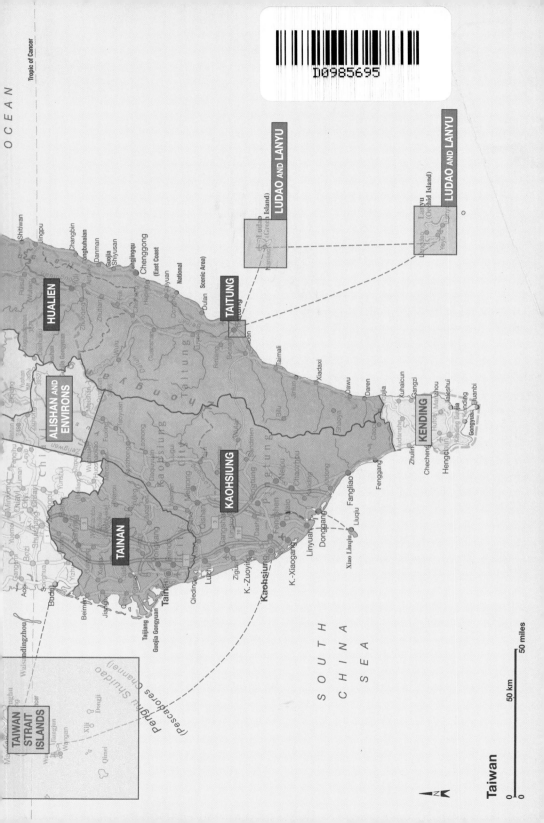

Taiwan

INSIGHT ⊙ GUIDES

TAIWAN

www.insightguides.com/Taiwan

⊙ Walking Eye App

YOUR FREE DESTINATION CONTENT AND EBOOK AVAILABLE THROUGH THE WALKING EYE APP

Your guide now includes a free eBook and destination content for your chosen destination, all for the same great price as before. Simply download the Walking Eye App from the App Store or Google Play to access your free eBook and destination content.

HOW THE WALKING EYE APP WORKS

Through the Walking Eye App, you can purchase a range of eBooks and destination content. However, when you buy this book, you can download the corresponding eBook and destination content for free. Just see below in the grey panels where to find your free content and then scan the QR code at the bottom of this page.

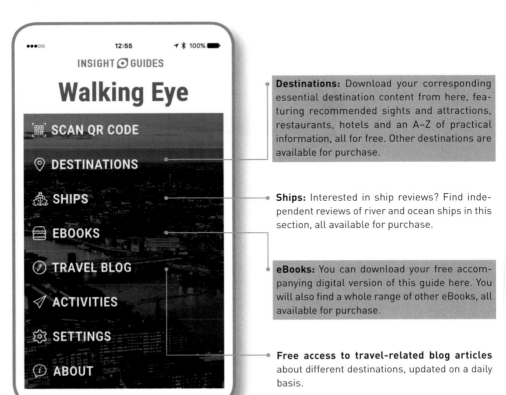

Destinations: Download your corresponding essential destination content from here, featuring recommended sights and attractions, restaurants, hotels and an A–Z of practical information, all for free. Other destinations are available for purchase.

Ships: Interested in ship reviews? Find independent reviews of river and ocean ships in this section, all available for purchase.

eBooks: You can download your free accompanying digital version of this guide here. You will also find a whole range of other eBooks, all available for purchase.

Free access to travel-related blog articles about different destinations, updated on a daily basis.

HOW THE DESTINATION CONTENT WORKS

Each destination includes a short introduction, an A–Z of practical information and recommended points of interest, split into 4 different categories:
- Highlights
- Accommodation
- Eating out
- What to do

You can view the location of every point of interest and save it by adding it to your Favourites. In the 'Around Me' section you can view all the points of interest within 5km.

HOW THE EBOOKS WORK

The eBooks are provided in EPUB file format. Please note that you will need an eBook reader installed on your device to open the file. Many devices come with this as standard, but you may still need to install one manually from Google Play.

The eBook content is identical to the content in the printed guide.

HOW TO DOWNLOAD THE WALKING EYE APP

1. Download the Walking Eye App from the App Store or Google Play.
2. Open the app and select the scanning function from the main menu.
3. Scan the QR code on this page – you will then be asked a security question to verify ownership of the book.
4. Once this has been verified, you will see your eBook and destination content in the purchased ebook and destination sections, where you will be able to download them.

Other destination apps and eBooks are available for purchase separately or are free with the purchase of the Insight Guide book.

Contents

THE BEST OF TAIWAN: TOP ATTRACTIONS

From dramatic mountain landscapes to white-sand beaches, via some of the world's best food and its finest collection of classical Chinese architecture, here is a shortlist of Taiwan's most alluring attractions.

△ **Chiang Kai-shek Memorial**. Built in memory of the general-issimo who long ruled over Taiwan, this is a grand architectural masterpiece built on an imperial scale that rivals Beijing's Forbidden Palace for magnifi-cence. See page 144.

△ **Cycling**. A high-quality nationwide system of dedicated paths and lanes has been built. Circle the entire city of Taipei by riverside, and head to the north coast, on inexpensive rental bikes. See page 189.

◁ **Taipei 101**. Soaring 101 stories and for a time the world's highest building, this is a wonder of engineering that offers tremendous views from its observa-tion deck near the top. See page 137.

△ **Taroko Gorge**. A deep, breathtaking 19km (12-mile) -long chasm of lofty, marble-laced cliffs and a cascading river strewn with massive boulders, traversed by a slow highway at the bottom literally chiseled from sheer rock. See page 279.

△ **Kending National Park**. At Taiwan's tropical southern tip, this top tourist destination with an emphasis on conservation is a natural playground of upraised coral, exotic flora and fauna, sandy beaches, and blue-water recreation. See page 260.

△ **Longshan Temple**. When China was busily destroying its cultural heritage, Taiwan's was being preserved and celebrated. Taipei's Longshan Temple is a place of beautiful art and ornate ritual. See page 141.

◁ **Yangmingshan National Park**. Just 40 minutes from downtown Taipei, overlooking the city, this is a large, easily reached getaway of volcanic landscapes, hot springs, pleasant trails, and colorful bird and butterfly life. See page 161.

▷ **National Palace Museum**. Home to the world's greatest repository of Chinese art, collected over the course of a thousand years by China's emperors, with approximately 700,000 individual works, each priceless. See page 149.

△ **Food**. The country's history and location has made it a crossroads of humanity – and a grand gourmet bazaar. The best initiation to Taiwan's fantastic traditional snack culture is Taipei's incredibly diversified Shilin Night Market. See page 133.

▽ **Matsu Islands**. The remote Matsu Islands in Taiwan's straits, within sight of China, are a living museum of military and traditional East Fujian history. See page 233.

THE BEST OF TAIWAN: EDITOR'S CHOICE

Mountain trails and railways, traditional markets and folk arts, and Taiwan's tea culture and tribal cultures are just some of the attractions of this small but endlessly diverse country. Here, at a glance, are the editor's top tips for making the most of your visit.

ONLY IN TAIWAN

Alishan Forest Railway. One of the world's only three remaining alpine railways, this tourist favorite presents both first-rate engineering feats and breathtaking mountain canvases. See page 225.

Glove puppetry. This colorful traditional art form is enjoying a renaissance, with TV shows and dedicated museums where house troupes present tourist-friendly shows. See page 78.

Night markets. Busy, colorful, and dirt cheap, these much-loved gathering spots present a whirlwind tour of Taiwan's dazzling range of traditional snack foods. See page 146.

Indigenous tribal culture. The distinctive cultures of the country's 14 tribes can be explored in quality museums, theme parks, and tourist-welcoming tribal villages. See page 57.

Hot springs. Many of the over 100 hot-spring locations in this land of rugged mountains have been developed into rustic, picturesque resorts. See page 154.

Tea plantations. Taiwan grows some of the world's best teas, and plantations – often perched on slopes in dramatic locations – offer inviting teahouses. See pages 157 and 210

Mountain vistas. The high ranges, home to popular parks and scenic areas, thrill you with a never-ending roll-out of sublimely beautiful panoramas. See pages 161 and 225.

Grazing buffalo.

BEST HIKES AND TRAILS

Qingtiangang. Found high on Yangmingshan, this wide plateau with ocean views passes fumaroles and idyllic pastures of water buffalo. See page 164.

Qixingshan Trail. This walk to Yangmingshan's highest peak takes hikers past fumaroles and through bamboo thickets and thick silvergrass to a widescreen Taipei Basin view. See page 164.

Yushan. With 11 peaks to climb, the overnight treks here to the roof of the island reward you with majestic views. See page 228.

Butterfly Corridor. The most popular trail on Yang-mingshan, colored pastel shades with many of the park's 151 species of butterfly. See page 163.

Qilai Ridge. Qilai Ridge is one of the most popular and challenging of the hiking locations in the Central Mountain Range. See page 229.

Caoling Historic Trail. The last coastal section of the pioneer trail over the hills from Taipei to Yilan, with imperial-era relics and striking ocean vistas. See page 178.

Baiyang Falls Trail. Taroko Gorge's most popular trail takes you through a tunnel bored through cliff and a marble-streaked canyon to a lovely high waterfall. See page 284.

An elaborate glove puppet performance.

BEST ARCHITECTURE

Taipei's Grand Hotel.

The Grand Hotel.
This classical Chinese palace-style artwork, sitting on a plateau overlooking Taipei, was long the city's defining icon. See page 132.
85 Sky Tower.
Looking like a giant rocket about to launch, the tower houses a hotel in the upper half. Many love it, many hate it. See page 249.
Lin Family Mansion and Garden. See how the rich lived hundreds of years

ago in an expansive preserved residential complex of great esthetic sophistication. See page 135.
Baoan Temple. This architectural masterpiece, featuring intricate stone and wood carving, is among Taiwan's most elaborate temples. See page 133.
Longshan Temple. Built in the 1730s, this is among the world's premier examples of exquisite Chinese temple art. See page 141.
Lin Family Gardens in Wufeng. Called one of the Four Great Gardens of Taiwan, this grand complex was home to central Taiwan's most powerful family in imperial days. See page 196.
Chung Tai Chan Monastery. This monumental Buddhist complex, which can be seen from throughout the Puli Basin, is bathed in glowing light at night. See page 206.

BEST VIEWS

Alishan. At 2,400 meters (7,875ft) up, witness sparkling sunrises over majestic Yushan and other great peaks, and the renowned 'sea of clouds' at your feet. See page 225.
Jiufen. A former mining town now filled with artists and old teahouses, buildings clinging to the steep hillside, the magnificent Pacific far below. See page 175.
Muzha Tourist Tea Plantations. The city sparkles and twinkles beneath your feet at night from the scores of teahouses perched on the highest slopes. See page 157.
Suao-Hualien Highway. One of the world's most exhilarating drives, etched from cliffs thousands of meters high rising straight up from the sea. See page 270.
Taipei 101 Observatory. On the 89th floor, Taipei becomes a giant scale

model, and you must look down to see toy-like planes landing at the local airport. See page 137.
Four Beasts Mountain. A mountain spur of four low peaks poking into Taipei's east side, the whole city is laid out before you like a carpet. See page 156.
Hehuanshan. The pass here is Taiwan's highest public road point, at 3,275 meters (10,745ft), and offers tremendous down-island eye-level views of scores of peaks past faraway Yushan. See page 201.

Taiwanese tea plantation terraces.

BEST FESTIVALS

Birthday of the City God. Enjoy raucous processions, opera, puppet shows, drumming, and other fun at Taipei's Xiahai City God Temple. See page 139.
Dajia Mazu. A celebration of Taiwan's most popular deity, the Goddess of the Sea, who protects sailors and fishermen. Colorful pageantry, fireworks, massive crowds. See page 66.

Spring Scream Festival. This is no traditional music party. It's an annual multi-day alfresco rock festival set in Kenting National Park. See page 263.
Baosheng Cultural Festival. This lively weeks-long tribute to the God of Medicine features grand processions, firewalking, lion-dance, drum and martial arts troupes. See page 134.

Burning of the Plague God Boats. A unique religious festival with a full-size mock-up of a traditional junk, groaning with spirit money, fired to carry away evil. See page 247.
Keelung Ghost Festival. Each year during Ghost Month, Keelung stages Taiwan's most colorful sacrificial processions, rituals, and feasts to placate visiting spirits. See page 173.

A performer at Baosheng Festival.

Dragonboat Festival at Dajia Park.

Guandu Temple's ornate roof.

Rush hour on bustling Taipei's Metro.

THE BEAUTIFUL ISLAND

This fertile island of tremendous natural esthetics
is home to a young and thriving democracy –
the first in the Chinese-speaking world.

Sunset over Dansui.

Taiwan's place in the popular imagination of the West has long been as a producer of computers and peripherals, as a political thorn in China's side and, more recently, as the small island that sprinted from the starting line of martial law to full-fledged democracy in little more than a decade. Its rich trove of natural scenic assets, and a vibrant culture that preserves the best of ancient traditions while passionately embracing the newest in high-tech modernity, are also now catching the attention of the international traveler.

The ruggedly mountainous island that the Portuguese named *Ilha Formosa* – the 'beautiful island' – in the 1500s is a place of countless pleasant surprises. The northern and western flatlands are densely populated, but just a short distance inland pristine mountain views await. The craggy east coast remains largely unspoilt, as are Taiwan's less-visited yet easily accessible offshore islands.

Enjoying public art in Taipei.

Lying close to China, the island became a refuge for Chinese migrants escaping legal and political persecution starting around four centuries ago, who joined the many indigenous tribes. Traders and adventurers, farmers and fishermen left behind south China's crowded coastal areas to start new lives here. They found that food grew abundantly in Taiwan's soil, a significant concern for a people accustomed to frequent famines and chronic food shortages. Furthermore, the island was fat with mineral resources – notably coal, sulfur, and iron.

Over the years, others have also come. The Dutch, Spanish, and Japanese have had colonies, and in the mid-20th century Taiwan became a refuge for those who lost the mainland to the Chinese Communist Party.

This mix of peoples has created a cultural mosaic unlike that found anywhere else on the planet. The country's natural and cultural wonders are also now more accessible to the tourist than ever before, for with the advent of democracy has come powerful pride of place, and systematic investment in tourism resources.

Note: This book uses the Hanyu Pinyin transliteration standard, the official standard in both Taiwan and China; non-Hanyu forms are used when official or more familiar.

Taiwan has considerable fertile land for farming.

LAND AND CLIMATE

A mountainous backbone, fertile plains, persistent
volcanic activity, and a complex weather system
provide the geographical backdrop to the island.

The island of Taiwan straddles the Tropic of Cancer, separated from China by the Taiwan Strait, 160km (99 miles) wide at its narrowest point. Taiwan lies 355km (221 miles) north of the Philippines and 595km (370 miles) southwest of Japan's Okinawa.

Taiwan is shaped like a tobacco leaf, with its tip pointing toward Japan. It stretches 390km (242 miles) in length and is about 140km (87 miles) wide at its broadest point. Its total area of nearly 36,000 sq km (13,900 sq miles) makes Taiwan about the size of the Netherlands.

Divisive mountains

Taiwan's most prominent topographical feature is the Central Mountain Range (Zhongyang Shanmo), a ridge of towering mountains that runs for about 270km (167 miles) of the island's length and which was formed by ancient tectonic, and, to a lesser extent, volcanic activity.

The mountain range bisects the island from north to south, covers two-thirds of the country, and is almost impenetrable because of its extreme ruggedness. More than 200 of the island's peaks rise 3,000 meters (9,843ft) or more in altitude. Taiwan's tallest peak is Yushan (Mt Jade) at 3,952 meters (12,966ft). Heavy rainfall has deeply scarred its face with rugged gorges and valleys.

A narrow valley of rich alluvial soil, 160km (99 miles) long, separates the middle bulge of mountains from a smaller line of crests that fronts the east coast. In many areas of the east coast cliffs drop sharply to the sea, forming the island's most spectacular scenery. The Central Cross-Island Highway dramatically slices its way through the central range to these east-coast escarpments.

Primeval plate activity pushed the island up from under the sea, as evidenced by coral from prehistoric seabeds lodged in igneous rock up

A sharp drop at Cape Longdong.

to 610 meters (2,000ft) high in the hills. While the related fiery volcanic activity ended eons ago, bubbling pools of hot sulfurous water and hissing steam vents still punctuate the terrain.

The most densely populated areas of Taiwan are the plains, tablelands and basins. The broad, sea-level plains that spread across the west of Taiwan are fed by short rivers that bring rainwater and alluvial soil from the mountains, making them extremely fertile. The largest plain is the Chianan (Jianan) Plain, which extends from Changhua to Kaohsiung, a distance of 180km (112 miles), and measuring 48km (30 miles) at its widest point. Taipei, Taichung, and Puli are situated in basins. The area stretching between Taoyuan and Hsinchu, on the other hand, is tableland.

Offshore islands

The rivers flowing down from the mountains into the western plains of Taiwan not only deposit fertile alluvial soil but also turn much of the western coast into tidal mud flats, a feature that military strategists claim would make the island very difficult to invade. Easier targets might be two island groups administered by Taiwan in the Taiwan Strait, which are much closer to China than to Taipei. Small, hilly Kinmen (Quemoy) is close enough to China's Fujian province (only 2,310 meters/yds) to afford views of the Chinese city of Xiamen,

The 1999 earthquake caused significant damage.

while Matsu lies close to the mouth of Fujian's Min River.

Also prominent are the Penghu Islands, or Pescadores, an archipelago of some 64 small islands located about midway between China and Taiwan and primarily formed by volcanic action forcing up basalt from the sea floor.

Taiwan is still characterized by seismological instability. The island sits where two plates grind together (the Eurasian Plate is folding under the Philippine Sea Plate at a rate of about 7cm/3ins a year), building up enormous pressure that occasionally results in earthquakes.

Hualien is closest to what geologists refer to as the subduction zone between the two plates, and indeed it is the east of Taiwan, in the vicinity of Hualien, that is most often rattled by tremors. Nevertheless, the entire island is riddled with fault lines, and major earthquakes (Taiwan has recorded 19 quakes measuring over 7 on the Richter scale since 1906) can strike anywhere on the island, the biggest in recent history being the 9-21 (September 21) earthquake of 1999, which measured 7.3 on the scale.

Climate

Due to Taiwan's mountainous topography, its weather is as diverse as its landscape. In the low areas the climate is subtropical and in the far south tropical, while in the heights of the Central Range the thermometer can dip to temperatures that allow snow.

There are two distinct seasons: hot (May–Oct) and cool (Nov–Mar). The island's excessive humidity exaggerates these seasonal changes. During the summer months, with average daytime temperatures in the north rising to 35°C (95°F) and humidity seldom dropping below 75 percent, the island's low-lying coastal areas seem like a giant sauna, making it a good time to escape to the relative cool of the mountains. Likewise, winter temperatures usually do not fall below 10°C (45°F), but the dampness chills. It is a good idea to bring warm clothes during the winter months, even if you are going to be spending the majority of your time in southern Taiwan.

The most pleasant times of the year are the brief spells of spring and fall, during April and May, and October and November. Skies are generally clear, nights are cool and days moderate. But, at any time of year, Taiwan's weather may change dramatically. High and low temperatures can vary as much as 10°C (15°F) from one day to the next.

TYPHOON WARNING

Even without watching the television weather reports, most Taiwanese know instinctively when a typhoon is on the way. Formed by low-pressure regions out to sea, typhoons suck Taiwan's clouds and dirty air away long before they make landfall, usually blessing the island with a day or so of brilliant sunshine. A beautiful sunny day in the months of September through October will usually have people remarking to each other about 'typhoon weather' – and invariably they're right. Two or three days later the island is battening down, and scouring winds will send torrential downpours lashing down on anyone foolhardy enough to venture outdoors.

Nature wrings an average annual rainfall level of 2,500mm to 5,000mm (100 to 200ins) from the cloak of humidity that hangs over Taiwan. At higher elevations, the average rainfall can be five times as great.

The northeast winter monsoon and the southwest summer monsoon provide the moisture. The northeast monsoon moves in from late October to late March, causing rain in the windward reaches of northeast Taiwan. The southwest monsoon takes its turn from early May until late September, causing wet weather in the south while the north enjoys drier spells. Nevertheless,

The earthquake on September 21, 1991 gave Taiwan such a shaking that it is thought that Yushan, the island's highest peak, may have gained a few meters in altitude.

than a half-dozen typhoons may cross or skirt Taiwan. At roughly three- to four-year intervals, a typhoon of major proportions crashes into Taiwan, with wind speeds of up to 160kmh (99mph) or more. Such fierce storms can capsize ships, flood low-lying city areas, trigger huge landslides,

Sheltering from the rain in Taipei.

it is not entirely wise to rely on such general formulations in predicting Taiwan's weather. Rain – often British-style incessant drizzle – is something to be prepared for at any time of the year.

The typhoon season

The most feared aberrations in Taiwan's moody weather are typhoons. *Taifeng* (the English word derives from the Chinese), meaning 'great wind,' tend to swell up in the open waters of the western Pacific off the Indonesian archipelago, then sweep through the Philippines and storm northwards toward Japan, often making landfall on Taiwan and/or the southern Chinese mainland.

The typhoon season lasts from mid-August until early October. During this time, no fewer

uproot trees, and blow down dwellings.

One of the worst typhoons to hit Taiwan occurred in August 1911. Barometric pressure at the southern city of Kaohsiung fell below 71cm (28ins), reportedly the lowest reading ever recorded in Taiwan. Winds of 250kmh (155mph) battered the island. And in 1968, a typhoon drowned downtown Taipei in nearly 4 meters (13ft) of water, and made rowboats the only form of practicable transportation.

Visitors caught in Taiwan during a typhoon need not panic, however. Taiwan's new steel-and-concrete structures and modern hotels are generally immune to any serious damage. But bear in mind that, while it's safe to watch from the windows, it is still risky to walk the streets.

A depiction on silk of a procession of the Ming emperor, Wuzong.

DECISIVE DATES

Island settlement

206 BC
The oldest Chinese historical record referring to Taiwan indicates the island was called the 'Land of Yangzhou.'

AD 239
The Chinese Kingdom of Wu sends a 10,000-man expeditionary force.

Ilha Formosa

15th and 16th centuries
Taiwan becomes a haven for pirates and traders. Portuguese sailors dub it *Ilha Formosa*, or 'beautiful island.'

1593
The first Japanese attempt to create a Taiwan colony.

Colonial interests

1622
Dutch forces capture the Pescadores archipelago (Penghu Islands) and attempt to control the Taiwan Strait.

1624
At Chinese instigation the Dutch evacuate the Pescadores and establish a colony on Taiwan.

1626
Spanish forces seize Keelung and from there expand control in northern Taiwan.

1642
The Dutch expel the Spanish, consolidating control over the island.

The Zheng Dynasty

1661
Zheng Cheng-gong (Koxinga) attacks, abruptly ending Dutch rule.

1662
Koxinga dies. His descendants rule until 1683, when defeated by the Manchu Qing dynasty.

Colonial intrusions

1839
China takes up arms to suppress the foreign opium trade in Canton (Guangzhou).

1858
Treaty ending the Second Opium War opens four Taiwanese ports to foreign trade.

1867
Foreign traders settle in northern Taiwan at Danshui and Keelung. Trade booms, notably in tea.

Japanese occupation

1874
The Japanese mount a punitive campaign against south Taiwan aborigines for killing Japanese sailors.

1895
The Treaty of Shimonoseki concludes the 1894-1895 Japanese War; Taiwan is ceded to Japan.

1945
Taiwan is taken over by the Republic of China after Japan's defeat in World War II.

1947
February 28 Incident sparks suppression and mass killing of Taiwanese by Kuomintang (Guomindang); beginning of White Terror period.

1949
The Republic of China government flees to Taiwan after defeat on the mainland.

American involvement

1950
The Korean War breaks out, Taiwan is placed under American protection against Communist attack, and substantial economic aid begins.

1955
The US and Taiwan ratify the Sino-American Mutual Defense Treaty.

1958
The second Offshore Island Crisis begins with the People's

A map of the Island Formosa and the Pescadores, c. 1640.

Chiang Kai-shek (standing) with his mentor, Dr Sun Yat-sen, 1924.

Republic of China bombarding Kinmen.

1959
Taiwan experiences its worst floods for more than half a century.

1965
Preferential trade status with the US is terminated; economic progress nevertheless accelerates.

1971
The Republic of China loses its United Nations membership, with the China seat given to the PRC.

1975
Chiang Kai-shek dies.

The growth of democracy
1978
Chiang Ching-kuo (Jiang Jing-guo), Chiang Kai-shek's son, is elected president. The US recognizes the People's Republic of China, and ends official diplomatic relations with Taiwan.

1979
The Kaohsiung Incident galvanizes the Taiwanese against martial law.

1980
The US–Republic of China Defense Treaty is terminated.

1986
The Democratic Progressive Party (DPP) establishes itself as an opposition force.

1987
Martial law is lifted.

1988
President Chiang Ching-kuo dies; the National Assembly elects Lee Teng-hui (Li Deng-hui), the first Taiwan-born president.

1991
Taiwan replaces Japan and the US as the number one investor in the People's Republic.

Modern era
1993
The first official governmental contacts between Taipei and Beijing take place in Singapore.

1996
Taiwan holds its first fully democratic presidential elections; Lee Teng-hui wins.

2000
The DPP's Chen Shui-bian is elected president, ending five-plus decades of KMT rule.

2001
DPP emerges as largest party in legislative elections.

2002
Taiwan gains entry into WTO.

2004
Chen Shui-bian pulls out a surprise victory against a united KMT-led opposition; street protests ensue.

2008
The KMT comes back into power with pro-China Ma Ying-jeou elected president; tensions with China ease. The first direct Taiwan-China flights since the late 1940s are inaugurated.

2010
Taiwan and China sign a landmark free-trade pact.

2012
Ma Ying-jeou wins a second term.

2016
The pro-independence DPP candidate Tsai Ing-wen wins the presidential election, becoming the first woman and first unmarried president of Taiwan.

President Tsai Ing-wen.

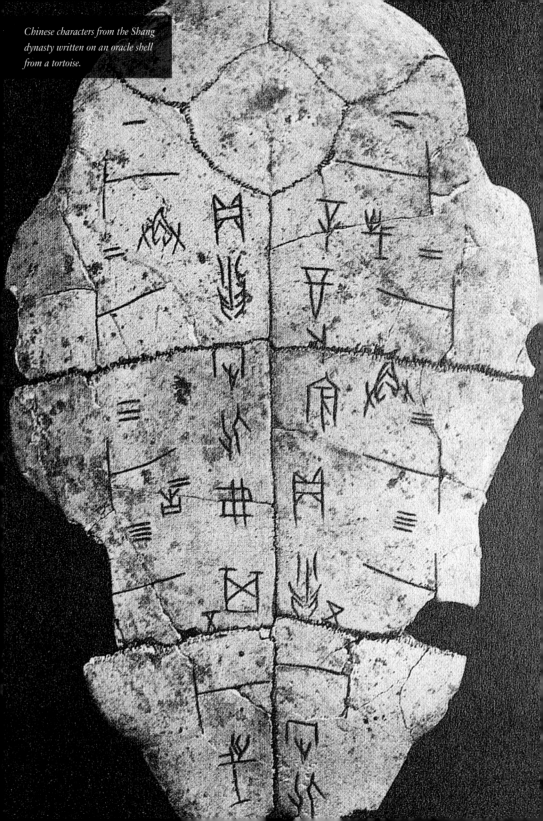

Chinese characters from the Shang dynasty written on an oracle shell from a tortoise.

ISLAND SETTLEMENT

The Portuguese may have openly declared its beauty,
but they were by no means the first or the last
people to stake a claim on this bountiful island.

Ilha formosa! Ilha formosa! Portuguese sailors shouted with admiration from their ships as they sailed past Taiwan, en route to Japan during the 16th century. The island thus became known to the West by the Portuguese word *formosa*, or beautiful.

This island off China's southeast coast has lured successive waves of people from Austronesia, Chinese immigrants from the mainland, explorers and exploiters from the West, and aggressive imperialists from Japan. All desired possession.

But of all Taiwan's suitors, China proved the best match for the feisty and fertile island. The marriage of China's sophisticated and esthetic culture with Taiwan's bountiful beauty and rich natural endowments has produced one of Asia's most dynamic lands. Like *yin* and *yang*, ancient Chinese heritage and the island's indigenous charms are the inseparable elements that define Taiwan.

Prehistoric development

Little is known about Taiwan's earliest history. Radioactive carbon dating of primitive utensils found in caves and other sites has indicated that prehistoric people appeared on the island at least 20,000 to 30,000 years ago. Archeologists believe Taiwan's links with mainland China may be just as old. They have identified four stages of prehistoric tool development that match those of the mainland. They have also identified two later stages suggesting that other prehistoric Southeast Asian cultures arrived on the southern and eastern coasts of Taiwan. These early peoples are believed to have had Malaysian and southern Chinese Miao ancestry; it has not been determined whether there is a direct line with the

Scene from Taiwan's prehistoric past.

indigenous peoples who now form an important part of Taiwan's culture.

The most ancient Chinese reference to Taiwan indicates that the island was called the Land of Yangzhou, during the rise of the Han dynasty, in 206 BC. There may even have been an attempt at that time to explore the island, according to the *Shiji* (historical records), which referred to Taiwan as Yizhou. The earliest attempt to establish a Chinese claim apparently occurred in AD 239, when the Kingdom of Wu sent a 10,000-man expeditionary force, according to the ancient *Sanguoji*, or the *History of the Three Kingdoms*.

In the early 1400s, a eunuch from the Ming court who also served as a diplomat and fleet admiral, Zheng He (Cheng Ho), reported his 'discovery' of the island to the emperor of China. But despite the obvious fertility of the land, the imperial court prevented the Ming empire's populace from emigrating to Taiwan – or elsewhere – on pain of death, out of fear of pirates and the fomenting of rebellions from abroad.

Two distinct groups of peoples were living on Taiwan at the time of the Chinese arrival. One group lived a sedentary existence on the rich alluvial plains, practicing hunting, fishing, and swidden cultivation (shifting agriculture), the majority in the central west and southwest.

The others were semi-nomadic mountain tribes. There was constant fighting among the tribes, many of which practiced ritual tattooing and headhunting.

Enter the Hakka

Although it is not known exactly when the Chinese first began to settle on Taiwan, the first mainland immigrants came from an ethnic group called the Hakka – literally 'guests' or 'strangers.' The Hakka, a minority group relentlessly persecuted in China since ancient times, were driven from Hunan province about 1,500

Bronze pitcher from China's Spring and Autumn period (722–481 BC).

A PIRATES' PARADISE

During the 15th and 16th centuries, Taiwan was a haven for marauding Chinese and Japanese pirates and freewheeling traders plying the eastern Chinese coast. The distinction between pirates and traders was gratuitous, as ships plied both trades and operated freely in Taiwan's waters. Because it was close to the trading centers and shipping lanes of China and Japan, yet free of outside political control – the populace governed itself on clan and village lines, without interference from Peking (Beijing) or elsewhere – Taiwan turned into a pirates' paradise. When times were good, they traded. When times were bad, they raided.

years ago and forced to flee to the Fujian and Guangdong coasts of the mainland. There, they successfully engaged in fishing and trading, activities that eventually brought them to the Pescadores archipelago, now known as Penghu, and then later to Taiwan. By AD 1000, some Hakka may have established themselves in the southern part of Taiwan. The Hakka primarily grew sugarcane, rice, and tea, and engaged in active trade with the mainland. Today, the Hakka rank among Taiwan's most enterprising people.

Other Chinese also set their sights on Taiwan. In the later years of the Ming dynasty (1368–1644), immigrants from Fujian province began to cross the Taiwan Strait in ever-increasing numbers. They pushed the Hakka further inland and steadily usurped the rich western plains. The settlers from Fujian adopted the term *benshengren*, which means 'this-province people,' or natives, to differentiate themselves from both the Hakka and the original indig-

> It is generally accepted that the name 'Taiwan' is the Chinese version of 'Tayouan,' what local natives called the long, thin, sandy peninsula on which the Dutch built Fort Zeelandia, in today's Tainan.

enous peoples, whom they called 'strangers.' Even today, the descendants of these early immigrants from Fujian refer to themselves as *benshengren*, thereby distinguishing themselves from the late 1940s influx of mainland refugees and their descendants, who they call *waishengren*, or 'outside-province people.'

Still, the only true natives of Taiwan are the aborigines. Like the Indians of America and the Aborigines of Australia, those not absorbed into the larger Chinese population now mostly live in relatively isolated protected areas, though many choose to live among the Han in search of work or education. The majority of Taiwan's populace, in contrast, is descended from the various groups of mainland Chinese immigrants. The Taiwanese dialect of Chinese, the mother tongue of about 70 percent of the population, is an offshoot of southern Fujianese.

Colonial interests

In 1590, the Portuguese arrived on the north coast of Taiwan, built a small fort, and established a short-lived trading settlement and port facilities. The Japanese also established a short-lived colony in 1593, after the warlord Hideyoshi Toyotomi unsuccessfully tried to conquer China by way of Korea. Hideyoshi's designs on Taiwan fared no better, as it proved too unruly to control.

This did not put off other Europeans, however. The Dutch turned to Taiwan after they failed to wrest Macau from the Portuguese. In 1622 they established themselves on the Pescadores, but in 1624, under threat of Chinese attack if they did not vacate, they established a fort and settlement on the southwestern coast of Taiwan.

The Dutch imposed heavy taxes and labor requirements on the island's inhabitants in areas they controlled, and imported missionaries to

preach Christianity. The Dutch East India Company gained exclusive commercial rights to the island, importing opium from Java (Batavia), which was part of the Dutch East Indies. The Dutch taught islanders to mix tobacco with opium and smoke it. The habit rapidly took root in Taiwan, later spreading to the mainland. (Two centuries later, opium would play a notorious role in the fall of the Qing dynasty, and would become the catalyst for war between China and Britain.)

In 1626, the Spanish took control of the natural harbor and surrounding area at Keelung,

The Dutch Fort Zeelandia (Anping Gubao), in today's Tainan, in the mid 1600s.

later building a fort in Tamsui. The jealous Dutch, wishing to achieve complete control over the island's foreign trade, finally drove the Spanish out of Taiwan in 1642. Two years later, the Manchu conquest of the mainland began, an event that exerted lasting impact on Taiwan.

Despite their heavy tax and labor demands, for a while the Dutch lived in relative harmony with both the indigenous residents of Taiwan and mainland immigrants. But after the Dutch imposed a poll tax, the Chinese revolted in 1652. The revolt was easily suppressed, with the help of native braves, with nearly 3,000 Chinese killed.

China's Ming dynasty reigned for 276 years, under 16 emperors. The creative arts and sciences flourished. But its glory faded under an administration that became increasingly corrupt. At the same time, Manchu leaders built a strong base of support and a huge army in what are today's northeastern provinces. They swept south, advancing against the crumbling Ming armies.

Before the Manchu reached Peking (Beijing), a Han Chinese rebel army took the capital. The emperor hanged himself, a humiliating final act in the saga of a glorious era. Loyalist Ming forces allowed the Manchu past the Great Wall to push the rebels from Peking, but soon

Porcelain jar from Qing dynasty, at Taipei's National Palace Museum.

found the Manchu had greater designs. As they were pushed south, the Ming loyalists brought a southeastern merchant/pirate named Zheng into their cause.

Son of Zheng

Zheng's forces, especially his navy, proved effective. He had earlier taken a Japanese wife, who bore him a son in 1624. The son inherited the Ming banner and with it a new name: Koxinga (Guoxingye) – Lord of the Imperial Surname.

With an army of 100,000 men and an armada of 3,000 ships, Koxinga carried on the mainland fight against the Manchu starting in 1646. At

one point he almost recaptured the ancient capital of Nanjing. But the Manchu finally forced Koxinga to retreat to the island bastion of Taiwan, an event that eerily foreshadowed Chiang Kai-shek's (Jiang Jie-shi) retreat across the Taiwan Strait three centuries later.

In Taiwan, Koxinga encountered the Dutch, whose leaders in Batavia (Indonesia) had discounted him as a mere pirate, incapable of mounting a serious threat. But Koxinga's spies, aided by Dutch deserters, provided valuable intelligence. In 1661, Koxinga sailed from Penghu with 30,000 armed men, engaging 600 Dutch settlers and 2,200 Dutch soldiers at the two southwestern coastal forts. Koxinga captured Fort Zeelandia (Anping Gubao), in present-day Tainan, and graciously permitted the Dutch governor and his surviving men to leave the island. Thus, Dutch rule in Taiwan ended less than four decades after it began.

Taiwan became Koxinga's personal domain. He gave the island its first formal Chinese government, turning it into a Ming enclave that continued to defy the Manchu, who by now had established firm control over the mainland. Koxinga's reign was brief but influential. He set up his court and government at Anping, and launched transport and education systems. Great strides were also made in agriculture. Tainan became the political and commercial center, and Anping grew into a prosperous harbor.

Perhaps Koxinga's greatest and most lasting contribution to Taiwan was his love for most things Chinese. His entourage included more than 1,000 scholars, artists, monks, and masters of every branch of Chinese culture. He ushered in a renaissance of Chinese laws, institutions, and customs.

Koxinga died suddenly in 1662, aged 38, mere months after his conquest of Taiwan. Centuries later, he was named a national hero and is venerated in Taiwan as a *junzi*, perfect man. His son and grandson maintained rule over Taiwan until 1683, when the Manchu finally succeeded in taking control of the island, snuffing out the last pocket of Ming patriotism. Taiwan officially became a part of the Chinese empire when the Manchu, or Qing, court conferred the status of *fu*, or prefecture, on the island. But Qing rule remained nominal at best. Manchu officials sent to govern Taiwan usually succumbed to intrigue and self-indulgence.

COLONIAL INTRUSIONS

As China's grip on Taiwan weakened, a succession of foreign powers cast hungry eyes on this strategic and fertile island and made bids for control.

Despite sometimes-strict prohibitions from the imperial court against further emigration to Taiwan, colonists continued to pour across from the mainland. During the first 150 years of Qing rule, the island's population increased sevenfold. Karl Gutzlaff, a Prussian missionary visiting Taiwan in 1831, observed: 'The island has flourished greatly since it has been in the possession of the Chinese. The rapidity with which this island has been colonized, and the advantages it affords for the colonists to throw off their allegiance, has induced the Chinese to adopt strict measures… The colonists are wealthy and unruly…'

One early point of contention between China and the West concerned the fate of shipwrecked European sailors who were frequently washed ashore on Taiwan. These involuntary visitors were routinely beaten, imprisoned and often beheaded, either by the Chinese authorities or by aborigines on the island. Whenever the Western powers petitioned the court at Peking (Beijing) to intervene in such incidents, they discovered that Peking had little real authority over island affairs, and even less interest. So Western nations resorted to gunboat diplomacy to punish locals for mistreatment of their crews, and dealt directly with the islanders rather than with Peking.

Economic potential

One of the first foreigners to recognize Taiwan's economic potential and to advocate its outright annexation was Dr William Jardine, scion of the powerful British trading firm Jardine Matheson and Company. Jardine was alarmed when China took up arms in 1839 to suppress the British opium trade in Canton (Guangzhou). He informed the British foreign

Matteo Ricci, an Italian Jesuit, was influential in the Chinese court.

secretary that 'we must proceed to take possession of three or four islands, say Formosa, Quemoy (Kinmen) and Amoy (Xiamen), in order to secure new markets and new footholds in China.'

When the first conflict, or Opium War, broke out between China and Britain, it further strained the relations between China and the West. Crews of British vessels subsequently shipwrecked off Taiwan faced even harsher treatment. The ships were plundered, and then burned. The crews were stripped naked and forced to walk painful distances to captivity.

The British were not the only foreign power to show an interest in Taiwan during the 19th century. Several American traders and diplomats also advocated annexation of the island. They included Commodore Matthew Perry, who understood Taiwan's strategic importance in East Asia. Gideon Nye, a wealthy American

> Taiwan was famously difficult to govern during the Qing dynasty, evidenced by the popular Chinese saying 'Every three years an uprising, every five years a rebellion.' The strife only began to subside in the 1860s.

Kaohsiung) in the south. During the ensuing decade, foreign trade in Taiwan grew rapidly, involving British and American firms. Primary export products were camphor, tea, rice, sugar, lumber, and coal. The primary import, sometimes exceeding exports in value, continued to be opium.

By 1867, 25 foreign traders lived in northern Taiwan at Tamsui and Keelung, and another dozen lived in the south at Tainan. Trade boomed, doubling in volume by 1869 and doubling again by 1870. Expatriate communities flourished around Taiwan's ports and they

The Qing emperor receives a foreign envoy in Peking.

merchant and a leading member of his country's expatriate community in Canton, proposed in 1857 that 'Formosa's eastern shores and southern point... in the direct route of commerce between China and California and Japan, and between Shanghai and Canton, should be protected by the United States of America.' Nye also had personal reasons for his proposal: he suspected that his brother, who mysteriously disappeared on the opium clipper *Kelpie* in 1849, had been captured and killed in Taiwan.

The treaty ending the Second Opium War, in 1858, opened four Taiwanese ports to foreign trade: Tamsui and Keelung in the north, and Taiwan Fu (now Tainan) and Takao (now

maintained close ties with their counterparts in Hong Kong, Canton, and Xiamen.

Increased violence

A negative aspect of the trade boom was the increased frequency of violent incidents, corresponding to the greater number of foreign trading vessels that called at the island's ports. Brawls between drunken foreign sailors and the local Chinese usually ignited the violence, and vendettas followed. Local magistrates refused to act in such cases, insisting that the foreigners petition authorities in Peking. But, because of Peking's lack of influence and interest in the island's affairs, nothing was accomplished through such 'legal channels.'

Yet one thing was clear to all the squabbling parties: Taiwan was indeed an alluring beauty. It was rich in resources and strategically located, but it was also untamed. There was a need for law and order that Peking could not provide. Expatriates clamored for foreign governments to step in. The Japanese did just that.

The Japanese

In 1871, a Japanese ship foundered and sank off the coast of Taiwan. Three of its crew drowned, and only 12 of the remaining crew survived. Botan aborigines slaughtered the

directly with ethnic minority tribes. But Washington had always ignored LeGendre's calls for greater American vigilance in Taiwan. So LeGendre advised Tokyo that it should prepare for war if its foreign minister's mission to Peking turned out to be unsuccessful.

Soyeshima obtained a formal audience with the Chinese emperor, a significant accomplishment. The emperor tacitly admitted that the minorities inhabiting parts of eastern and southern Taiwan were beyond his political control. All of Japan hailed that disclosure as a diplomatic victory, but Soyeshima's return to Tokyo was

The British negotiate to open China's ports to trade.

rest. When the news of the killings reached Tokyo, Japan immediately prepared to launch a punitive expedition against the Botan tribe. Only Foreign Minister Soyeshima Taneomi held back the impending attack, deciding first to try to work out a diplomatic resolution with Peking.

Soyeshima was accompanied on his trip to Peking by Charles LeGendre, an advisor to the planned military expedition to Taiwan who had earlier resigned as American consul to Amoy in order to enter the service of Japan's new Meiji emperor. LeGendre had extensive experience in the island, negotiating settlements involving several American ships wrecked there, and in some cases also dealing

MISSIONARY MAYHEM

The law and order situation in Taiwan, chaotic throughout the Qing dynasty, was further aggravated by the arrival of foreign missionaries in the early 1870s, who fanned out over the island and staked out territorial domains, creating more confusion than their conflicting religious doctrines. The missionaries, backed by home countries, competed for exclusive territories in much the way traders competed for export monopolies. Attacks on missionaries and their converts led to the same futile wrangling between local magistrates and foreign officials as incidents in the commercial sector. Only displays of force produced settlements.

marred by factional fighting over the military's long postponement of intervention in neighboring Korea, a Chinese vassal state. Soyeshima wiped his hands of the Taiwanese affair in disgust. In 1873 a Taiwanese tribe killed several sailors. A violent revolt of samurai protesting Meiji reforms in February 1874 finally impressed upon the Japanese government the urgent need for a foreign adventure to vent the frustrations of dissatisfied, and now masterless, samurai. So on April 27 that year, 2,500 troops, 1,000 laborers, and several foreign advisors, led by LeGendre, boarded warships bound for Taiwan.

decade after the departure of the Japanese. But the repercussions of the Japanese occupation continued to resound through the island. For one thing, Japan's bold military move, for the first time in the island's history, had created a semblance of law and order on parts of

After Japanese withdrawal in 1874, Taiwan was declared the 22nd province of China in 1885 and the population surpassed 2.5 million.

Qing dynasty's Empress Dowager Cixi.

France and China went to war in 1884.

The military expedition landed at two points in southern Taiwan, one clearly within Chinese jurisdiction. Japanese troops made a few forays into the mountains to punish the offending tribal groups, but their continued presence in the south prompted strong Chinese protests and a willingness to negotiate. After protracted talks in Peking, the Chinese government agreed to pay Japan to compensate the families of the dead crewmen, and four times as much additionally for the expenses incurred by the military expedition. In return, Japanese forces withdrew from Taiwan and returned to Tokyo in triumph.

China continued to run Taiwan as a prefecture of Fujian province for more than a

the island. In fact, some foreign traders even seemed to welcome the Japanese occupation of 1874, as it forced Chinese authorities to take more interest in the island's affairs and virtually eliminated attacks on its foreign settlements. Meanwhile, militarists in Tokyo soon began rattling their swords and demanding annexation of Taiwan, Korea, and the Ryukyu Islands (Okinawa).

Fighting between Japan and China again broke out in 1894, when the Japanese invaded Korea, which had long been a loyal Chinese tributary state. China sent battleships to Korea's aid, but the Japanese sank them in a humiliating rout. Earlier, China had managed to buy off Japan to avert war, but this time nothing short of territorial gains would satisfy Japan's burning desire for an overseas empire. In the 1894–5 war, China suffered total and ignoble defeat at the hands of a nation it had considered inferior and barbaric. China's navy had been made a complete mockery of in the war.

Not long before the war, vast sums of money that had been earmarked for modernizing China's navy had, in fact, been diverted by the Qing dynasty's Empress Dowager Cixi to restore the Summer Palace, northwest of Peking. Therefore, it came as no surprise to outsiders when the outgunned and humiliated Chinese navy was annihilated in the Sino-Japanese War.

Cession to Japan

The Treaty of Shimonoseki, written by Japan, ceded possession of Taiwan and the Pescadores to Japan. It marked the start of half a century of Japanese rule over Taiwan and much of Northeast Asia, giving Japan a decisive role in Korea that would culminate in its annexation 15 years later.

Japan's takeover of Taiwan did not go down well with some locals, who resisted for several months; over 7,000 Chinese soldiers and several thousand civilians were killed during this early resistance. (Later, in 1915, some 10,000 Chinese lost their lives during the Tapani revolt against the Japanese, again without success.)

The Japanese undertook an intensive modernization of Taiwan's infrastructure. A domestic network of railways and roads was constructed, linking major points of the island for the first time. The Japanese also built schools, hospitals, and industries, and updated agricultural methods. Most importantly, strict Japanese rule ended the factional bickering and futile debates that had always marked island politics and commerce. Still, Japanese occupation proved oppressive and ultimately unpopular.

Between 1918 and 1937, Japan consolidated its regime in Taiwan, exploiting its rich natural resources exclusively for the benefit of Japan. Resident Japanese officers and officials enjoyed elite privileges that were denied to local citizens. In the last stage of occupation, the naturalization of all Taiwanese as Japanese nationals was enforced. As in occupied Korea, the Japanese required everyone in Taiwan to adopt Japanese names and speak the Japanese language in an effort to remold Taiwan in its own image and to sever the island's ancient Chinese cultural roots. But, as in Korea, such cultural brutality would fail.

Retrocession Day

Taiwan toiled under Japanese occupation until the end of World War II. After Japan surrendered, Taiwan was restored to Chinese sovereignty on October 25, 1945, a date still recognized annually as Retrocession Day.

Following this return to Chinese sovereignty, hordes of adventurers from mainland

Civil war on the mainland drew a motley crew.

China stormed across the Taiwan Strait, dismantling the industrial infrastructure left by Japan and shipping items of value back to Shanghai.

Meanwhile, civil war had broken out on the mainland. The struggle for control matched the Communist Party of Mao Zedong and Zhou Enlai against the Nationalist Party, or Kuomintang (KMT; Guomindang). The KMT head was a fiery leader named Chiang Kai-shek (Jiang Jie-shi). The struggle for control of the mainland preceded World War II by decades, but both sides had reluctantly joined efforts to defeat the Japanese. With both the Japanese and the earlier colonial powers gone, China now had the opportunity to set its own course.

THE RISE OF THE REPUBLIC

The successful post-war emergence of Taiwan as an economic power while remaining a preserve of Chinese tradition is the legacy of one man.

C hiang Kai-shek's (Jiang Jie-shi) association with Taiwan bears striking similarities to the saga of Koxinga (Guoxingye) centuries earlier. Both men fought to preserve the traditional order in China, and both established a bastion of that order in Taiwan, in defiance of their adversaries on the mainland. Most significantly, both men successfully launched a renaissance of classical Chinese culture, which has made Taiwan a living repository of China's most ancient and cherished traditions.

Birth of a nationalist

Chiang Kai-shek was born on October 31, 1887, in Zhejiang province, China. His mother was a devout Buddhist; his father, a salt merchant, died when Chiang was only eight. Then, when he was at the tender age of 14, Chiang's mother arranged for him to marry Mao Fu-mei. In 1908, she gave birth to Chiang's first son, Chiang Ching-kuo (Jiang Jing-guo).

At the time, the Chinese imperial system was disintegrating. Nationalism became the dominant force, and revolution was in the air. Caught up in the rapidly changing swirl of events, young Chiang took up military studies – in Japan, ironically. It was there that he first met a revolutionary called Sun Yat-sen (Sun Yi-xian).

Chiang participated in Sun Yat-sen's revolutionary forays into China, completing his military studies in Japan in 1912. That same year, Dr Sun Yat-sen became the first provisional president of the Republic of China (ROC), when Puyi abdicated as emperor, ending the Qing dynasty and closing the history books on China's 50 centuries of imperial rule. Chiang returned to China shortly after his second son, Chiang Wei-kuo (Jiang Wei-guo), was born, out of wedlock.

Chiang Kai-shek in 1930.

Two episodes left permanent imprints on the character of young Chiang after his return. For 10 years he resided in Shanghai, where he socialized with the wealthy merchants and bankers of that commercial city, as well as its underworld elements. Those contacts helped Chiang to forge a political power base that would carry him through two decades of warfare, and also provided him with the backbone for the Nationalist, or Kuomintang (KMT; Guomindang), successes in Taiwan. The second influential episode occurred in 1923, when Sun Yat-sen sent Chiang to Moscow as his emissary. Chiang returned from this mission with a deep distrust of the Russians and Communist doctrine.

Chiang Kai-shek has been labeled a conservative revolutionary. His concept of changing China was to foster nationalism and end China's humiliation at the hands of foreign powers. Nevertheless his vision of a modern China remained grounded in traditional Confucian social values. A born-and-bred Confucian, he cherished values like loyalty and obedience. He believed that the rebirth rather than the destruction of traditional culture was the answer to China's woes.

After the successful Northern Expedition against the warlords who had partitioned China into personal fiefdoms, Chiang rode into Shanghai to consolidate his power. In 1927, Soong (Song) Mei-ling became his second wife. She was from a Shanghai merchant and banking family, one of China's most powerful, and younger sister of Sun Yat-sen's widow. (Dr Sun had died in Peking in March 1925, at the age of 59.) Madame Chiang, as she became known in the West, was an American-educated Christian. Before they married, Chiang Kai-shek fulfilled a vow to her parents and converted to Christianity. His new wife and his conversion were important influences during the remainder of his life.

Constant conflict

The story of Chiang Kai-shek's campaigns against the Chinese Communists, and his war against the invading Japanese, has been well documented in many history books. The Japanese succeeded in occupying Manchuria in 1931. In 1937, they took Tianjin and Peking, captured Chiang's beloved Shanghai, and then overran Nanjing, which then was the capital of China. Bombing raids conducted from Japanese airfields in Taiwan bolstered their advance. In 1943, the Generalissimo, as Chiang came to be called, met with American president Franklin D. Roosevelt and Britain's prime minister, Winston Churchill, in Cairo. The three men secretly pledged that Manchuria and Taiwan would be returned to China after the war.

Japan surrendered in 1945, but Chiang's problems continued. The Communists seized the opportunity of post-war chaos – and quantities of abandoned Japanese arms – to directly engage Chiang's Nationalist (Kuomintang or KMT) army in an all-out conflict. Civil war raged across the vast Chinese landscape for four long years. To make things worse,

Chiang's administration was plagued by corruption and incompetence.

Chiang Kai-shek was elected president of the Republic of China (ROC) in 1948. However, by then, the war was swinging in favor of the Communists; they eventually took Peking and established the rival People's Republic of China (PRC) in October 1949. Thus began the saga of the 'two Chinas' – the PRC and the ROC.

Retreat to Taiwan

On January 21, 1949, Chiang Kai-shek resigned from the ROC presidency. After nearly a year

Lugang in 1934. The Japanese tried hard to eliminate Taiwan's Chinese identity.

The book Formosa Betrayed is a powerful eyewitness account of the February 28 Incident period, and a damning indictment of the KMT, written by George Kerr, an American official. It is still available in print, as well as online.

of self-imposed solitude, in December 1949 Chiang returned to lead an exodus of Kuomintang soldiers and a rambling entourage of merchants, monks and masters of classical arts across the Taiwan Strait to Taiwan. Still calling his retreating government the Republic of

China (ROC), Chiang's army defeated pursuing Communists in a last-stand battle on Quemoy (Kinmen), holding that island, and the Matsu Islands to the north, ever since.

Chastened by his defeat on the mainland, and knowing there was growing discontent in the military and civilian ranks – as well as being pushed by a disapproving US administration – Chiang was determined to reform Kuomintang policies in Taiwan. One of his first acts was to execute the rapacious governor-general Chen Yi, who was held responsible for the looting of Taiwan's wealth and the terrorizing of its people in 1945 and after. Chen Yi was the Kuomintang governor of Taiwan when the tragic February 28 Incident occurred. Many Taiwanese were under the impression that Chen Yi was later killed for his misdeeds in Taiwan, but in fact Chiang had first sent Chen Yi to the mainland, afterwards promoted him, and it was only when Chiang later suspected him of colluding with the Communists to overthrow Chiang that he had him killed.

Next, Chiang initiated a land-reform policy that was as sweeping as the one instituted by the Communists on the mainland, but

Chiang Kai-shek and his wife at the Cairo Conference, 1943, with Franklin D. Roosevelt and Winston Churchill.

THE FEBRUARY 28 INCIDENT

Nationalist misrule on Taiwan led to a deep undercurrent of anger among the Taiwanese. On February 27, 1947, a minor incident led to a rupture of the dam holding back their discontent. On this fateful day, officials injured a poor widow on a Taipei street while attempting to confiscate her black-market cigarettes. A crowd rushed to her defense. In their panicked retreat, one of the monopoly bureau officers shot into the crowd – a man fell and died.

Word spread like wildfire. On the next day, the Taiwanese gathered in the streets, and there were more shootings. Around the island people rose in protest, and mainlanders caught alone and unprotected fell to the mobs. An ugly and clearly KMT-orchestrated crackdown came, with summary executions and arbitrary massacres, and the educated, in the thousands, 'disappeared.' Between 18,000 and 28,000 Taiwanese are said to have been murdered. On March 10, 1947 martial law was declared, and remained in existence for the next 40 years.

The February 28 Incident, commonly known as 'Er Er Ba' or '2-2-8,' long defined the Taiwan independence movement and still lies at the core of embittered feelings toward mainlanders by the Taiwanese, the wounds only slowly healing. Exactly 50 years after the February 28 Incident, in 1997, the day was proclaimed a national holiday.

with one vital difference. Instead of vilifying and killing landlords, the Kuomintang government paid them for their land, and then offered them funds and tax breaks to engage in non-agricultural business ventures. That move helped launch the industrial revolution

> In 1971, the Republic of China (ROC), a founding member of the United Nations, lost its membership and was replaced by the mainland's People's Republic of China (PRC).

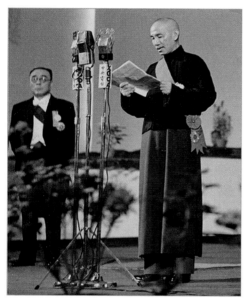

Chiang broadcasts the news of his Nationalist (Kuomintang) government's retreat to Taiwan, 1949.

that would become the catalyst for the island's phenomenal economic growth. Overnight, Taiwan found itself with an entrepreneurial elite of former landlords, who now had the money and the motivation to invest in Taiwan's future. Other reforms followed: the educational system was overhauled and students were sent abroad to absorb new technology and training.

Although national affairs remained firmly in the hands of the Kuomintang, more democratic institutions were established at local levels.

Chiang nominally governed the island according to Sun Yat-sen's *Sanminzhuyi* (Three Principles of the People). Still honored today

in both Communist China and Taiwan as the father of each respective country, Dr Sun built his framework for sensible government on three points: *minzu*, nationalism, or the liberation of China from foreigners; *minquan*, democracy; and *minsheng*, livelihood, or economic security for the people.

Of the three principles, Dr Sun considered nationalism the primary goal, and that the fastest way to obtaining that goal was through a democratic system that provided for the livelihood of the people – after an undefined period of 'political tutelage' by the KMT. Chiang amplified on Dr Sun's interpretations of the Three Principles in his book, *China's Destiny*, published in 1943.

With the outbreak of the Korean War in 1950, Taiwan was placed under the American protective umbrella from possible Communist attacks, and received substantial economic aid, too. In 1955, the United States and Taiwan ratified the Sino-American Mutual Defense Treaty.

Chiang's last years

Chiang Kai-shek continued to maintain strict political discipline and social order, crushing all dissent, potential and real, in the White Terror period and shutting out almost all non-KMT political participation at the central and provincial levels.

Although Chiang gave entrepreneurs free rein in the economic sphere, the domestic market for large-scale concerns was largely restricted and directed to those loyal to the regime in the early years.

Enthusiasm for capitalism propelled the private sector to grow from less than 50 percent of Taiwan's economy in 1953 to 75 percent in 1974, at the expense of state monopolies. During this time, the island's population doubled to 16 million.

The year 1965 proved a critical test of strength for Taiwan and its leadership. Financial aid from the United States, which had provided a springboard for economic development, was terminated. Nevertheless, industrialization, modernization, and economic progress continued to accelerate.

Chiang died shortly after midnight, on April 5, 1975. The vice president, Yan Jia-kan, succeeded him. In the next presidential election in 1978, Chiang Kai-shek's son, Chiang Ching-kuo, was elected president.

A statue of Chiang Ching-Kuo on Matzu Island.

MODERN TAIWAN

The transition to democracy has provided the framework for economic prosperity, with far-sighted governments stealing a march on Taiwan's near neighbors.

At the time of Chiang Kai-shek's (Jiang Jie-shi) death in 1975, Taiwan was a rising economic power, and had evolved from a pineapple- and sugarcane-growing country into a leading exporter of textiles, toys, and shoes. But material success came at a price. The ruthless Chiang had allowed only limited freedoms and dissent. His dictatorship was typified by executions without trial, midnight knocks on the door, long prison terms for political dissidents, and strict suppression of everything Taiwanese, including the Taiwanese and other native languages.

As the country prospered, and the people became richer and more educated, they grew restive. To the native Taiwanese, most of whose ancestors came from Fujian province in the 1600s and 1700s, Chiang and the China-born Nationalist (Kuomintang; Guomindang) Party 'mainlanders' were outsiders. During the 1970s, despite the persecutions of the martial-law era, dissent percolated, especially in the south, a native stronghold where Taiwanese was the common language, and where few mainlanders had settled. Resentment against martial law and the Nationalists boiled over in 1979 with the Kaohsiung Incident (see page 44).

Friendlier times

After the Kaohsiung Incident, the situation began to change. Chiang Kai-shek's son Chiang Ching-kuo (Jiang Jing-guo), declared president in 1978, steered the country toward greater freedoms. Unlike his autocratic father, the younger Chiang was friendly and personable, and made an effort to mix with the people. He brought native Taiwanese into the high echelons of the central government, including Lee Teng-hui (Li Deng-hui).

A member of the Taiwanese honor guards stands motionless at the Chiang Kai Shek Memorial Hall.

Chiang was re-appointed president in 1984, and Lee became vice-president. Within the next few years, Chiang clearly saw the need for reform. Across Asia, the tide was turning in favor of democracy. The Philippines had overthrown Ferdinand Marcos, and violent pro-democracy protests were underway in Korea and elsewhere. International pressure to end martial law was increasing as well.

As the island continued to prosper, Taiwan's people demanded a greater voice. In 1986, the Democratic Progressive Party (DPP) established itself as an opposition force. Though illegal, Chiang defied Nationalist hardliners and refrained from a crackdown.

In 1987 Chiang announced the lifting of martial law, and allowed travel to China for the first time since the end of the civil war in 1949. By the time Chiang died in 1988, Taiwan's transition from martial law to democracy was well underway. The ban on political parties ended the following year.

Lee Teng-hui took over as the island's president in 1988, and became party chairman the same year, outmaneuvering mainlander Nationalist hardliners. He continued the political reforms begun by Chiang Ching-kuo, but soon had to turn his attention to another issue: persistent bullying by mainland China, which considered Taiwan a breakaway province.

Years of resistance to the Nationalists had hardened the Taiwanese people, making them

The Kuomintang is the world's richest political party. After World War II, the assets of the Japanese colonial government and innumerable businesses and individuals were seized as the party's private property – not placed in the public coffers.

Taiwan's sovereignty from China remains a hot potato issue.

THE KAOHSIUNG INCIDENT

The Kaohsiung Incident was the landmark event in the development of Taiwan's democracy. It took place in December 1979, when a pro-democracy journal called *Formosa Magazine* organized a rally in Kaohsiung, to commemorate Human Rights Day.

The rally was repeatedly interrupted by riot police using tear-gas, and it soon became a violent confrontation between the martial-law government and the democracy activists, who numbered nearly 150,000. Between skirmishes, the protestors gave impassioned speeches, but the rally eventually turned into an all-out riot, and many activists and policemen were severely beaten.

Eight of the Kaohsiung rally organizers, including famous dissident Shih Ming-teh (Shi Ming-de) and later vice-president Annette Lu, were charged with sedition. They were defended by a team of lawyers including Chen Shui-bian, future president of Taiwan, and Frank Hsieh (Xie), later mayor of Kaohsiung and chairman of the Democratic Progressive Party (DPP). In the end the eight organizers were found guilty, and many received long jail terms. But the Kaohsiung Incident and subsequent trial received widespread publicity, and it galvanized the people of Taiwan against martial law. It was the crucible in which the DPP party was forged, and a turning point in modern Taiwanese history.

difficult to push around. The harsh rhetoric from China solidified their sense of a separate identity, and the DPP was loudly demanding a formal declaration of independence from China. By this time, millions of Taiwanese had visited China, and what they saw shocked them: grinding poverty, harsh repression, and corruption.

Provocative politician

Throughout the 1990s, the Taiwan–China dialogue was shaped by master politician Lee Teng-hui, president and Nationalist Party chairman from 1988 to 2000. The Taiwan-born Lee did much to provoke China, furthering his pro-independence sentiments along with those of a solid segment of the populace.

The Chinese had little success dealing with Lee, and took to calling him names like 'schemer.' In 1996, as Taiwan prepared for its first direct presidential election, China tried to derail Lee's campaign by launching missiles near the island. The move backfired, and Lee won by a huge majority, becoming the first president ever elected by the Taiwan people. In 1999, Lee took the offensive again, saying Taiwan and China were two separate states, a sharp break from his previous position that there was one state but with two governments. That speech has since loomed large in the ongoing debate on Taiwan's identity.

Democracy takes hold

In early 2000 the DPP candidate, Chen Shui-bian, won the presidency with just over 39 percent of the vote. This election ended 54 years of Nationalist rule, and marked the completion of Taiwan's journey from dictatorship to democracy. The Nationalists were further humiliated in the legislative elections of late 2001 when the DPP became the largest party.

Chen won re-election in 2004. During his years in power his actions were often deliberately provocative toward China, and without openly declaring so, it was clear he was intent on taking every step possible to move the country toward independence. The US saw him as a destabilizing influence, and attempted to curb him behind the scenes.

In 2008, the KMT took back power, in large part because of DPP scandals. President Ma Ying-jeou won a second term in 2012. Ma was pro-China, and desired eventual Taiwan/China reunification. He was seen by many as an appeaser, too feebly defending Taiwan's interests

in the international arena in the face of Chinese aggression. At the same time, however, there was overall satisfaction that relations between the two sides became more amicable, with significant cooperation in such areas as trade and tourism.

2016 saw the DPP come into power, winning both the presidential election (Tsai Ing-wen won with 56 percent of the vote and has become the first woman and the first unmarried person to hold the office) and a majority in the Legislative Yuan, making it possible for the DPP to govern alone for the first time. Thus, the official line towards mainland China has shifted again, from

Tsai Ing-wen is the island's first female president.

working with the PRC's 'One China' policy to stating firmly that Taiwan is a *de facto* independent state. Nevertheless, China continues to systematically stifle Taiwan's voice on the international stage, preventing Taiwan participation in any form in major international democratic institutions, notably the United Nations and World Health Organization. The major powers acquiesce, seeking to appease the dragon.

The economy

Taiwan's powerhouse economy is one of the envies of Asia. Even the Asian economic crisis of 1997–8, which plunged neighboring countries into recession, was barely a bump in the road for the country.

A world-class producer and exporter of ICT products, bicycles, plastics, chemicals, and many other goods, its foreign exchange reserves were about US$4,350 billion at the end of 2016, the fifth-highest in the world after China, Japan, the Eurozone, Switzerland, and Saudi Arabia.

The economy is a key topic in Taiwan because it fuels a high-flying lifestyle of lavish restaurants, mobile phones, cars, designer clothes, and overseas trips. Per capita GDP is about US$20,400 a year, less than half that of the United States and Western Europe, but far higher than countries such as Malaysia, Thailand, and China.

Taipei 101 is a symbol of the nation's prowess.

Much of the credit for Taiwan's economic success goes to the government, which avoided the prestige projects that typify other Asian countries. Instead, it built useful infrastructure that contributed to economic growth. In the 1950s, the government promoted agriculture through land reforms, and in the 1960s it emphasized the manufacture of labor-intensive exports such as textiles, paper and electrical goods. With its low labor costs and high quality control, Taiwan soon became a successful exporter. By the 1970s, the focus was on infrastructure projects like the first North-South Freeway, Chiang Kai-shek International Airport, railroads, harbors, and a nuclear power plant. In 1980, in a stroke of farsighted genius, and long before other countries

> *Chen Shui-bian's victory in the March 2000 presidential election was the first democratic change of power in 3,400 years of recorded Chinese history.*

in Asia realized the importance of electronics, government planners launched the Hsinchu Science-based Industrial Park (now Hsinchu Science Park), which became the epicenter of Taiwan's electronics industry.

In the 1980s, rising labor and land prices eroded Taiwan's advantage in cheap manufacturing, and much of such business fled to cheaper sites in China and Southeast Asia.

Decreased regulation

In the 1990s, the government's ambitious Asia-Pacific Regional Operations Center plan eased regulations and introduced competition to a variety of industries. The plan helped liberalize the economy, lower trade barriers, and clear away useless red tape. Hundreds of areas were targeted, ranging from banks to foreign exchange and telecommunications.

In the early 2000s Taiwan became a member of the World Trade Organization, and it is becoming even more competitive as it lowers trade barriers and ends subsidies. Some long-protected local industries were severely impacted, notably in the agricultural sector and in other low-tech sectors. For example, the tobacco-cultivation industry was wiped out, and the island's monopoly producer of cigarettes, beer, and spirits initially saw sales plummet. The overall effect, however, has been decidedly positive, with consumers enjoying a much wider range of choices, with local companies forced to upgrade and offer better value for money in the face of international competition, and with Taiwan companies granted easier access to overseas markets.

Taiwan, heavily dependent on exports, was severely impacted by the world financial crisis that began in 2008, and recovery was slow. However, the signing of the Economic Cooperation Framework Agreement with China in 2010 – which aimed to reduce tariffs and commercial barriers between the two – brought significant economic stimulus. Only recently has the trade between China and Taiwan begun to stagnate, which has reopened the dispute over the benefits and costs of the ECFA itself.

Cross-Strait relations

Taiwan faces an existential problem – its troubled relationship with China. Its de facto independence is intolerable to the latter, which considers Taiwan a breakaway province.

By insisting that Taiwan return to the motherland on its terms, and by threatening military force in order to achieve this, China has left itself little room for diplomatic maneuver.

Taiwan, on the other hand, wants full, internationally recognized independence. Polls show that the vast majority of people in Taiwan wish to remain separate from China. That stance has strengthened since the lifting of martial law, as the China-born 'mainlander' generation has lost influence, and a strong pro-Taiwan identity has emerged.

The Taiwanese see no reason to return to China, which they view as a badly governed country where business is dominated by corrupt officials, personal rights and freedoms can be snatched away, and the quality of life is poor.

However, despite having opposite goals, the two sides have talked. In 1992 and 1993 discussions were held under a One China platform, which maintained that Taiwan and China were part of one country, but with two governments. Then, in the mid-1990s, Taiwanese President Lee Teng-hui introduced rules restricting Taiwanese investment in China and refused to reopen direct air and shipping links, banned since 1949. In 1999, Lee broke from the One China policy, saying the two sides were separate states, and should negotiate as such.

The relationship's third major player, the US, officially endorses the One China policy and does not support Taiwanese independence. But the Taiwan Relations Act, enacted by the US Congress in 1979, implies that America will provide Taiwan with defensive weapons and defend it against attack. Though difficulties often arise, the US supplies Taiwan with much of its military materiel, though never quite state-of-the-art, including F-16 fighter jets. This is a constant source of tension in Sino-US relations, and China has at times threatened to withdraw military-to-military links.

China military build-up

China is in the midst of a rapid military build-up, with much of its defense budget secret, alarming

Taiwan and other Asian nations and intensifying China's strategic rivalry with the US in Asia. In the eyes of the Pentagon and many other military analysts, its acquisitions and training are now designed for the projection of power. The Pentagon now believes that if it does ever attack Taiwan its strategy is not focus on a frontal assault, but instead on suddenly enveloping the island, quickly starving it into submission, and presenting the US with a fait accompli. The assumption is that the US will not risk a full-scale war by attacking. Among the Chinese navy's key recent acquisitions is a new class of nuclear-powered ballistic-missile subma-

Taiwanese soldiers on maneuvers.

rines, and the Pentagon says its military now has 1,600 land-based missiles aimed at Taiwan. The China government denies it has aggressive intentions, stating its growing deep-water navy is for self-defense purposes only.

Meanwhile, Taiwan continues to behave like an independent country, conducting its own foreign policy. It is not a UN member, but it has a small core of diplomatic allies, and constantly seeks admission to world bodies such as the UN and WHO.

The war of words has done little to slow cross-strait trade. Business has grown steadily over the past two decades, and China is Taiwan's top trading partner, followed by Hong Kong and the US. Taiwan is also China's largest investor, with over 500,000 businesspeople and dependents living in China.

Enjoying the spring bloom in Tainan Shirakawa.

Bustling streets in Taipei's Xinyi District.

行人優先
Pedestrians Have Right of Way

THE TAIWANESE

The people of Taiwan may come from a variety of ethnic backgrounds, but they are united in their generous hospitality and their openness to visitors.

The population of Taiwan stands at just over 23.4 million. With much of the island taken up by uninhabitable mountainous regions, those people are squeezed into a relatively small amount of space, making Taiwan 16th in the world in terms of population density, among countries with a population of at least 10 million.

Unsurprisingly, it is Taipei where this population density is at its highest, with 10,000 people per square kilometer (nearly half a square mile). Having rapidly evolved from a largely agrarian society in the space of a few decades, over 70 percent of Taiwan's population today can be found in urban metropolitan areas with populations of 1 million or over. The largest by far is the greater Taipei area, which has a population of 8.5 million, followed by the Kaohsiung metropolitan area with 2.8 million and the Taichung- metropolitan area with 2.7 million.

The upshot of this is that Taiwan may be crowded, but, if you get out of the urban corridors into the mountains or the rural east coast, it suddenly becomes a lot more peaceful.

Ethnicity and politics

Taiwan's population is not as homogeneous as it might seem to the casual visitor, and the ethnic breakdown is an issue that is subject to sensitive political factors. Until around the turn of the century, asking someone whether they were Taiwanese was likely to result in a vehement denial, followed by the words 'I'm Chinese.' This is far less the case these days, and the opposite often applies, making it safer to ask people whether they are Taiwanese than Chinese.

The problem derives from the fact that, in modern times, the term Chinese refers to those

Most of Taiwan's population lives in the cities.

mainland Chinese who fled with Chiang Kai-shek (Jiang Jie-shi) to Taiwan in 1949 as well as their descendants. Called *waishengren*, literally 'outside-province people,' or *daluren* (mainlanders), they comprise about 14 percent of Taiwan's population. The remainder of the population are called *benshengren*, or 'this-province people' – whether Hakka, some of whose ancestors may have arrived from China as early as AD 1000 (comprising around 14 percent of the population), aborigine (about 2 percent), or descendants of the Minnan people of southern Fujian province (about 70 percent). This latter group began settling in Taiwan around four centuries ago, thus forming deeper connections with the island than most mainlanders, and are likely to perceive themselves as exclusively Taiwanese (as do the Hakka for the most part), with no connection to China.

The decisive moment in this change of consciousness came with the lifting of martial law in 1987. Suddenly, after 40 years of suppression of Taiwanese language and culture, the question of Taiwanese identity was something that could be discussed openly. Today, the Taiwanese dialect can be heard in popular music, television, movies and news broadcasts. Former president and Kuomintang (KMT; Guomindang) chairman Lee Teng-hui (Li Deng-hui), a Hakka who

themselves: *huaren*, a name that recalls the people who founded the legendary Hua dynasty near China's sacred Huashan (Mt Hua).

Taiwanese

Some 95–97 percent of Taiwan's population is ethnically Han Chinese, meaning at some point their ancestors – or they themselves – crossed the Taiwan Strait from China and made Taiwan their home. The Han Chinese may share a general common culture, but linguistically they are a very diverse people. The Cantonese dialect spoken in Hong Kong and

Alfresco ballroom dancing.

is more comfortable speaking Taiwanese than Mandarin, first used the term 'New Taiwanese', a rallying cry that has become somewhat definitive of the native sentiment that is growing ever stronger on the island.

With increasingly large numbers of citizens preferring to call themselves Taiwanese (*taiwanren*), the issue emerges of how to acknowledge the shared Chinese cultural legacy of the Taiwan people. A long-used Chinese term for the 'Chinese' is *zhongguoren*, but this literally means 'people of China' which, as explained, many people in Taiwan now argue is a separate political entity from Taiwan. More and more people are thus using the term used by Malaysian and Singaporean Chinese to refer to

southern China, for example, is as different from Mandarin (the standard 'national tongue' spoken in both China and Taiwan) as Dutch is from English. The same applies to Taiwanese, a polytonal dialect said to be older than Mandarin, which has evolved from the Fujian dialect known as Minnanyu.

Minnanyu-speaking immigrants from Fujian province started to arrive in Taiwan in large numbers early in the 17th century, a period that coincides with the earliest Dutch settlements on the island. When Koxinga (Guoxingye) fled to the island in the 1660s, there were about 50,000 Fujian immigrants living on Taiwan. By the time his descendants were ousted by the Manchu some 20 years later, the number had jumped to 100,000. They continued to come, so that by the 1895 Japanese annexation of the island there were more than 3 million.

In the early days, they were very clannish, and communal conflicts tended to break out on a regular basis between immigrants from different parts of Fujian, or these two main groups against Hakka from northern Guangdong. By the 1860s, however, such conflicts had almost disappeared, as the population assimilated through intermarriage.

Unless you can hear the difference between Mandarin and Taiwanese, it is near impossible

and communal meals are frequently accompanied by drinking sessions. Deeply religious, they pay regular visits to temples to pray for good luck and request the assistance of specific deities for specific concerns. In the aftermath of the 9-21 Earthquake in 1999, Western-trained psychiatrists from Taipei who went to the mostly Taiwanese-populated quake areas to offer counseling to victims largely found their services disregarded in favor of treatments by local soothsayers.

Today, Taiwan's Hakka population numbers around 4.6 million, though for the most

Cycling in Dajia Riverside Park.

If invited to a Taiwan home, bring a small gift. Gift-giving is far less institutionalized than in Japan, but is nevertheless important in cementing relationships. When offered a gift, always accept, to maintain the giver's face.

to distinguish between more recently arrived 'mainlanders' and those who can trace their Taiwanese ancestry back through many generations. In general, however, away from the cosmopolitan sophistication of Taipei, Taiwanese folk tend to be earthier.

The men often chew *binlang* (betel nut), especially in the countryside and smaller cities,

part they are not a very visible minority. The exception is in traditional countryside Hakka communities that have retained their language and customs, such as in the rural district of Meinong (see page 256) found in the south of Taiwan. The Hakka people have a well-known reputation for being thrifty and hardworking, and even more than most people of Chinese descent have a great love of education. Meinong claims to have produced more university graduates than any other rural community in Taiwan.

Traditionally, Hakka people have lived in villages made up of three-sided homes (*sanheyuan*) fronted by a wall to create a compound garden, reflecting what is perceived by other Chinese as their clannish nature. Most Hakka nowadays live in the same apartment blocks as other Taiwanese, but it's still possible to see such homes in the vicinity of Hsinchu and in Meinong.

Hakka *sanheyuan* buildings have three colors. The bottom section is made up of grey rounded stone, symbolizing the seeds of new generations and the desire for many children. The middle section features red brick, the red symbolizing the blood and toil of the working adult population. The top layer is white stucco, the white symbolizing the hair of the elderly generation, the layer's position atop the others indicating their elevated status. *Sanheyuan*

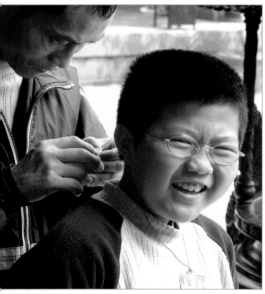
Traditions are kept alive among the young.

walls for other Taiwanese are generally one color, white stucco.

Hospitality and 'face'

The people of Taiwan like to think of themselves as *reqing*, a word that translates best as 'warm-hearted,' and possessing a spirit of *renqingwei*, which means, loosely, 'hospitality.' Few visitors would be able to dispute these qualities. Unlike nearby Japan, where foreigners too often feel clumsy in the face of mysterious social rules, in Taiwan the visitor is invariably greeted warmly and made to feel at ease. Foreigners, after all, are considered guests, and Taiwan folk pride themselves on being *haoke*, or 'good hosts.' Don't be surprised if locals make you the object

of uninvited hospitality or small favors. Even if at times it seems a little overwhelming, try to enjoy it. The thinking is that if they themselves were far from home they would very much appreciate it if locals went out of their way to take care of them. Taiwan folk – especially businesspeople – are often surprised that they are left on their own at night and on weekends by local hosts when they travel abroad.

Much is made about the Chinese concept of 'face' or *mianzi* as it's called in Chinese, but it's not a particularly complex concept. If, for example, somebody were to toast you at a banquet and you didn't toast in return, it would be a loss of 'face' for the toaster. If, on the other hand, you were to politely explain (with a smile) that you don't drink but would reciprocate the toast with some tea (which is invariably on hand), you would save the 'face' of the person toasting you. In other words, face boils down to showing respect and not embarrassing people.

Lastly, in Taiwan no social rules are carved in stone. Maintain an open mind and a smile, and you'll find local folk exceedingly welcoming and generous, even should you make the occasional social gaffe. Such gaffes simply reinforce their sense of having a unique and special culture.

Lifestyle

The women of Taiwan enjoy a high degree of equality, and a social status markedly higher than that enjoyed by their sisters in other East Asia countries. They commonly fill high positions in the workplace, and in most households control the family budget. There are two primary historical factors behind this phenomenon. Through much of its imperial-era frontier days Taiwan suffered a severe shortage of Han Chinese women, who were therefore able to establish a high degree of autonomy. In modern times, most factory jobs during the island's economic miracle era went to young women. Many of these women also needed to move away for their work. Their horizons were broadened and, even more importantly, they often earned more than the males in their families, and often were the key sources of family financial support. Elevated social status and personal freedom was a natural concomitant.

The middle-aged and senior generations have some of the world's highest personal savings rates, inspired by growing up in times when material goods were limited. The younger

> Taiwan folk – except young students – never 'go Dutch.' Dividing up a bill is considered unseemly. It's always someone's role – the oldest person, or most likely the person who suggested the outing – to qingke, or 'get the bill.'

The people of Taiwan have deep affection for the traditions of the past while at the same time pursuing the modern, especially the material modern, with a vengeance. On the same day a person may visit a temple to pray to a god for success in an exam, business venture, or some other important life event, then go out shopping for the latest smartphone or laptop. As throughout the rest of East Asia, there is a fascination with all high-tech consumer gadgetry, and it is common to purchase a new cellphone every few months, for example, to keep up with the newest specs and looks.

generation, however, is far more free-spending. These individuals are more highly educated, have been raised in smaller families, and have been pampered by parents and grandparents.

Taking part in the Dragonboat Festival at Dajia Park.

The family's pooled savings are intended for their use, and they access these savings freely. While their seniors have a collective perspective, younger citizens are more individualistic. Nevertheless, such traditional values as *reqing*, *renqingwei*, family loyalty, and responsibility toward their extended-family seniors remain at the core of young people's social life.

As per long-standing tradition, most young people still live with their parents until they get married, unless their choice of school or work obliges them to move away. The traditional family structure is undergoing change, with the extended family slowly being superseded by the nuclear family, though in most instances grandparents will still be located close by.

It is common with people of Chinese descent that one's self-image, and one's image and social status with others, is measured in terms of material success. And if one has achieved material success it is expected one flaunts it. Brands will be prominently shown on apparel and accoutrements, one's Rolex must be worn so that others can see. Taiwan's men, who because of crowding live in homes of limited size, compensate through a display of luxury in their cars. If one has 'made it' one says so by purchasing a Mercedes, referred to instead as a Benz in Taiwan, and vehicles begin to have luxurious additions such as leather-covered seating much further down the quality scale than in the West.

TRIBAL MINORITIES

Taiwan's earliest settlers are now finding their
voice, shaking off old, unfavorable reputations,
fighting back from long-term oppression, and
proudly celebrating their heritage.

Amid all the debate of recent decades as
to who are the 'real' Taiwanese, the voice
of Taiwan's original inhabitants has been
gathering strength. Once regarded by Taiwan's
Chinese settlers as 'savages,' Taiwan's indigenous
tribes are finally being recognized as the victims
of long oppression, and their arts and culture
taken with new seriousness. With the formal
recognition of five small tribes since 2014, there
are now officially 16 tribal groups.

Today, the indigenous peoples amount to
about 2.3 percent of Taiwan's total population,
numbering just over half a million. Until the
1990s they were called *shandiren*, or 'mountain
people,' a name derived from the fact that Chinese occupation of the fertile plains initially
left the mountain and other remote tribes
untouched. Today, however, the preferred appellation is *yuanzhumin*, or 'original inhabitants.'

Most of Taiwan's indigenous people have been
assimilated into modern life to the extent that
they have become almost indistinguishable from
their Chinese counterparts. But it is still possible in mountainous and other remote regions to
find villages where many of the old ways have
been preserved. These villagers grow traditional
crops like millet for brewing alcohol, sweet potatoes, and taro, a kind of root vegetable. In recent
times, cash crops like wild mushrooms, pears,
peaches and plums have become a popular and
lucrative form of income, though Taiwan's entry
into the WTO has resulted in severe price competition. The tribes are also benefiting somewhat
from enhanced tourism income opportunities.

The tribes

The origin of Taiwan's minorities is disputed
in anthropological circles. The consensus, however, is that the northern tribes are probably of

An Atayal tribeswoman weaving.

southern China origin and the southern tribes
of Austronesian origin. One thing is certain:
archeological digs have shown that aborigines
have inhabited Taiwan for at least 15,000 years,
much longer than their Chinese counterparts.

The largest ethnic minority group is the Ami,
which has around 200,600 members. They pop-
ulate the scenic valleys and flatlands in Hualien
and Taitung counties, on the east coast. The Ami
are mainly farmers: their annual harvest festival, held during the last weeks of July and early
August, brings out the best of their traditional
dance forms, music, costumes and customs.

The minority group most accessible to visitors
to Taipei are the Atayal, the closest of whom live
in the lush valleys of Wulai, just an hour's drive

south of the capital, but who can also be found in Taoyuan, Nantou, and other northern counties.

The Paiwan inhabit the mountains of eastern Pingtung and Taitung, in the south. The snake-worshiping cult of the *baibushe* or 'hundred-pacer' (victims, it is said, will only live 100 paces after being bitten) still remains strong in Paiwan tradition. The snake's visage appears in abstract form on almost all arts and crafts.

The Paiwan, in particular, are master wood carvers, making totems, doors, eaves, beams, smoking pipes, and other masterpieces from the trees of Taiwan's alpine forests. Another

attire, then swing the ladies until they sail like kites to dizzying heights. Afterwards, the girls are carried from their swings and dropped into the arms of their most ardent admirers.

The Puyuma tribe has traditions similar to the Ami. They live mainly in the foothills of the

> *Although long called shandiren, or 'mountain people,' official statistics show that over half of Taiwan's native people have left the mountains to seek opportunities on the plains nowadays.*

Paiwan women.

interesting tribe is the Rukai, whose largest cluster of hamlets is in Wutai township, Pingtung county, where the inhabitants engage primarily in agriculture.

An interesting feature of the village of Wutai is the buildings constructed from stone slabs quarried in the surrounding mountains. The architecture resembles the piled slate homes that dot the Himalayan highlands of western China, northern India, and Nepal.

One fascinating display of Rukai prowess is seen in their traditional 'swing contest,' one of the most entertaining tribal rituals in Taiwan. Prospective brides mount an enormous swing, with their legs bound to prevent them from flailing. Burly tribesmen, dressed in full ceremonial

Central Mountain Range, near Taitung city, and occasionally congregate on the city's outskirts for major festivals that include swing contests.

Another island tribe of note are the Bunun, who live in the southern Central Mountain Range. The Bunun still practice a ritual form of night worship that remains essentially unchanged from ancient times. There are, however, two exceptions: severed pig heads have replaced disembodied human heads as sacrificial offerings, and electricity has replaced traditional torches for lighting.

The ethnic group that has been least affected by Taiwan's headlong plunge into the 21st century are the Dao, who live on Orchid Island (Lanyu), off the southeast coast, and who are the only seafaring minority found in Taiwan. For half a century during their occupation of Taiwan, the Japanese deliberately isolated Orchid Island as a living anthropological museum. Dao fishing boats, pieced together with parts hewn from a single giant tree, are beautiful vessels that glide over the waters of the Pacific.

Trial husbands

Of particular interest are the marriage customs of the Dao. Women significantly outnumber the men on the island and have parlayed their numbers into a potent social force.

Upon engagement, the male moves into the family home of the female for a one-month trial marriage. During that time, the prospective groom must prove his prowess in hunting and fishing, exhibit his ability to build boats, and demonstrate other skills. If he fails the tests, he is sent packing in disgrace and another suitor is brought in. Even when the man successfully wins the bride, he is expected to continually prove his worth to his wife and her family. Otherwise, the Dao woman may exercise her unilateral right to divorce her husband – at any time and on any grounds – and seek a new mate.

A Dao man dries flying fish on Lanyu.

SO CLOSE, YET SO FAR

Orchid Island's Dao (also called 'Yami') people speak a language mutually intelligible with the language spoken by minority tribes on the Philippines' Batanes Islands. Some anthropologists think the word 'Yami' is an ancient Austronesian word meaning 'north.' Orchid Island lies north of the Batanes, though the Dao themselves refer to their island as Botel Tobago. Whatever the case, today the Dao are separated from their Philippine neighbors by politics. A journey once made on festive occasions by boat in a day, today requires flying from either Taipei or Kaohsiung to Manila and then a long journey to the northern Philippines.

Creativity

Taiwan's aborigines have been taking an increasingly active role in politics in recent years, but it is their creativity as singers and dancers, and their arts, that have chiefly caught the public eye in Taiwan. Popular Puyuma singer A-Mei has achieved much success with her R&B-influenced hits in Taiwan and throughout the Chinese world. She has been called a diva of the Mandarin pop world as well as the 'Pride of Taiwan.'

A number of high-quality museums and theme parks showcase aboriginal arts and crafts, in particular weaving, a tradition carried on by many tribal women. Motifs incorporate elements of the two regions from where anthropologists believe the tribes' ancestors may have come.

Devotees making offerings.

RELIGION AND RITUALS

Ancestor worship, Daoism, Buddhism, and popular
folk religion have bequeathed a mix of mysticism and
ritual that underscores the lives of the Taiwanese.

Traditional religion has flourished in Taiwan, despite the rapid development from a rural society into an industrialized complex of urban enclaves. Indeed, the temples of Taiwan are as much a feature of the skylines as are factories and office buildings.

Ancestor worship

The ancestor worship of the Chinese is based upon the assumption that a person has two souls. One of them is created at the time of conception, and when the person has died this soul stays in the grave and lives on sacrificial offerings. As the corpse decomposes, the strength of the soul dwindles, until it eventually leads a shadow existence in the underworld. However, it will return to earth as an ill-willed spirit and cause damage if no more sacrifices are offered.

The second soul only emerges at birth. During its heavenly voyage post-death, it is threatened by evil forces, and is also dependent upon the sacrifices and prayers of living descendants. If the sacrifices cease, then this soul, too, turns into an evil spirit. But if the descendants continue to make sacrificial offerings and tend the individual's grave, the soul of the deceased may offer them protection.

Originally, ancestor worship in Chinese history was exclusive to the king. Only later did peasants also begin to honor their ancestors. At first, people believed that, during the sacrificial ritual, the soul of the ancestor would search for a human substitute – usually the grandson – as an abode. Until 2,000 years ago, when genealogical tablets were introduced as homes for the soul during sacrificial acts, the king and noblemen used human sacrifices.

Even today, the Chinese worship their

A traditional Chinese altar at the Liudui Cultural Park.

ancestors and offer the deities sacrifices of food. However, the original religion of the people focused on the worship of natural forces. Later, people began to worship the Jade Emperor, a Daoist figure who became the highest god in the popular religion in the 11th century. Among the many other gods in popular Chinese religion, there were also earth deities, and every town worshipped its own unique city god. There were demons of illness, spirits of the house, and deities of streams and rivers. Apart from Confucianism (which scholars consider a code of ethics rather than a formal religion), Daoism, and Buddhism, there was also a working-class religion known as Daoist-Buddhism.

Daoism

Only when the Qin dynasty bested its last rival in 221 BC did the first emperor over a united China come to power. At the time, there were various schools of philosophical thought, but only Confucianism and Daoism gained wide acceptance in China.

Central concepts of Daoism are the *dao*, which means way or path, but also has a second meaning of method and principle, and *wuwei*, which is sometimes simply defined as 'swimming with the stream.' The concept of *de* (virtue) is closely linked to this, as a virtue that manifests itself

written by a single author. The earliest, and most significant, followers of Laozi were Liezi and Zhuangzi. Liezi (5th–4th centuries BC) was concerned with the relativity of experiences and strived to comprehend the concept of *dao* through meditation. Zhuangzi (4th century BC)

> As Buddhism became more and more popular, it borrowed ideas from Daoism, and vice versa, to the point where one might speak of a fusion between the two.

Buddhist monks at Jinguashi.

in daily life when *dao* is put into practice. The course of events is determined by the forces *yang* and *yin*. The masculine, brightness, activity, and heaven are considered *yang* forces; the feminine, weakness, darkness and passivity are *yin* forces.

Laozi was the founder of Daoism. He is said to have been born in a village in the province of Henan in 604 BC, the son of a distinguished family. For a time, he held the office of archivist in the capital of Luoyang. But Laozi later retreated into solitude and died in his village in 517. Since the 2nd century AD, many legends have been told about Laozi and experts argue about his historical existence.

The classic work of Daoism is called the *Daodejing*. It seems certain that this was not

is famous for his poetic allegories. The ordinary people were not particularly attracted by the abstract concepts and metaphysical reflections of Daoism. Even at the beginning of the Han period (206 BC–AD 220), there were signs of both a popular and religious Daoism.

Religious Daoism developed in various directions and into different schools. The ascetics retreated to the mountains and devoted their time to meditation, or lived in monasteries. In the Daoist world, priests were important medicine men and interpreters of oracles. They carried out exorcism and funeral rites, and perform rituals for the dead or for sacrificial offerings.

Historical and legendary figures were added to the Daoist pantheon. At the head were the Three

Commendables. The highest of the three deities, the heavenly god, is identical to the Jade Emperor, worshipped by the common people.

Buddhism

The Chinese initially encountered Buddhism at the start of the first century, when merchants and monks came to China over the Silk Road.

The type of Buddhism prevalent in China today is the *Mahayana* (Great Wheel), which – as opposed to *Hinayana* (Small Wheel) – promises all creatures redemption through the so-called *bodhisattva* (redemption deities). There were two aspects that were particularly attractive to the Chinese: the teachings of karma provided a better explanation for individual misfortune, and there was a hopeful promise for existence after death. Nevertheless, there was considerable opposition to Buddhism, which contrasted sharply with Confucian ethics and ancestor worship.

At the time of the Three Kingdoms (AD 220– 280), the religion spread across each of the three states. After tribes of foreign origin had founded states in the north, and the gentry from the north had sought refuge in the eastern Qin dynasty (317–420), Buddhism developed along very different lines in the north and south of China for about two centuries. During the rule of Emperor Wudi (502–549), rejection and hostility towards Buddhism spread among Confucianists. And during the relatively short-lived northern Zhou dynasty (557–581), Buddhism was officially banned for three years.

Buddhism was most influential in Chinese history during the Tang dynasty (618–907), when several emperors officially supported the religion. During the years 842 to 845, however, Chinese Buddhists also experienced the most severe persecutions in their entire history: 40,000 temples and monasteries were destroyed, and Buddhism was blamed for economic and moral decline. In the course of time, ten Chinese schools of Buddhism emerged, but only two remain influential today.

Key figures

In Chinese Buddhism, the center of religious attention is the Sakyamuni Buddha, the founder of Buddhism who was forced into the background in the 6th century by the Maitreya Buddha (who is called Milefo in China, or redeemer of the world). Since the 7th century, a *bodhisattva* deity has been a popular female figure of devotion in China.

She is known as Guanyin, a motherly Goddess of Mercy to the ordinary people. Guanyin means 'the one who listens to complaints.'

From the 14th century onwards, the Pure Land (Amitabha Buddhism) school has dominated the life and culture of the Chinese people, but the most influential Buddhist school has been the so-called School of Meditation (called Chan in China, Zen in Japan), which developed during the Tang dynasty. It preaches redemption through Buddhahood, which anyone is able to reach. It despises knowledge gained from books or dogmas, as well as rites. Guided meditation is

An altar God in rock on way up to Parrot Rock.

used in order to lead disciples toward enlightenment, but the most important method is dialogue with the master, who asks subtle and paradoxical questions, to which he expects equally subtle and paradoxical answers.

In 1949, the year the People's Republic of China was founded, there were approximately 500,000 Buddhist monks and nuns, and 50,000 temples and monasteries, in China. A number of well-known Buddhist temples were classified as historical monuments. But, during the Cultural Revolution started in 1966, it seemed as if the Red Guards were intent on completely eradicating Buddhism. Nominally autonomous Tibet – which practiced Tantric Buddhism or Lamaism, introduced from India in the 7th century AD – was hard-hit by these excesses. (Lamaism features Brahman and Hindu gods in its pantheon, as well as Buddhist deities; magic, prayers, and rituals help achieve redemption.)

Popular religion

Chinese folk religion is a blend of practices and beliefs that have developed out of animism, ancestor worship, Confucianism, Daoism, Buddhism, and various folk beliefs. In Taiwan, these forms of worship are generally similar to those still practiced by Chinese elsewhere in Asia. But despite the common thread that runs through traditional beliefs and rituals, local practices in Taiwan differ from region to region.

Although Taiwan has Buddhist, Daoist, and Confucian temples, the common person blends the practices of all three with superstition and ancestor worship. To further confuse matters, devotees refer to this religious blending by the umbrella term Buddhism, even as they visit local folk-religion temples to worship heroes and deities unknown to Buddhism. There is little concern for strict dogmatism in folk religion.

Most of the time incense is burned in temples, and devotees light paper offerings to the deities

Taking part in a fire ceremony to pray for peace and prosperity in Taipei.

CATALOG OF DEITIES

A huge pantheon of gods and goddesses are found in traditional Chinese religion, and the origins and legends that surround these deities go deep into Chinese history. Most are the heroes and notables of Chinese myth, legend and history, deified either by imperial order or popular choice (not unlike Christian saints). Some of these deities are so well-known that their images are found in many or most temples; others are unique to a single temple. Some communities even have cult followings, which have developed around a particular historical figure who is believed to have protected or guided the town, or to have worked a miracle in the locality.

or seek advice through the use of divining blocks or sticks. Religious solemnity is not a quality of temples, which are often retreats from the heat and where women and the elderly meet and chat with acquaintances, relax or play cards. Some village temples even double as schools, stores and recreation centers.

Because the supernatural and human worlds coexist in the folk religion of Taiwan, temples represent the place where the two worlds can meet and communicate. The living devotees provide the resident deities with incense, oils, and food offerings; in exchange, they receive advice and protection against demonic influences responsible for such earthly sorrows as plagues, disasters and illnesses.

Taiwanese temples

Taiwan, not China, is home to the world's greatest collection of Chinese temple architecture. Every neighborhood seems to possess a heritage-site temple of ornate beauty.

Many of Taiwan's temples were built in the 18th and 19th centuries, almost all of these by master craftsmen from China. China itself lost much of its temple heritage in the strife of the 20th century, notably the Cultural Revolution. Taiwan's temples range from small shrines containing one or two images or tablets to large establishments with several main halls flanked by minor ones, each holding separate altars. A temple is named after the chief deity on the main altar.

Insight into Chinese folk religion can be gleaned from the architecture and decor of the buildings themselves. One important element is the ornate roof, alive with images of deities, immortals, heroes and mythological animals, which attract good fortune and repel evil.

The roof's center is usually crowned with one of five symbols: a pagoda, representing a staircase to heaven; a flaming pearl, symbolizing the beneficial *yang* spirit; the sun, usually flanked by two dragons; a magic gourd, said to capture and trap evil spirits; or Fu, Lu, and Shou, the gods of Prosperity, Posterity, and Longevity. Beside them are the fantastic assortment of figures associated with Chinese temples, including the phoenix, which appears only in times of extreme peace and prosperity, and the dragon, symbol of strength, wisdom, and good luck.

These exterior features are, at first glimpse, very much the same in Buddhist and folk-religion temples. Inside, however, the differences are obvious. Buddhist temples contain few images, with one to three significant gilded Buddhas on a main altar. Confucian temples, severe by comparison, contain no images.

Interior decoration

The interior decoration of folk-religion temples varies considerably. Many contain fascinating murals of scenes from Chinese mythology and history. Pillars and balustrades may be intricately carved. Most have guardians painted on the outside of the main doors. The main altar bears the image of the major deity, attended by aides or servants. Fronting the principal deity is a smaller image of the same god; this miniature is taken from the temple occasionally to bless devotees in their home doorways, or is carried aloft during festivals to other temples.

Beneath the main altar, at ground level, are two forms of small altar. One contains a tablet dedicated to the protective spirit of the temple itself; the other contains stone or wooden 'white tigers' – the bringers or destroyers of luck. There are always five items on the table before a temple's main altar, the most sacred being a large incense pot. Filled with ash accumulated by years of worship, it is the repository for the spirit of the venerated Jade Emperor.

From right to left: Fu, Lu, Shou – gods of Prosperity, Posterity and Longevity.

Ancestral offerings

In addition to the gods, ancestors are also commonly at the receiving end of offerings. Traditionally, ancestral tablets were kept in family homes (sometimes in ancestral halls), with respects paid at a living-room altar. These tablets bear the ancestors' names and sometimes photographs, and are given regular offerings, lest they become troublesome hungry ghosts. Increasingly, however, families pay temples to house the tablets.

Like those of the human world, the inhabitants of the underworld require food, money, clothes, and a house. Food offerings give symbolic sustenance, and spirit money – bundles of 'Bank of the Underworld' notes – and paper artifacts representing material items are burned to release their essence.

DAJIA MAZU

Gongfu (Kungfu) exhibitions, dancing dragons, exploding firecrackers, crowds, and lots of noise are all hallmarks of the annual Mazu pilgrimage.

Every year, around midnight on a pre-determined day before the 23rd day of the third month of the lunar calendar, Taiwan's Dajia Mazu pilgrimage gets underway. Over the following nine days, a mass of pilgrims will walk, cycle, and drive with Mazu as bearers carry her statue some 300km (186 miles) around central Taiwan. By the time the pilgrimage ends, more than a million people will have watched the procession pass by.

The pilgrimage is easily Taiwan's grandest, noisiest, and most grueling – a mass exercise in medieval pageantry and a celebration of all that is uniquely Taiwanese. Chinese opera singers do wailing battle with the tinny trumpeting of marching bands. Knots of 'devil boys' jostle the crowds with spears and clubs, while spirit mediums go into convulsions. Entire villages make food offerings and burn incense, and jostle to prostrate themselves in seemingly endless lines for the good fortune of having Mazu's statue pass over them.

The cult of Mazu

It is thought that the worship of Mazu originated in coastal China and then spread throughout Southeast Asia. Some scholars think Mazu was a woman named Lin Mo-niang, born during the Song dynasty (960–1127) on Meizhou Island, in China's Fujian province, who died at 28. In Taiwan, she is the island's patron saint and most widely worshiped folk deity.

Mazu makes her triumphant return home to Dajia's Zhenlan Gong after eight days of traveling and being watched by up to a million people.

The Mazu pilgrimage is an aural assault, with firecrackers exploding every step of the way and truckloads of loud drummers crowding the streets.

Although frowned upon by pilgrimage organizers, jitong (spirit mediums) can still be seen during the festival flagellating themselves until they bleed.

Taking part in the annual Mazu Pilgrimage in costume.

PRAYERS AND PILGRIMS

At the front of the Mazu pilgrimage procession is the *Bobe-a*, banging a gong to notify temples, villages, and towns that it's time to light incense in anticipation of Mazu's arrival. *Bobe-a* (in Taiwanese) is an outlandish figure in a conical, helmet-shaped hat, sheepskin vest, bifocals, and black pajama-like costume. With a pig's trotter and spring onions tied to his waist, his attire is completed by wearing a sandal on one foot and nothing on the other. This symbolizes the ecstasy and absent-mindedness one naturally feels at the approach of the heavenly presence. The trotter symbolizes long life, for if a tiger attacks it will take the trotter and leave the marchers to live. Behind the *Bobe-a* are flag-bearing troupes of pilgrims from all over Taiwan, including the 36 Expectants and the Embroidered Flag Troupe. The performing troupes that follow the *Bobe-a* lend the pilgrimage much of its color and excitement. They include a troupe called the Holy Infants, comprising huge dancing babies, and the Drunken Buddha Troupe, who cavort drunkenly along the street taking imaginary swigs from hip flasks.

People crowd to touch the Matsu sculpture in order to receive good fortune.

Xingang, bundles of paper offerings ('spirit money') pile so h they have to be shoveled into trucks and burnt outside n for fear of sparking a major conflagration.

Marching bands trumpet their way through the processions.

THE ROLE OF CONFUCIANISM

One man born over 2,500 years ago continues to shape Chinese society with his philosophy of benevolence and social propriety.

'**W**hen friends visit from afar, Is this not indeed a pleasure?' For more than 2,000 years, Chinese scholars aspiring to government office were required to memorize *The Analects*, or *Lunyu*, the most hallowed of all Confucian classics. Today, copywriters with Taiwan tourism offices often borrow the above opening lines of the *Lunyu* for obvious reasons. The fact that Confucius began his great work with such a disarmingly simple and welcoming maxim emphasized the importance the philosopher placed on friendship and social etiquette.

Confucius believed that true pleasure cannot be found in selfish, sensual abandon or in personal gain, but in generosity to friends, in social intercourse and in social hierarchy. Thus, hospitality has long been one of the Chinese culture's finest arts.

Master Kong

Confucius, known to the Chinese as Kong Fuzi, or Master Kong, was born in the kingdom of Lu, in modern Shandong, in 551 BC. As a child, he demonstrated profound interest in ancient rituals. People admired his erudition and sincerity but, because he lived in a time of internal chaos, few men of influence were willing to adopt his pacifist ideas.

Without a platform from which to address the masses, Confucius set out to peddle his ideas on his own. While still a young man, he traveled throughout the Chinese empire, taking his message of peace, friendship and reform to the various petty princes. Most received him with interest and hospitality, but few showed intentions of changing their warring ways. While traveling, Confucius also gathered and studied materials that revealed

Laozi, founder of Daoism, is often depicted riding on his water buffalo.

the secrets of the earlier golden ages of Chinese culture – the Xia, Shang and Zhou dynasties. One of the men who assisted him was Li Dan, known to posterity and philosophy as Laozi, the Old One.

Laozi was the founder of Daoism. He was also in charge of the imperial archives of the Zhou dynasty, which housed all the surviving documents detailing events from the 23rd century BC up to his time. The records were preserved in archaic script on tiles, bamboo and tortoise shells. Laozi permitted Confucius to use the archives and copy as many records as he wished. The ancient documents formed the basis for his so-called Confucian classics.

'I never created or wrote anything original,' Confucius claimed. Instead, he considered himself an interpreter and transmitter of the profound ideas and deeds of the ancient kings of China's golden age. He is generally credited with putting the documents of the imperial archives into a common, contemporary language, and with publishing them.

The 'Five Classics' of Confucianism, the *Wujing*, are the *Yijing* (Book of Changes), *Shijing* (Book of Poetry), *Shujing* (Book of History), *Liji* (Book of Rites), and *Chunqiu* (Spring and Autumn Annals). Later works written by Confucius, or by

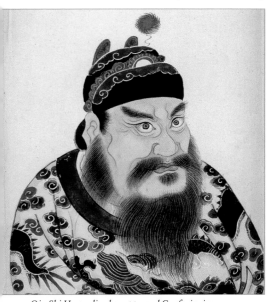

Qin Shi Huangdi, who suppressed Confucianism.

his disciples and believed to contain the master's original thoughts, are the *Great Learning*, *Doctrine of the Mean*, and *Classic of Filial Piety*.

The *Lunyu* consists of a collection of the notes and journals of the master's conversations, teachings and journeys. Believed to have been compiled by the disciples of his school, it is often regarded as the basic 'scripture' of Confucianism. Publication in itself was a bold move for Confucius. Never before in Chinese history had anyone but kings and ministers published books. But Confucius was a commoner, or at most, a member of an impoverished noble family. His years of writing and interpretation of hallowed doctrines followed by 44 years of teaching – yet another revolutionary course.

> *Although Confucianism is not generally considered a religion, temples to the great sage abound in Taiwan, always called 'Kong Miao.'*

Before he arrived on the scene, only aristocrats and royalty received formal education. Confucius, however, welcomed to his school of thought anyone who demonstrated a keen intellect and a sincere desire to learn.

By the time of his death at the age of 72, some 3,000 students had been attracted to the teachings of Confucius. Around 70 disciples are believed to have carried on his work, building on his ideas during the period of intellectual fervor known as the One Hundred Schools Period. Thousands of books were published, and tens of thousands of students educated as a result of the example set by Confucius.

Among them was Mencius. Considered second only to Confucius among the great sages of ancient China, Mencius further advanced the concepts of his predecessor and reaffirmed basic Confucian principles, particularly the notion that government should be conducted for the benefit of the people and not the ruler, and that human nature was basically good.

Dark ages

In 221 BC, what is commonly called the Age of Philosophers was buried under the militant Qin dynasty, which swept down from the northwest. Led by founding emperor Qin Shi Huangdi, China was united for the first time under a bureaucratic government. But Qin Shi Huangdi was contemptuous of learning and viewed the contending schools of philosophy as potential sources of sedition and a threat to his empire. He executed hundreds of scholars and ordered most books to be burned. Only tomes on agriculture, divination and medicine were spared.

It is a testimony to the strength and endurance of Confucius' doctrines that his works somehow survived. Private editions were secreted in walls and underground vaults. After the demise of the Qin dynasty, the subsequent Han dynasty collected the hidden works of Confucius during the 2nd century BC, and declared his writings to be the official canons of a new state philosophy. Until Confucian studies were formally abandoned in 1905, the Confucian classics remained the most sacrosanct source of knowledge and moral authority for every Chinese ruler and bureaucrat.

Li and ren

Confucianism is far too complex to cover in detail here. But a few highlights reveal its wisdom. Confucius' most celebrated concepts were those of *li* and *ren*. *Li* has been translated by various scholars as rites, ceremonies, etiquette, and propriety. Its combined implications underline all social behavior in the Chinese system, providing the appropriate behavior for every situation a person may face in life. If *li* conflicts

The Five Cardinal Relationships

Confucius established the Five Cardinal Relationships as a guide to the social behavior that would motivate followers to his utopia. These rules governed relations between subject and ruler, husband and wife, parent and child, elder sibling and younger sibling, and between friends. The last is the only social relationship of equality possible in a Confucian society. The rest demand the absolute obedience of inferior to superior, though superiors have a responsibility toward inferiors. Such common traits of Chinese society as authoritarian government,

Aristocratic life during the Ming dynasty.

with the law, a superior man will not hesitate to follow the dictates of *li*. Li also incorporates the many formal rituals by which a person symbolically expresses propriety, like sacrificial rites that honor deceased ancestors.

Even more important is the concept of *ren*. Its written form consists of the symbols for person and the number two. *Ren* thus dictates social relations. It can be roughly interpreted in English as benevolence and kindness. For Confucius, if all humankind followed the virtues of *ren* and *li*, all social behavior would become appropriate and benevolent, and the sources of friction among people would be eliminated. In his utopian prescription for humanity, he promoted peace and social harmony.

filial piety, patriarchal family structure, primogeniture, and the importance of friendships – all save the first are still important within the social life of Taiwan today – can be traced to the Five Cardinal Relationships.

At the top of society, the responsibility that superiors had for inferiors was manifested in imperial times in the Mandate of Heaven. Heaven would bless the authority of a just ruler, but widespread poverty and natural disasters were taken as signs that the ruler was neglecting his people, and in danger of losing his mandate and being overthrown.

Confucius also formulated a version of the universal Golden Rule. But like many things Chinese, it takes an opposite tack from the

Western concept. 'Do not do unto others what you would not have them do unto you' is a reasonably accurate translation of the Confucian version. To 'do unto others,' as the West does, would be far too aggressive and presumptuous. The practice of actively performing good deeds is considered a form of social interference in traditional Chinese society. Instead, the Chinese prefer simply to refrain from doing bad deeds.

Any individual who successfully follows the precepts of Confucian teaching can become a superior person. Confucius stressed that the superior individual was not necessarily an aris-

Children at a ritual ceremony honoring the birthday of Confucius.

tocrat or powerful politician, but simply a person of virtue. Learning is the key to that process. 'The superior man makes demands on himself; the inferior man makes demands on others,' the wise Confucius is said to have concluded.

In practice, this concept led to the system of appointing learned Confucian scholars to administrate China on behalf of the emperor, thus diminishing the role of hereditary princes and royal relatives. Rule by men of knowledge and virtue managed to hold the unwieldy empire together from the 2nd century BC until the birth of the republican form of government in 1912. The Confucian concept of the superior man also explains the respect that people

September 28 has been designated Teacher's Day, honoring Confucius. Teacher's Day is celebrated with elaborate ceremonies at Taiwan's many Confucian temples.

of Chinese descent have always maintained for the learned and scholars.

A way of life

Confucianism, as practiced by the Chinese, is not a religion in the strict sense of the word. Technically, it is not even a philosophy. It is a way of life with equal importance placed on theory and practice. Confucius himself rarely expounded on religious subjects. He did not deny the existence of gods and obviously felt there was some universal force on the side of right. But he felt that people should steer away from spiritual concerns and concentrate on creating a harmonious society in this world.

The people of his day were extremely superstitious, spending an inordinate amount of time on formal sacrifices that invoked spirits. When Confucius' ideas that humanity's most pressing concerns lay in this life were widely adopted, religious matters receded and social issues moved to the fore. Since Confucius's time, the Chinese have continued without feeling the need for a single omnipotent god or an exclusive, all-embracing religion. They have simply referred to the powers above as 'heaven', an impersonal, inscrutable force that drives the universe. Meanwhile, for the most part they have welcomed all religious faiths to their land – as long as they do not interfere with social or governmental concerns. But, to be on the safe side, many still pay homage to a variety of gods.

Contemporary influences

The most lasting of the legacies of Confucius has been the perseverance of the primacy of family and friends. This legacy persists in Chinese communities throughout the world. Family and friends provide many of the social and economic services performed by courts, police, banks, and lawyers in the West.

It is the family, not the individual, that has been the basic unit of social organization in China since the Zhou dynasty established the system of *baojia* during the 12th century BC. Society was divided into units of 10, 100, 1,000, and 10,000 families, according to neighbor-hoods and districts. Each unit chose a leader from its ranks who was responsible for the behavior and welfare of all families under his jurisdiction. This leader reported directly to the leader of the next highest *baojia* unit.

If someone committed a crime, the head of his household would initially be held accountable, followed by the head of the 10-family unit, then the leader of the 100-family group, and so on. Thus, minor crimes rarely were reported beyond the *baojia* organization. In this way, too, the entire family assumed collective responsibility for the conduct and well-being of its members.

Guanxi

In Chinese society, family comes first, state and occupation second. Close connections are main-tained with all family members, even those who have moved halfway around the world. Such extended networks provide sources of warmth and comfort, as well as a secure form of social welfare and future business links.

Friends form the other half of the Chinese social equation. People of Chinese descent have a network of carefully cultivated friendships, their *guanxi* or connections. Good *guanxi* in the right places often helps get things done on both sides – and across – the Taiwan Strait. It can open doors and help cut through red tape.

Westerners often view the cultivation of such connections as a form of cronyism, but the Chi-nese believe it is perfectly natural to perform favors for friends. Years of experience have taught the Chinese to trust friends and rela-tives to get things done, but they feel uneasy asking favors of strangers. The betrayal of a per-sonal friend is a heinous social offense, which can have serious repercussions throughout the offender's network of *guanxi*. That network is only as strong as its weakest link, so each new relationship is given careful consideration.

Confucian-style relationships proliferate in the Chinese business world – and virtually prevent it from unraveling. People of Chinese descent routinely select business associates from among established family members and friends, or ask these people for recommendations, unlike Westerners, who tend to choose their friends from business or professional groups.

A Chinese businessperson can invoke the social pressures of a *guanxi* network whenever an associ-ate defaults on contracts, thereby eliminating the

need for expensive court actions. Similarly, people are encouraged to settle personal disputes within their own families, neighborhoods and occupa-tional groups rather than impose their problems on the public. They understand a member's behavior and motivations better than a court, and share collective responsibility.

Rotating credit associations

Banks are another Western innovation frequently bypassed by the *guanxi* system. In Taiwan, many people participate in small private investment associations, called *biaohui*, often translated as

Guanxi, a network of cultivated friendships, goes a long way in business.

'rotating credit associations.' Friends, relatives, and colleagues pool their money in a mutual fund, which may last for years, with each con-tributing a set amount on a regular basis, usually once a month. Each round any member may bid for that round's money, the person offering the highest interest winning. No person may win a bid more than once. The personal closeness of the group minimizes fraud. Generally, all mem-bers are known to the organizer.

Taiwanese and Chinese communities overseas often appear to be paradigms of lawfulness. In truth, they suffer their share of criminal activities. The peaceful appearances are in part a result of prefering to settle matters among themselves.

CONTEMPORARY CULTURE

Newfound wealth, the opportunities of travel, and the lifting of martial law have jointly provided the impetus for Taiwan's thriving arts scene.

The past three decades have been a period of explosive creativity for Taiwan's contemporary artists. The end of martial law in 1987, the ever-increasing affluence of the island, and the large numbers of Taiwanese returning from overseas study, travel, and work have all conspired to create a vibrant arts scene, much of it exploring the increasingly confident nature of Taiwanese identity. Film and theatrical directors continually receive international attention, and in areas such as popular music the island has emerged as an Asian center for creativity and innovation, far belying its small size and relatively small population.

Cinema

In the 1960s and 1970s Taiwan had a healthy movie industry, very much in the mold of centers like Bombay, Hong Kong and, of course, Hollywood. But with the opening up of Taiwan to foreign cinema, audiences grew tired of the often predictable romances and dramas, and for decades thereafter local cinema was almost entirely the provenance of the art-house set.

Directors of the early 1980s were influenced by the *xiangtu* – 'native soil' – literary movement, which had also influenced a great many local painters. One of the most representative movies is *A Time to Live and a Time to Die* (1985), directed by Hou Hsiao-hsien, winner of the Golden Lion award at the Venice Film Festival in 1989 for his depiction of the oppression of native Taiwanese by the Nationalists in *City of Sadness*. *A Time to Live and a Time to Die* is a coming-of-age depiction of childhood in rural Taiwan during the 1950s and 1960s as it changed from an agrarian to an urbanized and industrialized society.

Hou is internationally the most famous of Taiwan's so-called 'new wave' directors.

Hollywood blockbusters at a high-tech movie theater in Ximending, Taipei.

He continues to make and produce movies, remaining true to his artistic vision despite limited interest and a continuing scarcity of funds.

Directors of the 'second new wave' that started in the 1990s exhibited visions that were less brooding, reflecting perhaps the new sense of buoyancy that has come with the lifting of martial law and increased affluence, and which continues to impact the rapid currents of change in local society. Ang Lee, who has gone on to international Hollywood success with *Sense and Sensibility*, *Crouching Tiger, Hidden Dragon* and *Brokeback Mountain*, and more recently and *Life of Pi*, took on broader issues such as homosexuality in *The Wedding Banquet* (1993), and the

Chinese obsession with food in *Eat Drink Man Woman* (1994). He is the first person of Asian descent to win the Academy Award for Best Director, which he has won twice to date.

The Taiwan film industry was nearly dead through the 2000s, with almost no public interest and no production money. A dramatic and unexpected renaissance came in 2008 with the comedic romance, *Cape No. 7*, the country's biggest-ever box-office success. Momentum has been maintained with such award-winning efforts as *Monga* (2010), a look at the tough, gang-influenced life in Taipei's old Wanhua district in the 1980s, and *Warriors of the Rainbow: Seediq Bale* (2011), the most expensive production in Taiwan's history, and *Our Times* (2015). The government now more systematically encourages young talent with seed money and mentor programs.

Dance

Tsai Jui-yueh (1921–2006) is generally acknowledged as the mother of modern dance in Taiwan. In 1936, at the age of 16, she left Taiwan for Tokyo to study with Ishii Midori, one of Japan's most famous modern dance instructors. She returned in 1945 and established Taiwan's first school of ballet in Tainan. Evicted from the premises on the grounds that Western-style dance was 'indecent,' she soon shifted to Taipei. Shortly after marrying in Taipei, her husband was deported for his political views and she herself was imprisoned for two years. Upon her release, she opened the China Dance Academy on Taipei's Zhongshan North Road, where it served as a center of dance until it burnt down in late 1999, the academy was later renovated as a heritage site and tourist attraction dedicated to her memory.

A performance by the Taipei Dance Circle.

PEOPLE, NOT POLITICS

Though Hou Hsiao-hsien has never backed away from politically sensitive subjects – filming his early movies in Taiwanese despite a Nationalist injunction against doing so, and portraying political oppression by the Nationalist forces in *City of Sadness* – he denies he is a political filmmaker. 'What really interests me is people,' he has been quoted as saying. 'I am emotional about people. Only people move me.' For anyone who has seen his films, with their moving depictions of ordinary people struggling against circumstance and history, such words ring true. His films (he now produces as well as directs) leave an emotional residue that lingers.

The most famous of Tsai's students today is Lin Hwai-min, whose Cloud Gate Dance Theatre has toured to international acclaim. Lin, who also studied in the US under Martha Graham, initially set out to combine modern Western dance, Chinese opera, and an expression of Taiwanese identity in the early 1970s. His later work, however, has embraced influences from as far afield as India, Java, and Tibet, taking on subjects that are not restricted to Taiwanese themes, such as China's Tiananmen massacre in *Requiem*. A Cloud Gate performance is a breathtaking experience, providing a far more exhilarating insight into the vibrancy of contemporary Taiwanese arts than tourist-oriented performances like Beijing opera.

Lin's Cloud Gate has been enormously influential in Taiwan, spawning many imitators and innovators. Most successful of these has been Liu Shao-lu's Taipei Dance Circle, whose oiled, near naked, squirming dancers caused controversy but won Liu the National Award for Arts nonetheless.

Lin Xiu-wei is another Lin protégé who has gone on to success with her Taigu Tales Dance Theater, whose brooding, studied performances have been compared to Japan's Butoh dance.

Puppetry

Taiwan's glove puppet theater, or *budaixi*, seems an unlikely candidate for a modern revival, but a modern revival of what was once one of the island's most popular forms of entertainment is precisely what has happened. In part the excitement is due to a feature-length, glove puppet movie, *Legend of the Sacred Stone* (1999), a hit amongst Taiwanese young and old, but the real reason lies with the group behind the movie, the High Energy Puppet Theater, which has its own cable-TV channel devoted to nothing but glove puppet dramas.

Reprising a 583-episode puppet TV series from the 1970s, High Energy has had enormous local success, spawning fan clubs and leading

quality museums dedicated to puppetry have been opened, with resident troupes that are invited to travel far abroad.

While it's possible to find performances of glove puppets today by channel surfing on Taiwanese television, nothing beats seeing an outdoor performance. The makeshift stage is usually a grandly colorful affair covered in swirling red and gold designs that make it look like the entrance to a temple. Meanwhile, the characters themselves strut about the stage in richly embroidered cloaks, carrying out pitched battles, intrigues, and romantic affairs.

A collection of traditional hand puppets.

to the unexpected spectacle of glove puppets sharing shelf space with Hello Kitty dolls in Taiwan's toy shops and handcrafted puppets fetching hefty sums in *tourist-oriented* boutiques.

Until this renaissance, *budaixi* was just one of many traditional Taiwan folk arts that had fallen into decline. In 1993, director Hou Hsiao-hsien made a movie about one of the island's leading protagonists, Li Tian-lu (now deceased), called *The Puppetmaster*, an elegiac piece of cinema that little anticipated the art form's revival in fortunes. Nevertheless, at the time the movie was made, some 200 puppet troupes were still active around Taiwan, usually reserving their performances for local festivals. Today there are even more, and a number of

Manga

The Japanese word *manga*, meaning comics, is pronounced *manhua* in Chinese, and, like many things Japanese, took the island by storm in the 1990s. As in Japan, comics have been a staple in the Taiwanese 'literary' diet for several decades, and a number of local artists have achieved regional renown in the art.

Japanese *manga* remain the most popular variety in Taiwan in spite of (or perhaps because of) their sometimes quite racy content, frequently featuring soft porn and sometimes surprisingly explicit sex. Taiwanese *manga* artists (or *manga-ka* in the parlance of fans, borrowing from Japanese) first achieved success in the late 1990s, some of them breaking into the

Japanese market. Local artists have since won the Grand Prize in Japan's prestigious Morning International Comic Competition on a number of occasions. Perhaps Taiwan's most celebrated *manga* creator is Chen Wen, whose adaptations of Chinese *gongfu* novels (*wuxia xiaoshuo*) have been a hit in Taiwan, Hong Kong, and Japan. For a glimpse of *manga* culture at its most vibrant, a stroll through Taipei's Ximending youth shopping and entertainment district will turn up numerous *manga*-devoted shops, as well as colorful youngsters sporting *manga*-inspired clothing designs.

Pop scene

Despite the perennial success of Hong Kong singers – most of whom release their albums in both Cantonese and Mandarin – Taiwan has emerged as the center of the Mandarin pop, or Mandopop, universe. This is a phenomenon that has led local cultural critics to proclaim that, while the two sides of the Taiwan Strait are divided politically, unification took place long ago on the cultural front.

The front-runner in the explosion of Taiwanese pop in the Chinese world was the late Teresa Teng, who, sharing the same surname as China's

Street singer in Taipei.

ALTERNATIVE MUSIC

One side of Taiwan few visiting foreigners see is its exciting alternative music scene. Whereas most Asian music cultures are almost entirely dominated by the corporate marketing of saccharine melodies, Taiwan indie fans have difficulty keeping track of the many acts jostling for attention in the vibrant local circuit.

The flowering of an indie-music consciousness – using your own style to express your own music, without kitsch or affectation, free of commercial influence – was kick-started in 1994 with Scum, a dingy Taipei basement bar in which, musically, almost anything went. The music created was more cultured in spirit, more experimental, and more free ranging. The listening market was initially very small, but acceptance has grown, and today it might even be said the genre is approaching mainstream, popular status. Such well-known contemporary singers as Wu Bai, Cheer Chen, and Deserts Xuan, and bands such as Mayday, Sticky Rice Ball, and Sodagreen, have risen from the indie sub-scene, bringing alternative modes of expression to the big scene.

Today, performances take place in more salubrious venues, listed in the Friday editions of Taiwan's English-language newspapers and on www.taiwannights.com. The top three venues, which have launched many acts into the mainstream over the years, are Taipei's The Wall Live House, Riverside Music Café, and Kafka by the Sea.

late party chairman, Deng Xiaoping, used to be jokingly referred to as Taiwan's 'little Deng.' Her popularity coincided with the reforms that began in 1978 in China, and her nostalgic Mandarin love songs struck a popular chord on both sides of the strait.

The Taiwan music scene has, however, come a long way from the days when it was content to simply export sweet love songs. The local music scene began to diversify in the late 1970s and 1980s, when Taiwan's so-called 'campus folk scene' started to permeate the corporate music world in what was called the 'sing my own song' movement. The unofficial spokesman for this generation of singer-songwriters, who voiced social concerns through music, was Luo Da-you, who influenced Beijing rocker Cui Jian, among others.

Broadening horizons

It was only in the 1990s that the Taiwanese pop industry truly started to broaden its horizons and come into its own. Corporate-groomed stars continue to be a phenomenon, but the industry is also marked by a large number of innovators who are able to turn their musical talents to considerable popular success. Many of these have emerged from the island's thriving underground music scene, which makes its biggest public-notice bang each year with the immensely popular Ho-Hai-Yan Rock Festival, held at Fulong Beach on the northeast coast. A prime example is Wu Bai, who writes his own music and who has gone from playing Taipei's alternative-music pubs to playing stadiums. His music is what he calls Taiwanese rock – melodic, foot-stomping crowd-pleasers sung in Taiwanese. His presence – if not his music – has inspired numerous more musically adventurous songwriting bands.

More surprises have occurred in the willingness of recent pop artists to break taboos and deal with subjects other than the Mandopop staples of broken hearts and wistful love. Zhang Zhen-yue, an aboriginal singer-songwriter popularly known as A-Yue, broke onto the scene with *Boring Day* in 1997 and then took the island by storm in 1999 with *Mom, Pa, Give Me Money*, a song that reflected Taiwanese society's materialism but was considered so unfilial overseas that it was banned in Malaysia. Like many other Taiwan artists, he now incorporates hip-hop elements into his music, and as frontman for the band Free9 tours the Chinese-speaking world.

More mainstream, but nevertheless breaking new musical ground, is aboriginal pop diva A-Mei, who surprised audiences with her gutsy, R&B-influenced voice when she released *Bad Boy*. A-Mei has since become one of Taiwan's

> Culture lovers should be in Taipei between April and June for the Taipei Traditional Arts Festival, which highlights crossover collaborations fusing traditional Oriental music with Western classical music.

Local pop group, the Fleabags, entertain visitors at the Dragon Boat Festival in Kaohsiung.

most successful musical exports in the Chinese world, although China banned her for a year after she sang the national anthem at the presidential inauguration of Taiwanese independence supporter Chen Shui-bian in 2000. She has since made successful visits, and is known as the 'Pride of Taiwan.'

When it comes to solo acts, edgy Jay Chou and diva Jolin Tsai continue to occupy the thrones of pop royalty. Chou is called Chairman Chou by his fans, reference to his long-term reign.

A phenomenon that arose in East Asia in the early 2010s is the embrace of Taiwanese music by local audiences, pushed by the popularity of Taiwan soap operas, in which pop stars take roles.

ARTS AND CRAFTS

Taiwan's artistic heritage may owe much to Chinese
tradition, but its galleries display a wealth of artworks
in various materials, and of varied inspiration.

Many visitors to Taiwan associate the island's art and crafts with the kind of traditional Chinese arts that can be found in the Gugong Bowuguan (National Palace Museum). Yes, Taiwan is perhaps the best place in the world to admire China's artistic tradition, but it is also worth remembering that Taiwan has its own artistic trends and traditions.

Calligraphy

Almost without exception, the artist of early China was a calligrapher, and from a privileged class. Otherwise, he would never have had the endless hours of time needed to acquire skill with the *maobi*, the brush used to write characters. Competence with the brush was an important reflection of an education in ancient China.

The Chinese have always regarded calligraphy as the highest art. With its abstract aesthetic, it is certainly the purest. In times past, the strength of a man's calligraphy was a key element in passing examination. Writing was regarded as a window to the soul. Few examples of ancient calligraphy still exist. Most ancient inscriptions are rubbings taken from cast-metal vessels, and the earliest examples of Chinese writing in Taipei's National Palace Museum (see page 149) are Shang-period oracle inscriptions, incised on tortoise shells or oxen scapulae.

One of the museum's earliest examples of work by famous calligraphers is *Bing-fu tie (On Recovering from Illness)*, by Lu Ji (261–303). Samples of post-Eastern Qin calligraphy are more common. Wang Xi-zhi, who lived during that dynasty, is regarded as the patriarch of the art of calligraphy.

The Song dynasty saw the rise of calligraphers carving on wood or stone, then making rubbings on paper and compiling their works

Yingge is synonymous with ceramics in Taiwan.

as copybooks, a practice that became a popular method of studying an artist's style. Even the short-lived Yuan dynasty produced several noted calligraphers. But the 300 years of the Ming dynasty generated numerous masters and masterpieces. The Qing dynasty introduced two distinctive styles of calligraphy, one that marked the era from 1796 to 1820, and the other from 1851 to 1874.

Porcelain

The Chinese invented porcelain sometime in the 7th century – 1,000 years before the Europeans obtained the secret. The most widespread form of ancient Chinese porcelain was celadon – a product made from a blending of iron oxide with a glaze that resulted, during the firing stage, in a characteristic greenish tone.

Sancai ceramics – ceramics with three-color glazes from the Tang dynasty – became world-famous. The colors were mostly strong green, yellow, and brown. *Sancai* ceramics have also

Jade bangles for sale at Taipei's weekend market.

been found among Tang-period tomb figurines in the shape of horses, camels, animal or human guardians, ladies of the court, and officials.

The Song-period celadons – ranging in color from pale or moss green, pale blue or pale grey to brown tones – were also technically excellent. As early as the Yuan period, a technique from Persia was used for underglaze painting in cobalt blue (commonly known as Ming porcelain). Some common themes seen throughout the subsequent Ming period were figures, landscapes, and theatrical scenes. At the beginning of the Qing dynasty, blue-and-white porcelain attained its highest level of quality.

Since the 14th century, Jingdezhen has been the center of porcelain manufacture, although today relatively inexpensive porcelain can be bought throughout China. However, antique pieces are still hard to come by because the Chinese government prohibits the export of articles older than 100 years.

Jade

With its soft sheen and rich nuances of color, jade is the most highly valued stone in Chinese culture. The Chinese have known jade since antiquity, but it became widely popular only in the 18th century, when it began to be mined in China. Colors vary from white to green, but there are also red, yellow, and lavender jades. A clear emerald-green stone is deemed most precious.

The oldest jades so far discovered are from the Neolithic Hemadu culture (about 5,000 BC). The finds were presumably ritual objects. Among them are circular disks called *bi*, given to the dead to carry into the afterworld. Centuries later, the corpses of high-ranking officials were clothed in suits made of more than 2,000 thin slivers of jade sewn together with gold wire.

Since the 11th century, the Jade Emperor has been revered as the godhead in folk religion. Today, the ring disk – a symbol of heaven – is still worn as a talisman, and jade bracelets are worn for good luck throughout Taiwan.

Lacquerware

The oldest lacquered objects date back to the 5th millennium BC. The glossy sheen of lacquerware is not only attractive to the eye but is also appealing to the touch.

The Chinese lacquer tree (*rhus verniciflua*) grows in central and southern China, Korea, and Japan. When the bark is cut, it exudes a milky sap that solidifies in moist air, dries, and turns brown. This dry layer of lacquer is impervious to moisture, acid, and scratches, and is ideal protection for materials such as wood or bamboo.

Bowls, tins, boxes, vases, and furniture made of wood, bamboo, wicker, leather, metal, clay, textiles, and paper are coated with a lacquer skin. A base coat is applied to the core material, followed by extremely thin layers of the finest lacquer, which, after drying in dust-free moist air, are smoothed and polished to a glossy sheen.

In the dry-lacquer method, the lacquer itself dictates the form: fabric or paper is saturated with lacquer and pressed into a wood or clay mold. After drying, the mold is removed and the piece coated with further layers of lacquer.

Items were already being made in this way in the Han period.

During the Tang dynasty, large Buddhist sculptures were produced by the lacquerware process. If soot or vinegar-soaked iron filings are added to the lacquer, it will dry into a black color; cinnabar turns it red. The color combination of red and black, first thought to have been applied in the 2nd century BC, is still considered a classic by aficionados of Chinese art.

In the Song and Yuan periods, simply shaped monochromatic lacquerware was valued, and, during the Ming period, the manufacture of

Cloisonné and ivory

The cloisonné technique – used to create metal objects with enamel decor – reached China from Persia in the 8th century AD, was lost, and was then rediscovered in the 13th century. Metal rods are soldered to the body of a metal object, forming the ornamentation outlines. The spaces between the rods are filled with enamel paste and fired in a kiln. Metal surfaces not covered with enamel are gilded.

As a craft material, ivory is as old as jade, and early pieces can be traced to 5,000 BC. During the Bronze Age there were wild elephants

Traditional Chinese cloisonné enamel.

lacquered objects was further refined.

The carved lacquer technique, which began at the time of the Tang dynasty, reached its highest peak during the Ming and Qing periods. The core, often of wood or tin, is coated with mostly red layers of lacquer. When the outermost coat has dried, decorative carving is applied, with the knife penetrating generally to the lowest layer so that the design stands out from the background in relief. The most well-known lacquerware is the Peking (Beijing) work, which goes back to the imperial courts of the Ming and Qing dynasties. Emperor Qianlong (1735–96) had a special liking for carved lacquerware; he was even buried in a coffin magnificently carved using this technique.

in northern China, and the old artist-carvers regarded elephant tusks as a most desirable material. As a result, the once-large herds of elephants shrank to a small number, and eventually ivory had to be imported. Ming dynasty carvings exemplified excellent craft skills and superior taste; during Qing times, ivory carving was further improved. Most countries today, seeking to reduce animal poaching, ban the import of items carved from ivory.

Painting

Chinese painting first blossomed during the Tang dynasty, from 618 to 907. The period's figure and horse paintings were particularly exquisite. Few have survived the centuries, but

Taipei's National Palace Museum has 65 paintings that date from the Tang dynasty and earlier.

Flowers, birds, and landscapes were the favorite subjects of artists who painted during the Five Dynasties and Song periods. Two of the greatest masters of the Southern Song imperial painting academy were Ma Yuan and Xia Gui. Their styles, which became popular in Japan, are typically asymmetrical. All the landscape elements and human figures are placed to one corner, the empty remaining surfaces suggesting an enveloping mist. Such masterpieces as Ma's *Springtime Promenade*, painted between 1190 and 1225, and Xia's *Chatting with a Guest by the Pine Cliff*, which dates to between 1180 and 1230, are typical examples.

Because of the short duration of the Yuan dynasty, the number of paintings produced was relatively small. One Yuan-era painting in the National Palace Museum collection is the masterpiece *Autumn Colors on the Qiao and Hua Mountains*, dated 1295.

The Ming dynasty saw the revitalization of traditional Chinese institutions, including painting. Among the myriad notables was Wu

In Taipei's Museum of Fine Art.

A GLIMPSE OF THE MODERN

Home to scores of galleries, Taipei is the best place to view Taiwan's vibrant modern art scene. One of the oldest, and most influential, is the Apollo Art Gallery. The Eslite Gallery is more eclectic in its offerings; it is in the basement of a 24-hour Eslite Bookstore that stocks many English art titles. The Chi-Wen Gallery focuses on Taiwan artists using digital media, while IT Park is among the city's most avant-garde galleries. A recent development is the proliferation of artist-in-residence programs, invariably in renovated heritage sites, with permanent galleries. Most significant are Taipei Artist Village and Treasure Hill Artist Village.

Wei, an ardent Daoist who so fully comprehended the mysteries of the *dao* that he came to be regarded as an immortal. Also prominent were Wen Zheng-ming, who excelled at images of old trees, and Dong Qi-chang, one of the most important artists of the late Ming period.

The Qing period saw the flourishing of the so-called Individualists, including Zhu Dao, Dao Ji, Gong Xian, Kun Can, and Hong Ren.

A Jesuit priest named Giuseppe Castiglione, who went to China as a missionary and was called to the imperial court, also became famous as a painter of figures, flowers, birds, and horses. Lang Shi-ning, as the priest became known, blended European naturalism with Chinese composition and media.

Public art

The legion of imaginative public artworks is one of the most visible manifestations of a cultural-creative beautification bloom in progress throughout the country.

With the lifting of martial law in the late 1980s, Taiwan's people were free to come and go from the country as they pleased. With significant disposable income saved and great thirst for international travel built up, they began venturing forth in substantial numbers to savor the world's great cities, returning with a desire for home-grown public art to beautify their own cities, which lacked green and inviting public spaces.

In 1998 Taipei led the way with ratification of its Public Art Establishment Measures, stipulating that public artworks be installed at metro stations, on traffic islands, along sidewalks, and at other highly visible locations; since that time, one city after another has launched contemporary public-art beautification projects. Private entities and scenic-site management are often partners.

Metro art

Among the most conspicuous and oft-seen works are in the stations of the Taipei and Kaohsiung metro systems, and what is perhaps the country's best-known and most celebrated individual work is in Kaohsiung's Formosa Boulevard Station. The *Dome of Light* is a magnificent cathedral-like dome of stained glass, created by Italian-American artist Narcissus Quagliata, that covers 667 sq meters (798 sq yds) of the station's ceiling, measuring 30 meters/yds in diameter, and said to be the world's largest-ever work of glass art. The inspired imagery represents the human life cycle, from birth, growth, and honor to destruction and rebirth.

Taipei public-art tours

Taipei has concentrated on creating corridors of art, and has introduced six Taipei Public Art Strolling Routes (http://taipeipublicart.culture.gov.tw). Three are located close together in the downtown area – along the Dunhua Public Art Vestibule on Dunhua Road, along Civic Boulevard, and in the Xinyi District – stringing together the art of the east district. Among the most noticeable and notable works are *Chess*, at the intersection of Shifu and Songshou

roads, a giant chess game which pedestrians are obliged to pass through that symbolizes the chessboard of life and the power of fate. *Garden*, just south of the Zhongxiao/Dunhua intersection, is a giant red birdcage with a sculpted tree growing in it and canaries staring at the big world outside, reminding viewers that we must live our lives to the full and avoid becoming a deluded caged bird.

Tainan old-area beautification

In Tainan, the Haian Road Public Art Street project is beautifying one of the city's older districts. Shuixian Temple Market, Taiwan's oldest, today still thrives,

The public artwork 'Garden'.

and in the 1990s the local government started work on an underground shopping complex along Haian here. Things did not go well, the project was abandoned, many old buildings were left partly demolished, and today the beautification project has resulted in a series of dynamic public artworks incorporating and celebrating these vestiges of yesteryear.

The Memory of Wall fronts an abandoned-now-renovated building home to artist-run Blueprint Lounge Bar. The facade is now a blueprint, with painted white windows and rafters creating an illusion of the interior space. Another, called *Great Yongchuan Palanquin*, is on the side of a heritage shop of the same name, where master Wang Yong-chuan has long been creating exquisite palanquins and other objects for Tainan's temples. The mural presents a cross-section view of the two-story shop interior.

CHINESE OPERA

**Although initially strange to the Western ear and eye,
Chinese opera has many conventions and traditions
that ease the appreciation of its drama and spectacle.**

Westerners usually cringe when first encountering the somewhat shrill tones of traditional Chinese opera. To the ears of aficionados, however, the high-pitched notes lend emotional strength to song lyrics, and the prolonged wails accentuate the singers' moods. When added to the traditional accompaniment of drums, gongs, flutes, and string instruments, the end result is an ancient sound so abstract it might have been concocted by an avant-garde composer of the 21st century.

The music provides the beat and the backing for a visual spectacle of electric shades of painted faces, glittering costumes, exquisite pantomime, and impossible acrobatics – a unique blend of sight and sound called *jingxi* (capital opera), and better known as Beijing opera.

Beijing opera was formally established in 1790. That was the year the most famous actors from all corners of the Chinese empire gathered in Peking (Beijing) to present a special variety show for the emperor. The performance proved so successful that the artists remained in the capital, combining their ancient individual disciplines of theater, music, and acrobatics into the form of Beijing opera that continues today.

Teahouse spectaculars

The first venues for these spectaculars were the teahouses of the city. With greater popularity and increasingly complex performances, the teahouses evolved into theaters. Yet the carnival atmosphere of the small teahouses persisted, and continues to do so even today.

Foreigners visiting an opera may be stunned to find that audiences eat, drink, and gossip their way through the show, only to fall silent during famous scenes and solo arias. But since audiences in Taiwan and in other Chinese communities

In performance.

know all the plots by heart – and all the performers by reputation – they know exactly when to pay undivided attention to the action.

Chinese opera has no equivalent in the West, and bears only minor similarities to European classical opera. Thematically, the stories play like high melodrama, with good guys and bad guys who are clearly defined by costumes and face paint. The themes are drawn from popular folklore, ancient legends, and historical events.

It is in terms of technique, however, that Chinese opera emerges unique among the world's theatrical forms. The vehicles of expression blend singing, dancing, mime, and acrobatics, and utilize sophisticated symbolism in costumes, make-up, and stage props.

Each of the vehicles of Chinese opera is an art form in itself. The use of face paint, for instance, is divided into 16 major categories representing more than 500 distinctive styles. Proper application of the paint imparts a character with a clear identity.

> Tang dynasty emperor Xuanzong is the patron saint of Chinese opera. His fickle consort Yang Guifei is celebrated in the popular opera The Drunken Concubine.

character; brown suggests strong character with stubborn temperament; green is reserved for ghosts, demons, and everything evil; and gold is the color of gods and benevolent spirits.

Water-sleeves and props

The extensive use of pantomime in Chinese opera virtually eliminates the need for elaborate stage sets. The few backdrops and props that are incorporated are put to ingenious uses.

One inventive prop that is actually part of a performer's costume is the water-sleeve, often used to mime emotion and imply environmental

A TaipeiEYE performance of Chinese opera.

History credits the invention of the make-up techniques to Prince Lanling, a ruler of the Northern Wei kingdom during the 6th century. As his own features were so effeminate, the prince successfully designed a fierce facemask to improve his appearance and his chances on the battlefield. His savage mask was later adapted for dramatic use. To facilitate the actors' movements and their ability to sing, the design was painted directly onto their faces.

Each color applied possesses its own basic properties: red is loyal, upright, and straightforward; white denotes craft, cunning, and resourcefulness – even a clown or a criminal; blue is vigorous, wild, brave, and enterprising; yellow indicates a dominant and intelligent but reserved

conditions. These long, white armlets of silk are attached to the standard sleeves of the costume and trail down to the floor when loose.

Although it is merely an extra length of cloth, the expressive power of the water-sleeve can be remarkable when flicked by expert wrists. To express surprise or shock, a performer simply throws up his arms. The sleeves fly backwards in an alarming manner. An actor wishing to convey embarrassment daintily holds one sleeve across the face, as if hiding behind it.

The range of symbolic gestures made possible by the water-sleeve is endless. These complement other expressive gestures in mime. Performers dust themselves off to indicate that they have just returned from a long journey. They form the sleeves into a muff around the clasped hands as protection against the cold weather of a winter scene. To cope with hot weather, the sleeves are flapped like a fan.

Simple devices like the water-sleeve, with its wide range of expression, make stage props generally unnecessary. The few that are used have obvious connotations. Spears and swords come into play during battle and action scenes. The long, quivering peacock plumes attached to the headgear of some actors identify them as warriors. Ornate riding crops with silk tassels tell any tuned-in audience that the actors are riding horses. Black pennants carried swiftly across the stage symbolize a thunderstorm, but four long pennants held aloft on poles represent a regiment of troops. A character riding a chariot holds up two yellow banners horizontally about waist high, each painted with a wheel. An actor bearing a banner with the character for *bao*, meaning report, is a courier delivering an important message.

Chinese opera also employs single props for a variety of uses. As simple an item as a chair is exactly what it appears to be when sat upon. But when placed upon a table, a chair is transformed into a mountain. Or it can be used as a throne. If an actor jumps off a chair, he has committed suicide by flinging himself into a well. After that, long strips of paper may be hung from just above his ears to indicate he has become a ghost.

With some basic grounding in the rich symbolism of the costumes, props, face paints, and mime gestures; even a spectator who doesn't understand a word of Chinese may be able to follow the outline of the plot.

Rousing acrobatics

While neon-colored costumes and dazzling make-up can enthrall audiences for hours, the long intervals of song and dialogue invariably induce bouts of boredom. But just as attention begins to drift, the performances are punctuated by rousing feats of athletics and prestidigitation.

Chinese operas don't unfold on a stage. They leap, bound and bounce into action. Performers appear to have an uncanny knack for doing one midair somersault more than is humanly possible before they return to earth.

The most thrilling portions of Chinese opera are the battle scenes. They employ every form of martial-art and acrobatic maneuver conceivable. Sabers, axes and fists fly around in a way that would end in bloodletting amid novices. A sword flung high in the air, quite miraculously, can be caught in the razor-thin slit of its scabbard.

Traditionally, men performed female roles in Chinese opera, but modern performances usually employ women to play women. Ironically, the old impersonators perfected such stylized feminine gestures that aspiring actresses have to learn to imitate a man imitating a woman.

The route to becoming an accomplished performer is a grueling one. Most children attend classes in opera schools as early as age seven, and instruction requires at least eight years.

The painted face, a distinguishing feature of all forms of Chinese opera.

TAIWANESE OPERA

In addition to Beijing opera, an offshoot called Taiwanese opera has become popular. It is usually performed outdoors on stages in the island's markets and temples and incorporates bright costumes and elaborate backdrops. Innovations in Taiwan opera range from the use of the Taiwanese dialect, instead of the difficult Hubei dialect of Beijing opera, to disco-style robes and Western make-up techniques. These changes have broadened the popularity of opera among the general public. Traditional Chinese puppet shows are also staged frequently in Taiwan, and are based on the themes, roles, music, and costumes of Beijing opera.

Taipei's parks are a good place to see martial arts practitioners.

MARTIAL ARTS

Chinese martial arts have a far softer, more deeply
spiritual basis than the high-kicking, brick-smashing
antics that the movie world tends to suggest.

A scene long played out in the hills of Taipei behind the Grand Hotel: It's three o'clock in the morning. An old man strides vigorously up to Round Mountain Park. There he begins the dance that wakes the dawn. His arms arch upward slowly in a giant circle that symbolically splits the primordial unity of the cosmos into *yin* and *yang*. He moves his hips, spine, and limbs in a harmony that animates the mystical ballet of *taiji*. With his circular movements synchronized to his abdominal breathing, he absorbs the potent *yang* energy that peaks between midnight and dawn.

The sun begins to rise. The old man, looking as spry as the new day, finishes with a regimen of *gongfu*. Back home, he sips the first of many cups of an herbal brew containing white ginseng and red jujube, sweetened with raw sugar, to help maintain the level of vital energy that pulses through his legs, spine and nervous system.

By the time the old man begins breakfast each morning, all Taipei had come alive with people jogging through the streets, stretching in the parks, and egging their bodies into heightened consciousness with an array of exercise. Today in downtown Taipei, 228 Memorial Peace Park is a particularly popular spot for this impressive display of physical culture.

From the slow-motion flourishes of *taiji* and the graceful thrusts and parries of classical sword-fighting, to innovative fighting techniques and Chinese versions of aerobic dancing, spirited residents of Taipei display an impressive range of athletic abilities.

Many of the movements hark back to that most noble of Chinese institutions, the martial arts. Contrary to popular misconception, the Chinese martial arts are collectively called *guoshu*, or national arts, not *gongfu*, which literally translates

A martial arts master works on his technique.

as 'time and energy spent on cultivating an art or skill.' In fact, it can refer to any skill. A great calligrapher has good *gongfu*. So does a master chef or master fighter.

The secrets of the martial arts have been handed down from master to disciple in an unbroken tradition reaching across tens of centuries. Many great masters joined the exodus to the island of Taiwan in 1949, bringing their secrets and skills with them. Here, they trained a new generation of experts.

Hong Yi-xiang

Two of the greats who came from the mainland were Zhang Jun-feng and Chen Pan-ling. Hong Wu-fan welcomed these homeless and destitute masters to his wealthy household. In gratitude, Zhang Jun-feng began to school Hong's five sons in the ways of the ancients. Subsequently, Chen let the Hong family in on the secrets of his mastery of *shaolin* and *taiji*.

Among Hong's five sons, the two masters discovered a sleeping dragon, someone with enormous talent not yet developed. Under the tutelage of Chen, Zhang, and 15 other renowned masters, the dragon awoke. Hong Yi-xiang, before his death in the 1990s, was considered one of the greatest masters of the ancient arts. His legacy still defines the martial-arts world in Taiwan.

Chinese that martial arts should be cultivated for spiritual development, not for superficial shows of force, and should be used exclusively for defense, never for offense. His blend of external fighting forms, derived from animal postures and internal breathing methods is the model for all Chinese martial arts.

These arts are based on the cosmic principles of *yin* and *yang*, and on the five elements of the cosmos: earth, water, metal, wood, and fire. The most fundamental concept is *qi*, which translates as vital energy or life force. But it also means air and breath. *Qi* is an invisible element contained

Young martial arts trainees in combat.

Hong Yi-xiang defied the typical image of a *gongfu* master. Packing more than 90kg (198lbs) of powerful bulk into a compact 1.7-meter (5ft-6in) tall body, he looked more like a stevedore than a master of the martial, medical, and fine arts. But to watch him perform his *taiji* forms, or demonstrate the circles of *bagua*, was like watching a gentle wind stir willow branches. Each move was smooth and fluid, yet swift and very sudden.

Spiritual development

In the 5th century, the Indian pilgrim Bodhidharma, known to the Chinese as Damo, introduced Zen Buddhism to China and enhanced Chinese fighting forms by teaching the deep-breathing methods of yoga. Damo also taught the

in air, food, water, and every living thing on Earth. Martial-arts exercises like *taiji* cultivate *qi* through deep breathing and direct it around the body with rhythmic motions. *Qi* is the force that fuels the martial arts. Proper breathing must be correctly cultivated before a student moves on to complex external movements.

The essence of classical Chinese martial arts can be defined in two words: *ruo* (softness) and *yuan* (roundness). By remaining soft and loose at all times, a person conserves vital energy while an opponent expends his by thrashing about. By using round, circular movements, the master combatant deflects his opponent's direct linear attacks, and all his parries naturally flow the full circle to become counterattacks.

> *The Chinese developed fighting forms by imitating the movements of animals, and it is said that taiji was invented when a master fighter stumbled upon an eagle and a snake locked in mortal combat.*

Softness and roundness are maintained and enhanced through rhythmic breathing. Breathing also permeates the body with *qi* during combat. The hard linear movements glorified by the modern Chinese *gongfu* movies do not promote the circulation of *qi*. Hard styles like Japanese karate, Korean *taekwondo*, and Chinese *shaolin* are better known in the West, but the soft rhythmic Chinese styles like *taiji*, *xingyi*, and *bagua* are more traditional.

Legacy of Master Peng

Hong Yi-xiang's mastery over his own *qi* came to the forefront under his last and greatest teacher, Master Peng. Peng was a mainlander who had never accepted a student after fleeing to Taiwan until, growing old, he realized he had to reveal his secrets before his death, or they would be lost to posterity. Scores of hopefuls rushed to his home in Taichung to be interviewed for the honor.

Master Peng conducted his audiences in a stark, dark room lit by a single candle. The candle stood on a low table between himself and his visitors. One by one, the eager hopefuls filed in, spoke briefly with the master, then left. Little did they know that they had been judged before uttering a word. Only one man passed the test. He managed to enter the room, approach the master and pay his respects without once causing the candle to flicker, so revealing full control of his *qi*. Master Peng had found his disciple: Hong Yi-xiang.

Master Hong not only took up the mantle of his great teachers, he also developed his own system of martial arts. Hong called his school *tangshoudao*, the Way of the Hands of Tang. It blends the finest elements of *xingyi*, *bagua*, *taiji*, and the more difficult *shaolin*. It takes its name from the so-called golden age of Chinese culture, the Tang dynasty of the 7th to early 10th centuries, which was also the formative age of Chinese *gongfu*. *Tangshoudao*, which is Chinese *gongfu* at its classical best – internal, subtle, and linked to Daoist philosophy – was Hong's personal attempt to restore Chinese martial arts to their authentic forms and traditions.

Master Hong, like Damo, believed that health and longevity are the true goals of martial arts. He said that self-defense techniques using martial arts can promote health by protecting one from bullies, but he emphasized that if one's internal powers of *qi* are strong and steady, bullies will instinctively steer clear. 'The most accomplished martial artists are those who never have to fight. No one dares challenge them,' Master Hong said. 'Concentrate on the inner meaning, not the outer strength.' He also elaborated on the apparent paradox that in softness there is strength, noting that water will wear down the hardest rock.

Outdoor exercises to start the day.

CONCRETE PROOF

Taiwan's Master Yi-xiang, one of the greatest martial artists of all time, once demonstrated the truths of the *Dao* and the explosions of power that his training enabled him to summon at will. Challenged to prove his might, he smashed three cement blocks with one blow. The blocks were stacked on a solid flat surface, rather than up on blocks. Focusing his *qi* within, Hong mustered intense concentration, then raised his fist and delivered a single devastating blow. He didn't break the blocks. He shattered them. A film replay showed that, at the moment of impact, every hair on his right arm and shoulder was erect – the power of *qi*, he later explained.

Weighing out herbal medicine.

TRADITIONAL MEDICINE

Time-honored Chinese herbal concoctions and
physical techniques both play their parts in keeping
the people of Taiwan healthy, vital, and long-lived.

Consider the case of the curious goatherd, who one day noticed that several of his billy goats were behaving in an unusually randy manner, mounting the nearest females repeatedly in remarkably brief spans of time. Concerned by their amorous behavior, perhaps even a bit envious of their prowess, the goatherd, in time-honored scientific tradition, kept careful watch on his horny herd for a few weeks. He soon detected a pattern. Whenever a billy goat ate from a particular patch of weeds, the goat's promiscuous proclivities peaked.

Before long, Chinese herbalists had determined what goats had long known: that a plant of the *aceranthus sagittatum* family was one of the most potent male aphrodisiacs. Many of China's most efficacious herbal remedies were discovered in much the same manner, and Chinese medicine now has the world's most comprehensive pharmacopoeia of herbal cures.

Historical roots

Popular history credits the genesis of herbal medicine to Shen Nong, the legendary emperor also known as the Divine Farmer, for his teaching of agricultural techniques, around 3,500 BC. References to various diseases and their herbal remedies first appeared on Shang dynasty oracle bones, c.1500 BC. They prove that medicine was a formal branch of study in China as long as 3,500 years ago. Later, books on medicine were among the few types spared during the infamous burning of books by Qin Shi Huangdi, in 220 BC.

The first volume that summarized and categorized the knowledge of herbal cures in China was first mentioned in the 2nd century BC. *The Yellow Emperor's Classic of Internal Medicine* contained the world's first scientific classification of medicinal plants, and is still used today.

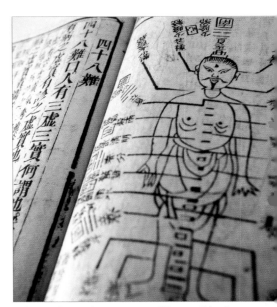

A drawing from a Qing Dynasty-era Chinese traditional herbal medicine book.

The quintessential herbal doctor, Sun Si-mo, appeared 800 years later. He established a pattern of practice still followed by Chinese physicians. 'Rich and poor, old and young, high and low are all alike in the clinic,' Sun wrote. Three emperors invited Sun to be their personal physician. He declined, preferring to practice among the commoners. Previously only the high and mighty had access to professional medical care, but Sun applied the Confucian virtue of *ren*, or benevolence, to his trade. He established the great tradition of *renshu renxin* (benevolent art, benevolent heart) that has guided Chinese physicians ever since.

FOOD AND DRINK

Few places can match Taiwan for culinary expertise, where the secrets of ethnic cuisines from the mainland are celebrated by Taiwanese chefs.

Many Taiwanese claim that their country has the best Chinese food on earth, and there's little point in arguing. While there are more and more visually attractive restaurants where care is taken to present pleasant and distinctive visual surroundings, the island has a huge selection of simple, undecorated restaurants, many of them local secrets and most serving great food.

When immigrants flooded into Taiwan after the civil war in China in 1949, they brought with them regional cuisines from all over the mainland. Many of the first restaurants in Taiwan were opened by retired soldiers, who plied their trade over hot woks in simple kitchens.

As Taiwan prospered, the people retained their taste for the regional dishes of China. Continued prosperity has brought a refined palate and an excellence seen only in the world's great dining cities. Taiwan is now a paradise for food lovers, and eating out is the top recreation.

Just about every type of Chinese food is available in Taiwan, including steamed Shanghai dumplings, salty beerhouse food, northern Chinese wheat-based snacks, Mongolian barbecue, Sichuan hotpots, night-market noodles, barbecued squid, Cantonese dim sum, dried Hunan honeyed ham – the list is virtually endless. No matter how many times you eat out in Taipei, every meal will feature something original: a new dish, a new ingredient, a new preparation.

Most Chinese restaurants in Taiwan are very casual. The lighting and decor are unremarkable, and the staff tend to be informal and friendly. Each dish arrives steaming hot as soon as it's ready, with little regard for order or decorum. The meals themselves are a frenzy of chopsticks and rice bowls, and afterwards the

Northern-style hot meat-filled dumplings are a favorite snack.

tablecloths are often badly stained and piled high with remnant bones and spilled food.

Gourmets will argue endlessly about Chinese regional cuisine: what dish belongs to which place, how the regions should be divided up, where the best seafood comes from, and so on. But generally speaking, five major mainland types are represented in Taiwan: Canton (Guangdong), Sichuan, Hakka, Shanghai, and Beijing.

Cantonese

Food-wise, the Cantonese have long been ahead of their time. In the past few decades, the world has discovered the virtues of fresh food with simple ingredients, quickly cooked and lightly seasoned. The Cantonese have been doing this for centuries. The classic Cantonese dish is lightly steamed fish doused in red-hot oil and topped with a mild sauce of fresh coriander (cilantro), ginger, pepper, sesame, and soy sauce. Other famous Cantonese dishes are too numerous to list – they include beef and broccoli with oyster sauce, diced chicken with cashew nuts, barbecued pork, steamed lobster, and the many kinds of *dim sum*.

Cantonese chefs like to mix fruit with meat or poultry, and lemon-roasted chicken and duck with pineapple are both typical. Another

quite mild compared with Thai or Indian food. Sichuan-style cuisine uses a variety of chili oils, hot sauces, and dried chili peppers to season its foods, but the chilis are not strong, and the dishes usually have a complementary sweet or sour flavor that provides balance.

As with the other cuisines, there are dozens of good Sichuanese dishes; *mapo dofu*, spicy bean curd with minced pork, is a staple, and so is *yinsi juan*, a delicate fried bread roll that sometimes serves as a substitute for rice.

Chicken or shrimp cooked with a hot and sweet sauce of peanuts and chili is a signature

Cooking in a flaming-hot wok.

quintessential dish is chicken strips dipped in egg white and cooked with fresh sweet peas. This delicate dish is typically Cantonese in character: mild, lightly spiced and full of subtle flavor.

Perhaps as a result of their competitive nature, the Cantonese repertoire also includes the most expensive, elaborate, and exotic foods of all the Chinese cuisines, including shark-fin soup, bird's nest soup and sea slug.

Sichuanese and Taiwanese

Sichuanese food, with its trademark flavorings of chili pepper and garlic, may be the most popular Chinese cuisine in Taiwan. While Sichuanese cooking is reputed for spiciness, it is

dish. Dried chilis are cut into long strips, fried in oil, then removed and cooked with the meat, and at the end a rich mixture of soy sauce, wine, vinegar, and sesame oil is added.

Hui guo rou, or 'twice-cooked' meat, is pork that is boiled with scallions (spring onions), wine, and ginger, then removed and stir-fried with garlic, chili peppers and a vegetable, usually cabbage. One especially popular Sichuanese dish is *mala huo guo* (numbing-spicy hotpot). This large pot of pig blood and pork broth, bubbling with brown peppercorns, red chili seeds, and chili oil is not for the faint of heart – it's a taste bud-destroying blaze of pungent pepper flavor. You can choose a pot with a firewall: with all the wicked spices kept in one half. Diners choose from a wide variety of ingredients to add, such as pork balls, egg and pork dumplings, mushrooms, tofu, beef, and duck blood.

In recent decades, Taiwanese food has enjoyed a renaissance. This cuisine combines the Fujianese and Japanese cooking styles with local ingredients such as sweet potato and indigenous species of clam, mullet, oyster, and freshwater shrimp.

Like many Chinese cuisines, the origins of Taiwanese cooking lie in scarcity. The most famous dish is probably *danzai mian*, or slack-season noodles. *Danzai* noodles were invented

Hakka

The Hakka are a migrant people who settled in Taiwan via Guangdong. Traditionally poor, and often on the move, their food features preserved meats and vegetables, sun-dried sausage and liver, bean curd, and plenty of cabbage and pork. The signature flavorings are vinegar, sliced ginger, pickle, and chili pepper.

Hakka food has enjoyed a revival in Taiwan, as the Taiwanese have rediscovered the virtues of simple peasant cooking. Pork features heavily. *Dibang* is a thick leg of stewed ham cooked with tangy vegetables and a rich,

Serving up steamed sesame seed-coated buns.

in 1895 by a fisherman from the southern city of Tainan as a way to stretch meager food supplies through the non-fishing season. It is made by boiling fresh noodles and beansprouts in a bamboo cup, after which the toppings are added: coriander, pork sauce, shrimp broth, vinegar, garlic, and two small shrimps. This might be the best bowl of noodles you could eat in Taiwan.

Taro cakes are also popular. The cooks slice and steam taro, a type of root vegetable, then douse it with a pork-based sauce. The *taro* cakes stay firm and chewy, and the sauce adds texture and flavor. Condiments include a mouthwatering choice of pungent garlic, tongue-searing wasabi and a smooth, sweet chili sauce.

sweet sauce. Stewed tofu with pork meatballs is typical, as is *mei gan kou rou*, or dry plum fatty bacon: thick slices of marbled pork in a salty, tangy sauce. The defining Hakka dish, shredded beef and ginger, is superb, and the thinly sliced ginger has a remarkable mildness. How cooks achieve this flavor remains a Hakka secret.

Shanghainese and Beijing

There is argument about whether Shanghai has a cuisine of its own, or whether it absorbed its food culture from surrounding territories. But who cares? In Taiwan, Shanghainese means a rich, sometimes-oily cuisine featuring gravies and stews made mostly with fish and pork.

Deservedly or not, Shanghai also gets credit for one of the most delicious of Chinese foods, the dumpling. *Xiao long bao*, the most popular type, is a mouthwatering mixture of green onion, ginger, pork, and sesame oil. Another delicacy is *tang bao*, or 'steamed buns with soup,' made with delicate dumplings that contain a warm and fragrant burst of gingery soup.

Shizi tou, or lion's head meatballs, are large meatballs of ground pork mixed with beaten egg, scallions (spring onions), ginger, minced mushrooms, and bamboo shoots, braised on a bed of cabbage. The cabbage absorbs the

on delicate wheat pancakes or in sesame seed-coated buns.

The most famous northern dish is Peking duck, which is one of the highlights of Chinese cuisine. It is sometimes called *yi ya san chi* (one duck three ways), because the crispy skin is served first, followed by the meat, and then the bones, which arrive last in a rich soup.

Peking duck takes days to prepare. The duck is boiled, brushed with wine and honey, hung up to dry for 24 hours, and then roasted and served with mild spring onion and sweet *hoisin* sauce on a thin pancake. The rich flaky skin

Family get-togethers are synonymous with feasting and drinking.

flavor from the meatballs, making this a very tasty dish.

Among the other well-known Shanghainese dishes is bean curd with pickled snow vegetable: a cold dish made from custard-like tofu, covered with the delicate snow vegetable, and sprinkled with seasonings. Shanghainese also cook many types of fish, the most famous being sweet-and-sour, where fish is coated in batter, deep-fried, and served with a tomato-based sauce.

Long the seat of the imperial court, Beijing once had a reputation as a gastronomic center, where mandarins and other privileged people ate rich and unusual foods.

In northern cooking, wheat flour largely replaces rice, and many of the dishes are served

GAOLIANG (KAOLIANG) LIQUOR

Gaoliang is a fiery spirit whose best-known brands are distilled on Kinmen and Matsu, islands off the China coast. Gaoliang is the Chinese for sorghum, from which the drink is distilled. It's a strong, explosive liquor that combines the earthy flavor of the sorghum with the heat and volatility of distilled liquor. Served in tiny glasses, about half the size of normal shot glasses, drink it as the Taiwanese do – down in one quick shot. Foreigners who can handle gaoliang, which is 58 proof, are held in high esteem. There's only one problem: every male at a banquet who thinks he is also proficient will come by and offer a toast, to see if it's true.

is the highlight. It should be crispy and fresh, with all the fat roasted away.

The best Chinese dessert is also a northern specialty. Pieces of fruit, usually banana or apple, are deep fried and then covered in a glaze of caramelized sugar and sesame seeds. Before they can cool, the fritters are plunged into a bowl of ice water and then served immediately.

Banquets

Banquet food qualifies as a separate cuisine. Because so many people must be served, many

> *The Chinese love of seafood has caused serious damage to Asia's oceans. The use of cyanide to stun fish has destroyed coral reefs and shark numbers are also in steep decline.*

That distinction belongs to bird's nest soup, made from the saliva of Asian cave swallows. The best-quality nest can be worth US$2,000 to US$10,000 per kilogram (2.2lbs), depending on type.

International beers at Taipei's Brass Monkey.

Taiwanese Kaoliang.

of the dishes are prepared in advance and served cold, while only one or two, normally fish or lobster, will be hot. Banquets feature expensive and unusual preparations. Shark-fin soup, for instance, takes three days to make. The shark fin is boiled for eight hours, then rinsed, then cooked again with ginger and scallion (spring onions), and then placed in stock made from ham, pork, and chicken. Abalone is almost as fussy to cook as shark fin, while lobster, another popular banquet dish, must be steamed for just a few seconds before it is served – a tall order when hundreds of people are waiting.

Those three dishes – lobster, shark fin, and abalone – are the crowning jewels of many banquets, but they are not the most expensive.

With rising incomes in the Chinese-speaking world, the demand for shark-fin and bird's nest soup has soared, with devastating environmental consequences.

Drinks

In Taiwan, drinking and eating out are usually combined. In night markets, diners often drink beer with their noodles, *you bing* (oil pancakes), and other snacks; in restaurants they might have gaoliang liquor or spirits like brandy or Scotch whisky. Red wine has made inroads in Taiwan, seen as a health drink, and beer is common, but two drinks are key for the Taiwanese: *gaoliang jiu* (sorghum liquor) and *shaoxing jiu* (yellow rice wine).

Gaoliang remains especially popular among the older generation, while golden-yellow *shaoxing* wine, comparatively sweet and mild, is more popular generally. Shaoxing wine is made from glutinous rice, and has the smooth nutty taste of a sweet sherry. It's generally served warm; sometimes a dried plum is added for extra sweetness.

Ordering

Never ask the waiter for suggestions, as you will end up with a dull selection of uninspiring dishes, or possibly some very expensive

polite to take the item nearest you, even if it's a bony chicken wing and not a mouth-watering slice of juicy breast meat.

One rule is inviolate: never leave your chopsticks stuck in the rice bowl. This resembles a funeral tradition, upright incense sticks, and is considered bad luck. Finally, there's the ritual of paying the bill. Often, local hosts will seem to fight and argue endlessly over who pays for the meal, but it's a farce: the 'honor' rests with whoever made the invitation, or is the responsibility of the boss or family patriarch.

Taiwanese feasts can be groan-inducingly filling.

ones. It's best to order yourself.

Select a variety of dishes: one chicken, one beef or pork, a vegetable one, possibly an egg, fish, or tofu dish, plus soup and an appetizer. The general rule is one dish for every diner, plus one extra. Each person will have a bowl of rice, while the accompanying dishes are all shared by the various diners at the table.

Etiquette

When it comes to eating Chinese food in Taiwan, few table manners apply, and the rules that do exist are often disregarded. Serving spoons are provided with each dish, and it is polite to use these common spoons, and not your personal chopsticks, to serve yourself. It is also

TOASTING

Toasting has a key role at Taiwan social gatherings, showing respect and cementing relationships. The host often stands to offer the first toast, touching the glass with both hands and sipping. Do the same, making eye contact. After this toast to the table, individual toasts are offered back and forth at will, toasters also often standing. As drinkers get red and flushed, toasts become more frequent and boisterous. If someone says 'gan bei' (dry glass) and you reply 'gan bei,' you must finish your glass. Most don't really want to drain their glasses again and again as, so it is polite to reply 'sui yi' (as you wish), allowing both drinkers to sip.

Night shopping in Taipei.

SHOPPING IN TAIPEI

The Taipei shopping experience is both international and parochial, ranging from famous haute couture and electronic gadgetry to local arts and crafts.

In Taiwan, as in much of Asia, shopping is a national pastime. As in Hong Kong and Singapore, shopping malls have taken over the island's large cities, serving as full-range shopping, entertainment, and dining destinations. Hotel arcades with high-end retail shops can be found in most five-star hotels, and there are also occasional boutique arcades near department stores. Locally owned department stores follow the Japanese model in terms of style, and many facilities are either jointly- or wholly-owned by Japanese groups. One of the biggest chains, Shin Kong Mitsukoshi, is a joint Taiwan-Japan enterprise.

Where do the Taipei locals shop? The youngest and trendiest shoppers, emulating the Japan-inspired fashions of their favorite pop stars, are in Ximending. Located near Taipei Railway Station in the older, western part of the city, Ximending (West Gate area) is extremely popular with teenagers and college students.

Young adults shop in the Dinghao area, in the eastern part of town, while more mature office ladies and salarymen can be found toting shopping bags through the designer boutiques along Zhongshan North Road, or around Renai Circle. On weekends and holidays Taipei offers a more interesting local experience, as lively temporary markets for jade, flowers, indie-designer fashion accessories, and other items open up.

Taipei's youngest and hottest shopping district is Xinyi, centered on Taipei 101, one of the world's tallest buildings. Numerous large-scale department stores and malls have sprouted here, as have outsized VieShow Cinemas and retail outlets. The massive Taipei 101 Mall and three stores of Shin Kong Mitsukoshi Xinyi New Life Square now form the area's shopping core.

Traditional products are available as well as the most cutting edge items.

Gargantuan mall complexes also dot other Taipei neighborhoods, including Breeze Center on Fuxing South Road; Core Pacific City Living Mall on Bade Road, Section 4; Miramar Entertainment Park in Neihu; and Dayeh Takashimaya in Tianmu.

Ximending and Dinghao

Hundreds of clothing stores, coffee shops, restaurants, and theaters dominate jam-packed Ximending, which has several pedestrian-only streets – a rarity in this vehicle-crazy town. Amid the neon lights, thumping music, and frosty air-conditioning is the energy associated with crowds of young and trendy people.

The Dinghao district lies along Zhongxiao East Road, near Fuxing North Road. Here, the shoppers are older, decidedly female, and often accompanied by their young families. Marked by Sogo Department Store at one end and the Ming Yao Department Store and Uniqlo Global Flagship Store near Yanji Street at the other, Dinghao is filled with high-end to mid-range boutique clothing and accessories stores such as Hang Ten, Pierre Cardin, Agatha Paris, and Benetton. Beauty and health-care stores are in abundance here as well, including Sasa and the Body Shop.

Stores such as Fendi and Gucci are found here alongside local designers like Shiatzy. High-end stores such as Tiffany's, Hermes, and Piaget are found in the nearby Grand Formosa Regent's shopping arcade.

In Xinyi district, outlets of two Taiwan glass-art enterprises with an international reputation are located in Shin Kong Mitsukoshi. Both offer exquisite pieces heavy in local cultural references, such as dragons and koji pottery. Tittot is the child of artist Heinrich Wang, and Liuli Gongfang the child of Loretta Yang, artist and former film actress.

Youth fashion dominates Ximending.

In the Dinghao-area alleys off Zhongxiao's Section 4 is Handicrafts Alley (Alley 29, Lane 205, Section 4), known for numerous boutiques creating handiworks found nowhere else. Figure 21 makes handmade leather items with nostalgia themes. McVing is both a shop and a brand, specializing in handcrafted bags that are both fashion statements and declarations of green-living commitment. The design team at AtWill makes personalized jewelry artworks that fuse rock 'n' roll and retro themes plus freewheeling ornate exuberance.

Zhongshan North Road has a number of exclusive designer boutiques that cater to well-heeled Japanese tourists and the local jet set.

Local markets

For a more traditional-style local experience, try the temporary markets. On weekends and national holidays, the Taipei Holiday Jade Market and Taipei Holiday Flower Market open up under the Jianguo Elevated Expressway where it passes over Renai Road.

The Jade Market is a packed, busy bazaar full of jade items of many different qualities and provenance. Jade dominates, but there are also freshwater pearls, amethyst, tiger's eye, and many other semi-precious stones and crystals.

The vendors are quite honest. They generally will tell you if a product is real jade or not. However, as when shopping for any expensive product, it's best to know what you're looking for and how to tell the genuine product from a well-made imitation. If you don't trust your instincts or your knowledge, you can go to one of the countless jewelry stores that line the streets in Taipei, as they offer an authentication certificate with the sales slip, albeit adding slightly to the cost.

Bargaining isn't encouraged, but it's not out of the question. The general rule of thumb is to offer half the asking price and work your way to a compromise. However, don't make an offer if you're not interested. Vendors

The two markets are open from 9am to 6pm on Saturdays and Sundays, as well as national holidays. It is crowded in the afternoons; mornings are a little quieter. Food vendors sell Chinese sausages, barbecued squid, sweet bean cakes, and other treats near the Renai and Xinyi entrances.

Trinkets and collectibles

The best place in Taipei to spend an afternoon browsing through antiques and collectibles is the area centered on the corner of Yongkang Street and Chaozhou Street. There is a large

Taipei Holiday Flower Market.

High-end shopping at the 101 Mall.

dislike having to go through the trouble of bargaining and coming to an agreement on price only to be met with the bargainer walking away.

Plants sprout everywhere in Taipei in luxurious profusion: from balconies and rooftops, in alleys and streets. The Taiwanese love their plants, and many of them come from the Taipei Holiday Flower Market.

Vendors at this market sell every kind of plant life imaginable. Bamboo, miniature maple trees, Japanese bonsai, bushes, leafy house plants, exotic ferns, gourds, and citrus trees form part of the endless variety that can be found among the profusion of orchids and other flowers.

JOINING THE TEA SET

The Taiwanese love their tea, and it shows. Teashops are a common sight, filled with silver barrels of tea leaves and dozens of brown-clay tea sets.

Traditional brown-clay tea sets come in many shapes and qualities. A set usually includes a teapot, cups, and a container with a lid, which is used to collect discarded tea leaves.

For those new to the Chinese tea tradition, selecting a tea set involves choosing a design that appeals to you. However, connoisseurs will look more closely at the quality of the clay, the thinness of the crockery, and how long it will take for the tea to 'flavor' the teapot.

cluster of shops here, with the 30 crowded shops of Zhaoheting Antique Market in old Jin'an Market the cluster's heart and soul. The shops have a wide array of Chinese antiques, as well as a wide range of interesting collectibles from 1950s and 1960s Taiwan.

Locals warn tourists to take extra care before purchasing Chinese antiques, as it's often difficult to tell the genuine antique from the fake. Taiwan has been scoured dry, and most pieces now come from China. On some bronze 'antiques,' what looks like a patina of dusty age may actually be a handful of clay rubbed

In Guang Hwa Digital Plaza.

on two weeks ago in China. As with expensive jewelry, be sure you're dealing with a legitimate licenced retailer, and/or bring along a knowledgeable friend, when purchasing high-priced antiques.

Dihua Street

Northwest of the Taipei Main Station is one of Taipei's oldest areas, Dihua Street. This area is rich in its variety of traditional wares such as Chinese herbal medicines, Taiwan-style fabrics, handmade crafts, and traditional treats.

In its day, Dihua was a Tamsui River port street, and the main conduit for trade in Taipei Basin. During the annual run-up to

the Chinese Lunar New Year, this classical building-lined street teems with hawkers and shoppers. The shops specialize in traditional holiday treats and paraphernalia to ring in the new year.

Other areas

North of Taipei Railway Station, on Chengde Road near Changan West Road, is another area of interest for the adventurous shopper. This district has a mixture of stores, from those supplying industrial equipment to ones selling Christmas decorations. In this neigh-

> *Buddhist bracelets – yellow jade or amethyst beads on an elasticized band – are popular accessories for Taiwanese men and women, and reputedly have protective qualities.*

borhood, two worthwhile stops are Lin Tian Barrel Store, a heritage shop making wooden buckets/barrels on the corner of Zhongshan North Road and Changan West Road, and the Taiwan Handicraft Paper Manufacturing Company at 47–2 Changan West Road, offering handmade crafts.

On Civic Boulevard at Xinsheng North Road is Guang Hua Digital Plaza. Hundreds of electronic goods shops are found in this young, specially built six-floor facility. Taiwan is one of the world's largest producers of computers and peripherals, as one look at this market immediately proves. Great deals can be found, but it's advisable to be armed with a knowledge of what you will require. Many shoppers end up spending more than they intended due to the enthusiasm of fast-talking salesmen. There are also specialist repair shops here.

Located at the corner of Zhongshan South Road and Xuzhou Road, the government-sponsored Chinese Handicraft Mart offers four floors of Taiwan-made Chinese, Taiwanese, and indigenous souvenirs. On the first three floors the merchandise includes jewelry, porcelain, wall hangings, painted fans, silk, teapots, and furniture, while the basement offers T-shirts, slippers, toys, and novelty items. The center handles international shipping.

Best buys

Taiwan offers myriad traditional Chinese handicraft items. Jade jewelry, engraved chops, and Chinese tea sets are essentials in local lives, and quintessential souvenir choices for tourists.

Tea sets, engraved chops, and jade jewelry are seen by Taiwan folk as an extension of their character and indispensable elements of their unique individual identity. As souvenir items, these iconic treasures bring a little bit of the Taiwan culture to your home.

Jewelry

The Taiwanese love their jewelry. There are jewelry and gold shops in almost every neighborhood. Jade is a prized semi-precious stone, and is believed by many to bring good luck. It comes in a variety of shapes. Round pieces with a hole in the middle are called *bi*, and were initially carved to honor the gods of heaven, while the elongated carved jade known as *cong* was made to honor more earthly spirits. As with many other stones, jade comes in a variety of different colors, some more valuable than others. The jade from Taiwan is dark green, while Burmese jade is a lighter green and is preferred by many Taiwanese. Unless you're an expert, simply buy within your budget, and to your taste.

Personalized chops

Chops are nearly as common today in Taiwan as they were hundreds of years ago in China. Engraved with a person's name and stamped on documents with a pasty red ink, they are used in place of a signature when conducting business such as banking, posting registered mail, and authorizing legal transactions, though use of signatures alone is now legally recognized.

Because they are so widely used, chops engravers can be found in almost every neighborhood. Their shops are identified by their displays of different chops, made from wood, plastic, stone, metal, and jade. The engraving style is as important as the composition of the characters. The traditional style of calligraphy used is called *zhuan shu*; others include the clerical script *li shu*, and regular script *kai shu*. There are also scripts unique to chop engraving, such as the 'bird,' 'insect,' and 'phoenix' styles. Prices of chops can vary enormously, and most engravers include a carrying case and red ink.

Pottery and porcelain

Some of the most beautiful pieces of pottery and porcelain ever made are on display in Taipei's National Palace Museum. However, those wishing to bring home a piece of quality china should look beyond the museum's expensive gift shop.

Yingge, southwest of Taipei, is famous for its fine ceramic works, including porcelain. Hundreds of small shops and large factories line its streets, and its artisans pride themselves on reproducing hand-painted works of art from centuries ago. Worth collecting are latticed vases in which craftsmen cut holes out of the clay to produce a basket effect.

Jade has always been a favorite gemstone in Chinese culture.

Another source of pottery and porcelain is the Chinese Handicraft Mart. The selection is not as varied, but it is conveniently located in Taipei.

Classic Chinese silk is an excellent gift purchase. Yongle Market at 21 Dihua Street sells all kinds of fabrics, and there are also boutiques in the neighborhood, particularly along Yanping North Road. These shops will also tailor-make clothing articles.

Electronic goods are a reasonably good buy and, generally, new products from Japan make it to Taiwan's shores faster than to North America or Europe. The greatest concentration of camera shops is on Boai Road, south of Zhongxiao West Road, near Taipei Railway Station. Prices here are somewhat lower than in most outlets in the US and Europe, and comparable to internet wholesale prices. A little browsing will help you discover the right price.

A stunning stretch of coastline in eastern Taiwan.

Kaohsiung's Dragon and Tiger Pagodas.

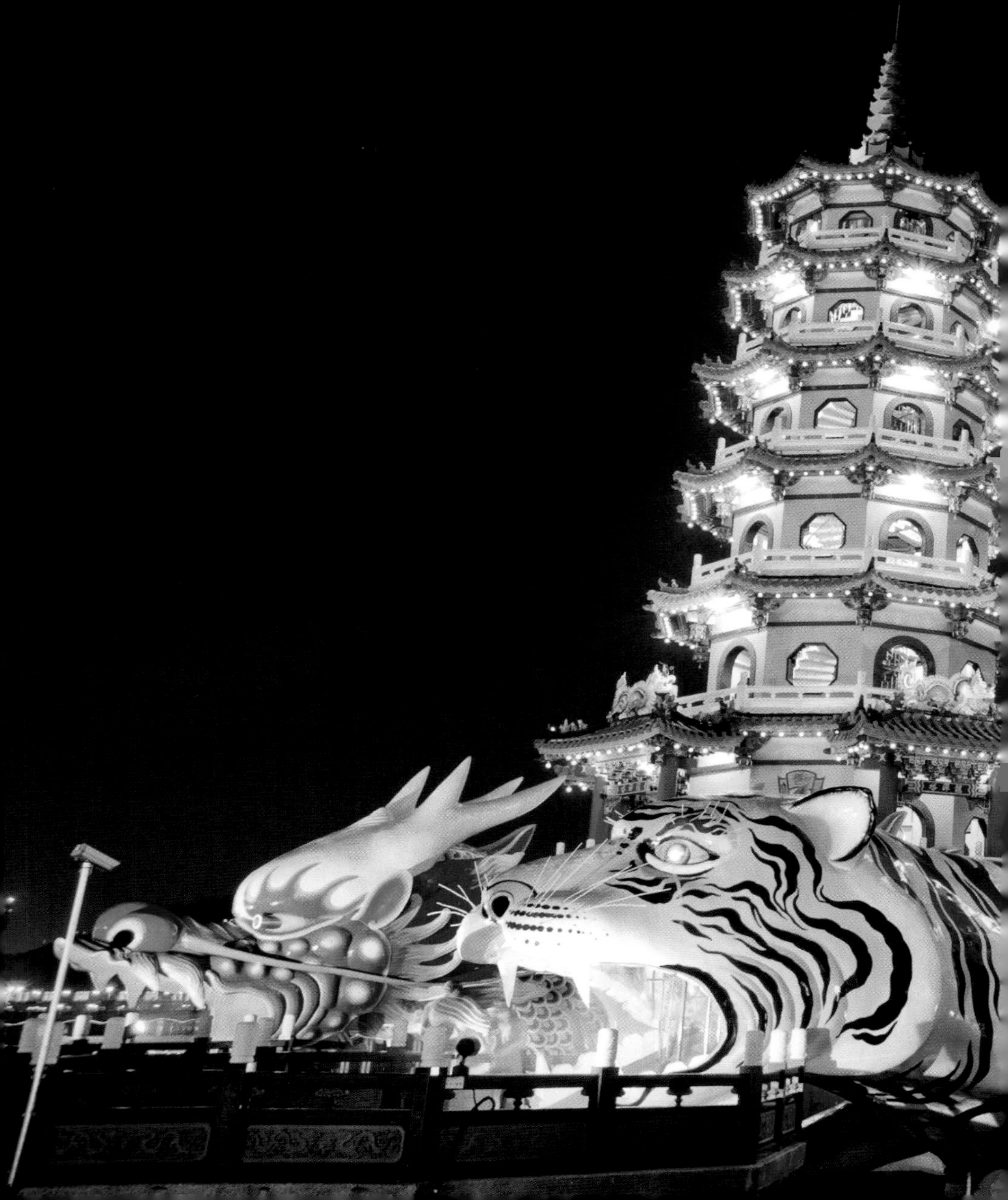

Taroko Gorge.

Chiang Kai Shek Memorial.

INTRODUCTION

A detailed guide to the entire island, with principal
sites clearly cross-referenced by number to the maps.

Taipei views from Four Beasts Mountain.

Despite the fact Taiwan has modernized at breakneck speed over the past half-century-plus, an expedition out of its major cities never fails to yield the lingering influences of old ways and spectacular natural vistas.

Little Taiwan features immense diversity in terrain and culture, and a first-rate highway system that encircles the island and gives easy access to the mountainous interior. Small it may be, but Taiwan is characterized by fascinating extremes, from periodic high-mountain snowfalls to wave-lashed rocky shores, from high-tech science parks to traditional Daoist rituals.

Northern Taiwan, a mix of flatland and foothills, is the upper terminus of the soaring central mountains that bisect the long, narrow island. The north-coast highway skirts a sculpted-sandstone seashore of haunting beauty. Taipei is Taiwan's largest city, its capital, and its economic and cultural heart.

West-central Taiwan has a tall central mountain backdrop for a wide plain that runs to the sea. The flatlands landscape is at turns agricultural and industrial. The major city, Taichung, is a small city with a leisurely pace.

Outside the main cities, Tainan and Kaohsiung, the south is primarily agricultural. The far south is tropical, blessed with soft, sandy beaches. Tainan is Taiwan's Kyoto, albeit in a modest way, while Kaohsiung is an industrial port city working hard on its cultural, creative side.

Travelers in search of Taiwan's raw beauty choose the east coast, where steep coastal cliffs on the north and south bracket a palm-tree environment akin to a South Sea paradise island. The most notable sight is Taroko Gorge, a fantastic marble chasm with an equally remarkable road sliced right through its walls.

A picturesque landscape on Juguang Island in the Matsu Islands.

Tremendous strides have been made in terms of tourist infrastructure and services in recent years to make all of the island's treasures easily and inexpensively accessible to the traveler from overseas.

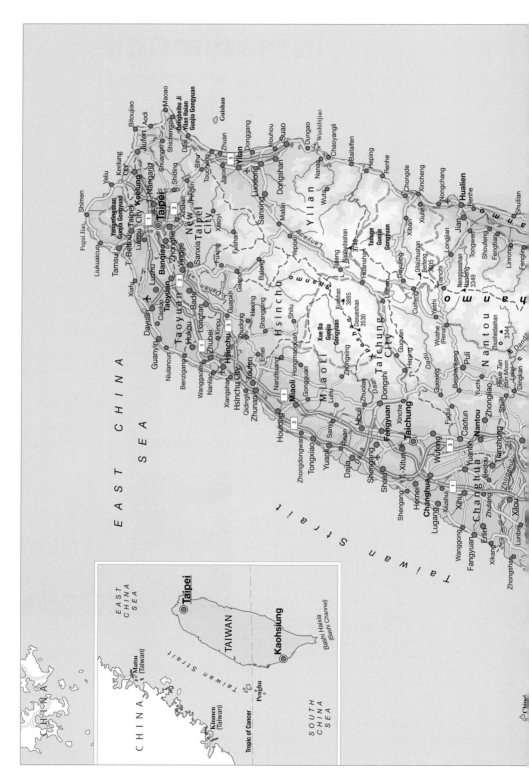

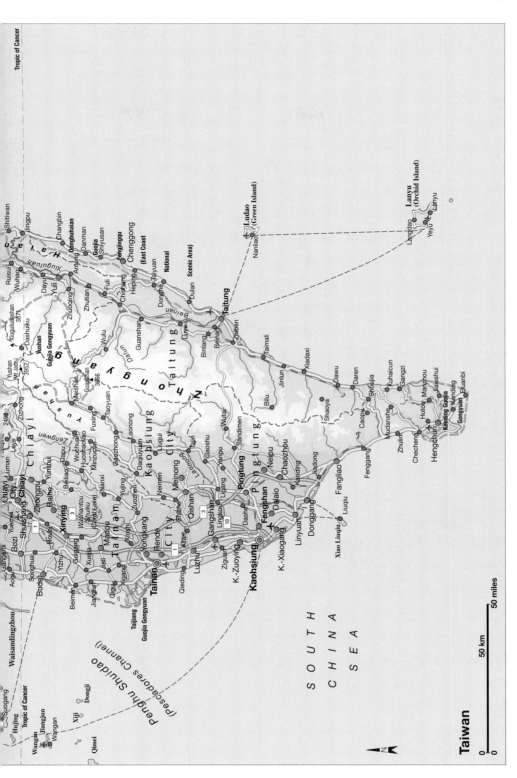

Taiwan

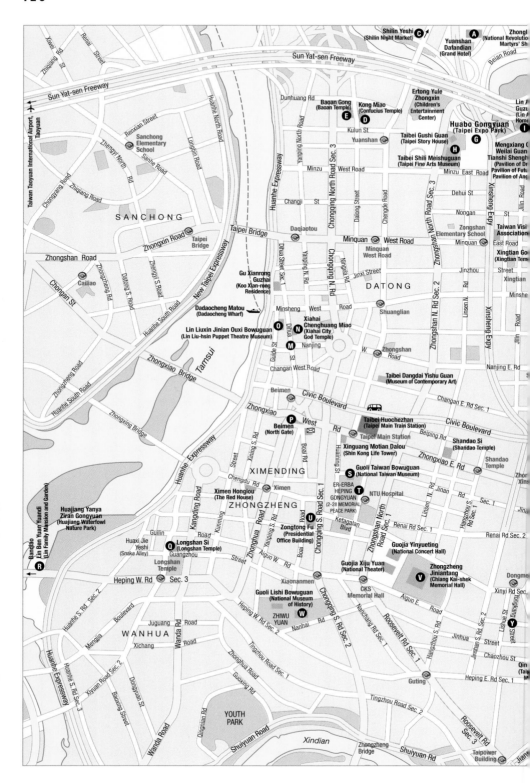

Shilin Yeshi (Shilin Night Market) **C**

Yuanshan Dafandian (Grand Hotel) **A**

Zhongl (National Revolutio Martyrs' Sh

Sun Yat-sen Freeway

Sun Yat-sen Freeway

Taiwan Taoyuan International Airport, Taoyuan

Renai Street

Zhiqiang St

Kwai Rd

Banxian Street

Renai Road

Sanhe Road

Sanchong Elementary School

Zhengyi North Rd

Longdin Road

Huanhe North Road

Dunhuang Rd

Baoan Gong (Baoan Temple) **E**

Kong Miao (Confucius Temple) **D**

Ertong Yule Zhongxin (Children's Entertainment Center)

Lin A Guzu (Lin A Hom **I**

Zhengri North Rd

Zhiqiang Road

Chongyang Road

Sanhe Road

Kulun St

Yanping North Road

Yuanshan

Taibei Gushi Guan (Taipei Story House) **H**

Huabo Gongyuan (Taipei Expo Park) **G**

Mengxiang G Weilai Guan Tianshi Shengh (Pavilion of Dr Pavilion of Futu Pavilion of Ang

Zhongyang Road

Zhiqiang Rd

Taipei Bridge

West Road

Minzu

Chongqing North Road Sec. 3

Taibei Shili Meishuguan (Taipei Fine Arts Museum)

Minzu East Road

Jilin R

SANCHONG

Huanhe Expressway

Changji St

Dalong Street

Chengde Road

Dehui St

Zhongshan North Road Sec. 3

Kinsheng Expy

Zhongshan Elementary School

Taiwan Visi Association

Nongan

Jinzhou

Rd

St

Taipei Bridge

Daqiaotou

Minquan West Road

Minquan West Road

Dihua Street Sec.

Ningxia Rd

Yanping N. Rd

Jinxi Street

DATONG

Minquan

East Road

Xingtian Go (Xingtian Tem Street

Zhongshan Road

Chongan St

Caiiliao

Datong S. Road

Zhongxi Road

Zhengyi Road

New Taipei Expressway

Huanhe South Road

Xingtian

Rd

Xinsheng Expy

Minshe

Gu Xianrong Guzhai (Koo Xian-rong Residence)

Dadaocheng Matou (Dadaocheng Wharf)

Minsheng West Road

Xiahai Chenghuang Miao (Xiahai City God Temple)

Shuanglian

Zhongshan N. Rd Sec. 2

Linsen N. Rd

Jilin

Road

Zhongzheng Road

Huanhe South Road

Tamsui

Zhongxiao Bridge

Lin Liuxin Jinian Ouxi Bowuguan (Lin Liu-hsin Puppet Theatre Museum)

Dihua

Guide Street

Nanjing

Zhongshan Road

Nanjing E. Rd

O
N
M

Zhongxiao Bridge

Changan West Road

Taibei Dangdai Yishu Guan (Museum of Contemporary Art)

Beimen

Civic Boulevard

Changan E. Rd Sec. 1

Zhongxiao

West

Rd

Taibei Huochezhan (Taipei Main Train Station)

Civic Boulevard

Beimen (North Gate) **P**

Taipei Main Station

Beiping Rd

Shandao Si (Shandao Temple)

Shandao Temple

Zhor Xins

Huanhe Expressway

Zhongxing Bridge

Xining S. Rd

Kangding Road

Boai Rd

Xinguang Motian Dalou (Shin Kong Life Tower)

Guoli Taiwan Bowuguan (National Taiwan Museum)

Zhongxiao E. Rd

XIMENDING

Chengdu Rd

Ximen

Yanping S. Rd

ER-ERBA HEPING GONGYUAN (2-28 MEMORIAL PEACE PARK)

NTU Hospital

Linsen N. Rd

Jinan

Rd

Sec. 1

Jina

Jina

Huajiang Yanya Ziran Gongyuan (Huajiang Waterfowl Nature Park)

Ximen Honglou (The Red House)

ZHONGZHENG

Kunming

Zhongshan North Road Sec. 1

S

T

Hangzhou S. Rd Sec. 1

Renai Rd Sec. 2

Bangqiao

Lin Ben Yuan Yuandi (Lin Family Mansion and Garden)

Huaxi Jie Yeshi (Snake Alley)

Longshan Si (Longshan Temple) **Q**

Guilin Road

Zhonghua Road

Yanping S. Rd

Chongqing S. Road Sec. 1

Ketagalan Blvd

Zongtong Fu (Presidential Office Building)

Renai Rd Sec. 1

Guojia Yinyueting (National Concert Hall)

U

Guojia Xiju Yuan (National Theater)

Zhongzheng Jiniantang (Chiang Kai-shek Memorial Hall) **V**

Dongme

R

Guangzhou Street

Aiguo W. Rd

Xiaonanmen

CKS Memorial Hall

Aiguo E. Road

Xinyi Rd Sec.

Longshan Temple

Heping W. Rd Sec. 3

Guoli Lishi Bowuguan (National Museum of History)

ZHIWU YUAN

W

Hangzhou S. Rd Sec. 2

Jinshan S. Rd Sec. 2

Shaoxing S. Street

Y

Chaozhou St

WANHUA

Juguang Road

Heping W. Rd Sec. 2

Nanhai Rd

Nanchang Rd Sec. 1

Roosevelt Rd Sec. 1

Jinhua

Street

Qin (Tai M

Mengjia Boulevard

Wanda Road

Xichang

Zhonghua Road Sec. 1

Tingzhou Road Sec. 1

Guting

Heping E. Rd Sec. 1

Dingnian Rd

Guoxing Rd

Shuiyuan Road

Xindian

Zhongzheng Bridge

Shuiyuan Rd

Roosevelt Rd Sec. 3

Jian

Taipower Building

YOUTH PARK

Tingzhou Road Sec. 2

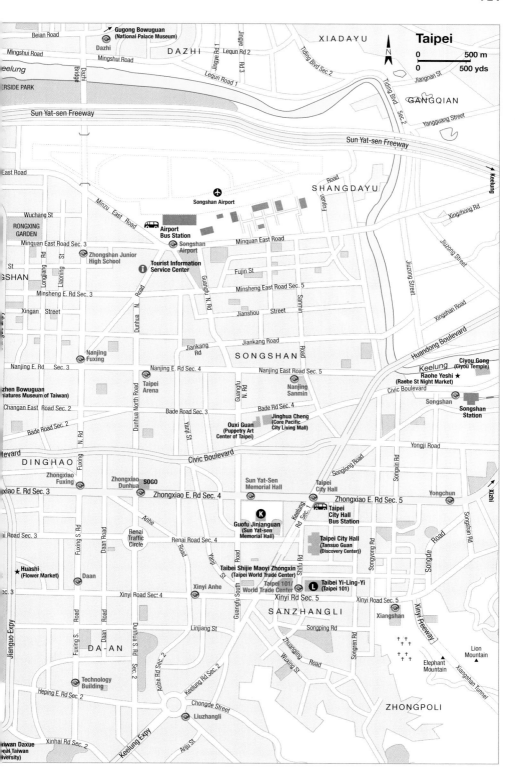

Taipei

0 — 500 m
0 — 500 yds

Beian Road
Mingshui Road
Gugong Bowuguan (National Palace Museum)
Dazhi
Mingshui Road
DAZHI
Jingye
Lequn Rd 2
Jingye Rd 1
Rd 3
Tiding Blvd Sec.2
XIADAYU
Keelung
Bridge
Dazhi
Lequn Road 1
Lequn Road 1
Jiangnan St
GANGQIAN
RIVERSIDE PARK
Sun Yat-sen Freeway
Tiding Blvd
Sec.2
Yangguang Street
Sun Yat-sen Freeway
Keelung
East Road
Minzu East Road
SHANGDAYU
Fuyuan Road
Xingzhong Rd
Songshan Airport
Wuchang St
RONGXING GARDEN
Minquan East Road Sec. 3
Airport Bus Station
Songshan Airport
Minquan East Road
Juzong Street
Juzong Street
Xingshan Road
SHAN
Rd
St
Longjiang
Liaoning
St
Zhongshan Junior High School
Tourist Information Service Center
Guangfu N. Rd
Fujin St
Minsheng East Road Sec. 5
Sanmin
Minsheng E. Rd Sec. 3
Dunhua N. Road
Jianshou
Street
Xingshan Road
Xingan Street
Jiankang
Rd
Jiankang Road
Huandong Boulevard
Nanjing Fuxing
SONGSHAN
Keelung
Ciyou Gong (Ciyou Temple)
Nanjing E. Rd Sec. 3
Nanjing E. Rd Sec. 4
Guangfu N. Rd
Nanjing East Road Sec. 5
Raohe Yeshi ★ (Raohe St Night Market)
zhen Bowuguan (Miniatures Museum of Taiwan)
Taipei Arena
Dunhua North Road
Nanjing Sanmin
Civic Boulevard
Songshan
Changan East Road Sec. 2
Bade Road Sec. 3
Bade Rd Sec. 4
Songshan Station
Bade Road Sec. 2
N. Rd
Fuxing
Yanji St
Jinghua Cheng (Core Pacific City Living Mall)
Ouxi Guan (Puppetry Art Center of Taipei)
Yongji Road
Boulevard
Civic Boulevard
Songlong Road
Songxin Rd
DINGHAO
Zhongxiao Fuxing
Zhongxiao Dunhua
SOGO
Sun Yat-Sen Memorial Hall
Taipei City Hall
Xizhi
Zhongxiao E. Rd Sec. 3
Zhongxiao E. Rd Sec. 4
Zhongxiao E. Rd Sec. 5
Yongchun
Songshan Rd
Anhe
Keelung Rd Sec. 1
Taipei City Hall Bus Station
Fuxing S. Rd
Daan Road
Renai Traffic Circle
Renai Road Sec. 4
Guofu Jinianguan (Sun Yat-sen Memorial Hall)
Shifu Rd
Taipei City Hall (Tansuo Guan (Discovery Center))
Songgong Rd
Songde Road
Songren Road
ai Road Sec. 3
Huashi (Flower Market)
Daan
Yanji St
Taibei Shijie Maoyi Zhongxin (Taipei World Trade Center)
ec. 3
Xinyi Road Sec. 4
Xinyi Anhe
Guangfu South Road
Taipei 101/ World Trade Center
Taibei Yi-Ling-Yi (Taipei 101)
Xinyi Road Sec. 5
Xinyi Road Sec. 5
Dunhua S. Rd
Linjiang St
SANZHANGLI
Xiangshan
Xinyi Freeway
Jianguo Expy
DA-AN
Fuxing S. Rd
Daan
Sec. 2
Anhe Rd Sec. 2
Keelung Rd Sec. 2
Songping Rd
Zhuangjing Road
Wuxing St
Songren Road
Lion Mountain
Elephant Mountain
Xiangshan Tunnel
Technology Building
Heping E. Rd Sec. 2
Chongde Street
ZHONGPOLI
Liuzhangli
iwan Daxue (nai Taiwan versity)
Xinhai Rd Sec. 2
Keelung Expy
Xinhai Rd Sec. 2
Anju St

TAIPEI

The booming, vibrant capital is a cosmopolitan city that nevertheless remains steeped in native Taiwanese, Chinese, and Japanese cultural elements – a compelling combination for visitors.

The capital of Taiwan is not an ancient city. Like Tokyo, Hong Kong, and Singapore, it's a new arrival. Just 300 years ago, it was a place of swamps, its only inhabitants the indigenous Ketagalan tribe, the only traces of whom today remain in the lingering influences of some of the old names for areas in the city. It was not until the first decade of the 18th century that Chinese immigrants from Quanzhou in Fujian province began to arrive in numbers. Over time they turned the area they called Mangka (renamed Wanhua by the Japanese), an elbow of land cradled by the Danshui and Xindian rivers, into a flourishing trading port.

By the late 19th century, the Chinese Qing dynasty had established most of its major administrative agencies in Taipei, and the city center had moved from Wanhua to today's Zhongzheng district, now home to the Presidential Office Building and Chiang Kai-shek Memorial Hall. And when the Japanese colonized Taiwan in 1895, they followed suit, making Taipei the capital. But even when the leaders of the Republic of China established their government in northern Taiwan in 1949, Taipei was still no more than a sleepy country town surrounded by rice fields and mud flats. As late as the mid-1960s, the city had few paved roads, and

Women protecting themselves from the hot sun.

pedicabs were the primary means of public transportation.

Frenzy of growth

The changes that forever altered the face of Taipei starting in the 1970s were truly dramatic. All the blessings and evils of modernization gripped the city in a frenzy of growth, which continues today. Hundreds of thousands of two- and four-wheeled vehicles today fill the streets, and the still-expanding Taipei Metro system now ferries Taipei residents around

Main Attractions
Shilin Night Market
Baoan Temple
Taipei Expo Park
Sun Yat-sen Memorial Hall
Taipei 101
Dihua Street
Longshan Temple
Lin Family Mansion and Garden
2-28 Memorial Peace Park
Chiang Kai-shek Memorial Hall

The ubiquitous scooter transports residents in and around Taipei.

In the Taipei 101 Observatory.

the city. The drab, gray compartments of concrete that once characterized Taipei architecture now squat in the shadows of high-rise glass and metal.

The remarkable change has also affected the city's residents. Utilitarian fashions were long ago mothballed in favor of the latest trends and designs from Paris, Hong Kong, and New York. Youths patronize Starbucks cafés, and dance in nightclubs to the latest international sounds. A catalyst for internationalism was a relaxation of restrictions on overseas travel. Prior to 1978, residents of Taiwan were prohibited from leaving the country, except to visit relatives, or for business or educational purposes. The change in policy permitted people to receive passports and exit visas purely for pleasure trips. Many Taipei residents had been saving for decades for the chance to taste foreign flavors firsthand, and they have been flocking overseas ever since. The new tastes in food, fashion, and recreation have turned Taipei into a cosmopolitan city.

At the same time, there have been serious government efforts to improve two of the side-effects of rapid modernization that have been a blight on the city's reputation: traffic congestion and pollution. Visitors to Taipei today who remember the mid-1990s are pleasantly surprised to see how the establishment of bus lanes, the addition of expressways, the opening of the metro system, and emissions controls have combined to not only make Taipei's notorious traffic less frightening but also help lift the pollution that once hung over the city.

New and old in harmony

Yet this veneer of 21st-century sophistication does not mask one implacable fact: Taipei remains one of the most staunchly traditional cities of Asia. Taipei may look increasingly like Westernized Asian cities such as Singapore and Hong Kong, but far more than its chief Asian rivals, Taipei has not forgotten its heritage – the beating heart of the city is a unique mix of indigenous Taiwanese, Chinese, and Japanese influences that makes the city ceaselessly fascinating for visitors.

Not unexpectedly, the greatest source of visitors to Taiwan annually are the overseas Chinese and Taiwanese communities of the world. Taiwan also remains a magnet for Japanese, who have borrowed heavily from classical Chinese culture during the past 1,000 years. Visitors to Taiwan are always impressed by the hospitality of the Taiwanese people. In the end, *renqingwei* – warmth, hospitality, and the flavor of human feelings – leaves many a visitor with thoughts of returning.

Into the city

Modern visitors to Taipei, like the settlers of old, experience the city's outskirts first. Taiwan Taoyuan International Airport (CKS) is in Taoyuan, 45km (28 miles) southwest of the capital. The airport cannot compare with the gleaming new airports of Asian cities like Singapore, Kuala Lumpur, Osaka, and Hong Kong, but ongoing renovations go some way to remedying this state of affairs. Buses and taxis whisk – traffic permitting – new arrivals along one of the two north-south freeways, linking the airport to Taipei

in the north and to other destinations in the south.

Taipei was once described as the ugly duckling of Asian cities – an impression founded during the 1960s on the city's drab, hastily erected buildings, dusty streets, open gutters, and battered pedicabs. It has come a long way since, transforming itself into a modern city that at its best rivals its Asian neighbors. Spacious six-lane boulevards shaded by islands of tropical trees provide breathing space between the walls of new buildings, and a slew of young parks, large and small, have given Taipei residents a green escape.

Wandering aimlessly through Taipei's streets is a good way of familiarizing oneself with the city and its people. It will uncover many surprises that could never be duplicated on guided tours around the main attractions. Bear in mind, though, that because of the city's size it would take weeks rather than days to explore all the city on foot. Therefore, concentrate on some of the more interesting districts for walking forays. For a broad-brush impression of Taipei, consider taking a trip on the

FACT

As Taipei has developed physically, so too has its population increased dramatically, with Taiwanese from other parts flooding in to find work. The Taipei greater metropolitan area is home to 7.4 million people, almost a third of Taiwan's population.

In Carnegies bar, one of the city's most popular.

A guard at Martyrs' Shrine.

Grand Hotel.

MRT Wenshan Line, which runs high above the traffic from the wooded hills of Muzha in the south into the heart of the city along fashionable Fuxing North/South Road, or slide along the base of the Yangmingshan massif on the north side on the MRT Tamsui and Xinbeitou lines, through upscale residential areas, to the Beitou hot-springs resort area.

The north side

One of the city's most visible landmarks for orientation is the **Grand Hotel** Ⓐ (Yuanshan Dafandian). Located atop a ridge on the north side of the city core, this 530-room hotel looks somewhat like an ancient palace, built in the classical imperial style of old China and patterned specifically on Beijing's Forbidden City. The massive multi-story newest wing, finished in 1973, is crowned by the largest classical Chinese roof on earth. Once the most fashionable place to be seen in Taipei, the hotel was looking aged by the 1990s, and then a fire destroyed the original roof in 1995, but new management teams have since had some success in restoring the hotel's fortunes and good looks.

The Grand Hotel is as good a spot as any to begin touring Taipei. About half a kilometer (0.2 mile) east of the hotel is the **Martyrs' Shrine** Ⓑ (Zhonglie Zi; daily 9am–5pm), on Beian Road. The complex is built in the palace style of the Ming dynasty, each structure attempting to recreate a similar hall or pavilion in Beijing. Dedicated to the fallen heroes of the Republic of China's wars, the arched portals of the main gate open onto a vast courtyard, past guest pavilions and drums and bell towers. Two gigantic brass-studded doors stand before the main shrine, where the names of the heroes are inscribed beside murals depicting their feats. The late Chiang Kai-shek, Taiwan's first president, considered this a favorite retreat, often spending entire afternoons strolling through the grounds and halls. The changing of the guard on the hour (9am–4pm) is as much an attraction for visitors as the shrine itself.

Just to the northwest of the hotel, beside MRT Jiantan Station, is the best

BE STREETWISE

Before setting out on a street ramble, it's worth remembering a couple of points about Taipei's street system, which invariably confuses newcomers. The city has in the past moved decisively to standardize the English street names, but there remains significant confusion because there are many signs with street names put up by the central government's various bodies, indicating government sites, tourist sites. These are less standardized. Thus, you may see the 'Zhongshan' of 'Zhongshan Road' also spelled Jungshan, Jhongshan, and Chungshan.

A second point of confusion is the habit of dividing roads into sections and then tagging them either 'north,' 'south,' 'east,' or 'west,' depending on what part of the city they happen to run through. Thus, an address on Zhongxiao Road, which effectively cuts Taipei into northern and southern districts, might, say, be 143 Zhongxiao East Road, Section 1. There could also very well be the following address: 143 Zhongxiao West Road, Section 1. Miss the 'East/West' difference and you're lost.

Any addresses on Section 1 of a road will be close to the city center, while an address on Section 5 will be farther out. Looking at an address, therefore, will immediately give you a general idea of which sector of the city you should look at if referring to a map.

night market in the city and perhaps all of Taiwan, **Shilin Night Market**  (Shilin Yeshi; daily 5pm–midnight; free). With a history of over 100 years, it is known for the quality of its food, which represents Taiwanese snacks at their best. The food market is housed in a purpose-built multi-story building, and the streets in the adjoining area are home to scores of shops and still more food-sellers. The market's signature food treats are giant deep-fried chicken steaks, oyster omelets, and thick squid soup.

Further north, next to the Astronomical Museum and Science Education Centre is the **Taipei Children's Amusement Park** (http://english.tcap.taipei; Tue–Fri, Sun 9am–5pm, Sat until 8pm), which opened in 2014 and is a place you should know of if traveling with children. In addition to the indoor playground and rollercoasters, children may enjoy a play in the Children's Theatre and a family meal in one of the food courts. It is always busy, so reservations for the attractions (which can also be made through the reservation app) are recommended.

Contrasting temples

To the southwest of the hotel is **Taipei Confucius Temple** (Taipei Kong Miao; www.ct.taipei.gov.tw; Tue–Sun 8.30am–9pm; free), on Dalong Street. Built in 1925, it's a tranquil retreat. Absent are the throngs of worshipers supplicating their gods with prayer and offerings, the cacophony of gongs and drums, and the gaudy idols – unless you happen to visit on September 28, Teacher's Day (Confucius' birthday), when the temple is host to colorful Confucius Ceremony rituals and dance performances by children. Absent, too, are images of Confucius. The tranquility is fitting – Confucius preached, among other things, the virtues of peace and quiet. The temple's architecture is subtle yet exquisite in its simplicity, and highlighted by magnificent roofs. There are videos daily in English on Confucius and the temple at 10.30am and 3.30pm, an exhibit on the classic Confucian Six Arts, and regular educational activities on Confucianism.

By contrast, the 200-year-old Daoist **Baoan Temple** (Baoan Gong; www.

Martyr's Shrine.

baoan.org.tw; daily 6.30am–100pm; free), on Hami Street and next to the Confucius Temple, is a gaudy monument to Baosheng Dadi, the folk religion God of Medicine. Carved dragons decorate the main support columns, and the interior is crowded with the images of many deities. The main one of Baosheng Dadi was brought from Fujian province in China by early settlers in 1805. The Baosheng Cultural Festival, which goes on for weeks generally starting in April, brims with diversity. Highlights are the Traditional Three Consecrations Ceremony and Feasting of the Kings Ceremony, showcases of ancient rites. Among the classic theatrical martial-arts arrays are the Song Jiang Battle Array, Twelve Grannies Formation, and Flower Drum Formation. Magnificent deity parades stretch kilometers, and great bedazzling bursts of Fire Lion firecrackers dispel sickness and evil.

Another north-sector temple of note, near a metro station of the same name, is **Xingtian Temple** ❻ (Xingtian Gong; www.ht.org.tw; daily 6am–9pm; free), on Minquan East Road,

Section 2. Dedicated to the red-faced, black-bearded Guangong, the God of War and patron saint of merchants because of his skill with strategy and numbers, the temple throngs with businesspeople praying for good fortune. It is unique for discouraging the burning of paper money and taking no donations. Built in the 1960s, it's a popular destination for those seeking advice from the spirit world. Tiny fortune-teller 'offices' line the pedestrian underpass outside.

Taipei Expo Park

Directly south of the Grand Hotel is the expansive **Taipei Expo Park** ❼ (Huabo Gongyuan; www.taipei-expopark.tw; 9am–6pm; free). The city hosted the large-scale Taipei International Flora Exposition in late 2010 to early 2011, connecting four large park areas on the south side of the Keelung River to serve as the expo grounds. Existing buildings underwent major renovations and alterations, and numerous new and attractive modern-design exhibition structures were erected. Three of the original four park areas

Taipei Story House.

now make up the popular Taipei Expo Park, which has all original floral-theme landscaping still in place, plants changed with the seasons.

Within the park is the **Taipei Fine Arts Museum** ❶ (Taipei Shili Meishuguan; www.tfam.museum; Tue–Sun 9.30am–5.30pm, Sat until 8.30pm), with 24 galleries of modern art, featuring local artists as well as changing exhibits from abroad. It claims to be the largest modern art museum in Asia and, if you're interested in the subject, is worth a visit for an overview of the local modern art scene. While you're there, visit the adjacent **Taipei Story House** (Taipei Gushi Guan; Tue–Sun 10am–5pm), a quaint Tudor-style building, originally built in 1913 as a summer villa for a local tea merchant, that now houses an art showroom and a history showroom focused on the 'Taipei story', everyday life, and the economic development of the Taipei Basin There is also a café with comfortable outdoor seating.

Another major local attraction is the **Lin An Tai Homestead** ❶ (Lin An Tai Guzuo; http://english.linantai. taipei; Tue–Sun 9am–5pm), on the park's east side, an original 30-room family home of a wealthy merchant from the Qing-dynasty era. Built built between 1783 and 1823, the graceful, somewhat minimalist structure was originally constructed entirely with materials brought from Fujian province in China. The buildings were moved and reconstructed at their current location after Dunhua South Road was widened in the late 1970s. A number of other elements were added for the flora expo, including an imperial-style landscaped stone garden and a two-tier teahouse overlooking a landscaped pond.

The many new pavilions purpose built for the flora expo were all designed as bold statements on green-architecture possibilities intended to serve as models for the rest of the country. Perhaps most impressive are the visually dynamic, interlinked

Pavilion of Dreams, Pavilion of Future, and **Pavilion of Angel Life** ❶ (Mengxiang Guan, Weilai Guan, and Tianshi Shenghuo Guan; Tue–Sun 9am–6pm; separate charge for each), which are interlinked. The buildings blend with the surrounding natural environs, are lower than the treetops, and simulate natural ecosystems. Wood from Taiwan's China fir trees have been used extensively in construction, and not a single nail used, with mortise connections opted for instead. Walls, chairs and tables are made of industrial paper tubing, armrests and railings of bamboo, and all materials recycled. Roofs are slanted and covered with green life to echo the display themes inside.

Beyond the concrete pathways originally in place, no concrete has been used. The surface of the welcoming pathway is made with tree-trunk cross-sections, and underneath a rainwater collection pool is visible, which provides site-use irrigation water. Electricity comes from rooftop solar panels, and water is brought in directly from the nearby Keelung River and run

Festivities at Baoan Temple.

Taipei's architecture

Taipei has become a dynamic creator of striking modern structures, green building models, and forgotten heritage sites made cultural-creative hubs.

During the martial-law era, little attention was paid to esthetics in architecture. The KMT deemed Taiwan's culture and heritage of little value, while glorifying China's. A selection of Japanese-built government buildings survived, preserved and maintained for purely practical reasons.

An intrinsic element of the democratization movement was the *xiangtu* or 'native-soil' movement, and today great pride is taken in all things local – both the unique Taiwan heritage and the 'new' heritage being exuberantly created. There are three primary architectural trends: making bold statements in new, large-scale works; saving heritage buildings of historical and/or architectural value; and beautifying functional structures built on the cheap during the martial-law era, notably residential high-rises. The preponderance of such structures helped earn Taipei (and Taiwan) its much-disliked 'ugly duckling of Asia' reputation – now part of the past.

Modern architecture

The Taipei 101 tower, in the Xinyi district, is the country's beacon of inspiration for bold architectural statements – along with the district as a whole. In 1990 this area, also home to Taipei City Hall, was largely scrubland and small farm plots. Today it brims with gleaming large-scale structures each of distinctive face and personality.

Another beacon of inspiration is the young set of above-ground metro and high-speed rail stations, many designed as works of art and symbols of local cultural character. Taipei's MRT Jiantan Station looks like a stylized dragon boat; the city's annual international races are held nearby. HSR Taichung Station resembles a shuttle loom, symbolizing the area's thriving textile industry.

A third major focus is green structures that serve as blueprints. The most celebrated model is the Taipei Public Library Beitou Branch. The popular Taipei Expo Park's interconnected Pavilion of Dreams, Pavilion of Future, and Pavilion of Angel Life, along with a number of other buildings, were purpose-built as green models for the 2010–2011 Taipei International Flora Exposition.

Saving heritage architecture

Government has been heavily involved in the renaissance of heritage buildings, and a major theme is making sites wholly or substantially self-supporting, with management turned over to private concerns. The majority have been transformed into cultural-creative attractions. Two prime examples are Huashan 1914 Creative Park (www.huashan1914.com) and Treasure Hill Artist Village (www.artistvillage.org), part of an effort to create a 'necklace of cultural pearls' by the city of Taipei's Department of Cultural Affairs. The former, in the old Taipei Brewery complex, is today home to a creative design workshop, creative works exhibition center, performance stage area, and movie theater, all dedicated to non-mainstream art. The latter, in a military dependents' village once slated for demolition where over 20 families still live, is a model eco-sustainable urban community where artists from around the world live in residence. There are studios, exhibit areas, public art, and art-related public events. Another noteworthy initiative is the Urban Regeneration Station (www.urstaipei.net) initiative overseen by the city's Urban Regeneration Office, which has reintegrated numerous forgotten places and spaces into city life and made them cultural hubs.

Taipei's modern MRT trains.

through a natural gravel-filter purification system for irrigation use. A small rooftop weather observation station sends information to interior monitors, allowing adjustment of plant-display sprinkler and watering systems to ambient natural conditions.

The east district

In the eastern part of the city is an important memorial to the man known in both China and Taiwan as the 'National Father', Dr Sun Yat-sen, considered the founder of modern China in both the PRC and ROC. On Section 4 of Renai Road, just outside a Taipei Metro station, the **Sun Yat-sen Memorial Hall ⓚ** (Guofu Jinianguan; www.yatsen.gov.tw; daily 9am–6pm) is distinguished by a sweeping Chinese roof of glazed yellow tiles. A 6-meter (20ft) high bronze statue of Sun Yat-sen graces the main lobby. Exhibit rooms feature photographs taken in mainland China during the early years of the 20th century, as well as personal items and other artifacts depicting Sun's life and times. There are also art galleries

and regular stage-arts performances. Perhaps the most interesting time to visit is at daybreak or dusk, when the extensive grounds fill with Taiwanese people flying kites, jogging, practicing martial arts, and even disco dancing.

The facility is in the Xinyi district, an area in east Taipei that is one of the most vibrant parts of the city. Just over a block southeast is the **Taipei World Trade Center** (Taipei Shijie Maoyi Zhongxin; daily 9am–5pm; www.twtc.org.tw; charge during exhibitions); floors 2 through 6 have a permanent Export Market, floor 7 an Import Market, with over 1,000 companies displaying their wares (Mon–Fri 9am–5pm). Dominating the area is 508-meter (1,667ft) **Taipei 101 ⓛ** (Taipei Yi-Ling-Yi), a financial-center skyscraper with the Taipei 101 Mall (Taipei Yi-Ling-Yi Gouwu Zhongxin) at its base and quality restaurants and cafés with splendid views on higher floors. **The Taipei 101 Observatory** (Taipei Yi-Ling-Yi Guanjing Tai; daily 9am–10pm) located on floors 89 to 91 of the tower, has panoramic views of the city and mountains from an

TIP

Carry a card displaying your hotel's name in Chinese, just in case you get lost. When walking in Taipei, never take zebra crossings or even walk signals for granted: drivers reluctantly give right-of-way to pedestrians and sometimes ignore red lights.

Shin Kong Observatory.

Indulging your taste buds is one of the main attractions of a visit to Taiwan. The large, comfortable food court on Taipei Main Railway Station's second level is a good stop.

The North Gate.

indoor and outdoor deck, and visitors can also view the huge typhoon and earthquake motion-damper sphere on level 88.

Just north of the Xinyi district is **Raohe Street Night Market** (Raohe Jie Yeshi; 5pm–midnight), on Raohe Street near Songshan Railway Station. Scores of food stalls are lined up back to back down the middle of the street, which in turn has scores of shops lining both sides, selling clothes, curios, toys, and much else. The market's signature foods are black pepper cakes, which are buns filled with seasoned meat baked in clay ovens, and medicinal pork ribs, stewed in Chinese medicinal herbs.

The Dihua Street area

The Xinyi district emerged as the city's new Downtown in the 1990s. The old downtown area, centered on **Taipei Main Railway Station** (Taipei Huochezhan), has experienced a renaissance since the mid-2000s and is a good place to launch walking tours. The busy station is where the metro, regular railway, and High Speed Rail

systems meet, and the city's main intercity bus station is right beside It has an attractive second-floor food court and connects with large underground retail area, with hundreds of shops, that stretches north to MRT Zhongshan Station.

North of the station is **Dihua Street** Ⓜ (Dihua Jie), a traditional Taiwanese shopping district. Taipei's most important historical street, Dihua Street parallels Yanping Road in the Dadaocheng neighborhood, near the Tamsui River – after Wanhua, Taipei's oldest commercial district. The area has its origins in the mid-1800s when a power struggle among Fujian immigrants in Wanhua drove the losers here. Business prospered, first in the form of rice mills, and then later in the trade of tea, camphor, and other products. Most of the old buildings that can be seen in this area, which has been extensively refurbished, date from the late 1800 and early 1900s.

The construction is typical of early establishments in Taiwan: the shop houses look very small from the front but extend quite a way back. Here, the

merchant's family lived, inventory was stored, and often products were manufactured. Today, Dihua Street sells an unbelievable variety of Chinese products, from dried fruits and nuts of all sorts to traditional candies, colorful Taiwanese floral fabrics, and herbal medicines.

The air is thick with incense at the small and unpretentious **Xiahai City God Temple** Ⓝ (Xiahai Chenghuang Miao; www.tpecitygod.org; daily 6.30am–9pm; free), also on Dihua Street. Traditionally every Chinese city and town has its city god, and Xiahai is home to Taipei's. The temple, built in the 1850s, may be small, but it's never short of worshipers and on the 13th day of the fifth lunar month it becomes the focus of massive street celebrations, when the city god tours the surrounding streets in a palanquin, accompanied by folk-art performance troupes.

The **Lin Liu-hsin Puppet Theatre Museum** Ⓞ (Lin Liuxin Jinian Ouxi Bowuguan; www.taipeipuppet.com; Tue–Sun 10am–5pm) houses over 5,000 puppetry artifacts spread over four floors. Displays are primarily focused on Taiwan, but explore other cultures as well. The museum is very dynamic, with puppet-carving workshops, puppet-master demonstration shows, DIY puppet theater, and traditional puppetry skills teaching sessions. The facility's Nadou Theatre is home to two troupes, which put on regular shows where English introductions and subtitle assistance is given.

East of the railway station

Just east of the railway station is the **Sun Yat-sen Historic Events Memorial Hall** (Guofu Lishi Jiniantang; daily 9am–6pm; free), at the intersection of Zhongshan North Road and Civic Boulevard. The modest exhibition is housed in a delightful Japanese-style building, once a luxury inn where Sun Yat-sen stayed when he visited Taiwan in 1913 seeking support for his revolutionary blueprint, tolerated by the Japanese because they sought continuing unrest and a weakened China. The grounds are a relaxing escape from the surrounding city bustle.

The fashionable district of Ximending.

A short walk from here, in front of a metro station of the same name, is **Shandao Temple** (Shandao Si; Tue–Sun 9am–5pm; free), built by Japanese Buddhists early in the 20th century. It's not much to look at from the outside, but worth visiting for the museum superb collection of Chinese Buddhist art in its museum.

Ximending

West from the railway station and opposite the main post office (which offers a good philatelic section) stands the restored **North Gate** ❷ (Beimen), one of the four remaining city gates and the only one still fully intact. Built in 1884, it was once part of a system of walls and gates that were mostly torn down by the Japanese to improve public hygiene and facilitate military movement. It may look like something of an anachronism, nestled against a major flyover at the intersection of Zhongxiao and Zhonghua roads, just before Zhongxiao crosses the river, but for some it is more impressive than the other imposing monuments around town.

Anyone who has spent time in Tokyo will find the area directly southwest of the North Gate, on the other side of broad Zhonghua Road, particularly fascinating. **Ximending**, the shopping and entertainment district most popular with Taipei youth along with the new **Xinyi** district, is the apotheosis of Taiwan youth's fascination with all things Japanese. Take a stroll around the area to soak up its bustling atmosphere and its bizarre fashions, and to take a look at its niche boutiques selling everything from Hello Kitty products to Japanese manga, or *manhua*, as comics are known in Mandarin. A number of streets right outside MRT Ximen Station are closed to vehicles on weeknights and non-work days. It's perhaps fitting that Ximending should have a Japanese flavor, given that the Japanese jump-started the area's fortunes by building **The Red House** (Ximen Honglou; www.redhouse.org.tw; Sun–Thu 11am–10.30pm, Fri–Sat 11am–10pm; free), Taipei's first modern market and then movie theater, in 1908. The second-floor

National Concert Hall.

theater has now been converted into a live performance venue concentrated on traditional stage arts, and there is a café, history exhibit, and cultural-creative shop area on the main level. The rear-area courtyard, a popular nighttime hangout, is filled with bars and eateries, and there is a regular weekend indie-designer market in the front plaza.

Wanhua, Taipei's oldest district

Directly south of Ximending is Wanhua, the heart of old Taipei. The focus of the area is the oldest and most famous of Taipei's myriad temples, **Longshan Temple** **Q** (Longshan Si; http://lungshan.org.tw; daily 6am–10pm; free), or Dragon Mountain Temple, a reference to a mountain and sacred temple in Fujian province where the area's immigrants originated. The temple is on Guangzhou Street, close to the Tamsui River. Owing its origins to a diverse community of Fujian immigrants, Longshan is unusually multi-denominational in character.

Originally constructed in 1738, the temple was hit by an Allied air raid in 1945 – supposedly inadvertently, but the Allies knew the Japanese deliberately used religious facilities as barracks and for weapons storage, and thus (not publicly announced) considered them legitimate military targets. So intense were the flames from the incendiary bomb that they melted the iron railings surrounding the large camphor-wood statue of Guanyin, the Goddess of Mercy. The hall was totally destroyed – yet the wooden statue somehow withstood the searing flames, except for a bit of ash and debris around its feet. The main hall was rebuilt, in 1957, enveloping the statue that gazes with unceasing equanimity at worshipers from the main altar. Devotees attribute the survival of the statue to the supernatural powers of the deity.

In addition to the miraculous carving of Guanyin, the temple is renowned for its fine stone sculpture, woodcarving, and bronze work. Only the island's best craftsmen are permitted to perform maintenance and

Taipei Grand Mosque.

Longshan Temple has intricate roofs embellished with dragons.

restoration work on the temple buildings. Especially striking are the 12 main support columns that hold up the central hall, which feature dragons hewn from solid stone. Open until late, Longshan is usually packed with worshipers. The tables groan with gifts for the gods, who are partial to anything and everything, from oranges to potato chips, but mostly to cash, which is consecrated and then burnt in an urn at the rear of the complex.

If you're wondering where all the temple's colorful, intricately crafted religious paraphernalia comes from, take a stroll over to **Xiyuan Road** – which runs north-south along the western flank of the temple. This is where Taiwan's biggest collection of religious supplies shops is located, and the section by the temple is popularly called **Buddhist Implement Street** (Foju Jie). The oldest shops have been in business since the early 19th century, when many of the supplies had to be brought in from southern China's Guangdong province. The predominant colors are red and gold, although gleaming white porcelain

(mainly used for images of Guanyin, the *bodhisattva* of compassion, and the Buddha) can be seen, too, under the bright glare of fluorescent lights. All items are for sale to individuals, because not yet consecrated: aside from bundles of spirit money and incense, choose from lotus-pod-shaped electric lamps, menacing 'protector gods', brass incense holders, and votive plaques while somnolent Buddhist chant music plays in the background.

Just west of the temple is **Snake Alley** (Huaxi Jie Yeshi; daily 7pm–midnight; free). The cramped, covered arcade announces itself with a sign that reads 'Taipei Hwahsi Tourist Night Market'. Not so long ago, the alley heaved with shops stacked with cages of hissing snakes, whose blood and bile was mixed with spirits and herbs and drunk by men who believed the potion strengthened the eyes and spine and promoted male virility. Today, less than a handful of such shops remain, but the tourists still come. The meat is served up in soup or stir-fried with vegetables. The market was the center of a legal red-light district until 1997, and vestiges of the trade linger on down the side alleys; do not patronize the foot-massage parlors off the main market alley.

Just south of Wanhua, in New Taipei City's Banqiao district, is the exquisite **Lin Family Mansion and Garden** Ⓡ (Lin Ben Yuan Yuandi; www.linfamily.ntpc.gov.tw; daily 9am–5pm, closed on the 1st Mon of the month), a short walk from MRT Fuzhong Station, four stations south of Wanhua's MRT Longshan Temple Station. It is known as one of the Four Great Gardens of Taiwan, home to north Taiwan's most powerful family in imperial days. In Wufeng is another: the Lin Family Gardens. The complex, built up over 40 years in the 1800s, was crafted with both esthetic beauty and defense in mind. It sits on low-lying Banqiao's highest point, enabling the clan to watch over their lands and also watch for bandits and

narauders from rival Han Chinese ub-ethnic groups. Visitors enjoy a pleasing exploration of majestically crafted buildings, pavilions, and other architectural works. Every turn reveals a corridor or courtyard designed with esthetics in mind, and each nook and cranny contains a delicate and complete miniature world. The complex is loaded with auspicious symbolism, a prime example the wide, undulating wall that protects the inner sanctum, shaped with the curves of a protective dragon that at the same time invited good fortune. The walkway atop has low railings giving defenders a clear field of view and some protection. The wall is tunneled, with openings for archers facing the outer complex. Access to top and tunnel was only possible via the inner complex.

Free guided tours are given to a regular schedule from 9.30am to 3.30pm. Only visitors on guided tours may enter the main mansion.

Old walled city area

Directly south of Taipei Main Railway Station, on Hsiangyang Road, stands the **National Taiwan Museum** ⑤ (Guoli Taiwan Bowuguan; www.ntm. gov.tw; Tue–Sun 9.30am–5pm), eye-catching in Greek Revival style. It is noted for its collection of over 40,000 items related to Taiwan's natural history and also has displays of aboriginal handicrafts, clothes, and artifacts.

The museum is in **2-28 Memorial Peace Park** ⑦ (Er-Erba Heping Gongyuan; http://english.pslo.taipei.gov. tw), originally laid out by the Japanese in the early 1900s and known as Taipei New Park. It was renamed in memory of the Taiwanese who perished in an uprising against the mainland Kuomintang (KMT) forces that started on February 28, 1947. The park is home to the 2-28 Memorial, a post-modern erection looking like two boxes mounted by a huge knitting needle, and the **2-28 Memorial Museum** (Tue–Sun 10am–5pm), an essential stop for anyone interested in the side of KMT rule that was kept quiet until after the end of martial law (see page 40).

Oddities also featured in the park include a pair of old steam trains,

Longshan Temple.

Worshippers making offerings of joss sticks, fruit, and spirit money at Longshan Temple.

A number of power-attesting miracles are associated with Wanhua's Longshan Temple. Its Guanyin statue miraculously survived an Allied air raid in World War II, and also survived an earthquake that flattened the temple in 1815. The temple was originally built here after a merchant stopped at the spot and his sacred incense pouch from China's original Longshan Temple began to glow.

A snake handler.

seven cannons, and even a megalithic tomb. The best time to walk the grounds is at dawn, when thousands of city residents stretch, dance, exercise, and practice *taiji*, *gongfu*, and other Chinese disciplines. Visitors are welcome to join in.

Surrounding the park are most of the important government ministries and offices. Just off the southwestern end is the governmental center of Taiwan. Most prominent is the **Presidential Office Building** Ⓤ (Zongtong Fu; free guided Chinese tours Mon–Fri 9am–noon, register before 11.30am; photo ID required), fronting an enormous plaza that is the site of colorful celebrations on Double Tenth: October 10, or National Day. The five-story complex, finished in 1919, has a central tower 60 meters (197ft) high and is Taipei's most famous example of Japanese colonial architecture.

Facing this building at the other end of short Ketagalan Boulevard is the impressive **East Gate** (Dongmen), the biggest of the original five gates of the 19th-century city wall. It was renovated in 1966, and its once very simple facade was ornately embellished.

Chiang Kai-shek Memorial

Just southeast of the gate is a massive visually compelling monument, the **Chiang Kai-shek Memorial Hall** Ⓥ (Zhongzheng Jiniantang; www.cksmh.gov.tw; memorial hall daily 9am–6pm; grounds 24 hours; free). Dedicated in 1980, the fifth anniversary of Chiang's death, the 76-meter (249ft) high hall dominates the expansive landscaped grounds. Inside is an imposing bronze statue of the president. In times now gone by, the memorial teemed with locals paying their respects, as well as tourists; nowadays it's the park that attracts all the people. From morning until late evening, it's full of life – seniors chatting under a shady tree or feeding the beautiful fat carps in the placid ponds, mothers with children strolling the paths, newlyweds taking wedding photos, and students in groups practicing their dance routines dreaming of stardom.

The main entrance to the grounds is a magnificent arch, in traditional Ming style, that towers 30 meters (98ft) high and stretches 75 meters (246ft) across. Eighteen different styles of traditional Chinese windows run, at eye level, along the entire length of the memorial's perimeter wall. There are two other magnificent structures on the grounds, the **National Theater** and **National Concert Hall**, built in classic Chinese-palace style.

South of the old walled city area

The **National Museum of History** Ⓦ (Guoli Lishi Bowuguan; www.nmh.gov.tw; Tue–Sun 10am–6pm) is on Nanhai Road. The permanent display offers around 10,000 Chinese objects dating from 2000 BC to modern times, including a fine sampling of Chinese currency, but the museum is also frequently host to fascinating exhibitions from overseas. It is less crowded than its more famous counterpart, the

National Palace Museum. Tours in English must be booked at least two weeks in advance by email. There is a fine coffee shop outside and a teashop on the fourth floor, both relaxing places in which to forget the bustle of the city.

Next door is the **Taipei Botanical Garden** (Taipei Zhiwu Yuan; http://pbg.tfri.gov.tw; daily 5.30am–10pm; free), established by the Japanese in 1921, which has hundreds of species of trees, shrubs, palms, and bamboo. There are 17 areas and 9 ponds, all dedicated to showcasing different tropical and sub-tropical species, with the large Lotus Pond the most popular attraction. Counterintuitively, this is a prime bird-watching spot, with many migratory species visiting, notably the rarely seen Malayan Night Heron.

The south sector

In the city core's south area is Taipei's biggest park, **Daan Forest Park ⓧ** (Daan Senlin Gongyuan; daily), one of the most popular places to take a walk, jog or, especially for young couples, lounge in the sun. There are myriad facilities, with basketball courts, an outdoor auditorium with regular performances, eateries, and a large eco-pond on the north side.

Just northeast of the park, under the Jianguo Elevated Expressway, is where two of Taipei's most popular weekend markets spring into life – the **Taipei Holiday Flower Market** (Taipei Jiari Huashi) and the **Taipei Holiday Jade Market** (Taipei Jiari Yushi). Both are open 9am to 6pm.

Opposite the park across Xinsheng South Road is Taiwan's largest mosque, the **Taipei Grand Mosque** (Qingzhen Si; open to public Mon–Fri outside prayer times; free), built in 1960 and the focus for Taiwan's 100,000 Muslims. The area behind the mosque, centered on popular **Yongkang Street ⓨ**, is a favorite nighttime gathering area. Yongkang and its side streets brim with European-style coffee shops and restaurants, Shanghai-style dumpling houses, indie designer boutiques, Chinese antiques and curio stores, and toy shops.

South of Yongkang Street, on the south side of Heping East Road, is the student district known colloquially after the Mandarin name of Guoli Taiwan Shifan Daxue (National Taiwan Normal University) – **Shida**. Shida Road is the focus of the area, though most of the action is on narrow, parallel Longquan Street. By day, like many Taipei mixed residential/commercial neighborhoods, the area is somewhat nondescript, but at night Longquan Street becomes a bustling night market selling Taiwanese snacks, bordered by innumerable coffee shops, pubs, and restaurants. Another lively student area can be found close by in Gongguan, the area south of **National Taiwan University ❷** (Guoli Taiwan Daxue), between Dingzhou Road and Roosevelt Road. It features outlets for discounted clothing, CDs, and jewelry, budget Chinese and Southeast Asian ethnic restaurants, and two cinema complexes. The sprawling university campus is attractively landscaped, and is home to numerous heritage buildings from the Japanese era.

Snake Alley night market.

NIGHT MARKETS

Lit up like pinball machines and full of carnival atmosphere, the night markets of Taiwan are the brightest lights in town after the sun goes down.

Night markets are an essential element of Taiwanese life and a top visitor attraction. They burst into life every night in towns and neighborhoods around the country. Every city in Taiwan has a number of night markets, but Taipei's Shilin Night Market (Shilin Yeshi) is the undisputed king. Trading and selling began here over 100 years ago – as with many such markets, outside a local temple. The market is a vast sprawl of aisles in and around a purpose-built multi-story complex; in this good-humored chaos wafts the smells of a thousand delights, hawkers' cries enticing customers to reach for their wallets.

Just about anything can be bought in a night market, from T-shirts to toys, but the main attraction is food. Vendors sell squid and pork, candied tomatoes, roast chestnuts, oyster omelets, juices, and dumplings, and tables almost topple over with fruit and tofu and hundreds of other foods. Feeling adventurous? Try the duck tongue or chicken feet. Not feeling adventurous? Have a submarine sandwich. Night markets are often the last stop on a late night out, faithful all-night eateries where revelers can down a hot bowl of noodles to soak up the night's excesses before going to bed. The markets often open at sundown, although they are most crowded after 10pm or 11pm. All operate into the wee hours.

Food is cheaper in the night markets because most of the vendors pay little rent. Many people do their grocery shopping at street stalls.

The most famous night market in Taiwan, Taipei's Shilin.

Calligrapher at work in Jishan Street Market.

Playing majong at Tainan's night market.

THE MAGIC OF SNAKE ALLEY

This covered market, located near Longshan Temple in Taipei's oldest area, Longshan Temple, runs two blocks long. Snake Alley (Huaxi Jie Yeshi) is best-known for medicinal delicacies today rarely found elsewhere in Taiwan, notably snake blood and meat, turtle blood and meat, and deer penis wine. The traditionally minded believe these increase virility. The snake and turtle are served in a variety of ways, from soups to medicinal mixtures to wines and a medley of cooked dishes. In the past a notorious red-light district, the market has been largely cleaned up for the benefit of tourists, some of whom may wonder about the supposed healing and virility-enhancing properties of the various snake concoctions. The brave of heart can drink a cup of steaming snake bile and find out for themselves. Another of the market's specialties is fresh seafood; among the more popular delicacies are squid, shellfish, fish head, and fish-steak stew. Along the narrow passageways are also fortunetellers, vendors of herbal potions, tattooists, massage parlors, jewelry shops, and craft stores. The market is open from 7pm until after midnight.

pers with an eye for quality can find many bargains. But you buy something, there is no refund. You may not even the vendor the next night.

an has made an effort to crack down on pirated goods, but lk through any night market will yield a treasure trove of cat products.

Snake soup and wine are popular in the winter. Despite a lack of medical evidence, many Chinese believe in the healing qualities of snake.

Taking in the view from a Muzha tea plantation terrace.

TAIPEI'S OUTSKIRTS

The island's best museum, hot springs, tea plantations, and stunning mountain views encourage visitors to leave the downtown bustle behind and head for the suburbs.

Taipei

Main Attractions

National Palace Museum
Shung Ye Museum of
  Formosan Aborigines
Beitou Hot Spring Museum
Beitou Museum
Four Beasts Mountain
Zhinan Temple
Muzha Tourist Tea
  Plantations

The district of Shilin, in Taipei's north, is home to the city's best night market, mentioned in the previous chapter. It is also home to some of the best museums, including the island's most famous.

An imposing complex of beige brick buildings, topped with green and imperial-yellow ceramic tile roofs, houses the **National Palace Museum** ① (Guoli Gugong Bowuguan; www.npm.gov.tw; daily 8.30am–6.30pm). The main building is impressive, the treasures within unimaginable. Beside is a small but perfectly styled recreation of a Song dynasty Chinese garden called **Zhishan Garden** (Zhishan Yuan; Tue–Sun 7am–7pm; free with NPM ticket stub), well worth a stroll.

The museum displays some 6,000 works of art representing the zenith of 5,000 years of Chinese creativity. And these are just a fraction of the more than 700,000 paintings, porcelains, bronzes, rubbings, tapestries, books, and other objects stored in nearly 4,000 crates located in vaults tunneled into the mountain behind the museum.

The museum opened in 1965. But the history of its treasures, which reads like a John le Carré thriller, can be traced back more than 1,000 years, to the beginning of the Song dynasty (AD 960–1279). The founder of that dynasty established the Hanlin Academy to encourage literature and the arts. The emperor's brother and successor later opened a gallery, where some of the items in the current collection were first housed. The gallery was then established as a government department for the preservation of rare books, old paintings, and calligraphy, and became the prototype for Taipei's collection.

The Song collection was transported from Beijing to Nanjing during the Ming dynasty, then back again, foreshadowing the collection's many

Zhinan Temple.

moves in the 20th century. The collection was expanded considerably during the Qing dynasty (1644–1911), whose emperors were avid art collectors. The majority of items in the present collection are the result of their effort to seek out China's most important treasures.

Art on the run

The real intrigues began in November 1924. Warlord Feng Yu-xiang, who had taken Beijing, gave the last surviving Manchu emperor, Puyi, and his entourage of 2,000 eunuchs and ladies two hours to evacuate the Forbidden City. Then the government had 30 young Chinese scholars and art experts identify and inventory the overwhelming collection of art treasures that had been hoarded within the palace for more than 500 years.

It took the scholars two years just to sort out and organize the collection. In the meantime, the government formally established the National Beijing Palace Museum and began displaying some of the treasures. By the time the task of identifying all the priceless

Browsing the National Palace Museum's gift shop.

objects was completed in 1931, the Japanese had attacked northwest China, and were threatening Beijing. The art collection had, and still has enormous symbolic value for whoever possesses it, bestowing a measure of political legitimacy upon its owners. To prevent the Japanese from seizing the collection, everything was carefully packed into 20,000 cases and shipped in five trains, south to Nanjing.

Thus began a 16-year-long odyssey. The priceless treasures were shuttled back and forth across the war-torn face of China by rail, truck, ox cart, raft, and foot, always a few steps ahead of pursuing Japanese and, later, Communist troops. A representative selection of the best items was shipped to London for a major art exhibition in 1936 – prompting an uproar among China's intellectuals, who feared the foreigners would never return the works. But all made it back to China. The following year, the Japanese occupied Beijing and threatened Nanjing. Once again, the precious collection was loaded aboard trucks and transported in three shipments over hills

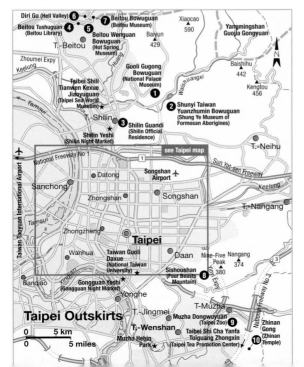

rivers, and streams to China's rugged western mountains.

Safe in Taiwan

After the Japanese surrender in 1945, the Nationalist government brought the pieces back to Nanjing. But when Communist control of the mainland appeared imminent in 1948, some 4,800 cases of the most valuable pieces were culled from the original 20,000 cases and sent for safekeeping to Taiwan. They were stored in a sugar warehouse in Taichung, where they remained hidden until the Zhongshan (Sun Yat-sen) Museum Building in Shilin's Waishuangxi area opened in 1965.

Among the original items cached are 4,400 ancient bronzes, 24,000 pieces of porcelain, 13,000 paintings, 14,000 works of calligraphy, 4,600 pieces of jade, 153,000 rare books from the imperial library, and 390,000 documents, diaries, and old palace records. Massive steel doors lead to the catacombs in the mountain behind, where the steel trunks are stacked one atop the other. One semicircular tunnel is 190 meters (620ft) long, the other 150 meters (490ft). The temperature is kept at a constant 18°C (64°F), and dehumidifiers line the corridors.

The secrets of the vaults are revealed fraction by fraction, but it would take a lifetime to see everything, especially since the museum has been adding systematically to the collection in recent decades. Paintings are rotated in special exhibitions every three months; other objects, like Hindustan jades and *ding* bronzes, are rotated at two-year intervals. Among the most famous pieces in the collection, which includes artifacts from tombs in Hunan province, bronzes, oracle bones, ceramics, porcelains, and paintings, are the *Jadeite Cabbage with Insects* – carved during the Qing dynasty, complete with camouflaged grasshopper – and 79 wooden cups carved paper-thin so that all can be held in a single large cup. There's also an amazing collection of miniatures carved from wood and ivory. One tiny cruising yacht, only 5cm (2ins) long and 3cm (1.2.ins) high, has both carved crew and guests in its interior cabin.

The grand National Palace Museum.

The museum now displays its treasures according to historical dynastic period rather than artwork type. In addition, it is adding works specific to Taiwan's cultural experience as well as works from outside greater China showing the impact of Chinese culture in the region.

Indigenous collection

Close to the National Palace Museum is the **Shung Ye Museum of Formosan Aborigines** ❷ (Shunyi Taiwan Yuanzhumin Bowuguan; www.museum. org.tw; Tue–Sun 9am–5pm, closed over Chinese New Year), a fascinating and tastefully presented introduction to the cultures of Taiwan's indigenous tribes. The museum has exhibitions on the belief systems, artifacts, and daily lives of the tribes, who are thought to have settled the island as much as 8,000 years ago, long predating the Han Chinese who now make up the vast majority of Taiwan's population.

Heading back toward central Shilin, on Lane 460 off Section 5 of Zhongshan North Road is the **Shilin Official Residence** ❸ (Shilin Guandi; www.culture.gov.taipei/front site/shilin; Tue–Sun 9.30am–noon, 1–5pm), the second and main home of Chiang Kai-shek (Jiang Jie-shi) in Taiwan. Long shrouded in mystery, the spacious grounds are now open to the public. The landscaped gardens – more in the European than Chinese style – are a popular location for wedding photographs, but it's possible to escape the crowds by taking a long flight of stairs to the top of a hill on the grounds for views of nearby Qixing Mountain. There is a pleasant café with outdoor seating and splendid views of the grounds.

Beitou hot-spring resort

North of Shilin, easily reached by the MRT Tamsui Line and then short MRT Xinbeitou Line, is the enclave of Beitou, nestled snugly in a valley between lush green hills. Beitou started out as a hot spring resort established by the Japanese administration, but the World War II and Vietnam War eras were its heydays, when its hot-spring hotels and drinking establishments made it a fully fledged R & R destination for troops. With the end of the Vietnam War, Beitou fell into neglect. Japanese tour groups would still arrive but, by the early 1990s, Beitou's hotels, which once numbered more than 70, had been reduced to little more than a dozen, most of them poorly maintained. Two things have since changed Beitou's fortunes. One was the arrival of the MRT line, and the other has been the revival of all things Taiwanese since the end of the martial-law era, which has led to a hot-spring boom across the island.

Beitou is easy to explore on foot, and is a favorite day-trip destination for international visitors in the city. The entrance to the Beitou valley is almost directly before MRT Xinbeitou Station, leading up into the Yangmingshan massif. Carved by the Beitou Stream, the narrow Beitou Park stretches along its banks, with most of the area's tourists attractions

Shung Ye Museum of Formosan Aborigines.

lined up one after another in the park or just beside. A walk to the top of the valley without stopping takes about 30 minutes.

The first attraction encountered, in the park, is the **Public Library Beitou Branch** ❹ (Taipei Shili Tushuguan Beitou Fenguan). This, regarded by many as the country's premier work of green architecture, is a place of stimulating innovation. Built of wood and steel, everything recyclable, it looks more like a giant ski lodge in the North American Rockies than a library. Rooftop greenery keeps things cool, rainwater is gathered for interior use, and there are tree-shaded reading balconies, plus many other impressive green-architecture highlights.

Facing the library, outside the park, is **Ketagalan Culture Center** (Kaidagelan Wenhuaguan; www.english.katagalan.gov.taipei; Tue–Sun 9am–5pm). The flatland-dwelling Ketagalan tribe were Beitou's original inhabitants. The center hosts myriad temporary and permanent displays, performances, symposiums, and other activities introducing Taiwan's tribal peoples and the

flatland peoples now mostly absorbed. Especially attractive is the exhibit on the well-crafted traditional dress, and contemporary arts and crafts.

Back in the park, perhaps the best place to get a glimpse of the area's history and a feel for its revival of fortune is the **Beitou Hot Spring Museum** ❺ (Beitou Wenquan Bowuguan; http://hotspringmuseum.taipei; Tue–Sun 9am–5pm; closed national holidays), housed in the former Beitou Public Baths, a Japanese building that dates from 1913. Exhibits feature the history of the area, and in a classic Japanese-style hall, complete with what looks like an acre of tatami matting, guides hold forth on the culture of hot-spring bathing. Downstairs, the original public bath is preserved in a cavernous room overlooked by stained-glass windows and Romanesque arches.

Outside the park, just above the museum, is **Longnaitang**, Beitou's oldest operational bathhouse (1907). Small and simple by today's standards, this is a purist's delight, the 'old days' still in place – separate male and

Preparing to dip toes in.

A steaming pool in Hell Valley.

Hot springs

One of the best ways to enjoy the splendid local mountain scenery is while sitting in a soothing, steaming pool of mineral water.

The people of Taiwan have a passion for hot-spring soaking, firmly believing their mineral waters do wonders for the body and that the scenic settings do wonders for the spirit. The rugged country, enjoying the benefits of sitting on the Pacific Ring of Fire, has one of the world's highest concentrations of thermal springs on the planet, as well as the greatest variation. There are over 100 hot-spring locations, the majority in the north, and there are also cold springs, mud springs, and salt-water coastal springs. The waters are generally high in temperature and crystal clear, and safe to drink. At a few locations, such as Suao on the northeast coast, it is bottled.

Japanese legacy

Though it was known that the indigenous peoples would soak in the mineral waters to assuage

Taking a dip in a Beitou pool.

physical ailments, it was the Japanese who planted the hot-spring culture during their 1895 to 1945 period of colonial rule. After taking over, they systematically mapped all locations and got to work developing resorts, the first in Beitou on Taipei's doorstep. Beitou enjoyed a surge of development in 1905 when the Japanese decided to ship soldiers wounded in the Russo-Japanese War for convalescence. The island's first public baths were also opened here in 1913, today's Beitou Hot Spring Museum. Many original Japanese-built facilities remain in place in Beitou and other locations, a number still in operation as bathhouses or inns.

After the Kuomintang took over Taiwan in 1945, all things Japanese were discouraged. Resorts became rundown, and places such as Beitou acquired a red-light tinge. Recognizing the springs and resorts as a quintessential element of the Taiwanese culture in the late 1990s, government at different levels began cleaning and fixing up resort areas, and hot-spring fever has taken hold.

The joy of old-time traditions

Many Japanese practices are still followed. There are indoor and outdoor, private and communal baths. Most resort hotels will have tubs in rooms, and separate men's and women's communal pools. In some hotels swimwear in communal pools is requisite, in others you can choose to wear it, but at most such baths soaking is done au naturel. Showers are taken before and after soaking, generally in the Japanese style, meaning pouring water over yourself with a wooden bucket or ladle while sitting on a small wooden stool. At hot-spring inns and hotels guests commonly move about in public areas dressed in the bathrobes and slippers provided, and most resorts offer massage facilities for post-soaking revitalization. The ceremonial drinking of tea is common during and after soaking, often in the Japanese rather than Chinese style.

Many resort hotels, especially near large urban areas, operate more as public bathhouses, renting rooms by the hour and allowing non-guests access to communal pools and spa and massage facilities. These facilities will be open into the late night, or even 24 hours. Places such as Yangmingshan or Wulai, both close to central Taipei, sometimes have traffic jams late at night on weekends or holidays as city folk enjoy a late-night soak and a snack or meal.

female pools (swimwear now obligatory), and the original 'Beitou Stone' pools. The stone has hokutolite, a weakly radioactive crystalline substance that forms on stone in crusts, found only in Beitou and Japan. Immerse yourself in history here – literally – for just NT$100.

Beitou's hot-spring hotels feature hot sulfur-spring water that runs directly from the taps into tiled tubs in rooms, either sunken or above ground, along with communal pools. After a soak in tub or pool, a professional massage completes the revival.

Further up the valley, a short side path leads to the source of the steaming Beitou Stream, **Hell Valley** ❻ (Diri Gu; Tue–Sun 9am–5pm; free), also called Thermal Valley, where the large, bubbling, steam-covered sulfur pit offers a first-hand look at the natural activity responsible for the area's hot springs. The original natives called the valley 'Patauw,' meaning 'sorceress,' sure that dangerous magic-wielders caused the strange otherworldly phenomena. This name became 'Beitou' in Mandarin Chinese. The Chinese came in the late 1600s to extract sulfur for munitions; there were once 27 sulfur mines in the area.

At the valley's top is one of Taiwan's prettiest museums, the **Beitou Museum** ❼ (Beitou Bowuguan; www.beitoumuseum.org.tw; Tue–Sun 10am–5.30pm). Housed in a former Japanese hot-spring inn (1921) that served as an imperial officers' club and once entertained kamikaze pilots on their final nights of mortality, the complex is among Taiwan's largest examples of Japanese wood-built architecture. Built in Chinese Tang Dynasty style, it is a work of art in itself. Exhibits are on early Taiwan life and culture, with a Beitou focus. Beitou was once a key area in Taiwan ceramics production, the mineral-rich local earth much valued, and many exquisite high-end works are displayed, with historical background provided. Another exhibit of black and white photos shows the area in its Japanese colonial-period heyday, when the valley looked nothing like it does today.

Ascending for a great view.

In-the-know Beitou visitors take the Beitou Museum's regular shuttle bus from the metro's Xinbeitou and Beitou stations, and then tour the valley with a downhill rather than an uphill walk.

On the city's east

The Taipei World Trade Center roughly marks the eastern extent of the city core. Rising above this, the Xinyi district, are the wooded hills of the Songshan Nature Reserve, which includes the **Four Beasts Mountain** ❽ (Sishoushan). The 'animals' are a fanciful reference to the shapes of the four peaks here, which to those with a fertile imagination look like a tiger, an elephant, a lion, and a panther.

Apart from stunning views of Taipei, the attraction of Songshan's hiking trails is their accessibility. Most of Taipei's nearby rural attractions require at least an hour of travel, sometimes spent sitting in choking traffic conditions. Songshan's trails, on the other hand, start less than a 5-minute taxi ride from the World Trade Center, at the end of Zhuangjing Road (which

begins opposite the trade center). From here it's possible to warm up with a relatively untaxing ascent up the 180-meter (590ft) Elephant Mountain.

Walkers looking for a slightly more strenuous workout, and the best panoramas, should follow the trail to Nine-Five Peak, named after a hardy 95-year-old Kuomintang (Guomindang) general who climbed to its 380-meter (1,247ft) summit.

The main trails are wide and well maintained, with maps. The best maps are at the trailheads. Some trails are lit up at night, rewarding walkers with tremendous twinkling city panoramas. Bring a flashlight and water.

On the city's south

The elevated MRT Wenshan Line makes an excursion to the hilly Muzha area an easy feat. The first stop for most visitors is the MRT's last stop, at **Taipei Zoo** ❾ (Taipei Muzha Dongwuyuan; www.zoo.taipei.gov.tw; daily 9am–5pm). As zoos go it's not world-class, but the animals for the most part do have spacious enclosures and

Muzha Tourist Tea Plantation terraces.

liveable habitats, and it's a good place to take children. It also represents a rare opportunity to see Taiwan's black bear, an animal that is seldom seen in the wild these days, as well as other indigenous Taiwan species.

For most visitors, however, the real attraction of Muzha is not its zoo but its surrounding hills, studded with tea plantations. Zhinan Road heads up to the area, but today many day-trippers take the scenic **Maokong Gondola** (Maolan; gondola.trtc.com.tw; Tue–Fri 9am–6pm, Sat–Sun 8.30am–8pm), which heads uphill from the zoo. First make a stop at **Zhinan Temple ⑩** (Zhinan Gong; daily) which, nestled in wooded hills, is easily the most stately and photogenic of Taipei's many temples. Dedicated to Lu Dong-bin, one of the Eight Immortals of Chinese mythology and figuring in both the Daoist and Buddhist pantheons, legend has it that lovers should never visit the temple together, as Lu, an immortal of amorous disposition, has been known to snatch beautiful women from the men who love them. The temple can be approached from the flatlands by a very long flight of steps starting outside National Chengchi University (Zhengzhi Daxue); those who accomplish the feat are automatically blessed for a year.

The **Muzha Tourist Tea Plantations**, in what is called the Maokong area, have become a popular escape for people from Taipei over the past few decades. Not so long ago, they restricted their business to growing tea. Today, scores have opened atmospheric teahouses that usually offer entrancing views of the surrounding countryside and city beyond, with the rich smell of tea in the air. All are open into the night, some 24 hours. Most of the teahouses are on Zhinan Road, Section 3. The **Taipei Tea Promotion Center** (Taipei Shi Cha Yanfa Tuiguang Zhongxin; Tue–Sun 9am–5pm; tours in English are provided with two days' notice) has a tearoom, and offers demonstrations of the tea production and brewing process. The famous local variety is known as *tieguanyin* (Iron Goddess), a variety of *oolong*.

TIP

The Maokong tea-plantation area can be explored via No. 10 or 11 minibuses from MRT Wanfang Station, which regularly loop the plantation road in one direction. Hop on and off wherever you like.

The Maokong Gondola.

MAOKONG TRAIL SYSTEM

A system of well-marked trails has been developed in the Maokong area, and 33 guide signs with English information on scenic spots and trails have been set up. Maps are available at the Maokong Gondola's Maokong Station. One of the most popular is the **Camphor Tree Trail** (Zhangshu Budao), which starts near the station. It stretches 1.2km (0.75 miles), and its grades are gentle. Also popular is the **Tea Promotion Center Trail** (Cha Tuiguang Zhongxin Budao). It descends a half-kilometer or so to the valley's main stream and Maokong's renowned potholes. The name 'Maokong' literally means 'cat's hollows'; the water-erosion potholes in the stream-bed rocks here reminded people of imprints left by cats' paws. The holes, of course, were eroded over the eons by rushing stream waters.

YANGMINGSHAN AND TAMSUI

A tour of Taiwan's northern coast, or even just a day trip out of bustling Taipei, provides an insight into both the natural glory of the island and its colonial past.

The sights and traffic in **Taipei** ❶ monopolize most of a traveler's time in northern Taiwan, but an excursion beyond the city and its suburbs will offer another side of life on the island. The nearby port of Tamsui is home to a fort and other remnants of the island's modern colonial history, superb seafood dining, the timeless rhythms of an old port, boardwalk strolling, riverside bicycling, and silky red sunsets. Yangmingshan National Park is often referred to as metropolitan Taipei's 'backyard garden,' a place of endless natural adventure that offers a network of hiking trails, steaming fumaroles, hot springs, birdwatching, and landscaped gardens.

The Yangmingshan massif

Yangmingshan ❷ is the closest northern attraction to downtown Taipei, about 40 minutes' drive along a winding road. Large numbers of wealthy industrial tycoons, movie stars, and entrepreneurs, as well as expatriate businesspeople, live here in luxurious villas clinging to the slopes in the cool climes above Taipei, while artists seek out the abandoned farmsteads that dot the area as subjects for their work. Originally called Grass Mountain, the name was changed by Chiang Kaishek to honor his favorite philosopher, Wang Yangming (1472–1529).

The mountain is also dotted with teahouses, tourist farms, and restaurants that offer grand views of mountain and/or twinkling city far below.

For visitors to Taipei, however, the main attraction is sprawling **Yangmingshan National Park** (Yangmingshan Guojia Gongyuan; www.ymsnp.gov.tw; free), which takes up the upper section of the Yangmingshan massif. The park comprises its crowning Yangming Park, along with Datun Nature Park and a host of other natural features. Yangmingshan is far

In Yangmingshan National Park.

North Taiwan

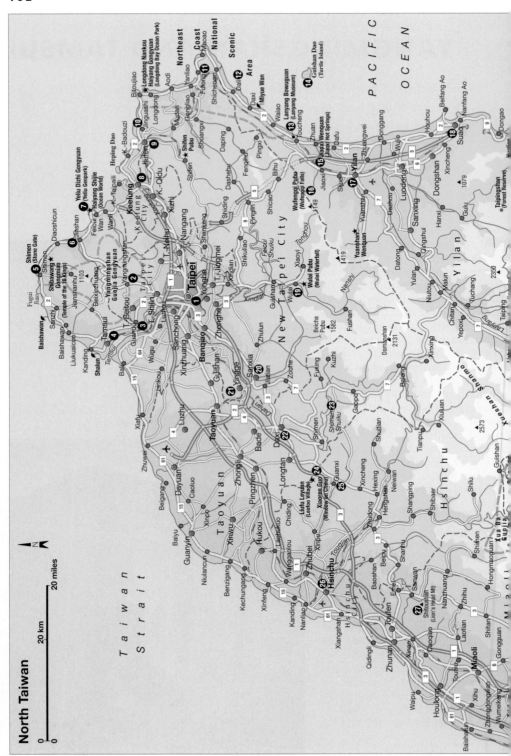

more than just a pleasant park with landscaped walks sitting at the summits of Taipei's most famous nearby peaks, and it's worth making the time to visit it.

Comprising the westernmost peaks of the Datun Mountain Range, Yangmingshan came into existence through volcanic activity around 2 million years ago. The lingering evidence of the mountains' volcanic origins is one of the chief draws for Taipei residents today, especially in winter, when they flock to Yangmingshan's many hot-spring resorts.

Park gardens and walking trails

Those with limited time should restrict their excursion to **Yangming Park** (Yangming Gongyuan; daily 5am–9pm), rather than venture farther afield within the much larger national park. This well-maintained park features walkways that wind through colorful gardens of trees, bushes, fragrant flowers, and grottoes. From the middle of February until the end of March, an annual spring flower festival is held in the park, with the entire mountainside awash with cherry blossoms and carpeted with bright, flowering azaleas. Just north of the park is the **Yangmingshan National Park Visitor Center** (Youke Fuwu Zhongxin; daily 8.30am–4.30pm; free), which has a display room on the area's geology, computer information consoles, and tourist information – a useful stop for those planning a hike in the area.

Deeper into the national park, popular walks include the **Bird Watching Trail** (one hour, round-trip) and **Butterfly Corridor** (two hours), though keen lepidopterists will probably be disappointed unless they visit during the top butterfly months of May and June. The latter walk terminates on the outskirts of the 350-hectare (860-acre) **Datun Nature Park** (Datun Ziran Gongyuan), which also features hiking trails and observation decks, and lies to the northwest of Yangming Park.

Northeast of the Yangmingshan Visitor Center is the striking volcanic landscape of **Lengshuikeng**, and

On the trail in Datun Nature Park.

a little farther east **Qingtiangang**, which pulls in the crowds with its alpine-like meadow and encircling ridge (which features a hiking trail), something of a novelty in Taiwan. To the northwest is **Xiaoyoukeng** (parking charge), with its large fumarole, wafting sulfurous clouds, and dense stands of bamboo. The park's highest point is **Seven Stars Mountain** (Qixingshan), at 1,200 meters (4,000ft), and a steep, but not dangerous, path leads from Xiaoyoukeng to the top, where the view over the city is remarkable. Check trail conditions at the park's Visitors' Center before setting out. Note that Datun Nature Park, Lengshuikeng, Qingtiangang, and Xiaoyoukeng are open daily 9am–4.30pm and closed the last Monday of each month.

On the road to Tamsui

The old port town of Tamsui, near the sea at the mouth of the Tamsui River, is a favorite destination for Taipei weekend day-trippers. The Taipei Metro's Tamsui Line makes it possible to avoid the often congested traffic on the single motor-vehicle route along the Tamsui River, with a trip from downtown Taipei taking just 25 minutes.

On the way, accessed by both highway and metro, is riverside **Guandu ❸**, home to the eye-catching 550-meter (1,700ft) long, bright-red Guandu Bridge. Directly on the river and close to a cliff is an extremely large temple complex, **Guandu Temple** (Guandu Gong; www.kuantu.org. tw), one of Taiwan's three oldest and most important Mazu temples (along with Lugang's Tianhou Temple and Beigang's Chaotian Temple). Built in 1712, the temple is a 15-minute walk from MRT Guandu Station, and also features a small adjacent Buddhist temple dedicated to Guanyin, the Goddess of Mercy. It's also worth taking a stroll around the vicinity of the temple – a viewpoint high above the river can be accessed via a tunnel through the cliff.

A short walk south of the temple is **Guandu Nature Park** (Guandu Daziran Gongyuan; www.gd-park.org. tw; Mon–Fri 9am–5pm, Sat–Sun until

pm in summer and 5.30pm in winter), which, occupying the confluence of the Tamsui and Keelung rivers, is a haven for migratory birds. Those visiting the nature center or taking any of the park's walking trails should make as little noise as possible; viewing shelters are provided along the trails for wildlife observation. Two stops further north is MRT Honghulin Station, jumping-off point for the **Hongshulin Mangrove Conservation Area** (Hongshulin Baohu Qu). Like Guandu Nature Park, this is another good place for birdwatching. Bike paths (with rentals) move along both sides of the Tamsui River from Taipei past Guandu and on toward the coast.

Tamsui

The port town of **Tamsui** ④, where the MRT Tamsui Line terminates, has a rich historical heritage. This was the main point of contact in northern Taiwan between the Chinese and foreign traders during its heyday as the island's major port in the late 19th century. Even before that, the

Spanish – who had occupied Keelung – extended their claim to Tamsui, where, in 1629, they built a fort, **Fort San Domingo** (Hongmao Cheng; http://en.tshs.ntpc.gov.tw; Mon–Fri 9.30am–5pm, Sat–Sun 9.30am–6pm), on one of the hills close to the river. After the Spanish were booted out, Tamsui was occupied by the Dutch until 1662, bombarded by French warships in 1884, and claimed by the Japanese in 1895. The Japanese built the island's first golf course in Tamsui, on a plateau just above the fort, now known as the Taiwan Golf and Country Club. Opened in 1919, the club remains popular among visitors and residents alike.

Today, the fort is a primary Tamsui attraction. It may be a relatively modest affair, but the bright orange-red structure atop a small hill overlooking the mouth of the Tamsui River encapsulates much of Taiwan's history: first built by the Spanish, rebuilt by the Dutch, taken over by Chinese Ming and Qing dynasty administrations, before serving as part of the British consulate in the late 19th

Octopuses for sale.

The Former British Consulate.

A tribute to George Lesley Mackay.

An evening on the Tamsui waterfront.

and early 20th centuries. It's known locally as the Hongmao Cheng, the 'fort of the red-haired barbarians,' a name that dates back to the Dutch. How much it resembles the original, however, is difficult to say after the Dutch rebuilt it. It's also difficult to ascertain whether it even started out red, or whether later Taiwanese renovations took a lead from the fort's popular name. But, idle musings aside, it is a place of scenic charm. Displays inside the fort feature old maps of Tamsui and reproductions of trade treaties.

Former British Consulate

Also on the grounds is the **Former British Consulate** (Yuan Yingguo Lingshiguan; Tue–Sun 9am–5pm; free), which was built as an annex in 1867, when the British took out a lease on the fort from the Qing dynasty government. It is a splendid two-story colonnaded structure, cooled by sea breezes that flow from one flung-open bay window to the next, the empty fireplaces hinting at an insulated expatriate coziness

through the brief winter months. Gazing at the dining room and the well-preserved bedrooms, it's easy to imagine the lives of the consular staff posted here in the days when there were no quick flights to more exotic destinations, and a journey home took many weeks.

The town the consular staff was surrounded by, a busy Taiwanese trading port in which the locals regarded the residents on the hill as 'red-haired barbarians,' can be seen pictured in black and white photographs in various rooms around the building.

The old town

Although Tamsui nowadays is a bustling, fairly modern town, it is still worth taking a stroll in search of the atmosphere of old Tamsui. The **Tamsui Old Street** (Danshui Laojie) and waterfront boardwalk area can be found a short walk southwest from the fort, next to the metro station and ferry pier. From here it is possible to take a waterside stroll (popular at sunset) or to strike north up to the **Tamsui Presbyterian Church**

(Danshui Jiaotang), a legacy of the famous foreigner whose name, for many Taiwanese, is almost synonymous with Tamsui – George Leslie Mackay.

A Canadian missionary, Mackay's efforts to improve health and education in Tamsui from 1872 until his death in 1901 have left it with a number of Western-inspired buildings. Opposite the church is the **Mackay Hospital,** Taiwan's first modern hospital, now converted into a memorial to Mackay. Just to the north of the fort is the **Octagonal Tower** (Bajiao Ta), which looks like a Renaissance-inspired pagoda and is the pride of the Danjiang (sometimes spelled Tamkang) High School. Opposite the school, on the grounds of Aletheia University, is **Oxford College,** designed by Mackay and Taiwan's first venue for Western-style education.

The river's mouth

At the mouth of the Tamsui is one of the town's most popular attractions, **Fisherman's Wharf** (Yuren Matou;

daily 9am–5.30pm). The wharf is a 20-minute direct bus ride (Red No. 26) from the MRT Tamsui Line terminus, and there is a ferry service from below the MRT terminus. The wharf houses traditional eateries and a coffee shop with grand views of the river and Yangmingshan behind. Perhaps the main attraction for tourists, however, is the chance to head out on one of the **Blue Highway** (Lanse Gonglu) 50-minute cruise-boat rides. There are hourly cruises taking in the river mouth and nearby coast, making it obvious why the Portuguese called Taiwan the 'beautiful island' when passing by in the 1500s.

Just before the wharf, on a high point along the river, is another major Tamsui draw, **Huwei Fort** (Huwei Baotai; Tue–Sun 9.30am–6pm). The Qing government built the fort, with the guidance of German engineers, after the 1884 to 1885 Sino-French War, during which the French blockaded and attacked Tamsui and held Keelung for many months. Never attacked, it is in fine condition.

A BALI EXCURSION

Bali, an old, small fishing community directly across the mouth of the river from Tamsui has become a popular day-trip destination with the opening of attractive tourist facilities. Many take the small ferry from below MRT Tamsui Station over to Bali Wharf. Bicycles may be brought on board. A pleasant riverside ride with boardwalk sections heads south along the river, and round the river mouth on the north. There are comfortable cafés and eateries along the south section to Guandu Bridge, bike-rental shops by Bali Wharf, and grand views of the Yangmingshan massif across the river. On the north section the boardwalk goes through Wazihwei Conservation Area, home of the world's northernmost mangrove swamp.

The path extends along the coast to the first-rate **Shihsanhang Museum of Archaeology** (www.sshm.ntpc.gov.tw; daily Nov–Mar 9.30am–5pm, Apr–Oct Mon-Fri 9.30am–6pm, Sat–Sun until 7pm; closed 1st Mon of month; free), facing out to sea, set amid expansive landscaped grounds with viewing platforms. The museum is built around one of Taiwan's key digs, which can be viewed on the grounds. The Shihsanhang culture knew iron smelting, the only such culture from more than a thousand years ago, seeming to prove regular contact with mainland Asia. There is a regular shuttle-bus service between the museum and Bali Wharf.

Path on Shimen (Stone) Arch beach.

THE NORTH COAST

The north coast is characterized by bathing beaches, unusual rock formations, and the occasional temple and museum, while its only city is home to possibly the best night market in Taiwan.

Taipei

he north coast area tends to get short shrift with many Taiwan visitors, largely due to the fact that the island's more famous sights like Taroko Gorge, Sun Moon Lake, and Alishan overshadow its attractions. This is a pity because, for those who make the effort, there is much natural beauty and history to be found within easy striking distance of Taipei's city limits. Should the bustle of downtown Taipei at any point prove overwhelming, it is worth bearing in mind that in less than an hour it is possible to reach destinations that move to far more traditional rhythms.

The immediate stretch of the North Coast Highway (Shengdao 2) that travels north of Tamsui has comparatively low-key, quiet attractions, most being swimming beaches geared to summer crowds fleeing Taipei's heat. The Tourism Bureau has created seaside parking facilities and viewing platforms, and licensed numerous coffee and snack kiosks featuring cool, umbrella-shaded seating. The roadway has also been widened, making cycling safer.

The most popular beach is **Baishawan Beach** (Baishawan Haishui Yuchang; daily 8am–sundown). Because of its proximity to Taipei, it pulls huge crowds on summer weekends. Otherwise, it is a convenient

spot to swim and sunbathe. The beach has snack bars and changing rooms, and is also known for windsurfing.

From Baishawan, the highway rounds Taiwan's northernmost nib at **Fugui Cape** (Fugui Jiao), marked by a picturesque lighthouse and pleasant park with paths and signboards above the cliffs. The lighthouse is part of a military installation and is off limits. Here, the Taiwan Strait is on the left, Pacific Ocean on the right, and East China Sea to the north.

Main Attractions
Stone Gate
Jinshan
Ju Ming Museum
Yeliu Geopark
Keelung

Sandstone formations at Yeliu.

Natural wonder

About 4km (2.5 miles) on from Fugui Cape, a natural wonder appears: **Stone Gate ❺** (Shimen), an impressive stone arch formed by tidal erosion, with an 8-meter (26ft) high opening. Tidal erosion may have created it, but it's now far removed from the tides, tectonic forces having pushed the land here beyond their reach. Locals say the name derives from the fact that, from a distance, the arch looks like the gates of a vast stone city. Atop are seats affording splendid views of the coastline and the sea, while a stroll around the area is a good introduction to the wind- and tide-eroded geology of Taiwan's northern coast. Walkways, small bridges, and viewing platforms make exploration easy.

Not far away, by the highway along a parallel side road at the 31km (19-mile) point is the **Temple of the 18 Kings** (Shibawang Gongmiao; 5am–10.30pm; accompanying games arcade and night market). It's a small affair, but almost always bustling, with incense thick in the air. Legend has it that 17 merchants and a dog were killed in a rough crossing from China during the Qing dynasty, and when this temple was founded in their memory the dog, who died trying to save his master, was made a god too.

As the highway turns southeast, it follows the stretch of coast that in Chinese is poetically known as Diaoshi Haian 'the thrown rock coast', on account of the fact that the beach is strewn with jumbled large rocks and boulders.

The next point of interest is the old town of **Jinshan ❻**, worth pausing at for several reasons. Jinbaoli Street is one of the few places in Taiwan where it is still possible to see Qing-era architecture. There is also a viewing area overlooking the **Candlestick Islands** (Lazhu Yu), a cluster of coral outcrops around 400 meters/yds offshore. Another interesting site is **Jinshan Youth Activity Center** (Qingnian Huodong Zhongxin), which – unpromising though it sounds – has an excellent beach and swimming facilities and a superb hot spring.

Sculpture tours

Those with their own transportation might consider making a very

Jinbaoshan's neat row of tombs.

worthwhile detour just before reaching Jinshan. Just past the 39km mark on the North Coast Highway, a signposted side road turns inland and, after a 15-minute drive uphill, passes the **Ju Ming Museum** (Ju Ming Meishuguan; www.juming.org.tw; Tue–Sun 10am–6pm, Nov–Apr until 5pm; children free). The museum is a celebration of the work of Ju Ming, Taiwan's most celebrated sculptor, and features around 500 of his works. The landscaped grounds host works by other sculptors, too.

Higher along the same road is the **Jinbaoshan Cemetery** (Jinbaoshan Fenchang; 24 hours), a site of pilgrimage for local music lovers, as Teresa Teng, Taiwan's most famous musical export, who died suddenly in 1995, is buried here. Vistas of the valley below, and coast beyond, are stunning.

Farther down the coast, the wave-buffeted geology of Taiwan's northern coastline finds one of its most unique manifestations at **Yeliu Scenic Area** (Yeliu Fengjing Teding Qu), in **Yeliu Geopark ❼** (Yeliu Dizhi Gongyuan; www.ylgeopark.org.tw; daily 8am–5pm, May–Aug until 6pm; free). The white,

yellow, and brownish sandstone promontory here, directly in front of the pounding ocean, has been etched into all manner of artistic shapes by the weather and erosion. The terrain is otherworldly.

Most of the rock formations have fanciful names, and for Taiwanese visitors half the fun of visiting is identifying them. The Queen's Head Rock could pass for the profile of the ancient Egyptian sovereign Nefertiti, while other rocks are variously dinosaurs, griffins, fish, candles, and even, in one case, the famous lost shoe of

The much-revered 'King of Beasts' is, quite literally, found everywhere as guardian of important buildings and temples.

Seascape at Yeliu.

Cinderella. A marked trail, used by few visitors, heads along a high bluff to the tip of the long promontory, revealing grand views.

Besides a crowded fishing village with many seafood restaurants, the other main scenic area attraction is **Ocean World** (Haiyang Shijie; daily 9am–5pm, Sat–Sun until 5.30pm). Here, the usual contingent of dolphins, seals, and other aquatic animals perform as at any sea park around the world. There is also an interesting 100-meter/yd underwater aquarium tunnel.

Just a short distance south of Yeliu is the beach resort of **Feicui Bay** (Feicui Wan), which goes by the English name of Green Bay Seashore Recreation Club (clubhouse: daily 8am–11pm; beach: May–Oct daily 8am–11pm). In the height of summer, enjoy a glimpse of the hurly-burly of Taiwanese beach culture – a little like Taipei-by-the-sea. There is beach volleyball, sailing, water-skiing, snorkeling, diving, surfing, and parasailing. Equipment for these activities can be rented. The Green Bay Club also provides an amusement park for children and several dozen beachside bungalows. This expensive overnight accommodation should be booked well in advance. Another upscale place to stay is the Howard Beach Resort Pacific Green Bay.

Keelung

From Green Bay, the highway runs on to the port of Keelung, Taiwan's northernmost city and second-largest port. **Keelung** ❽ is the junction for the North Coast and Northeast Coast highways, and the northern terminus of both north-south national freeways. Its natural harbor has 57 deep-water piers and three mooring buoys that handle vessels up to the 27,000-metric ton (30,000-ton) class. The port has excellent facilities for the loading and unloading of container ships; the container depots are massive. About 70 million metric tons (77 million tons) of freight are handled here annually. Only Kaohsiung, in the south, has more extensive port facilities.

Keelung's nearly 372,000 inhabitants are basically wedded to the port trade and its offspring industries, but its setting and history make it an interesting stop. Like Tamsui, Keelung has long

In Heping Island Park.

been a center for Taiwan's contacts with the rest of the world. Japanese pirates, Spanish conquistadors, Dutch soldiers, American traders, French marines, and Japanese imperialists have all made Keelung a base over the past three centuries.

Keelung's most famous landmark is an enormous white statue of Guanyin, the Goddess of Mercy. The 22.5-meter (74ft) statue is propped up on a 4-meter (13ft) high pedestal that enables the deity to watch over the entire city. Her stature is increased by the statue's position high on a hill in Zhongzheng Park (daily 24 hrs). Two finely proportioned pavilions grace a knoll next to the statue, inside which stairs lead to a viewing perch. Farther up the hill from the park is Keelung's most important historical attraction: the remains of **Ershawan Fort** (Haimen Tianxian). Built in 1840, the only intact segment of the fort today is the restored fort gate, but the grounds, with replica cannon emplacements, make for an interesting stroll.

Peace Island, Lover's Lake

On the southern edge of the harbor mouth is Peace Island (Heping Dao), connected to Keelung proper by Peace Bridge. Its chief attraction is the dramatic coastline in **Heping Island Park** (Heping Dao Gongyuan; daily 8am–5pm) on the seaward side of the island, which features more of the oddly weathered rock formations that distinguish the northeast coast. There are signposted walkways.

Farther afield, next to the scenic **Qingren Lake** (Qingren Hu), to the north of Keelung, are the remains of **Dawulun Fort** (Dawulun Baotai), another 19th-century cannon emplacement. It gets few tourists and is an atmospheric place to visit, with a majestic coastal overlook.

For most Taiwanese visitors, however, Keelung's chief attraction is its bustling main night market, universally lauded as the best in northern Taiwan. Located near the harbor base before Dianji Temple, **Miaokou Yeshi** ('Temple Mouth' Night Market; 24 hours; most vendors dusk–3am; free) has more than 300 food stalls, with all Taiwanese snack varieties represented. A day in Keelung is not complete without a visit, if only to soak up the atmosphere.

Shoppers in Keelung's Night Market.

KEELUNG GHOST FESTIVAL

Each year during Ghost Month, the seventh month in the lunar calendar (generally falling in August), the Gates of Hell are opened and all hell breaks loose, with spirits of the deceased let out on vacation and heading out to wander the mortal realm. Those without family to make sacrifices to them may cause trouble – these are euphemistically called 'hungry ghosts' and 'good brethren' – and thus individual and collective rites are performed and feasts given to appease them. Keelung's Ghost Month activities are the most elaborate, and attract tens of thousands on the key dates.

The main draws are on the evening of the 14th, with the national broadcast of a ceremonial gate-opening at a Laodagong Temple tower housing funeral urns, followed by a splendid raucous parade through the streets (especially the harbor area) of floats bearing family names, organized around fishing clans, reference to imperial-day fighting among local Han Chinese and communal reconciliation afterwards. The floats wend their way to Badouzi Fishing Harbor, where the elaborate float-top lanterns are taken down, set aflame, and guided out to sea. The blazes guide the ghosts of the drowned ashore, to share in the feasting. The full Ghost Month is also filled with evil-dispelling fireworks, traditional-arts performances, kids' shows, acrobatics, and many other spectacles.

Jiufen's laddered streets are lined with tea shops and antique buildings.

THE NORTHEAST COAST

The nostalgic town of Jiufen is just the start of
the attractions along the northeast coast, an
area with impressive waterfalls, fine beaches,
hot springs, and peaceful countryside.

South of the mountain-ridge town of Jiufen begins Taiwan's dramatically beautiful eastern coast, and even for those not planning to follow it as far as Taitung, it's worth traveling at least to Suao, renowned for its cold springs – the perfect antidote to the stifling heat of the summer months.

There is little flat land along the northeast coast from Jiufen to the top of the Yilan Plain; mountains line up shoulder to shoulder right along the shore, and fishing villages have been built wherever a flat spot opens up. Where no spots exist, shorelines strewn with great boulders from ancient rockfalls and bizarre sandstone formations caused by wave, wind, and rain are the norm. The small, triangle-shaped Yilan Plain, framed by mountains on two sides and bright-blue ocean on the third, was formed by tectonic activity lifting up the land and by mineral-rich silt carried down from the high hills by short rivers. Extremely fertile, this is one of Taiwan's most successful agricultural areas, carpeted in small farms raising cash crops. With the opening up of the heavily tunnelled National Freeway No. 5 through the mountains, the area has become a favorite playground for the people of greater Taipei.

Jishan Road is lined with interesting stalls.

Historic Jiufen

Not far south of Keelung is the small inland town of Ruifang, the jumping-off point for one of northern Taiwan's most picturesque getaways. Its name meaning literally 'nine parts', **Jiufen** ❾ is an arts and crafts mountain retreat overlooking the sea that began life as a gold-rush town. Today, it might be little more than a ghost town if nostalgia hadn't reclaimed it.

Before the 1890s, locals claim that just nine families lived up in these hills northeast of Taipei – hence the

Main Attractions
Jiufen
Gold Ecological Park
Pingxi Branch Railway
Fulong
Caoling Historic Trail
Lanyang Museum
Turtle Island
Jiaoxi Hot Springs
Wufengqi Falls

name, which is a reference to provisions being brought by boat and divided into nine portions for the climb up from the shore. It was the discovery of gold dust in the sand by local women, who used the sediment that washed down from the hills to scour their cooking woks, that kickstarted the tiny town's fortunes. By the mid-1930s, Jiufen was known as 'little Shanghai,' a place of bright lights, windfalls, and desperate toil. A decade later, the gold was gone and so were the bright lights.

The town first captured urban Taiwan's attention when it was featured in a television advertisement in the 1980s. Moviemakers also had their eye on the place, with its picturesque laddered streets and antique homes, at around the same time. In 1989 Hou Hsiao-hsien, then Taiwan's pre-eminent film director, clinched Jiufen's status as one of Taiwan's top-billed memory-lane travel destinations when he filmed his groundbreaking art-house portrayal of Taiwan's tragic 2-28 Incident (see page 40), *City of Sadness*, here.

See if you can pick up a bar of solid gold at the Gold Mining Museum.

Today, the chief attraction is its narrow streets lined with teahouses, souvenir shops, and snack sellers. A popular retreat for artists, it is also a good place to buy pottery – the **Jiufen Folk Art Gallery** (Jiufen Minsuguan; daily 10am–midnight) has items for sale. Most of the sights are of minor interest – the **Jiufen Gold Mining Museum** (Jiufen Kuangshi Bowuguan; daily 10am–6pm), the **Shengping Theater** (Shengping Juchang), once the focal point of Jiufen's bustling nightlife (old Jiufen-nostalgia films are shown Fri/Sat/Sun afternoons), the **City of Sadness Restaurant** (24 hours), a teahouse used as a movie set – but cumulatively they evoke a charm that is second to none in Taiwan. On the east edge of town is a short trail that snakes along the shoulder of Mt Keelung, offering superlative views of the northeast coast.

Many visitors like to stay overnight here; locals rent rooms for about NT$400 per night – watch for signs along Jishan and Qingbian roads – and some teahouses stay open all night.

Mining and POW camp relics

In a narrow valley opening to the sea just behind Jiufen, on Mt Keelung's south side, is sleepy **Jinguashi** ⑩ The **Gold Ecological Park** (Huangjin Bowuyuanqu; Mon–Fri 9.30am–5pm, Sat–Sun until 6pm), a history buff's delight, has sites spread along the valley, which is filled with closed-down mines first opened long ago by the Japanese. Visitors take in old Japanese-built heritage buildings, including renovated wood-built dormitory residences for high-level staff and the Crown Prince Chalet, built in 1922 for a visit by future Emperor Hirohito. A mine-tunnel experience is offered in Benshan Fifth Tunnel, and visitors can touch the world's largest gold nugget in the Gold Building museum, as well as enjoy a gold-panning experience. Vestiges of the infamous World War II Kinkaseki POW camp, where Allied soldiers were forced to work the mines, can also be seen.

Train to 'Little Niagara'

Ruifang is not only a staging post for Jiufen: it also sits at the head of the picturesque **Pingxi Branch Railway** (Pingxi Xian), originally built to carry coal from the upper reaches of the Keelung River to Keelung. The line now ferries nostalgic tourists on its narrow-gauge tracks about once an hour between 7am and 11.15pm (day passes available). Apart from the pleasures of a rustic train journey, the main reason to take a ride is to visit **Shifen Waterfall** (Shifen Pubu; daily 8am–6.30pm, Feb–Oct until 7pm), a short trip from Ruifang and around 10 minutes' on foot from Shifen's station. Shifen Pubu is known locally as the 'Niagara Falls of Taiwan' because of their shape, and while there's obviously more than a trace of hyperbole in such an appellation, the falls are nevertheless impressive.

Back on the coast, the Northeast Coast Highway (Shengdao 2) moves out eastward from Keelung to coastal enclaves like Bitoujiao, a high-bluff cape with an attractive historic lighthouse overlooking the Pacific Ocean. Like Yeliu, to the northwest of Keelung, its rock formations make for a spectacular blend of land and sea. There are walkways atop and below the cape. On the cape's south side are the cliffs of Longdong, with an attractive tourist trail along the edge with spectacular views; this is one of northern Taiwan's most popular destinations for serious climbing enthusiasts, as well as for scuba divers. **Longdong Bay Ocean Park** (Longdong Nankou Haiyang Gongyuan; daily 8am–5.30pm) offers outdoor seawater swimming pools, an aquarium, and snorkeling.

Fulong ⓫, the next stop on the Northeast Coast Highway, belies the notion that Taiwan's best beaches lie only in the southern reaches of the island. The white-sand beach here hugs the northern shore of a cape that juts into the Pacific Ocean. Because of its north-facing location, the sun rises on the right and sets on the left as one looks out to sea. To further enhance the setting, the cove is entirely surrounded by rolling green hills. Enthusiastic strollers will find that accessible shoreline stretches for kilometers in both directions. About 100 meters/yds inland, a stream runs parallel to **Fulong Beach** (Fulong Haishui Yuchang; facilities: May–Oct daily 9am–5pm), in effect forming a secondary beach. A bridge leads to the seashore, and sailing boats and windsurfing boards can be rented.

Historic mountain trail

A little south of Fulong, at **Dali ⓬**, look out for the wonderfully ornate Daoist temple known as Tiangong Miao, or the Jade Emperor Temple. The temple is worth a stop in its own right, and adding to its significance is that it marks the trailhead of the

TIP

Trains run directly to Fulong from Taipei, via Ruifang, before continuing down the east coast, making it possible to visit Fulong as a full day's outing. The National Freeway No. 5 from Taipei to Yilan also makes road access much easier.

GOLD IN THE HILLS

Jiufen, a popular tourist town of craft shops, traditional snack-food sellers, and teahouses, is perched dramatically on a mountain ridge looking almost straight down at the Pacific on the northeast coast. It may once have been a gold-rush town, but the only gold nowadays is in the tourist industry. According to Zeng Shui-chi, the curator and owner of Jiufen Gold Mining Museum, the old methods by which gold was extracted from the sediment that washed down from the hills are forgotten by all but one man – Mr Zeng himself.

Mr Zeng recreates the gold extraction process in his small museum, reliving the skills he first learned at the age of 14. He first grinds sediment with a huge pestle and mortar, adding water and grinding again with a pedal-powered serrated metal wheel, transferring the results to a wooden slat that he splashes with water, allowing the chaff to flow away into a large pot. After a while, the occasional sparkle begins to appear in the grit. Not long after that his work will have reduced a bucketful of sediment to half a small bowl of black mud, a miniature night sky twinkling with golden stars. Jiufen may, as he says, be slowly forgetting its past in its quest for the tourist dollar, but Mr Zeng is determined to do his bit to make sure that visitors who stray from the gift shops and teahouses get a glimpse of the days when hopefuls toiled under the sharp-eyed gaze of overseers to extract gold from the sand.

now been abandoned, but the rustic section between Fulong and Dali has been restored, and takes around three to four hours on foot. Stone markers engraved with Chinese characters mark the way, there are several pavilions en route to rest, and there are old bridges, the ruins of a travelers' inn, and other sights. Best of all are the tremendous views of ocean and coast.

Toucheng attractions

Between Daxi and **Toucheng**, a tiny coastal village with a modest beach resort that is usually less crowded than Fulong or other northern beaches, is Miyue Wan or Honeymoon Bay, a pleasant strip of beach that offers the best surfing in north Taiwan. There are surf shops and café/bar hangouts along the shore.

Toucheng's main attraction, beside the highway just north of the village, is the young, large **Lanyang Museum** ⓭ (Lanyang Bowuguan; www.lym.gov.tw; Thu–Tue 9am–5pm) is housed in a visually dynamic purpose-built work of architecture. The

Taiwan's biggest rock festival, the Ho-Hai-Yan Rock Festival, is held over three days at Fulong Beach each summer. Some 20,000 revelers attend at any one time. Admission is free and trains run hourly between Taipei and Fulong.

In the grounds of the Crown Prince Chalet.

Caoling Historic Trail (Caoling Gudao), a meandering and, in parts, flagstoned path that was cleared in 1807 to facilitate the migration of Chinese immigrants from Taipei Basin to the fertile Yilan or Lanyang Plain of Yilan County.

In its time, this was a pioneering route that enabled passage through the mountains that separate north and northeast Taiwan, thereby obviating the need for a dangerous sea journey along the windswept northern coastline. Most of the trail has

ngled tiers of the structure seem to hoot out of the ground, mimicking he northeast coast's great natural culptures of stratified rock hurled p from the seabed by tectonic activity. Inside, the sunlit, airy floors are lso staggered and open to each ther, cascading like the tiered-rock ormations of the coast. The museum xplores the heart and hardiness of ilan's peoples, telling the story of s indigenous peoples, pioneers, and nodern-day inhabitants, as well as he local geology, farming and fishng traditions, and the biology of nd and sea.

Between coast and museum is large lagoon busy with waterowl. This was the site of the origial Wushi Fishing Harbor (Wushi ugang). Pioneers drained the lagoon n the 1800s, and after the harbor was verwhelmed by a massive typhoon few decades ago it was decided > let it return to its (more or less) riginal state. The Wushi Fishing Iarbor, just beyond on the north de, is the launch point for tours > large **Turtle Island** ⓮ (Guishan

Dao), a volcanic outcrop so named for obvious reasons that are visible from all over Yilan County. Formerly site of an off-limits military garrison, the island is open to tourists during the day (March–Nov). Now a nature park, the island is today uninhabited. Visit the ruins of a century-old fishing village evacuated in 1977, inspect abandoned military facilities and tunnels with old weaponry, view steaming hot springs, and hike to the main summit. A permit is needed to visit the island; contact the Taiwan Tourism Bureau for guidance with the advance application required. International visitors are exempted from the 500 visitors per day limit. Alternatively, take a whale- and dolphin-watching tour that cruises by but does not visit the island.

Another area attraction lies in the hills behind Toucheng. About 5km (3 miles) west of the village is **New Peak Falls** (Xinfeng Pubu). The falls are found 500 meters/yds) beyond the main entrance to the tourist park, inside a canyon. By stepping carefully down the rocky ledge,

TIP

On weekdays, the popular Caoling Historic Trail, which connects the settlements of Gongliao and Dali on the northeast coast, presents a rare opportunity to peacefully enjoy the mountainous countryside, but be warned that there are none of the usual amenities associated with tourism – bring plenty of water and possibly a picnic lunch.

The rocky cliffs of Cape Bitou.

swimmers can slide into the refreshing water that cascades 50 meters (165ft) down a stone chute.

Hot-spring resort soaking

Another chief attraction of the lovely north Yilan Plain region is the **Jiaoxi Hot Springs** 🏷 (Jiaoxi Wenquan), located around 7km (4 miles) north of the small city of Yilan. In the past, after the Japanese left – like many of the island's hot-spring resorts – it became somewhat rundown, and an infamous red-light district. Those days are now gone, hot-spring soaking has become a favorite family-getaway activity, and scores of quality hotels offer the opportunity for a refreshing soak in the area's health-bestowing waters. Small restaurants scattered about the town specialize in tasty, fresh seafood. In the middle of town a small, pleasant park has been built around one of the original hot springs, which in Jiaoxi bubble up directly from the plain, not located in the wall of mountains against which the town is built. There is free foot-soaking here.

Less than 10 minutes' drive int the hills behind the Jiaoxi Wenqua is **Five Peaks Flag Scenic Area** (Wu engqi Fengjingqu). Vendors aroun the parking lot sell the area's sough after products of dried mushroom honey, preserved plums and othe fruits, fresh ginger, and medicin herbs. Among the last is a furry li tle doll with four 'legs' formed b roots, and two 'eyes' made with bu tons. The vendors call it *jingouma* (Golden Dog Fur). It's actually fern-plant that roots in stone an grows from remote cliff sides. Whe rubbed into cuts, scrapes, laceration and other festering skin wounds, stops the bleeding immediately an promotes rapid healing with a min mum of unsightly scarring.

The trail from the parking lot lead to **Wufengqi Falls** 🏷 (Wufengo Pubu), a vine-and-fern-spangle three-section waterfall in which th largest and uppermost section ca cades musically in sprays and shee down a 60-meter (200ft) cliff. A pi turesque viewing pavilion faces th falls from across the stream.

Hiking the Caoling Historical Trail.

Shengdao 9 continues south from iaoxi to the bright little city of **Yilan** 7. Although this is the county seat, nd a good place to stop for lunch r perhaps overnight at one of the nany hotels, Yilan has little to hold he visitor for long. Taiwanese visiors generally descend on the town o pick up supplies of the local speialities known as 'Yilan's four treasres.' Of these only *yashang* – duck ured in brine and smoked in bamoo cane – is likely to be of interest o the foreign palate.

On to Suao

ifteen minutes south of Yilan, at he bottom of the Yilan Plain where nountain meets sea, lies the interational seaport of **Suao** 18, though y no means on the same scale as Keelung or Kaohsiung. It's worth a top for two reasons: its famous cold prings and the nearby fishing port f Nanfang Ao.

Suao's cold springs (daily midun–Aug 8am–10pm, Sep–mid-June am–6pm) were discovered by the apanese in 1928. Rich in bubbling carbon dioxide, locals compare it to soaking in natural 'soda water' and have even taken to bottling the stuff as a drink. Definitely only an experience for the hardy in the cold winter months, a dip in the cold springs is a perfect antidote to the heat of summer – once the initial shock wears off. Unusually for Taiwan, a large outdoor communal pool is available (the sexes are segregated). It's expected that you wear a swimsuit; you will be required to rent one if you don't have your own.

Suao's international harbor is a dull affair, but that's all the more reason to head approximately 3km (2 miles) south of town to the bustling fishing port of **Nanfang Ao**. It is famous mostly for its seafood, which is cooked fresh in innumerable restaurants, but foreign visitors are inevitably charmed by the town's timeless and bustling harbor crowded with gaily colored, high-prowed fishing boats, along with its busy market and adjoining seafood restaurants, which will cook your catch if you bring your own.

Boats crowd Suao's harbor.

Wulai waterfall.

SOUTH OF TAIPEI

Close to the capital, a surprising mix of attractions
can be found, from displays of aboriginal culture
and fascinating cave temples to a ceramics town
filled with kilns and shops.

T he area immediately south and southwest of Taipei, marked by low mountains and valleys, is less compelling than the northern coastline, but is nevertheless a place of many worthy attractions. In the vicinity of the Shimen Reservoir, a popular escape for Taipei residents, are the theme parks of Window on China, which presents the architectural triumphs of China, Taiwan, and the Western world, in miniature, and the sprawling Leofoo Village. Also situated close by are the fascinating compounds of Taiwan's Hakka minority at Guanxi, one of the few places in Taiwan, along with Meinong in the deep south, where it is possible to get a glimpse of traditional Hakka culture.

Meanwhile, farther south again, past the city of Hsinchu, with its world-famous Hsinchu Science Park, is the Buddhist retreat of Lion's Head Mountain (Shitoushan), a mountain cluster of temples where it is possible to stay overnight in a Buddhist monastery.

A lovely ride back to Taipei is in store for travelers who double back up the Northeast Coast Highway from Suao to the north side of the Yilan Plain, then head inland over the mountains along Provincial Highway No. 9 (Shengdao 9), instead of taking

the much faster National Freeway No. 5, towards Pinglin and beyond to Xindian, just south of Taipei. The highway twists and turns through the spectacular Central Mountain Range, revealing vistas of spellbinding beauty as it zigzags back to Taipei, taking in the tea-growing area of Pinglin en route.

Wulai hot-spring resort

South from Xindian, in the opposite direction from Taipei, the mountainous retreat of **Wulai** ⑲ is popular for

Main Attractions
Wulai
Sanxia Temple of the Divine Progenitor
Old Pottery Street
Yingge Ceramics Museum
Daxi
Hsinchu
Lion's Head Mountain

A performance at Wulai Aboriginal Cultural Village.

FACT

One of Sanxia Temple's 122 intricate Sanxia Temple stone columns – each carved from a single slab of stone – depicts a plum tree, with 50 different kinds of birds on its branches.

its Atayal aboriginal performances and hot springs. **Wulai Aboriginal Culture Village** (Wulai Yuanzhumin Wenhua Cun; www.nine.com.tw; daily 9.30am–5pm) has performances of the traditional songs and symbolic dances of the Atayal and other tribes four times a day, with admission to a small folk art museum included in the theater charge. Traditional tribal arts and crafts, wild mountain mushrooms, Taiwan-grown Chinese herbs, and souvenirs are available in stores, and restaurants offer exotic fare like snake and freshwater eel and, intermittently, wild boar and deer.

A cable car (daily 7.30am–10pm) carries visitors from the indigenous-theme tourist section across the gorge and by spectacular **Wulai Waterfall** (Wulai Pubu) to a plateau and **Yun Hsien Resort** (Yunxian Leyuan; daily 8.30am–5pm), which has additional ethnic performances, a pond for rowing and fishing, a small amusement and exercise park, restaurant and coffee shop (open until 10 or 11pm), spa, outdoor swimming pool, and hotel.

During the winter, Wulai is favored for its outdoor hot springs. In the popular resorts of Yangmingshan and Beitou, hot-spring water is piped into hotels. Here it's possible to soak in an outdoor pool of piping-hot water and commune with nature. The springs can be found in the resort's lower section (the first reached from Taipei) below the indigenous culture village. There are also a number of quality hot-spring hotels here, along with many eateries and the **Wulai Atayal Museum** (Wulai Taiya Minzu Bowuguan; Mon–Fri 9.30am–5pm, Sat–Sun until 6pm). The attractive facility has displays on the Atayal people's history, cultural traditions and customs, religious beliefs, and festivals, and has a specific focus on the Wulai band and the area's ecology.

A mini-train originally used for timber transportation from further up the gorge now hauls tourists between the lower section and culture village. Another draw is the hiking trail that leads further up the gorge into **Doll Valley** (Wawa Gu) for

Pottery found on Yingge Old Street.

a round-trip of about 5km (3 miles), presenting mountain views, abundant bird life, waterfalls, and genuine Atayal hamlets.

Temple and heritage street restoration

Southwest of Taipei are several other places well worth a stop. Only 20km (12 miles) away is the busy old town of **Sanxia** ⓴. Narrow Minquan Street, also called **Sanxia Old Street** (Sanxia Laojie), is lined with renovated early-1900s business buildings put up by the Japanese. There are going concerns within, selling handicrafts and snacks.

Sanxia's chief claim to fame is **Sanxia Temple of the Divine Progenitor** (Sanxia Zushi Miao; daily 4am–10pm; free), originally built in 1769. It is among Taiwan's most renowned, due to the efforts of Li Mei-shu, a master craftsman who dedicated 36 years to restoring it after its 1948 destruction by fire. It is said that each of the celebrated 122 stone columns took 1,000 days to complete. Today, the results are commonly lauded as the best example of temple art in Taiwan and among the best in the Chinese world. The **Li Mei-shu Memorial Gallery** (Li Mei-shu Jinian Guan; www.limeishu.org; Sat–Sun, holidays 10am–5.30pm; groups by arrangement Mon–Fri) can be found at 10, Lane 43, Zhonghua Road.

Taiwan's pottery mecca

A short hop away is **Yingge** ㉑ town, a potter's haven. Some factories conduct tours, providing a chance to watch how 'muddy' clay is transformed into a beautifully painted Chinese vase, treasured in the Ming or Qing courts of old. Many shops line pedestrian-only, cobblestoned **Old Pottery Street** (Taoci Laojie), selling everything from simple earthenware to the finest porcelain, ordinary teapots to delicate figures – some predictable, others exquisite.

The town's artistic masterpiece is a rather large one – **Yingge Ceramics Museum** (Yingge Taoci Bowuguan; www.ceramics.ntpc.gov.tw; Mon–Fri 9.30am–5pm, Sat–Sun until 6pm).

An unusual display at Yingge Ceramics Museum.

*Window on China is
a park that contains
replicas of world-
famous architectural
wonders.*

The large, airy structure, itself a work of spatial art, is part of an impressive display on the Taiwan ceramics story, surrounded by a 14-hectare (35-acre) park filled with ceramics artworks. Audio guidance is provided in English. The museum is very family-friendly, with many DIY activities on weekends and holidays.

Several other attractions just to Yingge's south also beckon travelers. On Provincial Highway No. 3 (Shengdao 3) is the old town of **Daxi** ㉒. On the Dahan River, main branch of the Tamsui River that flows through Taipei and out to sea, Daxi is a history buff's delight. Up until the days of Japan's colonial rule the waters were navigable this far upstream. Trade was brisk, and camphor was the main draw. The main dock was by today's Heping Road. In the old commercial area formed by Heping and Zhongshan roads, old baroque-facade commercial establishments stand shoulder to shoulder, many built by Western trading firms and, later, by Japanese. Facades bear the names of the

business concerns and wonderful carvings of birds, animals, flowers and plants.

Today the narrow-front, deep shophouse-style locations house traditional businesses producing dried bean curd, religious-worship items and old-style wooden furniture, and also engaged in iron and stone working, the goings-on visible from the street. Tourists are welcome to come in and watch. The entire district has been refurbished, street wiring put underground, making for a stimulating step back into the past. Local tourists snap up the dried bean curd for which Daxi is renowned. The secret is said to be in the mineral-rich waters of the surrounding hills.

Nearby **Shimen Reservoir** ㉓ (Shimen Shuiku; daily 8am–6pm) offers pathways, bicycling, gardens, viewing pavilions, eco-tours from the visitor center (Chinese), history displays, motorboat rides, fishing, and restaurants specializing in the reservoir's very large deep-water carp. Though Shimen Dam, completed in 1964 with American aid, is impressive, the

area is more an attraction for locals than for foreign visitors.

Theme parks

Quirky **Window on China** ❷❹ (Xiaoren Guo; www.woc.com.tw; Mon–Fri 9am–4.30pm, Sat–Sun and holidays 9.30am–5pm) is near the town of Longtan. The sprawling site is best known for its miniature versions of well-known works of architecture. The front, original section is focused on Taiwan, and is now somewhat run-down though interesting. Next is the China section, with fine renditions of the Forbidden Palace and other sites. The newest section, at the rear, has splendid replicas of the Sphinx, Leaning Tower of Pisa, and other architectural triumphs from around the globe. Countless bonsai trees grown to proportionally correct sizes provide vegetation.

There is also an amusement park in the rear section, best suited for families with kids up to the teens, which includes Asia's tallest water flume. Reactions to the park tend to be mixed; some visitors come away enchanted, others find it all somewhat tacky.

If Window on China is not enough fun, close by is **Leofoo Village** (Liufu Leyuan; www.leofoo.com.tw/village; July–Aug daily 9am–8pm, shorter hours other seasons), which packs in Wild West, Arabia, African Safari, South Pacific, and a Greek island-theme water park area, along with carnival rides, cabaret, and stunt shows with imported talent, and much else.

A more traditional experience can be found just off Shengdao 3 south of Leofoo, at **Guanxi** ❷❺. After Meinong (see page 256) in south Taiwan, Guanxi is Taiwan's best-preserved Hakka village, with impressive ancestral homes built in the Hakka courtyard style the Chinese call *sanheyuan*. The oldest, the **Fan Family Home**, at 47 Pinglin Village, dates from 1700.

The city of **Hsinchu** ❷❻, best known for its science park, is not without its attractions. The City Moat and Riverside Park, a favorite local leisure spot, has many eateries along the canal's banks. The **Military**

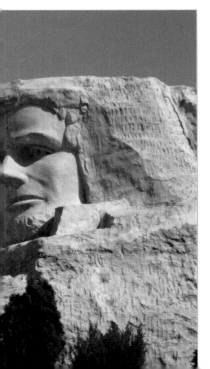

NEIWAN BRANCH RAILWAY

The Neiwan Branch Railway (Neiwan Zhixian Tiedao) heads east from Hsinchu Railway Station into the mining towns of the central mountains. This is one of Taiwan's four branch railways, all of which head from lowland into the hills, all popular with tourists. The Neiwan line's original raisons d'etre: camphor, limestone, timber, and coal. It stretches 27.9km (17.3 miles) with travel one way taking 50 minutes. The small air-conditioned trains roll past a total of nine small stations, halting at the town of Neiwan.

In Neiwan, the first tourist site encountered is the attractive small wooden station itself, built in the 1950s. The town is home to the only wooden police substation still extant. Stepping into the old Neiwan Theater (Neiwan Xiyuan; daily 11am–2pm, 4–9pm) is like stepping through a time portal; the facility has been renovated, taking on its original appearance, and is now run as a nostalgia restaurant, brimming with period items and with old Taiwanese films screened at all times.

Hsinchu and Miaoli counties form a major area of Hakka settlement, and the Neiwan trains roll right through the rural Hakka heartland. Many culture-vultures specifically travel the route to experience Hakka existence first-hand – especially in the many town eateries serving up authentic Hakka cuisine.

Dependents' Villages Museum (Juancun Bowuguan; Tue–Sun 9am–5pm; free) explores the lives of the military families set up in such villages – Hsinchu still has 11 – when the Kuomintang retreated from China en masse in the late 1940s. The **Glass Museum** (Boli Gongyi Bowuguan; Tue–Sun 9am–4.30pm), housed in a 1936 Japanese-built club building, details Hsinchu's longstanding success in glass-making and glass arts.

On the Lion's Head

Not far south of Hsinchu – on Sheng-dao 3, about halfway between Taipei and Taichung – is **Lion's Head Mountain** ㉗ (Shitoushan). When viewed from the proper angle, the mountain does resemble the king of beasts. It has been an important Buddhist center since the early 1900s; a number of the many temples here were built directly in natural caves. There are also small shrines and pagodas.

From the old stone-arch entrance above the parking lot, a sometimes steep 1,500-step path moves up the lion's head, then down its spine, visiting the temples and other sites and, near the tail, flower-scented forest and bamboo patches. The round-trip walk takes about three hours.

Feel free to inspect the ornate temples, observe monks and nuns at their daily duties, and listen to the forest sounds. Healthy vegetarian meals cooked by Buddhist nuns are available in several temples. The first main temple visited is the Zhonghua Tang. The main shrine hall, just above the dining room, rises on beautifully sculpted stone columns that depict celestial animals and ancient Buddhist legends. The massive multistoried structure just beyond is the **Kaishan Monastery,** a study and activities center for resident monks and nuns.

Up on the lion's 'mane' is the **Moon-Gazing Pavilion,** serving well its purpose on moonlit nights. From there, the trail moves past several cave-temples, the Pagoda of Inspiration, monastic quarters, a bridge, and viewing terraces. The rustic cave-shrines of the **Water Screen Convent** are the last major sights.

Pagoda below Shitoushan.

The kingdom of bicycles

The country now has myriad bike-outing options that make for scenic and healthy exploration of city and country, mountain and seaside.

In the mid-1990s Taiwan had no dedicated bike lanes or pathways. Today it is interlaced with thousands of kilometers of inviting bikeways, many individual systems in the form of easy-grade loops. The overarching theme has been to make the country a 'kingdom of bicycles,' denoting a land where citizens conveniently get healthy exercise out of doors on two wheels.

Country routes

Many of the most visually compelling routes are in the countryside. The first dedicated loop path was created in 1997 in the small farming town of Guanshan in the lyrically pretty East Rift Valley, carpeted in farms. Taiwan was then seeking entry into the WTO, Guanshan's leaders knew many farmers would be deeply impacted, and they decided to diversify to attract tourist dollars. The long loop meanders through small, well-tended farms cut up into a pastel mosaic when crops are maturing, along rice paddies and by old farmhouses and irrigation streams, offering classic tableaux with straw-hatted farmers bent over at the day's work, the close-in central and coastal mountain ranges as majestic backdrops. There are numerous bike-rental shops at the route's launch point.

This remains one of the prettiest countryside bikeways. With successful Guanshan serving as model, many other townships have followed suit, finding that fellow Taiwan citizens seem to have an unslakable thirst for new getaway options. Among the most scenic and enjoyable is a loop bikeway in Chishang, north of Guanshan, similar in theme to the latter's. Another is the network of theme routes on the sleepy side roads of Meinong, at the base of the southwest foothills, showcasing the area's strong Hakka culture, its tobacco-growing past, and so on. The rolling highway that encircles picturesque Sun Moon Lake has been called one of the world's 10 best cycling routes by a leading Western travel website; riders here can also jump on the popular shoreline boardwalk that spans much of the lake.

There is also especially good, safe highway biking along the east coast, in the East Rift Valley, Taroko Gorge, and Kenting National Park, as well as on all offshore islands save for the hilly Matsu islands.

City routes

Taipei has led the way amongst local cities in setting up bikeways. A loop now encircles the urban core, meandering through landscaped parks along the Jingmei, Xindian, Tamsui, and Keelung rivers, the loop completed with a jump over the Nangang hills. The system connects with other bikeways, enabling jaunts down the Tamsui to the coast, up the Tamsui all the way to Yingge, and up the Xindian to New Taipei City's Xindian district. Kaohsiung has been described as one of the five best biking cities in Asia by the same website mentioned above, and its system has expanded rapidly as it has ripped up downtown railway tracks in the harbor area and elsewhere.

All of the country's bike-route systems have rentals readily available, and both Taipei (www.youbike.com.tw) and Kaohsiung (www.c-bike.com.tw) have set up special rental-station webs in their central cores as well. Taipei's service has over 70 stations, fees are low, and payment is easy, via credit card or EasyCard. Rental bikes can be dropped off at any other station, and kept overnight. Both cities also allow bikes on metro trains.

Cycling along Dadaocheng Wharf.

Late President Chiang Kai-Shek's private wharf on Sun Moon Lake.

TAICHUNG AND ENVIRONS

With cosmopolitan Taichung as a convenient base, the visitor can explore the arts and crafts of a region that has its fair share of striking temples, shrines, and museums.

Less than an hour out of Taipei, travelers on the two main southbound freeways begin to see dramatic changes in the surrounding countryside. Factories are fewer, and lush farmland more prevalent. The congestion and steel-and-cement tones of the capital give way to green patchworks of ripening rice, fruit plantations, and vegetable plots.

The urban center of central Taiwan is **Taichung** ❶, which means, not coincidentally, Taiwan Central. As Taiwanese cities go, Taichung may be a long way from rivaling Tainan in terms of cultural attractions, but it is a far more leisurely paced city than, say, Taipei. Comparisons to Taipei before the big boom of the 1970s are to a certain extent inevitable but, as any Taichungite will be quick to point out, Taichung has its own style and flavor. Taiwanese is spoken here far more than in the capital and, with more space to spread out – the city lies in a wide basin that has low hills on three sides and is open to the central plains on the south – Taichung tends to do things on a grander scale than Taipei does, offering some of the island's biggest restaurants, nightclubs, and karaoke parlors.

City origins

Taiwan's third-largest city, **Taichung** has a population of over 2.7 million people. With an urban core located about 20km (12 miles) from the coast and 150km (93 miles) south of Taipei, it enjoys the island's best year-round climate, without the seasonal extremes of heat and cold that mark the north and south.

Chinese immigrants founded Taichung in 1721. They originally named it Datun, or 'Big Mound.' The city's current name was adopted by the Japanese after they took possession of Taiwan in 1895. Today, 20-hectare (49-acre) **Zhongshan Park** (Zhongshan

Main Attractions
Taichung Folk Park
National Museum of Natural
  Science
National Taiwan Museum of
  Fine Arts
Art Museum Parkway
Jingming 1st Street
Sanyi
Sanyi Wood Sculpture
  Museum
Zhenlan Temple

The exotic Hu Xin Pavilion is the most significant landmark inside Taichung Park.

Gongyuan), also called Taichung Park, occupies the hillock upon which the original settlement was built. The two pavilions rising above the lotus-filled lake are a city landmark.

The city has a number of pleasant attractions, and is known for its dining and nightlife, making it a good base while exploring more interesting scenic and cultural destinations around the region.

Places of prayer and reflection

The **Martyrs' Shrine** (Zhonglie Zi; daily 9am–5pm; free) on Lixing Road northeast of Zhongshan Park was erected in 1970. Its design provides a superb example of the harmony and balance inherent in classical Chinese

architecture. Many locals claim it is even more outstanding than the famous martyrs' shrines in Hualien and Taipei. Protected by two bronze guardian lions, it commemorates the 72 Chinese beheaded in 1911 by the Manchu court, on the eve of the republican revolution.

Next door, on Shuangshi Road, is Taichung's tranquil **Confucius Temple** (Kong Miao; Tue–Sun 9am–5pm; free), notable for the constrained design of its roof. The eaves curve gently downward, cleaving close to the earth, rather than flaring audaciously heavenward. Earth, not Heaven, was indeed the sage's prime concern. On the altar is a black stone stele with 'Confucius' engraved in gold on its smooth, unadorned

The Chinese words meaning 'goldfish' are phonetically identical with the two words meaning 'gold in abundance'.

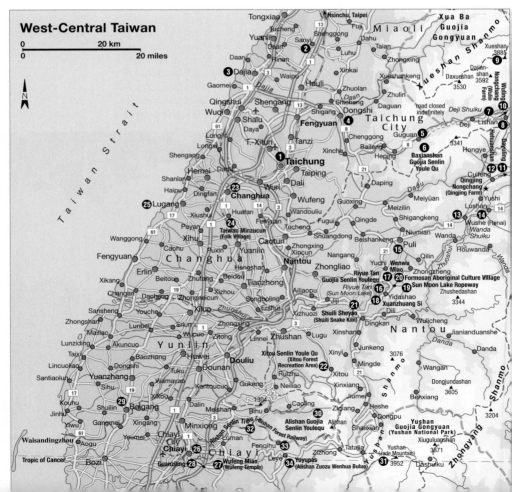

urface. Although he believed in pirits and deities, Confucius insisted people should steer clear of them. Every year on his birthday, September 28 (Teacher's Day), the temple hosts a colorful spectacle of ancient rituals nd archaic costumes.

Baojue Temple (Baojue Si; daily 8am-5pm; free), on the northern edge of the city on Jianxing Road, contains one of the largest and fattest Buddha images in all Taiwan. This is the proverbial happy Buddha, the golden shimmering Milefo, who sits laughing on a massive pedestal in one corner of the compound, towering 30 meters (100ft). Smaller Milefo statues are also scattered around the complex. Within the hollow pedestal of the giant pot-bellied Milefo is a room used for meetings, while in the adjacent building are several thousand cremation urns.

Art and science attractions

Appealing **Taichung Folk Park** Taichung Minsu Gongyuan; Tue–Sun 9am–5pm) is on Luxun Road.

Established in 1979, it features traditional Minnan, or Hokkien, architecture and arts and crafts exhibits. The buildings, with their sweeping needle-pointed roofs, are exquisite, and the works of folk art inside number over 3,000. Of particular interest are the exhibitions of Taiwanese crafts presented by artists in residence.

The **National Museum of Natural Science** (Guoli Ziran Kexue Bowuguan; www.nmns.edu.tw; Tue–Sun 9am–5pm; free) on Guanqian Road, northwest of Zhongshan Park, is aimed at young children, as is the adjoining Space Theater. The large **National Taiwan Museum of Fine Arts** (Guoli Taiwan Meishuguan; www.ntmofa.gov.tw; Tue–Fri 9am–5pm, Sat–Sun until 6pm; English tours available with advance notice, English audio for permanent exhibits; free), west of Zhongshan Park on Wuquan West Road, went through five years of renovations after being damaged in the 9-21 Earthquake, taking on a dynamic look. It stages over 30 exhibitions a year featuring Taiwanese and foreign art, and sits amid a large,

Night market shopping.

grassy park with an interesting outdoor sculpture park.

Dining and nightlife

Across from the entrance to the fine arts museum is the beginning of the **Art Museum Parkway** (Meishuguan Luyuandao), a green belt along Wuquan West Road lined on either side by art galleries, boutiques, and restaurants. A pedestrian/bicycle pathway traverses the middle, bringing visitors past dozens of compelling large-scale public artworks. At night the scores of restaurants, each of unique theme decor and personality, sit in the soft, romantic glow of atmospheric street lighting. A global buffet is offered: among the culinary choices available are Taiwanese, Taiwan indigenous, Shanghainese, Indian, American, Italian, Greek, and more.

Taichung residents are particularly proud of leafy, cobblestoned **Jingming 1st Street** (Jingming Yi Jie), in the downtown center, Taiwan's first-created pedestrian mall. There are cafés, restaurants, pubs, bookshops, and boutiques, with outdoor seating.

The Christian chapel at Donghai University was designed by I. M. Pei.

It's a popular place for Taichung' chic set to promenade, and a recom mended spot to relax over a drink and people-watch.

In the evening Taichung's most fam ous night market, **Zhonghua Nigh Market** (Zhonghua Yeshi) comes int action on Zhonghua Road. It stay open until the early morning hour and features numerous long-estab lished food stalls picked out by thei large numbers of diners.

Elsewhere, Taichung's nightlife i less cosmopolitan than Taipei's, bu no less lively.

Just beyond Downtown

A 20-minute drive northwest o downtown Taichung, on Taichun Harbor Road, is **Donghai Univer sity** (Donghai Daxue). The woode 139-hectare (343-acre) campus wa built in Tang dynasty style, China golden age of culture and the art This subtle and restrained style differ radically from the sometimes-garish style that prevailed in China afte the Ming period. Almost all cam pus buildings are constructed in th

SAVING LIN HISTORY

While the tragedy of the 9-21 Earthquake – so-called because it took place on September 21, 1999 – was overwhelmingly human, it also caused an important cultural loss. Various cultural relics have disappeared for good. It was long feared that chief among them would be the 200-year-old Lin Family Gardens in Wufeng, just a 10-minute drive from downtown Taichung. The Lins were one of Taiwan's wealthiest aristocratic families. Most of the clan emigrated after the Nationalists took over the island, leaving behind their sprawling, classically designed home, complete with ponds and gardens, known as one of the Four Great Gardens of Taiwan. One of the other four is the Lin Family Mansion and Garden, in New Taipei City's Banqiao district (see page 142). In the two years before the earthquake struck, NT$100 million had been spent restoring the complex to its former splendor, and it was poised to open to the public. In less than a minute, the earthquake practically leveled the mansions. Tragically, two members of the Lin family were also killed when their home collapsed. Restoration work on the national historic site has long been underway, with financial support from the national Executive Yuan's 921 Rebuilding Committee and Taichung's Cultural Affairs Bureau, and with experts brought in. Work is nearly complete, this priceless national inheritance has been saved, and some parts of the site have already been opened to the public.

quare, squat, colonnaded Tang style, with plain tiled roofs. A modern departure is the abstract Christian Chapel, designed by Sino-American architect I.M. Pei to symbolize a pair of hands touching in prayer.

Just 10km (6 miles) northeast of downtown Taichung lies **Encore Garden Theme Park**, which was seriously damaged by the 921 earthquake. The park finally closed in 2008 due to financial reasons. The area has remained unused and has not been sold since, so it attracts ruins photographers and adventurous youngsters, drawn by its eerie look, although venturing here is treated as trespassing.

Outside the urban core

Some 40km (25 miles) north of Taichung is **Sanyi ❷**, a small town stretched along one main road that parallels National Freeway No. 1. The town is famous throughout Taiwan as the island's woodcarving center, and indeed this is such a booming business here that it is estimated around half the local population support themselves through the craft. It is fascinating to stroll around the shops, and perhaps to stop and watch a local craftsman transform a large tree root, for example, into a masterpiece. The young **Sanyi Wood Sculpture Museum** (Sanyi Wudiao Bowuguan; http://wood.mlc.gov.tw; Tue–Sun 9am–5pm) provides both inspiring art and a good introduction to the craft and region.

On Provincial Highway No. 17 (Shengdao 17), 25km (16 miles) southwest of Sanyi, is the small town of **Dajia ❸**. It is significant for its **Zhenlan Temple** (Zhenlan Gong; daily 6am–9.30pm; free), which houses one of Taiwan's most revered images of Mazu (see page 66), the Maternal Ancestor, protector of fishermen, and the island's patron saint. The image was brought to Taiwan centuries ago by fishermen from Fujian province, and before her birthday on the 23rd day of the third lunar month the image sets off on a nine-day pilgrimage around central Taiwan in a palanquin accompanied by thousands of pilgrims.

Celebrants at the Mazu festival in Dajia.

An icey winter road on
Hehuanshan mountain.

THE CENTRAL CROSS-ISLAND HIGHWAY

Mountain resorts, farms, and hot springs punctuate the spectacular Central Cross-Island Highway, which weaves its way past the island's rich geographical features.

Taipei

North and then east of Taichung, the Central Cross-Island Highway stretches for 200km (120 miles) from Dongshi through Taroko Gorge to the east coast. The islanders claim no visit to Taiwan is complete without a trip across this road, for it displays – with striking beauty – the full gamut of the island's natural attractions: lush subtropical valleys and snow-capped peaks, alpine forests and rocky ravines, steamy hot springs and roaring rivers, mountain lakes and the shimmering sea.

The highway was completed in 1960 at great human cost. Ten thousand laborers, most retired servicemen who had fought on the mainland in the 1940s, struggled for four years to complete the road and hundreds either lost their lives or were injured (see page 280).

In two places, the highway forks. At Lishan, the north route traverses the upper spine of the Central Mountain Range to reach Yilan and the Northeast Coast Highway, 110km (68 miles) away; the south route heads to Dayuling. At Dayuling, the location of the second fork, one route moves east through Taroko Gorge; the other cuts south 40 km (25 miles) around Hehuanshan, the Mountain of Harmonious Happiness, to Wushe and Lushan hot-springs resort, leading back to Taichung or on to Sun Moon Lake.

After the 9-21 Earthquake, landslides and structural damage blocked off a long section of the main highway for quite some time. Not long after reopening, further weakening from typhoons caused another collapse. The government has closed, indefinitely, the section from just east of Guguan to just east of Deji. All sites listed in this chapter are still open and accessible, however, with a detour via Shengdao 14 through Puli.

The western section of the Central Mountain Range accessed via

A winding mountain road.

A road sign to warn drivers of the risk of falling rocks.

Fortunate Life Mountain Farm from above.

the highway, between Guguan and Lishan, sometimes resembles Switzerland more than a subtropical country. Visitors should let the terrain guide their choice of clothes: a sweater or jacket is often welcome at these altitudes.

Earthquake devastation

The first 20km (12 miles) from **Dongshi** ❹, the most devastated town in Taiwan's 1999 earthquake, lead past a series of alternating rice fields and vineyards. The first notable village is **Guguan** ❺, or Valley Pass, a hot-springs resort that is located approximately 1,000 meters (3,280ft) above sea level. Guguan has undergone major tourist development, and features numerous hotels and inns with piped hot-spring water, restaurants, and handicraft shops. At Guguan, a side road leads to the **Eight Immortals Mountain National Forest Recreation Area** ❻ (Baxianshan Guojia Senlin Youle Qu; daily 8am–5pm). The virgin forest here is a popular destination for birdwatchers. Beyond Guguan, the

highway climbs steeply for a few kilometers into the Central Mountain Range. At the **Deji Reservoir** ❼ (Deji Shuiku), Taiwan's highest, a torrent of water gushes beneath the impressive hydroelectric plant. The reservoir is currently only accessible from the east.

Lishan

East of Deji is **Lishan** ❽, on the crest of the Central Mountain Range near the Central Cross-Island Highway's halfway point. Shengdao 7, to Yilan in the northeast, begins here.

Swept by alpine breezes and drifting mists, lodges and restaurants dot the slopes of this mountain village, settled by decommissioned soldiers and Atayal aborigines after the highway was pushed through. The **Lishan Guest House**, an alpine version of Taipei's Grand Hotel, features terraces, pavilions, and sculpted shrubbery in its spacious grounds. This was one of Chiang Kai-shek's scores of villas, like most others rarely visited but with staff always at the ready. Severely damaged in the 1999 earthquake and a later typhoon, it has been completely renovated and reopened. Lishan is enchanting in spring (February to April), with apple, pear, and peach trees in full blossom.

An interesting side trip from Lishan is **Fortunate Life Mountain Farm** (Fushoushan Nongchang; www.fushoushan.com.tw; daily 6.30am–9pm; guided tours daily 8.30am, 4.30pm; free). Essentially a large fruit orchard spread across a hilltop, Fushoushan appears more European than Asian. The entrance is through an arched gate less than 1km (1,100yds) south of Lishan village. From there, a pine-lined drive leads past a church and steeple in a 5km (3-mile) ascent. Terraced acres of apple and pear orchards surround Western-style farmhouses. Trees are braced against the stiff mountain wind by elaborate bamboo scaffolding; individual fruits are protected in bags from insects and

birds. When in season, these fruits are on sale. At the farm entrance is a small museum displaying local artifacts and illustrations.

Mountain resort

Lishan is the staging point for mountaineering expeditions to **Snow Mountain** ❾ (Xueshan), Taiwan's second-highest peak at 3,886 meters (12,749ft). The climbing season is October to December and March to April. January and February on occasion see snowfalls, which make the trails impassable, and at other times of the year rain, winds and the risk of landslides make an ascent too dangerous.

Apart from spectacular mountain views, for many climbers, one of the reasons to visit this remote part is to see some of Taiwan's native flora and fauna. This, after all, is the habitat of the Formosan black bear, though sightings are extremely rare these days even for those who know where to look. Lucky hikers, however, may see deer and white-faced flying squirrels.

The ascent of the mountain begins at **Wuling Farm** ❿ (Wuling Nongchang; daily; cash only; www.wulingfarm.com.tw), a popular mountain resort – originally founded by the government for retired servicemen – offering spectacular views of the surrounding peaks. A 2.5-hour hike from the farm is a hostel at 2,440 meters (8,000ft) that climbers use as an overnight staging post for the final 2.5-hour assault on the summit.

Still on Shengdao 8 and 30km (19 miles) beyond Lishan, **Dayuling** ⓫ village straddles the highest point of the highway, at an elevation of 2,600 meters (8,530ft). East of here, the highway descends rapidly past Wenshan Wenquan (Wenshan Hot Springs) and through the Taroko Gorge to the east coast.

Dayuling is the junction for Shengdao 14, which heads southward from **Hehuanshan** ⓬, the Mountain of

Harmonious Happiness, and continues to the Lushan Hot Springs and Renai (Wushe). Hehuanshan, looming 3,420 meters (11,220ft) above sea level, is just 9km (6 miles) south of Dayuling. From January to early March, slushy snowfalls sometimes turn the mountain white temporarily. This, Taiwan's highest highway point at 3,275 meters (10,745ft), is also its only vehicle-accessible site where snow can be enjoyed, and locals flock here whenever there are reports of a coming downfall. Needless to say, at such times the driving can be treacherous. Even in the heat of summer, temperatures up here rarely rise above 15°C (59°F). Hiking, mountain climbing, and hot-spring bathing are the most attractive activities at this time.

Renai

Further on, the settlement of **Renai** ⓭ (Wushe) is embraced by the tall peaks of the Central Mountain Range. Although its name means 'foggy community', it is renowned for its crystal-clear alpine air, as well as a profusion

TIP

Hikes up Snow Mountain, Taiwan's second-highest peak located in the central mountains, are launched from the town of Lishan, on the Central Cross-Island Highway. The four-day, round-trip requires a special permit (for three people minimum) and prior permission from the National Police Agency, 7 Zhongxiao East Road, Section 1, Taipei; tel: (02) 2357-7377; www.npa.gov.tw.

High on Hehuanshan mountain.

TIP

Adventurous travelers should ask for a guide in Renai (Wushe) to take them to nearby Hongxiang village. Approachable only on foot, Hongxiang has a non-commercial hot spring where bathers can bask in natural surroundings.

of wild cherry and plum blossoms in early spring. Far below, the green mirror of **Wanda Reservoir** (Wanda Shuiku) is surrounded by abrupt mountain escarpments. The Chinese word for landscape is *shanshui* – literally, mountains and water – and this lake is a perfect example of that expression. A trail leads from the village to the lake, where only shore fishing is permitted. In Renai village are a few local inns and ethnic minority handicraft shops.

Wushe made its mark on Taiwan's history in 1930, when the Atayal minority tribal group residing there staged a bloody but futile uprising against Japanese occupation forces. The Japanese, with modern weaponry, killed more than 1,000 of the tribesmen, but not before losing 200 of their own people. A memorial plaque in highway-side Mona Rudao Memorial Park (Mouna Ludao Jinian Bei) commemorates the massacre.

About 3km (2 miles) before Renai, on Shengdao 14, is **Qingjing Farm** (Qingjing Nongchang; Mon–Fri 8am–4pm, holidays until 5pm), a major attraction giving Taiwanese a rare opportunity to see cows grazing in green fields and even to hug sheep and sit on a horse. Servicemen who were members of Yunnan's Bai ethnic minority and fled into Burma, Laos, and Thailand after 1949 settled this farm; among other things this makes for delicious Chinese-Bai dishes at local restaurants.

Hot springs and more

Lushan ⓮ village straddles a turbulent stream traversed by a suspension footbridge. Hot-spring inns lie along both banks of the river. On the far side of the river, just beyond the last hotel, a trail leads past a pair of waterfalls to the smoldering source of the area's hot springs. The simmering puddles that have formed in crevices around the source are hot enough to boil eggs, and many visitors do just that. The water lends flavor and vital minerals to the eggs, making them highly nutritional. Lushan village is famous for its tea, medicinal herbs, petrified-wood canes, wild-blossom honey, and dried mushrooms.

Driving through Taiwan's interior mountainous scenery offers beautiful views.

WUSHE INCIDENT

The Ayatal-tribe town of Renai (Wushe), in the central mountains on the Central Cross-Island Highway, was the site of a key uprising against the Japanese during their period of colonial rule. On October 27, 1930, local chief Mona Rudao and over 300 warriors ambushed Japanese officials and family members gathered for a sports meet at Wushe Elementary School, in retaliation for ongoing Japanese repression and slights. After days of fighting, with Japanese reinforcements expected, they retreated to the mountains and fought on for two months, hiding in caves to escape air bombing. The Japanese eventually resorted to poisonous gas, and many tribal members, sick and starving, committed suicide rather than be taken prisoner.

Hikers can make the most of the hill trails.

Morning on Sun Moon Lake.

NANTOU COUNTY

Romantic Sun Moon Lake, shrines housing miraculous relics, experimental forests, and leafy tea plantations are major features of Nantou County, home to the geographical center of the island.

antou County covers the middle of Taiwan, the only landlocked county in the country. A mountainous region, there are few flat areas, save for a number of mountain-basin areas and valley bottoms. This is the region with the best access to the magnificent Central Mountain Range.

This county was the area hit hardest by the devastating earthquake on September 21, 1999, and although complete recovery has been impossible, great strides have been made. The celebrated tourist area of Riyue Tan, or Sun Moon Lake, was made a national scenic area and has enjoyed a strong renaissance, and the government has systematically poured resources into other areas as well to stimulate tourism. In the past the majority of the local population relied on farming and resource extraction, with incomes comparatively low.

With much of the mountain region's topsoil rendered unstable by the terrific shaking it received in the 9-21 Earthquake, and by the great rains of later typhoons, landslides can be expected to occasionally shut down roads during the wet summer months from May through September.

Puli Basin

The sprawling town of **Puli** ⑮, in the wide and fertile Puli Basin, is known as the exact geographical center of the island. A monument (Taiwan Dili Zhongxi Bei), approached by a flight of stairs to the northeast of town, marks the actual point.

Puli is famous throughout Taiwan for the quality of its water and the beauty of its women. There are a few notable attractions in the town itself, which was badly damaged in the 9-21 Earthquake. **Puli Winery** (Puli Jiuchang; Mon–Fri 8.30am–5pm, Sat–Sun until 6pm; free) is the famed producer of Taiwan's version of Shaohsing Wine,

Sun Moon Lake's picturesque setting makes it popular with honeymooners.

made from rice. There is an interesting 'wine culture' museum on the second level, with quantity and quality English translations. The downstairs food-vendor court sells such inventions as Shaohsing popsicles and Shaohsing-flavored 'salmon snack cubes' and sausages.

On the outskirts of town are a large number of temples, notably the massive **Chung Tai Chan Monastery** (Zhongtai Chan Si; www.ctworld.org; Mar–Oct daily 8am–5.30pm, Nov–Feb until 5pm; free). The monastery, seeming to soar into the sky, is in the shape of a Buddhist cultivator in the lotus position. The large halls and pretty parkland are home to statuary of striking size and wonderful esthetic accomplishment, and the museum to priceless Buddhist antiquities. In the tower, visible through massive windows from far away, is a seven-story pagoda made without nails from Vietnamese teak.

Sun Moon Lake

It's a short drive from Puli to Taiwan's most enduringly popular honeymoon resort **Sun Moon Lake** ⑯ (Riyue Tan; www.sunmoonlake.gov.tw), 750 meters (2,460ft) above sea level in the western foothills of the Central Range. Entirely enfolded in mountains and dense tropical foliage, there were actually two lakes here – the Sun and Moon – before the Japanese built a hydroelectric dam and raised the basin's water level. Under sunny skies, the dreamy landscape of turquoise waters, jade-green hills, and drifting mountain mists lends itself well to the moods and passions of honeymooners and other amorous couples flocking to the lake's shores.

Before the Japanese built the dam, the aboriginal tribe that once flourished here, the Thao, had their major village on the slopes of the hill between Sun and Moon lakes. After the basin was flooded, only the upper reaches of the hill, where the Thao sacred burial grounds are located, still showed. The village was moved to the south shore, and was later moved again to higher ground – to the present site, Ita Thao village

Wenwu Temple.

when the Nationalists decided to raise the water level.

Needless to say, none of this sat very well with the Thao. Adding insult was the fact that the government refused to recognize them as an 'official' tribe. Thankfully, their numbers have risen to over 500, after dropping below 200 at one stage. The Thao are now one of Taiwan's 14 officially recognized tribes, and have gained control of their village lands and the tip of their sacred mountain (with a name change from Guanghua Island to Lalu Island). Today, the Tourism Bureau includes the tribe in planning for Sun Moon Lake National Scenic Area, set up to help revive local fortunes after the 9-21 earthquake pummeled the region and almost sank a local economy heavily dependent on tourism.

Daoist shrine

A good starting point for an exploration of the lake is **Wenwu Temple** ⑰ (Wenwu Miao; daily, use side entrance after 8pm; free), a temple of martial and literary arts located high on a promontory overlooking the lake. This Daoist shrine, dedicated to Confucius and the two great warrior deities Guangong and Yue Fei, is built into the hillside in three ascending levels. The two largest stone lions in Asia stand sentry at the entrance, and two full-relief windows of carved stone, depicting the celestial dragon and tiger grace the portico. A viewing terrace at the rear allows unimpeded vistas of the lake. The temple, like everything in the area, which was close to the epicenter of the quake, was badly damaged in September 1999, but has been fully restored.

The shrine to Confucius occupies the upper rear hall, with decorative motifs drawn from Chinese folklore predating by centuries the arrival of Buddhism in China. Symbolic of the ultimate subservice of the sword to the pen, the temple's martial shrine sits slightly lower than the literary shrine. Contained within are the red-faced Guangong, the God of War, but more likely to be worshipped by practical businesspeople on account of the god's legendary strategizing and mathematical skills, and the white-faced Yue Fei, a Song-dynasty patriot and military hero who attempted, without success, to recover the empire from the barbarian Mongol nomads.

The temple complex is interesting for its complicated layout, with various pavilions and side halls connected by ornate passages and stairways. Throughout the grounds stand potted bonsai trees, tropical flowers, and shrubs sculpted to resemble animals. The pair of 4.5-meter (15ft) tall gods at the entrance, carved from solid wood and colorfully painted, rank among the best in Taiwan.

Preserved Buddhist relics

High on a hill near the southern end of the lake, lovely **Xuanzang Temple** ⑱ (Xuanzang Si; daily 5am–6pm; free), built in Tang dynasty style, houses some of Asia's most precious

TIP

Sun Moon Lake (Riyue Tan) is at its best just after daybreak, the perfect time to drive around its circumference – it is too big to walk. However, regular on/off shuttle buses travel the loop road, and bicycles can be rented at the two main villages and other points.

Lion-guardian at Wenwu Temple.

Pixiu is a Chinese mythical hybrid creature considered to be a very powerful protector to practitioners of Feng Shui.

Ascend Cien Ta for great views.

Buddhist relics, known as *si-li-zi*. Devout Buddhists believe the small kernel-shaped stones – found among the ashes of highly accomplished Buddhist monks and Daoist adepts after cremation – are formed by the forging of spirit and energy after a lifetime of intensive meditation and other spiritual disciplines. The ashes of the historical Buddha, Sakyamuni, yielded 12 cups of these tiny black-and-white pebbles, some of which are enshrined here. Flames will not consume them, it is said, nor will sledgehammers crack them. Doubters say they are kidney- or gallstones, or perhaps crystallized remains from the cremation process.

The nuggets are said to have other unusual properties. The two carried to this site by monks during the Nationalist retreat of 1949 have not remained static over the centuries. It is claimed that they have expanded, contracted, or even generated new kernels, depending upon how much prayer and offering is performed. There are now seven enshrined at the temple, kept within a miniature

jewel-encrusted pagoda of solid gold on the altar in the main hall.

Also in the main hall are a gilded reclining Buddha and a handsome statue of Xuanzang himself. This Tang-dynasty monk made a pilgrimage to India immortalized in the classical Chinese novel *Journey to the West*. After 17 years of Buddhist study, lecturing, and traveling in India, he returned to the imperial Chinese capital of Changan (now Xian) in 645. Over the next two decades, he translated 1,335 *sutras* from the Sanskrit language into classical Chinese, playing a major part in bringing Buddhism to China.

On the third floor, another small golden pagoda protects a shard of what is believed to be Xuanzang's skull, looted from China by the Japanese during World War II. In 1955 a Japanese monk was dispatched to return the bone – both its age and authenticity have been verified – at Chiang Kai-shek's request. Upon handing over the relic, the monk-messenger died. His ashes are now kept in a wooden pagoda nearby.

9-21 EARTHQUAKE

At 1.47am on September 21, 1999, the sleeping population of Taiwan was jolted awake. An earthquake measuring 7.3 on the Richter scale had struck on the Chelungpu fault line, running right through Nantou County's tourist playground of Sun Moon Lake. The earthquake was so severe that it even toppled buildings in Taipei, 150km (93 miles) away. Thousands of aftershocks, some measuring more than 6 on the Richter scale, later rumbled across the island. The aftermath left 2,405 dead, 10,718 injured, more than 30,000 homes leveled and more than 25,000 damaged. The number of homeless was uncertain, but news reports generally quoted more than 100,000. The quake and subsequent typhoons have left many hillsides and mountainsides unstable, and high-mountain road blockages caused by landslides after heavy rains are frequent. A long section of the Central Cross-Island Highway is now closed to general traffic, perhaps permanently. Some residents are still suffering psychological problems. According to geologists, the earthquake resulted in major topographical changes in the mountains of central Taiwan – a crunch of 1.4 to 7 meters (4.5 to 23ft) horizontally and 1.3 to 3 meters (4.5 to 10ft) vertically. The 921 Earthquake Education Park (www.921emt.edu.tw) in Taichung's Wufeng district, which has a museum on the disaster, is built on the site of a destroyed school left as is. There is also a fault rupture and raised riverbank on-site.

Other lake highlights

Atop the peak behind Xuanzang Si stands the ornate, nine-tiered **Cien Ta** (Pagoda of Filial Virtue; daily 6am–10pm; free), erected by Chiang Kai-shek in memory of his mother, reached with an uphill walk through cool glades of bamboo, fern, maple, and pine. Those who climb to the top are rewarded with spectacular lake views.

Pleasant, tourist-friendly **Ita Thao** village is at the lake's south end. It is home to scores of gift outlets and eateries, many with indigenous themes. Regular Thao-theme entertainment is offered into the evening at the attractive pier area, with its sparkling yacht-shaped visitor center.

Just east of the village is the **Sun Moon Lake Ropeway** ⑲ (Riyuetan Lanche; www.ropeway.com.tw; daily 10.30am–4pm, Sat–Sun until 4.30pm; closed 1st Wed of month), a popular cable car attraction opened in 2010. The aerial ride between Sun Moon Lake and **Formosan Aboriginal Culture Village** ⑳ (Jiuzu Wenhua Cun; www.nine.com.tw; daily 9.30am–5.30pm) takes riders over two mountain passes, and brings stunning panoramas. A combined cable car and cultural village ticket brings a significant discount. The culture village is a large theme park spread over a gently sloping mountain valley. The informative Aboriginal Villages section celebrates Taiwan's indigenous peoples with scores of architectural replicas, song-and-dance shows, and demos of traditional cooking methods, weaving, pestle music, and more. There's also an amusement area and landscaped European Garden area.

A boat tour of Sun Moon Lake is highly recommended, and there are regular outings from Ita Thao and other locations. This is also one of Taiwan's most popular bicycling areas, and there are rental stations around the lake. The two-line highway, which has a low vehicle-speed limit, offers lovely views, and there is a dedicated lakeside pedestrian/bike path that encircles much of the lake, with long boardwalk sections that are sometimes right over the water.

Houseboats on Sun Moon Lake.

Kiln and forest area explorations

A short drive southwest of Sun Moon Lake is the **Shuili Snake Kiln**  (Shuili Sheyao; www.snakekiln.com.tw; daily 8am–5.30pm). Nantou County was once a major ceramics producing center, a main reason the free availability of the timber needed for firing, rolling out roof tiles, myriad household items, and large ceramic vessels for aging liquor. The highlight of the big, rambling wood-built kiln complex, opened in 1927, is a price-less historical relic – a snake-like kiln 40 meters (120ft) long, resting on a hillside, that takes three to four days to fire up. There is also a museum, multimedia exhibition room, pottery demonstration area, and DIY area.

The **Xitou Forest Recreation Area**  (Xitou Senlin Youle Qu; daily 8am–5pm; www.exfo.ntu.edu.tw) is within the Xitou Bamboo Forest. Forty percent of Taiwan's supply of raw bamboo and bamboo products comes from this 2,485-hectare (6,140-acre) forest research station, operated by National Taiwan University; the forest

Xitou Bamboo Forest.

recreation area is open to tourists. There are many varieties of bamboo here, along with vast tracts of cypress, cedar, and pine. The station cultivates and distributes more than one million tree shoots annually for Taiwan's extensive reforestation projects.

Visitors to the forest recreation area can stroll along paved footpaths shaded by leafy canopies. At 1,150 meters (3,773ft) above sea level, this is a favorite spot for both families and more serious hikers. One of the most popular walks leads to the remains of a sacred tree, over 3,800 years old and 46 meters (150ft) high. University Pond features a bamboo bridge arching gracefully over carp-filled water, there is a very popular raised boardwalk (charge) stretching 180 meters (590ft) through the tree-tops, 22.6 meters (74ft) at its highest, and a 7km (4-mile) trek leads to a remote ravine with a waterfall. For the hardy, the resort of Alishan, to the south, is a full day away by foot, but this excursion requires a permit and equipment.

Vehicles are prohibited; all facilities are outside the main gate, in Xitou village, a popular honeymoon retreat. Souvenir shops sell bamboo products and other mountain goods – mushrooms, tea, and herbs. Bamboo shoots are, of course, the specialty of the resort's restaurants. There are numerous accommodations options, most built with wood themes.

Songboling's teashops and farms

Returning toward Taichung, and just before the town of Nantou, at the village of Mingqian, Shengdao 16 meets Shengdao 3. About 10km (6 miles) further, the **Pine Bluff** (Songboling) tea-production region spreads across a hilly plateau. Despite the name, there aren't many pines on this bluff. Instead, groves of areca palm and giant bamboo shelter large tea plantations. Women wearing straw hats and bandannas can be seen plucking the ender leaves from these green shrubs, dropping them into huge baskets carried on their backs. Between the tea plantations are fields of pineapple and banana trees.

The main street of Songboling village is lined with teashops offering a service known locally as Old Folks' Tea, as only old folks (and presumably idle travelers) seem to have the time to enjoy this leisurely pursuit. Samples of many varieties of tea are brewed in tiny clay pots and poured into thimble-sized cups; as the tea is too coarse, the first infusion in the pots is always poured away. A variety of fragrant loose teas as well as teabags are available for purchase.

Dongding (Frozen Peak), a young Oolong leaf from the highest plantations above Songboling, is regarded by many as Taiwan's best tea. It has a superb flavor, subtle fragrance, and practically no bite. Those who buy bulk tea in Songboling get the same wholesale price as major Taipei retailers, which varies a great deal, depending on quality. The more expensive the blend, the better the bargain.

In addition to its famous tea, Songboling has one other attraction: a Daoist temple known as the **Palace of the Celestial Mandate** (Shoutian Gong; daily 6am–9pm; free). Some of the most exquisite stone sculptures in central Taiwan, depicting Daoist legends and Chinese folklore, comprise the portico.

Of special interest, carved in full relief from solid stone, are two huge, round windows that brace the temple. One depicts the celestial dragon and the other the tiger, a duo found in all Daoist temples. The intricate ceiling inside the hall and the finely painted 4.5-meter (15ft) solid wood doors are impressive. The temple comes with an attached guesthouse, should you be tempted to spend a meditative night there.

South of Songboling is Yuanquan, a station on the famous **Jiji Branch Railway** (Jiji Xian). Named after the picturesque small town of **Jiji** to the east, tourist/commuter trains on this line take 50 minutes to travel the less than 30km (19 miles) of narrow gauge that span the rustic countryside between Changhua and Nantou counties.

An exquisite tea set is a nice memento of your visit. Shops all over the island overflow with tea-brewing paraphernalia of all sorts.

Picking tea near Songboling.

SOUTH OF TAICHUNG

To visit some particularly ornate temples, witness how Taiwan life used to be, and enjoy some of the most extravagant religious celebrations, make the journey south of Taichung.

The alluvial plain that divides the highlands from the Taiwan Strait is filled by vast green rice fields and plantations of bananas, pineapples, papayas, sugar cane, tea, and other crops. Yet the same alluvial plain is one of Taiwan's key urban heartlands. Picturesque scenes of rural idyll are wont to give way with surprising rapidity to sprawling towns and cities, smoke-belching factories, and ugly garbage dumps.

This region was one of the earliest settled by the Han Chinese. The land is primarily flat, with a few hills suddenly rising from the plain. The short rivers, rushing out of the nearby mountains, are generally almost dry on either side of heavy rains. The earth is rich, and the lack of consistent rainfall is compensated for with a massive reservoir and irrigation system built up by the Japanese that has made this the country's breadbasket. There are few good ports in this region, for the heavy rains engender constant silt buildup along the coastline.

The towns and villages are centuries old, and still move to older rhythms, with a noticeably slower pace than in the cities. The land given over to farming is steadily shrinking, and many of the young leave village or town to pursue education and then work, with only some returning to their roots when older.

Buddha statue at Baguashan.

Crafts and model construction

About 20km (12 miles) from the city is **Caotun**, where the **Taiwan Craft Culture Park** (Taiwan Gongyi Wenhua Yuanqu; www.ntcri.gov.tw; Tue–Sun 9am–5pm; free) contains an extensive display of local handicrafts and modern manufactured goods. The site's four-story, air-conditioned building houses bamboo and rattan furniture, Chinese lanterns, lacquerware, ceramics, stonecraft, woodcraft, curios, jewelry, cloisonné, and textiles.

Main Attractions

Baguashan
Taiwan Folk Village
Lugang
Beimen Station
Chiayi Old Prison
Guanziling
Palace Facing Heaven

Lugang

West beyond Changhua, the ancient inland port of **Lugang** ㉕ lies sleepily near the shores of the Taiwan Strait. A main port of entry during the Qing dynasty (1644–1911) for waves of Chinese immigrants from Fujian province, Lugang was abruptly closed down by the Japanese in 1895. Thereafter, silt and sand rendered the port useless for commercial shipping; fishing is now the major maritime activity. The town is a day excursion from Taichung.

Lugang is interesting for its insight into old Taiwan. Along with some impressive temple architecture, it is an area where traditions live on. Although most of the town is recognizably modern, many of the narrow residential lanes have changed little since the Qing dynasty days. Artisans can still be seen fashioning furniture with ancient tools and techniques in open-front shops, and here and there are shops specializing in forgotten crafts such as Chinese lantern making.

Altar tables, shelves, ornaments, beams, eaves, and other furnishings and fixtures are hewn into shape, then finished with elaborate detail at numerous workshops lining the main street. The fragrance of freshly sawn camphor and wet lacquer drifts everywhere. Incense is also produced in Lugang, and it is interesting to see how the enormous coils that hang from temple ceilings and burn for days are produced by hand.

The oldest temple in Lugang, and one of the oldest in Taiwan, is Longshan or **Dragon Mountain Temple** (Longshan Si; www.lungshan.org.tw; daily 6am–10pm; free), dating from the 18th century. Located on Sanmin Road, just off the main avenue of Zhongshan Road, the temple was constructed by early Chinese settlers as an expression of gratitude to Guanyin, the Goddess of Mercy, for their safe passage from the mainland. Guanyin is enshrined in the main hall.

Longshan may not be quite the oldest temple on the island, but it is regarded as the most artistically significant, earning it the appellation 'Taiwan's Forbidden Palace.' Of particular note is the circular, carved

Lanterns are so important they have an entire festival dedicated to them.

Lugang Old Street.

dome ceiling over the main altar. Appearing on postcards and in brochures, it is as close as Taiwan gets to having a Sistine Chapel. The wall murals are the work of master artist Guo Xin-lin. The benches beneath them are usually occupied by lolling groups of elderly men – often the subject of photographic portraits, both professional and amateur. Also worth noting are the elaborately carved stone-dragon pillars.

The first Mazu center?

Down Zhongshan Road from the Longshan Si is the impressive, and old, **Tianhou Temple** (Tianhou Gong; www.lugangmazu.org; daily 6.30am– 9.30pm; free). The image of Mazu, Goddess of the Sea, on the main altar, is said to have been brought here in 1684 from the original Mazu shrine on Meizhou Island by Admiral Shi Lang, who captured Taiwan for the Qing emperor. If true, this story substantiates the claim of Lugang's people that this was the first center of the Mazu cult in Taiwan. There are numerous other exotic icons here. Among them is the magnificent Jade Emperor in a temple of his own, in the same compound. At the rear of the temple is a small Mazu Culture Museum. Signs to many more temples and shrines are posted throughout the residential maze.

Also well worth a visit is the **Lugang Folk Arts Museum** (Lugang Minsu Wenwuguan; www.lukangarts. org.tw; Tue–Sun 9am–5pm), a 30-room European-style villa that couldn't look more out of place in Lugang if it tried. Designed as a private residence in 1919 for a wealthy landowner by a Japanese architect in Orientalized Edwardian style, it is one of the most unusual mansions on the island. Inside is an interesting collection of old furniture and household fixtures, vintage photos, paintings, personal effects, costumes, books, musical instruments, hand puppets, and other items reflecting the lifestyle of Taiwan's people.

Heritage shops

West of the museum, on Qingyun Street, is the unusual triumvirate of the **Wenkai Academy** (Wenkai Shuyuan), **Civil Shrine** (Wen Zi), and **Martial Temple** (Wu Miao). Together they form a compound that brings together an academy that, in its day, produced a large number of Taiwan's cultural elite, a shrine that once served as a meeting place for one of the island's first literary associations, and a temple dedicated to Guangong, who is worshiped both as the God of War and as the God of Commerce.

Turn right out of the Wenkai Shuyuan, continue straight ahead, and the first intersection is at **Zhongshan Road**, Lugang's main thoroughfare. This is where most of the town's bestknown and longest-established shops can be found. Highlights include the **Wanneng Tin Shop** (Wanneng Xipu), where the Chen family has been creating traditional Taiwanese crafts out of tin for generations. Also famous is the **Shi Chin-yu Incense Shop** (Shi Chin-yu Xiangpu), which has been making and selling incense for more than 200 years.

TIP

The entrance to Tianhou Temple in Lugang is clustered with stalls serving famous local snacks. The specialty in this part of town is e-a-jian – oyster omelet – which is available all over the island, but nowhere is it quite like Lugang's, say locals.

Traditional beliefs remain strong.

TIP

If visiting Beigang during the Mazu celebrations, remember to bring earplugs: the staccato bursts of firecrackers, gongs, and drums are ear splitting.

extravagant of Taiwan's over 500 temples dedicated to the island's patron deity. Koxinga (Guoxingye) attributed the safe passage of his war fleet across the Taiwan Strait to the divine protection of Mazu; ever since then, she has been highly revered in Taiwan.

The Palace Facing Heaven

More than 3 million pilgrims visit Chaotian Gong, the Palace Facing Heaven, every year, leaving large sums of cash in annual donations. During the April or May festival week commemorating Mazu's birth, the town is the site of a fascinating display of ancient folk religion and traditional customs.

Beigang is not as lively as it once was during Mazu's birthday celebrations, as a dispute between temples has resulted in Beigang being taken off the Dajia Mazu's annual pilgrimage circuit. Nevertheless, it is still an exciting time to visit, and the crowds are not nearly as overwhelming as in Xingang. Religious rites are performed with a pomp and ceremony that has not changed significantly in 1,000 years. One particularly colorful (and frequent) ritual involves the parading of a holy icon in a gilded, silk-tasseled palanquin. When the procession returns to the temple gates, the deity is welcomed back amid thick clouds of incense, exploding firecrackers, and a cacophonous din of gongs, cymbals, drums, and flutes.

Four stone lions and the four Immortals mounted on dragons guard the front gate of the temple, but it is the roof that demands study. There may not be a livelier, more colorful set of eaves and gables on the island. Hundreds of glazed ceramic figures cavort among miniature mountains, palaces, pagodas, and trees, depicting tale after tale from folklore. On the central roof are the Three Star Gods of Longevity, Prosperity, and Posterity – the three cherished goals of the Taiwanese people in this life. The pagoda on the main beam of the central shrine hall symbolizes the communion of Heaven and Earth. The roof beams on the side halls have pairs of gamboling dragons pursuing the elusive Pearl of Wisdom.

Within the temple courtyard stands a three-tiered pagoda, where paper offerings are burned. Pilgrims pay real money to temple vendors for ersatz paper money, incense, and other gifts for the gods. Thus, the temple fills its coffers with legal tender, the gods benefit from the symbolic offerings, and the pilgrim is blessed by both.

There are many tall image-cones (known as Buddha mountains) bearing the names of the temple's financial patrons. Lit up like Christmas trees, they stand in pairs at the temple's altars. Most temples have only two such cones, but the Beigang temple has no fewer than 12, clear evidence of its immense following and generous patronage. Offering tables are heaped high with meat, fish, poultry, fruit, candy, incense, wine, real cash, and even soft drinks, left conveniently uncapped so that their essence might reach the gods. An open-air market occupies the streets that surround the temple, selling everything imaginable.

LUGANG – DEER HARBOUR

The name 'Lugang' means 'Deer Harbor.' In the 1600s millions of deer inhabited Taiwan's central plains, the export of deer products was a major moneymaker, and Lugang was the main entrepot. Pelts were sent to Japan, where samurai used them for quivers, leggings, and elsewhere, and venison was sent to the China mainland, along with antler and phalli for use as aphrodisiacs. The deer were hunted out by the mid-1700s, but Lugang still thrived. It became central Taiwan's port for agricultural exports, and was long one of Taiwan's three main ports. Silting was already causing trouble, with barges bringing goods to and from ships waiting out in open water, when the Japanese closed the port in 1895 to stop all contact with China. It became completely silted over. The town was frozen in time – especially when the north-south railway was built and bypassed it. With limited money for new building, old structures were left standing, to the benefit of later generations of tourists. Their trade cut off, local firms turned to manufacturing handicrafts for island sale. Lugang soon emerged as a key center for traditional handicraft production, and today scores of shops feature talented artisans wielding age-old skills introduced to Taiwan hundreds of years ago by their ancestors – religious icons and other paraphernalia, incense, kites, lanterns, oil-paper, and bamboo umbrellas, tinware, fans, pottery, carved wooden furniture, and more.

ALISHAN AND ENVIRONS

Alishan is the gateway to Taiwan's highest peaks, providing the opportunity for viewing spectacular sunrises, catching a glimpse of abundant wildlife, and enjoying a relaxing soak in a hot spring.

The fame of the south-central plains city of Chiayi in Taiwan is due less to its indigenous sights than to the fact it is the gateway to one of the island's most famous sights, **Alishan**, in the central mountains. When locals say they are traveling to 'Alishan,' which means 'Mt Ali,' they inevitably mean the **Alishan National Forest Recreation Area** ➌⓪ (Alishan Guojia Senlin Youlequ; daily 24 hours), a well-developed tourist resort area that is an object of pilgrimage for its sunrises over what the Taiwanese refer to poetically as the *yunhai*, or 'sea of clouds.'

The forest recreation area sits within the much larger, and much younger, Alishan National Scenic Area (Alisan Guojia Fengjingqu; www.ali-nsa.net; free), which is more pristine and undeveloped, defined by lofty peaks in the distance, Tsou indigenous villages, picturesque tea plantations, tall-tree forests, and trails far quieter than in the forest recreation area. The national scenic area abuts Yushan National Park (www.ysnp.gov.tw; Shuili Visitor Center daily 9am–4.30pm, closed Chinese New Year's Eve and announced holidays; free), providing easy access to Taiwan's loftiest peak, **Mt Jade** ➌① or Yushan.

Alishan Forest Railway

Perhaps Alishan's greatest attraction for Western travelers is the three-hour train ride (you'll need to stay overnight) on the **Alishan Forest Railway** ➌② (Alishan Senlin Tielu) to the mountain resort from Chiayi's Beimen Station. This magnificent feat of engineering was accomplished by the Japanese in the early 1900s, who built the line to gain access to the region's virgin timber. Today antique, specially restored diesel and steam locomotives chug along the zigzagging 70km (44 miles) narrow-gauge railway hauling colorful restored carriages, crossing 114 bridges and

Main Attractions
Alishan National Forest
   Recreation Area
Yushan National Park
Alishan Forest Railway
Fenqihu
YuYuPas

Mountain scenery in Alishan.

Morning at the parks sheds light on the social traditions and rituals of the local people. Qigong is a form of exercise involving coordination of the mind, breathing pace, and soft slowing movements, performed to help lower tension.

Admiring sunset in Alishan.

passing through 49 tunnels, one of them 770 meters (2,530ft) long. Unless visiting on the weekend (not recommended if avoidable), there is no need to book ahead. On weekends trains leave at 9.10am, with an additional Sunday departure at 10.10am. The return journeys are at 2pm and 3pm; from Monday through Friday there is a single departure at 9.10am and return journey at 2pm. You can get on and off the line at any point along the way, as on a regular rail line.

Alishan National Forest Recreation Area

The popularity of this area is due primarily to the famous sunrise view from the summit of nearby **Celebration Mountain** (Zhushan). Indeed, it is a spectacular event. As visitors stand shivering in jackets 2,490 meters (8,170ft) above sea level, gazing into the mist, the sun suddenly

peers over the horizon. Golden shafts of light pierce the dawn, skipping across the thick carpet of clouds that cover the valleys to the east. This, Alishan's famed 'sea of clouds,' springs to life like a silver screen the moment the sun glances across it, undulating in vivid hues of gold and silver, red and orange. On holidays and weekends, the summit is overcrowded with thousands of excited and noisy visitors – these are not the days to witness an idyllic sunrise. On any given day hundreds of people make the pre-dawn ascent, usually by tour bus. There is also a narrow-gauge railway from Alishan village (30 minutes one way), the recreation area's hub. Many people will take the bus or train and then enjoy the pleasant walk back downhill, which takes about two hours, through secondary forest.

The region is blanketed with thick forests of red cypress, cedar, and pine some thousands of years old. When these ancient plants finally fall to rest the Taiwanese let sleeping logs lie. The great gnarled stumps and petrified logs form some of Alishan's most

xotic sights, viewed when out on the boardwalks and wide, unpaved trails that traverse the area. A highlight is the huge **Three-Generation Tree**, a natural wonder with a tree growing in a tree that is growing within yet another tree.

Alishan National Scenic Area

The scenic village of **Fenqihu** ③ has a duo of raisons d'etre: it was close to great timber stands, and a halfway-point storage and repair depot was needed by the Japanese for the forest railway. A place of low wooden houses, it is fitted snugly onto a high slope where two mountain bodies meet, just below a pass that leads into the next valley. At the top of the village, just above the tracks, is a clutch of rustic wood-built cafés with splendid views of forest and valley. Just below, on the lower side, is a large old railway storage and repair shed. Running downhill past the shed, parallel to the tracks, is narrow Old Street; Fenqihu has been 'discovered' by flatlanders in recent years, and Old

Street is a prime draw. Lined tightly with heritage shops selling iconic Alishan foods and crafts, it becomes exceedingly narrow at its far (western) end, facing shops so close the sellers can almost reach out and shake hands across what is more corridor than street, eaves overlapping to create a tunnel effect where day feels much like night—a night at the fair. At the far end of the street is the original Japanese-era railway station, now retired. The new station is right beside it.

The Alishan area is home to the Tsou tribe. **YuYuPas** ④ (Alishan Zuozu Wenhua Buluo; daily 8.30am–9.30pm), a young native-run theme park dedicated to the preservation and promotion of the tribe's culture, is located on the slope below Leye village. It seems to hover above magnificent Rainbow Valley (Caihong Shangu), sometimes decorated with multiple rainbows. The village-style park is defined by two lines of large, thatched-roof buildings running down the slope, copies of traditional Tsou meeting halls, wood stilts replaced by sturdy steel girders,

TIP

Travelers arriving in Alishan will be met by professional 'sunrise hunters,' who organize tours for the next morning. It's best to use their services: they know the best places to see the sunrise given the mercurial weather conditions.

Take a train to the mountains.

open-air sides replaced by glass walls that allow in the panoramic mountain views. There are regular song-and-dance performances, a good museum that has English signage, crafts demonstrations, boutique areas with Alishan specialty produce such as coffee and merchandise created by Tsou artists and craftsmen, and a large, airy restaurant highlighting Tsou cuisine.

Ascent of Mt Jade

Alishan is the billeting post of mountaineering expeditions to **Mt Jade** (Yushan). At 3,950 meters (12,960ft) in altitude, Yushan is the highest peak in Asia east of the Himalayas, south of Russia's Kamchatka Peninsula, and north of Borneo's Mt Kinabalu. Even higher than Japan's majestic Mt Fuji, this peak was called New High Mountain during the 50 years of Japanese occupation. The Chinese restored its original name in 1945. Yushan is far more visited than the others, however, and physically fit individuals will find their endurance challenged by the overnight expedition to ascend its main summit.

Wildlife galore

Yushan actually has 11 peaks, of which the highest is Main Peak Climbing to the top is no afternoon stroll. The rock face is often crumbly, and rockfalls are not unknown It's also a long way up. But, even for those who do not attempt the summit, walks at lower altitudes in Yushan National Park are rewarding. Wildlife is abundant, with more than 150 bird species and 220 butterfly species recorded. There is also a strong likelihood that visitors will catch a glimpse of wild monkeys not to mention wild boar, mountain goats, and flying squirrels – the park is home to 34 different kinds of mammal.

At Tataka hamlet, on the Mt Jade Scenic Highway section of the New Central Cross-Island Highway, there is a visitor center (daily 9am–4.30pm closed 2nd and 4th Tue of month free) that presents multimedia exhibitions on the park. A number of trails emanate from the center, ranging from easy to challenging.

This is also the staging post for assaults on the mountain (permit are required; detail is given on the park's website). From here it is a 9km (5.5-mile) uphill trudge to the Paiyun Cottage (a hostel with camp site), where climbers spend the night before tackling the main summit of the mountain, leaving the hostel a around 3am in order to reach the summit in time for the sunrise.

The ascent from Paiyun follows the west face of the peak, and, for those who decide not to return the way they came, a treat is in store Down the east face of the mountain winds the **Batongguan Historic Trail** (Batongguan Gudao), which after around 6km (4 miles) joins up with another trail leading down to the hot-spring town of Dongpu a 2,600 meters (8,530ft). What better way could there be to finish up a climb of East Asia's highest peak than with a soak in a hot spring?

THE ALISHAN NSA TRAIL SYSTEM

Alishan National Scenic Area now has a fine trail system. Each is signposted, with clear English and trail-and-area maps with distances. Some of the best trails are along, or close to, Shengdao 18, the area's access road:

In Fenqihu the Cedar Trail, traversing tall stands of Taiwan fir outside the village's lower section, is defined by raised wooden walkways. The Fenqi Trail, defined by railway tie steps, is above the village. On the latter are ruins of the area's Japanese Shinto shrine, with tall fir planted by Chiang Kai-shek himself, pining for his mountainous China home.

The 800-meter/yd Eryanping Trail has wooden steps and platforms and some short, steep grades. It is set amid bamboo stands and tea fields, and offers grand views off to the plains.

The Miyang Stream Trail/Mihu Trail runs 2.3km (1.4 miles) along a rushing stream strewn with huge boulders. An old native trail, there are bamboo stands, pavilions, and a pretty suspension bridge. The highlight is a huge old tree lined with nails that once held steps in place. The Tsou climb such trees for wild jelly figs used in delicious *aiyu* jelly.

The shady, cool, easy-grade Dadongshan Trail is 10km (6 miles) long. Most just walk 50 minutes (one way) to the massive Tree-Stone Alliance – an ancient monster cypress with tremendous roots wrapped around a monster slope-hugging boulder larger than a three-story house.

Taiwan's top hikes

To most people, Taiwan means hot coastal cities and smoke-belching factories. But two-thirds of the island is covered with remote and beautiful peaks laced with good hiking trails.

Taiwan is home to the highest mountain in East Asia – Yushan (Mt Jade) – while well over 200 peaks soar above 3,000 meters (9,800ft). Protected by national parks, and home to rare Formosan black bears, landlocked salmon, and other wildlife, the mountains are among Taiwan's top attractions.

Trekking in Taiwan is not for the faint-hearted. The Central Mountain Range is steep and wild, and much of it is covered with thick forest. Summer thunderstorms rise unseen, and facilities are few and far between. But, for those willing to carry their own gear, the mountains are among the most beautiful in Asia. The trails, though steep, are generally well kept.

Easier outings

There are some easy walks to do in Taiwan. Yangmingshan National Park, for instance, is on Taipei's doorstep, and daytime hikes through its sulfur fumaroles and thick forests can end with a hot dinner and a cold drink in the suburb of Tianmu.

Taroko National Park (see page 279) is also full of trails. These lead to alpine lakes, Atayal tribal villages, peach and pear orchards, and hidden swimming holes. The trails wind across high suspension bridges, along sheer cliffs, up and down steep switchbacks, and sometimes through tunnels. Here, too, a hiker can finish the day by soaking in a hot spring, or relaxing in a five-star hotel or a comfortable hostel.

Challenging hikes

But the top hikes in Taiwan – Qilai Ridge and Yushan – require a strong back, some experience, and proper equipment, which includes a tent and stove, food and water, a sleeping bag, good boots, and warm clothes.

Yushan is one of the most popular hikes in the country. The trail starts near the top of the new section of the Central Cross-Island Highway, and winds steadily upward through magnificent forests of fir and cedar. The first day's trek is a long one – 1,000

meters (3,300ft) to Paiyun Cottage, a couple of hours below the summit. Most trekkers spend the night in or near the hostel, and leave before daylight to catch the sunrise from the main summit of Yushan. The view from the top is amazing, though you're likely to have lots of company.

To really get away from it all, try the Qilai Ridge trail, a lovely, treacherous meander straight down the rocky spine of Taiwan's rugged Central Mountain Range.

It takes four hours and a lot of legwork to hike to the top of Qilai Ridge from Hehuanshan on the Central Cross-Island Highway section to the north. The ridge trail then goes up and over a succession of rocky peaks, and is regarded as the most dangerous trek in Taiwan, but one that is unrivaled in beauty.

From Qilai Ridge, much of Taiwan is on display: to the east are Taroko Gorge and the broad blue Pacific, and to the west are the rolling green foothills and the city of Taichung. In the north is the famous rock spike of Dabajianshan, and far to the south, barely visible, is Yushan.

Hiking in Yushan National Park.

THE TAIWAN STRAIT ISLANDS

Taipei

If you ever need evidence of the friction that exists between Taiwan and China, visit the islands of the Taiwan Strait, which are also home to unspoilt fishing communities and fine beaches.

Main Attractions
Mashan Observation Station
Zhaishan Tunnel
Qinbi
Beihai Tunnel
Dongyin Island
Andong Tunnel
Penghu Aquarium
Tongliang Banyan Tree
Erkan Hamlet

Taiwan has administrative control of a number of surrounding islands. Little visited by Western travelers, some, like Kinmen and Matsu in the Taiwan Strait, are fascinating for their south Fujian-style fishing villages, their rugged beauty, and their place in the standoff with mainland China.

Both Matsu and Kinmen (formerly known as Quemoy) lie just kilometers off the coast of China's Fujian province. Heavily fortified, they were long considered by Taiwanese a hardship

posting for young men doing their compulsory military service. All that changed in 1992, when the islands were suddenly opened to tourism after nearly 50 years as an off-limits military secret.

Kinmen

Kinmen ❶, the southernmost of the islands, lies 280km (174 miles) from the coast of central Taiwan and just 2km (1.2 miles) off the coast of China's Fujian port city of Xiamen. It is actually an archipelago of 15 islands. Three, however, are controlled by China, and only two of the Taiwan-controlled islands – Kinmen main island and **Little Kinmen** (Xiao Kinmen) – are open to tourism. Kinmen's main town is **Jincheng**, little more than a sprawling village in the southwest corner of the main island. It has a large number of hotels – though accommodations are usually two-star – restaurants, and souvenir shops, making it a good base for island exploration by taxi, hired car/motorcycle, or bicycle (Kinmen is predominantly flat and has little traffic, making it perfect for meandering about on two wheels).

Military attractions

The most famous attractions on the island are **Guningtou Battle**

Alcohol-filled jars line the long corridor of Tunnel 88, a former military shelter now used to store locally produced wines and spirits.

Museum (Guningtou Zhanshiguan; daily 8.30am–5pm; free) and **Guningtou Battlefield** (Guningtou Zhanchang; daily; free) to the north of Jincheng. Propaganda rules the day, but the story is compelling all the same. Mainland Chinese troops – 12,000–17,000 of them, nobody is absolutely sure – sailed across from Fujian to Guningtou in fishing boats around 2am on October 25, 1949. By 8am the next day, the Chinese troops had dug in, and a Taiwanese counter-attack by the 14th, 18th, and 114th divisions was underway, as Taiwanese aircraft bombed artillery positions on the Chinese shore.

At 2pm on October 26, Chinese troops took the village of Beishan. Some of the buildings there still stand, riddled with bullet holes, weeds sprouting among the rubble inside. The village soon became the site of heavy fighting, and was recaptured in the night. The conflict resulted in some 15,000 dead, around 3,000 of them Kuomintang (Guomindang) troops (though the figures are impossible to verify), and around 6,000 Chinese prisoners of war.

Another military site is the **August 23rd Artillery Battle Museum** (Baersan Zhanshiguan; daily 8.30am–5pm; free), in the far east of the island. Established in 1988, the museum commemorates the 1958 artillery war between China and Kinmen. It started on August 23 with a sudden burst of artillery fire from Fujian, and within two hours the mainland artillery had rained more than 57,000 shells on the small island. The bombardment continued until October 6, by which time the Chinese had fired nearly 500,000 shells at Kinmen. Meanwhile, the Taiwanese military replied in kind, forcing – according to the

Chinese architecture on Kinmen.

A soldier on guard at Mashan Observation Station on Kinmen island.

FACT

An interesting feature of Kinmen, which is blasted by strong winds for much of the winter, are the so-called protective Wind Lions that stand at the edge of every village. They come in all shapes and sizes, looking like Tolkienesque trolls, some of them 'dressed' in red bibs.

The Matsu Islands boast dramatic and beautiful coastline.

Taiwanese view of things – the Chinese to call a cease-fire. The museum, which has a well-done sound-and-light show, black-and-white film taken during the event, and a collection of tanks, artillery emplacements and fighter aircraft in a grassy field, is a fascinating reminder of the simmering standoff between China and Taiwan.

North of here is another interesting military sight: **Mashan Observation Station** ❷ (Mashan Guancesuo; daily 8am–12pm, 1pm–5pm; free). Kinmen's closest point to China is still a military outpost, and visitors are required to relinquish their passport before entering. A winding tunnel, dank and narrow, leads to a pillbox with telescopes, from where it is possible to view the pale hills of China in the distance, and, on a good day, the outline of the city of Xiamen.

Easily the island's most fascinating military sight is an obligatory stop for tour buses. **Zhaishan Tunnel** ❸ (Zhaishan Kengdao; daily 8.30am–5pm; free), not far from Guningtou Zhanchang, is a hollowed-out small

mountain with seven barracks rooms that offers a glimpse of just how fortified Kinmen is – underground. Inside, two 360-meter (1,180ft) waterways open the sea, providing a safe haven for naval boats.

Quaint, Fujian-style fishing villages

After the military sights, Kinmen's most winning attraction is its old south Fujian-style fishing villages. For a look at one in immaculate condition, visit **Shanhou Folk Culture Village** (Shanhou Minsu Wenhuacun; daily 8am–5pm), a picturesque section of the larger Shanhou settlement that, despite the fact it has been turned into a tourist attraction, has little of the tackiness found in similar 'cultural villages' on the Taiwan mainland. The section dates from the turn of the 20th century, and many of the houses here are still lived in by their owners, who eke out a living selling souvenirs and local snacks to tourists. The houses, with their sweeping eaves and courtyards, are extremely photogenic.

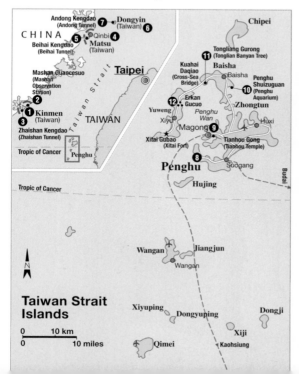

Matsu

Only a limited number of travelers, either Taiwanese or foreign, visit the remote and strikingly picturesque archipelago of **Matsu**, the northernmost of Taiwan's islands, which are solid granite. Numbers are slowly growing, however, with steady improvement in tourism facilities. Flights to the two main islands, Beigan and Nangan, are now regular, though often cancelled by fog. Amenities are limited, though steadily improving, and English barely spoken.

Matsu's culture and architecture are markedly different from the rest of Taiwan, which has its main roots in south Fujian. Matsu is a better showcase of traditional east Fujian culture than east Fujian itself, where the infamous attacks on all 'feudal olds' during Mao Zedong's reign created turmoil and destruction.

Stone houses

The most visually distinctive east Fujian cultural expression is the heritage stone houses. Four old villages are now protected, and stone houses are ubiquitous elsewhere. Beigan's Qinbi and Nangan's Niujiao are the most popular stone-house villages. Snuggled up between beach and mountain, **Qinbi** ❹ reminds you of old tiered, hill-clinging European villages by the Mediterranean. There are now attractive homestays and cafés here.

Tourist-friendly military sites

The **Beihai Tunnel** ❺ (Beihai Kengdao; daily 8am–5.30pm; accessible when tides are favorable, otherwise accessible by boat), on Nangan Island, is an extraordinary tunnel complex, a hidden port hewn from solid granite, hacked out by conscripts in the 1960s armed with not much more than picks and tremendous willpower. Many forfeited their lives in the effort, notably because of faulty use of explosives. Gouged out of a mountainside, it fit 120 smaller-sized vessels.

Dongyin Island ❻ (Dongyin Dao), at the north end of the archipelago, is Matsu's most visually dramatic, a place of sheer granite cliffs and stunning seascapes. The impressive **Andong Tunnel** ❼ (Andong Kengdao; daily 8am–5.30pm; free) shoots right through a small mountain from high on the inland side, exiting far down below at sea level. It's steep, built at a 30-degree angle. Inside are now-unused barracks, bathrooms, a kitchen, a meeting hall, even a pigsty. Matsu is known for birdwatching, and this is a prime site. On the right of the entrance is protected habitat for the Black-tailed Gull and Black-naped Tern. Inside, side tunnels lead to openings on sheer cliff sides, formerly used for gun emplacements. Black-tailed Gulls nest in number on these cliffs in summer, crashing surf far below. The tunnel's bottom opens out onto a large platform right above the sea, with tern nests on the rocky cliffs all about, so close that binoculars are unnecessary.

MATSU'S ARCHITECTURE

The granite blocks used in the walls of Matsu's old east Fujian-style stone residences have rough, curved surfaces; those used in traditional south Fujian architecture are flat. The red-tiled roofs are covered with large rocks for protection from the booming winter winds that come howling in along the China coast, holding the tiles down. The houses are said to 'breathe,' for no mortar is used to fasten the tiles, facilitating ventilation. This also enables easy roof repair. There are no overhanging eaves, avoiding upward wind pressure on roofs.

The granite blocks come in two shades, yellow and blue. The yellow is from Matsu, blue from the China mainland. As a rough rule, blue meant the family was more prosperous. Most stone homes are two-storied, the second floor providing views, allowing breeze access, and bringing relief from damp at ground level. Interior walls and beams are of wood. Windows tend to be small and higher up, for defense against attack; in imperial times pirates were a constant menace. Bright-blue painted strips high up on end walls are called 'fire-sealing walls.' The blue symbolizes water, dousing fires. Some residences are also topped with exaggerated vertical eaves that help block sparks from nearby actual fires. Many local temples have distinctive bright-orange walls. This is a fire-sealing wall variation. The color symbolizes flames, and since the temple is already on fire, there is no need for a real fire to visit.

TIP

The Penghu Youth Activity Center lays out tables on its patio overlooking the sea and serves drinks – the perfect place to watch the sun sink over the horizon. Liquid Sports now also has a popular bay-view café.

Pescadores Islands

One of Taiwan's best-kept secrets, the **Pescadores Islands**  (Penghu) are far enough off the beaten trail that you'll see few other Western faces while you are there. During the winter, ferocious winds scour the archipelago's 64 islands, but, with the onset of summer, the islands become a subtropical island getaway, with pristine beaches, tiny, picturesque fishing villages, and superb seafood.

Penghu has a long history. Nearly every military force that has ever attacked Taiwan has used it as a springboard, including the Dutch, Koxinga (Guoxingye), the Manchu Qing, and the Japanese, who took control of the archipelago as part of their annexation of mainland Taiwan.

Over the years, treacherous coastal shoals surrounding the Pescadores Islands have claimed countless ships. These shipwrecks help to account for the nearly 150 temples and assorted monuments dotting the otherwise barren islands, made up of lava and exposed coral. Half the archipelago's population of around 110,000 live in Magong, the Pescadores county seat, on the main island of Penghu. Fishing is the primary source of income; the only crops that grow here are peanuts, sweet potatoes, and sorghum, used for making potent Kaoliang (Gaoliang) liquor.

Magong

Magong, which is close to the islands' main airport, makes a convenient base for explorations farther afield. Hotels and restaurants are plentiful, and the small town even has a surprisingly active nightlife. The town also has a smattering of sights to fill a leisurely afternoon. In the south are the remains of the Qing dynasty **City Walls** (Magong Cheng), which are in surprisingly good shape. Close by, on Chenyi Street, is the **Tianhou Temple** ❾ (Tianhou Gong; daily 7am–5.30pm). Taiwan's oldest temple. Built in 1592, it is dedicated to Mazu. Its interior stone carvings are more impressive than its unassuming exterior lets on. Close by the small temple (just follow the crowds), on Zhongyang Street, are a pair of ancient wells. The one farthest up the street, the **Four-Eyed Well** (Siyan Jing), so named because it has four openings, is the oldest on the island, and Taiwanese tourists line up here for photo shoots.

On the beachfront western part of town, the modern white building is the **Penghu Youth Activity Center** (Penghu Qingnian Huodong Zhongxin). Brochures about the island's attractions are available at the front desk, help is given with tour packages, and tastefully appointed rooms are available for those who book ahead (http://penghu.cyh.org.tw). Beneath the center, on the waterfront, is the small **Guanyin Temple** (Guanyin Ting; daily), from which haunting chants can be heard at dusk. There is good windsurfing in the bay here; look for the Liquid

A traditional Matsu Fujian house.

Sports (www.liquidsportpenghu.com) shop, where English is spoken.

Other islands

From Magong, the best way to explore the main island of Penghu, nearby **White Sand** (Baisha) Island, and **West Island** (Xiyu; also known as Yuweng Dao – Old Fisherman Island), which are attached to each other by bridges, is to hire a motorcycle or rent a taxi and follow the coastline. The islands are blessed with some stunning and usually deserted beaches, which are often fronted by traditional fishing villages where little seems to have changed since the 19th century.

The main attractions on Baisha are the **Penghu Aquarium** ❿ (Penghu Shuizuguan; daily 9am–5pm) and the **Tongliang Banyan Tree** ⓫ (Tongli-ang Gurong). The first-rate aquarium, which unfortunately has no English signage, tells the story of the islands with such intriguing displays as mock-ups of local boats (which sway and pitch), the famed local stone-weir fish traps, and Qing dynasty architecture. The magnificent banyan tree,

over 300 years old, has created a great floating forest of branches and vines above a temple courtyard. There are over 100 trunks.

Xiyu is reached by the 5.5km (3.5-mile) **Cross-Sea Bridge** (Kuahai Daqiao). Close to the southernmost extent of the island is **Western Fort** (Xitai Gubao; 24 hours). Built in 1887, all that remains are its sturdy walls, which provide a fine view of the coastline. Tourist-friendly **Erkan Hamlet** ⓬ (Erkan Gucuo; daily 8am–5pm) is a preserved living-museum village of 50 houses.

If Penghu's main island is not quite remote enough, regular flights and tour boats depart from Magong to the tiny **Isle of Seven Beauties** (Qimei Yu). According to local lore, seven virtuous Ming dynasty beauties were said to have drowned themselves in a well on this island to protect their chastity from marauding pirates. **Wangan Island** (Wangan Dao) is approached by boat. It is famous for its turtles, but is also home to some quaint fishing villages, and features an impressive, craggy coastline.

Riding along a quiet road on Penghu.

TAINAN

The island's fourth-largest city is clean and cultured, combining a modern social scene with a deep respect for tradition in a maze of narrow lanes and an abundance of historic sites.

Taiwan's southwest is recognized – even in the self-confident north – as the cradle of the island's culture and traditions. **Tainan ❶** is to Taiwan what Kyoto is to Japan, and Kyongju to Korea. The city was capital of the island from 1683 to 1885, and its history, and thus its modern flavor, is inextricably linked with the exploits of Koxinga.

Known in Taiwan by his given name, Zheng Cheng-gong, Koxinga (Guoxingye; Lord of the Imperial Surname) was a Ming loyalist who was at odds with the new Qing court. He fled to Taiwan, landing near Tainan in 1661 with 25,000 troops in 400 war junks. He besieged the Dutch fort at today's Anping, eventually driving the *hongmao fan* (redhaired barbarians) from the island. The Ming stronghold that he established lasted through two more generations of Zheng leadership, until his grandson finally capitulated to the Qing court in 1683.

Koxinga brought more than troops to Taiwan. He carried a camphorwood icon of Mazu, said to be the one that sits in the shrine to this goddess at Luermen (Deer Ear Gate), where Koxinga first landed. Moreover, his entourage included about 1,000 writers, artists, musicians, craftsmen, and master chefs, whose function was to launch a Chinese

cultural renaissance in Taiwan. (A similar group of scholars and artisans followed Chiang Kai-shek (Jiang Jie-shi) to Taiwan in 1949.)

Today, Tainan remains highly conscious of its rich cultural legacy. Long a sleepy town of temples, old ruins, and pleasant memories, Tainan is hard at work restoring elements of its former glory. Taiwan's fourth-largest city, with almost 1,200,000 people, it has become a tourist attraction with a strong focus on history. Light industry, agriculture, fishing,

Main Attractions

Confucius Temple
City God Temple
Museum of Taiwan
    Literature
Chikan Tower
God of War Temple
Great Queen of Heaven
    Temple
Anping Fort
Anping Treehouse
Xiaobei Night Market

Confucius Temple.

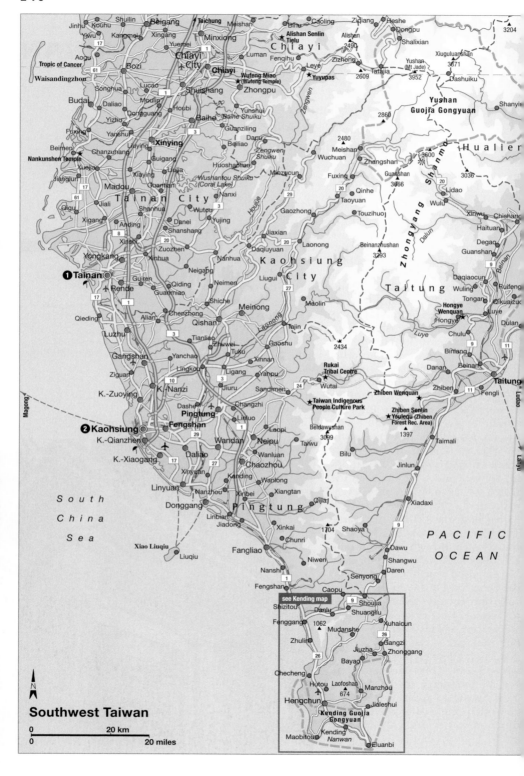

Southwest Taiwan

0   20 km
0   20 miles

nd tourism are all encouraged in the area, and a sci-tech park has been launched, but large industrial plants and their accompanying pollution are kept at arm's length. The goal is to maintain a clean and cultured city, a showcase for visitors.

Traditional and civilized

While Tainan is one of Taiwan's most socially progressive cities, it is also decidedly its most traditional. A maze of narrow lanes, courtyards, and garden walls are tucked around hundreds of shrines and temples. Native *bai-bai* religious worship festivals are observed far more frequently and extravagantly than in the north, and most residents prefer to speak the native Taiwanese dialect instead of Mandarin.

As the most 'civilized' city in Taiwan, Tainan naturally excels in that most civilized of all Chinese pursuits - food. After dinner, many Tainanese retire to sip coffee at the cozy, chic cafés found all over the city, or relish a cup of tea in one of Tainan's unique teahouses. Overall, the city is far more sedate at night than Taipei, Taichung, or Kaohsiung.

Tainan is a pleasant city to explore by foot, day or night. Most of its chief points of interest are concentrated in the old downtown section, and temples are the city's hallmark. There are 220 major temples and countless minor shrines scattered throughout the city core and its surrounding rural areas.

Shrine to a national hero

It is perhaps appropriate to begin at **Koxinga Shrine Ⓐ** (Yanping Zhengwangsi; daily 8.30am–5.30pm). Set in a garden compound of tropical trees and breezy pavilions on Kaishan Road, the shrine was built in 1875 by imperial edict from the Qing court in Beijing – the former Ming resistance leader had been forgiven. Today he is deified as a national hero on both sides of the Taiwan Strait. The building housing the shrine went up in 1662.

A statue of Koxinga stands in the central shrine hall, flanked by those of his two most trusted generals.

TIP

Try these Tainan specialty dishes: *duxiaoyue danzi mian* (passing-the-lean-months noodles); *guancai ban* (coffin cakes); *dingbiancuo* (pot-side pancake soup); or *shuijing jiao* (crystal pork dumplings). Intrigued?

A night market stroll.

In the colonnades are enshrined the 114 loyal officers who followed him to Taiwan. Major festivities for this father of modern Taiwan are held three times a year – on February 12 (the Dutch surrender to Koxinga), April 29 (Memorial Day), and August 27 (Koxinga's birthday). In the shrine's Tainan Folk Culture Hall are displays on the area's archeological finds, geography, Koxinga and Tainan's history, and on daily life in the city, the last including old street signs, bedding, land deeds, and money bills.

Dragons – frequently found on temple roofs – rank top in the Chinese almanac of creatures and are a symbol of natural male vigor.

At Chikan Tower.

Three blocks from the shrine, on Nanmen Road, is Tainan's **Confucius Temple B** (Kong Miao; daily 8.30am–5.30pm; free), the oldest

temple dedicated to the sage in Taiwan. Also serving as the first – and long the premier – educational institution in Taiwan, it was built in 1665 by Zheng Jing, Koxinga's son, as a center for the Chinese cultural renaissance in Taiwan. Restored 16 times since it was built, it still stands out as Taiwan's foremost shrine to the great teacher, reflecting a classical architectural style otherwise seldom seen on the island.

The temple is set in a garden compound, divided by arched gates and corniced walls into a series of courtyards, each with its own halls. Originally, these courtyards served as schools for the branches of classical Chinese studies. Confucius is enshrined in the central Dachengtian (Hall of Great Success), with a simple gilded stele of stone, adorned with flowers and incense. Plaques bearing honorific inscriptions to Confucius from various Qing-dynasty emperors also hang here. Ancient costumes, books, and musical instruments – used in formal ceremonies marking Confucius birthday each year – are displayed.

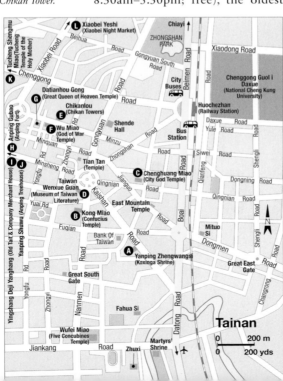

The city god

Tainan's residents believe their behavior is reported to the emperors of heaven and hell by Chenghuang, the city deity (in imperial times each prefecture had its own separate city god, akin to a government official). His small, old, and very original temple, the **City God Temple** Ⓒ (Chenghuang Miao; daily 7am–9pm; free), is located on Qingnian Road, between Jianguo and Boai roads. The main shrine is a fascinating jumble of smoke-stained icons, antique hardwood fixtures, and intricately hewn beams. Within is a solemn bearded statue of the deity, with life-size statues of a warrior and scholar standing guard. In the side-wall niches are two dozen smaller icons of smooth camphor-wood, clothed in silk brocade.

The open-beam work on the ceiling is noteworthy. Unlike other ceilings, this is varnished rather than painted, its surface etched with fine filigree. Relics and ritual objects hang everywhere, notably two giant abaci with hardwood beads the size of melons, used to tally the merits and faults of each citizen for Chenghuang's 'annual reports.' By the front door a sign with a gold inscription reads *Erlaile* (So you have finally come), for this is also the place where your spirit has its final judgment day.

Taiwan's literary history

The **Museum of Taiwan Literature** Ⓓ (Taiwan Wenxue Guan; www.nmtl.gov.tw; Tue–Sun 9am–6pm, Fri, Sat until 9pm; free) is housed in an impressive Second Empire-style structure built in 1916 by the Japanese, and which last served as Tainan's city hall. This is Taiwan's only museum focused on Taiwan literature. The museum tells the story of Taiwan's history through the words of writers and commoners, including the indigenous peoples. There is also an intriguing exhibit on the building itself, including its first role as seat of Japan-controlled Tainan prefecture, World War II damage, plus modern-day renovations, with exposed sections. There is English signage and a free 1.5-hour audio tour.

City God Temple.

Chikan Tower

The two Chinese-style pavilions of the **Chikan Tower** (Chikanlou; daily 8.30am–9pm) were built during the Qing Dynasty, on the site of Fort Provintia, an old Dutch fort. Located on Minzu Road, Section 2, little remains today of the original fortification, once known to local Taiwanese as Hongmaolou (Tower of the Red-haired Barbarians). It was built in 1653 as a Dutch stronghold, then taken over as Koxinga's initial administrative headquarters in 1661.

The pavilions house visual displays of Koxinga sailing across the Taiwan Strait and ousting the Dutch. Bronze statues in the adjoining park depict the surrender. Nine memorial steles in the park, borne by stone turtles, were inscribed by imperial edict in 1786 and presented to a Chinese magistrate in Taiwan for successfully suppressing an uprising.

An indispensable stop on any Tainan temple tour is the **God of War Temple** (Wu Miao; daily 5am–9pm), one of Taiwan's oldest and most authentic Daoist temples.

Located almost directly across Minzu from the tower, a highly detailed facade of stone, carved in deep relief, graces the entrance to the central hall of this gaudy complex. Inside, an elevated shrine is dedicated to the red-faced warrior-god Guangong. It is an exquisite shrine with finely painted door gods and attendant dragons, side panels of sculpted stone depicting animals and Daoist immortals, a large center pagoda for burning offerings, and a circular ceiling featuring hundreds of carved, gilded gods. Wu Miao is one of the most ritually active temples on the island. Exorcisms and other rites are frequently held. On some days you can follow the sound of drums, gongs, cymbals, and loud incantations to the rear courtyard to find trance mediums trying to contact the spirits of the deceased friends and relatives of anxious supplicants.

Temple of the patron saint

Great Queen of Heaven Temple (Datianhou Gong; daily 6am–8pm

Tainanese residents wear protective helmets and jackets as they light firecrackers to ward off bad fortune.

free), Tainan's downtown Mazu shrine on Yongfu Street, is just past Wu Miao down Ererqi Xiang (Lane 227). Fortunetellers line the narrow artery. Opened in 1683 to enshrine Taiwan's patron saint, this temple claims to be the oldest Mazu shrine on Taiwan proper, a boast disputed by a Lugang temple. Tall, well-wrought, smoke-stained statues of Mazu and her two bodyguards grace the shrine hall. Worshiped by unmarried men and women, Yuexia Laoren (Old Man Under the Moon) is a secondary deity; it is believed a prayer to this god will help to find a mate.

Vestiges of the Western presence

At **Anping Fort** ❶ (Anping Gubao; daily 8.30am–5.30pm), on Guosheng Road, a 10-minute taxi ride from the railway station, are more reminders of Tainan's military past. Fort Zeelandia was built by the Dutch in 1624, then heavily reinforced between 1627 and 1634. Bricks were held in place with a mixture of sugarcane syrup, glutinous rice, and crushed

oyster shells; a large section of one wall, covered with banyan roots, is still intact. After Koxinga took possession of Fort Provintia he laid siege to this bastion, with the Dutch surrendering only after nine months. He renamed the site Anping, which means 'peace.' During the Opium Wars of the 1840s and 1850s the Chinese installed cannons, and during the Japanese era a red-brick platform was constructed with a Western-style residence atop for Japanese customs officials. In the 1970s an observation tower was erected beside (silting has moved the coastline several kilometers to the west since the early 1800s). There are two small museums, with paintings, maps, and relics of Tainan's colonial past. The one by the entrance has good English. There is also good English on the signage around the grounds.

On nearby Gubao Street is the **Old Tait & Company Merchant House** ❶ (Yingshang Deji Yanghang; daily 8.30am–5.30pm), opened by a British trading firm after the Second Opium War forced Tainan and

YANSHUI 'BEEHIVE ROCKETS'

The Yanshui Beehive Rockets Festival certainly ranks as one of the island's, and the world's, more unusual celebrations. The madness takes place each year in the Tainan City rural district of Yanshui, to the north of the city's center, on the 15th day of the lunar New Year – the Lantern Festival. Hundreds of thousands of people converge on the old town's streets. Large platforms laced with honeycombs stuffed with thousands of rockets – the beehive rockets – are fired, all hell breaks loose, and the town is taken over by a Dantesque fervor.

Why? Early in the 1800s plague hit Yanshui. Townsfolk called on Guangong, the God of War, to drive off the demons causing the trouble. People set off fireworks to help him wage battle, and when the plague disappeared they decided to continue the practice.

The fireworks begin at dusk and continue until 4am. Smart folk wear motorcycle helmets and thick gloves (sold on the street), along with layers of old clothing (there are sparks and minor injuries galore).

It's impossible to book accommodations in the immediate area at this time of the year, so take the train to the nearest stop at Xinying (7km/4 miles away), switch to a taxi or local bus to Yanshui, rock(et) the night away, and head home next morning a bona fide 'Taiwan hand.'

TIP

If not self-driving, the easiest way to get around Tainan is by scooter. There are rental outlets right behind Tainan Railway Station (Tainan Rear Station). An international license and passport must be presented.

other Chinese ports open in 1858. The firm eventually abandoned the attractive colonial-style arcaded structure, and Taiwan, after the Japanese took over the highly profitable opium and camphor trades. The structure was later used by a salt company, and is today a museum. In behind is **Anping Treehouse Ⓙ** (Anping Shuwu), which served as a Tait & Company warehouse, abandoned after World War II. It has been completely overrun by banyan trees, creating a surrealistic maze which visitors can now safely enter.

The region's largest temple

In the city's rural area north of Anping district is what Tainan bills as the largest temple structure in this part of Asia: **Tucheng Temple of the Holy Mother ⓚ** (Tucheng Shengmu Miao; daily 5.30am–9.30pm; free). The entry is formed by an immense two-story facade braced by a pair of large pagodas. The sculpted-dragon columns that support the portico were hewn from solid stone

by Taiwan's finest temple artisans. An equally magnificent shrine hall stands behind the first, with six major shrines in the walls. The small black wooden icons are paraded about town on elaborate palanquins during festivals. Follow Chenggong Road west from the railway station, then bear right onto Anming Road, which becomes Provincial Highway No. 17 (Shengdao 17). The temple is on the left, in the urban area's outskirts.

The famous **Xiaobei Night Market ⓛ** (Xiaobei Yeshi; Tue, Fri approximately 4pm–1am; free), located some 10 minutes northwest of Downtown by taxi on Ximen Road, Section 3, features numerous stalls offering clothing and over 200 tiny, open-air eateries. Take the opportunity to crowd in together with half the city's populace on a warm, sultry Tainan night to quaff draft beer and feast on the city's many renowned *xiaochi* (snack-food) selections. There is always at least one large night market open in Tainan each night.

The classic lines of Tainan's Tucheng Temple of the Holy Mother.

Plague God Boats

The Burning of the Plague God Boats is a fiery spectacle that happens just once every three years, in rural towns located through Taiwan.

Occurring in the Chinese zodiac years of the Ox, Dragon, Goat, and Dog, The Burning of the Plague Boats – Shao Wangchuan – rewards the traveler with vivid and lifelong memories. The largest celebration takes place in Donggang, one of Taiwan's three biggest fishing ports, a half-hour drive south of Kaohsiung. It is centered on Donglong Gong (Donglong Temple), dedicated to the plague gods – called Wangye (kings) in Chinese – who have been worshiped for as long as 2,000 years as protectors against pestilence and disease. The weeklong festival leading up to the burning of the boats, filled with the parading of Wangye images, takes place in the ninth lunar month (October or November).

Colorful rituals

A nearly full-size mock-up of a junk is constructed for the festival, outfitted with masts and sails. Life-size icons of the Wangye are placed aboard the extravagantly decorated craft, which is then heaped high with sacrificial offerings that range from tasty foods to practical things such as televisions and fancy cars. In Chinese culture it is believed the world beyond is much like our own, and folk there need practical necessities as well; when burned, the essence of the offerings is transported and can then be used on the other side – in this case, by the helpful gods.

Prior to being burned, the boat, with the gods aboard, is paraded around town to drive out pestilence. On the final day it is brought from the temple to the shoreline, surrounded by a mountain of spirit money, and, after elaborate ceremonies conducted by the Daoist temple's six high priests, is set alight with firecracker strings at 3 or 4 o'clock in the morning. The ship's varnish cracks, the cloth of the sails snaps, and the temple complex is lit up as bright as day by the flames. *Jitong*, or spirit mediums, flagellate themselves and go into trances, indicating that the plague gods are indeed present. Smoke and ash drift skyward, to the other world, and revelers slowly drift home, feeling protected. Those who have not worshiped at the boat at least once that day, it is believed, are sure to suffer illness.

Plague god origins

Taiwan's southwestern coast is home to almost all of the island's 700-plus plague god temples. In the old days, when people in disease- and pestilence-racked southern China set Wangye boats adrift, the currents would often bring them, if they did not sink, to the Penghu Islands or to southwestern Taiwan. Locals, filled with both fear and reverence, would build temples to the gods. This being an expensive game, and the people being exceedingly practical as well as religious, the practice arose of burning the boats on shore rather than setting them off at sea to deliver their cargo of misery elsewhere.

Several legends relate the origins of the plague gods. In each, the gods begin life as scholars. In one, several scholars throw themselves down a well poisoned by plague demons in order to save a town; in others they are wrongfully killed by an emperor, who deifies them after their ghosts begin wreaking vengeful havoc.

Burning a boat.

KAOHSIUNG

The city of Kaohsiung's urban core and rural hinterland offer intrigue, with remarkable temples, interesting colonial relics, and quality outdoor leisure pursuits.

The Shuen-sanzi-ten Temple marks the start of the bridge to Dragon Pagoda on Lotus Lake.

Kaohsiung ❷ is Taiwan's industrial showcase and a city of superlatives. It is Taiwan's largest international seaport, its major industrial center, and the only city on the island besides Taipei with a true international airport. Kaohsiung is also Taiwan's largest container port and one of the largest in the world, with an extremely large dry dock for ship repairs and maintenance. It has a total population of over 2.5 million inhabitants.

The city is the southern terminus of the Zhongshan Gaosu Gonglu (Sun Yat-sen Freeway), the first north-south artery, about a six-hour drive from Taipei. It can be reached from Taipei by high-speed rail, regular train, or express bus. Visitors from abroad can also fly direct to Kaohsiung from Hong Kong and a number of other regional destinations. Long an overnight stop on the way to see the other attractions of southwest Taiwan, the urban core has become a destination in itself.

A city of humble origins, Kaohsiung experienced meteoric economic growth during Taiwan's economic miracle, but the concentration of heavy industry caused considerable pollution. The local government is now concentrating on attracting high-technology and other service industries to its central districts, and moving smokestack factories out to suburban industrial zones. Many factories have also been closed down, with operations moved to lower-cost China. The result is a much-improved living environment. Fishing remains a major enterprise, with thousands of vessels registered in urban-core and outlying ports. The city is Taiwan's center for deep-sea fishing, with local vessels plying waters as far as South Africa.

The southwest is Taiwan's 'Big Sky' country, a fertile land of big skies and open spaces, and within sight of Kaohsiung's skyscrapers the visitor enters a slower-paced realm of big

vistas, small settlements, old community temples, and great swathes of sugarcane, fruit trees, and betel-nut trees, which serve as evidence of a traditional culture that revels in its agricultural roots as it meshes, selectively, with the 21st century.

Temple touring

The city center is dominated by modern tower blocks, including the magnificent rocket-shaped 85 Sky Tower, once the tallest building in Taiwan, whose 85 stories house a major international hotel in the upper half (viewing deck on 75F; www.85observatory. com; 10am–10pm). **Longevity Mountain ❹** (Shoushan) overlooks Kaohsiung harbor and the oldest section of the city. Early-morning photo shoots are best, before the heat of the day creates a haze.

On top of Shoushan, which serves as a park and a nature reserve with hiking trails, is the Martyrs' Shrine (Zhonglie Zi; Tue–Sun 8am–5pm; free), and next to it a series of other temples, pavilions, historical monuments, and terraces. Among these is **Yuanheng Temple ❺** (Yuanhengsi; daily 5am–9pm), found on the eastern slopes of Shoushan. This grand and solemn temple, originally built in 1679, was rebuilt in 1926. It is an important religious center, and is dedicated to the Goddess of Mercy. Besides providing insight into modern Chinese Buddhism, a visit to Yuanhengsi reveals a dazzling array of golden Buddha statues in the imposing main hall.

Temple addicts may also want to include two other complexes on their rounds in Kaohsiung. The **Three Phoenix Palace ❻** (Sanfeng Gong; daily 5am–10pm; free), on Hebei Road, is the largest temple in Taiwan devoted to the demon suppressor, Nacha San Taizi. Stone lions stand sentry at the foot of the steps, which lead up to an elaborately carved stone facade. The central hall contains three major icons, exquisite altar tables,

and 10 large image-cones that glow warmly, bearing the names of the temple's financial patrons.

At the corner of Taren and Yancheng roads is the **Temple of the Three Mountain Kings ❼** (Sanshan Guowang Miao; daily 5.30am–9pm; free). This 300-year-old Buddhist temple is dedicated to three brothers, private tutors to a man who saved the life of a Chinese emperor. When the emperor rewarded the man, he gave credit to his three teachers, consequently making each brother 'King of the Mountain' in three mountainous regions of Fujian province. The exquisite shrine hall houses a dozen deities in a complex panoply of ornamentation.

Qijin island

There are two beaches within Kaohsiung city limits. One, in **Qijin Beach** (**Qijin Haishui Yuchang**) in Qijin Seaside Park (Qijin Haian Gongyuan), is a black-sand beach that is insulated not only from the bustle of downtown Kaohsiung, but also from the murky waters of the harbor, being located on the seaward side of a long

TIP

Avoid traveling on the two national freeways on long weekends and holidays. They become heavily backed up, with impatient drivers placing others in peril. Normal travel times can triple. The extra expense of a short high-speed train ride is worth it (book ahead).

The looming 85 Sky Tower.

TIP

Meal prices on
Kaohsiung's Qijin island
are often not listed, or
are unclear. There will
be little or no English, so
bring a local friend if
possible, and be sure to
confirm the price of
each individual dish
before it is served.

island that forms a breakwater for the harbor. This is **Qijin** Ⓔ island, one of the city's oldest and most popular tourist areas, which the government has done much to spruce up. A four-minute ferry ride from the mainland's Gushan Ferry Pier takes visitors to the north end. The island can also be reached by car, via the harbor tunnel, at the south end.

The island is 11km (7 miles) long, but only 200 meters (660ft) wide. There are a number of attractions besides the seaside park. At the foot of the ferry landing lies raucous **Qijin Seafood Street** (Qijin Haiyangjie), which provides a quick glimpse (and taste and smell) of Taiwan's seagoing past and present. As Taiwan's number-one fishing port, Kaohsiung naturally

offers excellent fresh seafood. Dozens of seafood restaurants stand cheek-by-jowl on this short road. Whether kept on ice or alive in tanks waiting for customers to make their choice, the sheer variety of seafood is unbelievable.

Nearby the seafood area is **Empress of Heaven Temple** Ⓕ (Tianhou Gong; daily 5am–10pm; free), one of the oldest architectural structures in the city. Erected in 1691 and dedicated to the protector of mariners and fishermen, this is a lively temple that is in constant use by Qijin islanders, who are often obliged to risk the sea's moods. Up the small mount behind the temple is **Qihou Lighthouse** Ⓖ (Qihou Dengta; Tue–Sun 9am–4pm, Oct–Mar until 5pm; free), a pristine 11-meter (36ft) -high structure that

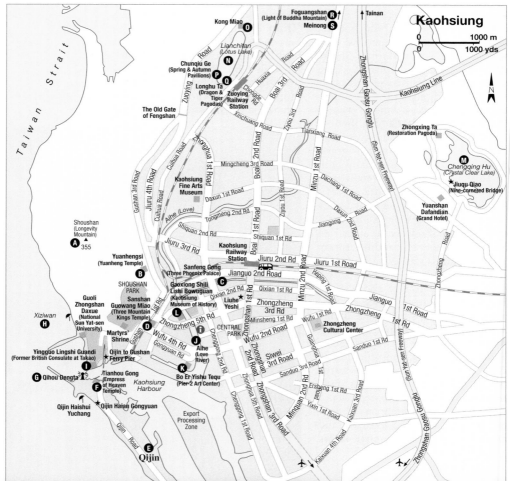

guards the harbor's exceedingly narrow north-end mouth. Constructed in 1883, riveting views of the tightly packed harbor can be enjoyed as ships squeeze by below. Another experience to be savored on the island is a ride in a traditional *sanlunche*. These rickety three-wheeled carts, which wait by the ferry, were the main form of wheeled transportation in Taiwan until the 1960s, and are now rarely seen elsewhere.

Xizi Bay area

Back on the mainland, beyond Shoushan near the northern entrance to the harbor lies **Xizi Bay** ⓗ (Xiziwan; daily 10am–6pm), whose main attractions are a long breakwater and a soft-sand beach. The water is not as clean as Qijin's, but it is still a pleasant enough place for seaside strolls. It is located near **National Sun Yat-sen University** (Guoli Zhongshan Daxue), with its modern buildings: sports grounds and other facilities have been developed on reclaimed land. From the Gushan Ferry Pier area, pedestrians can reach the bay and university grounds by the short shore-side road or through a 230-meter (755ft) -long foot tunnel, a cool but windy retreat during hot summer days.

On the steep hill overlooking the harbor entrance stands the **Former British Consulate at Takao** ⓘ (Dagou Yingguo Lingshi Guandi; daily 9am–9pm, closed on the third Monday of every month), the oldest complete example of colonial architecture extant in Taiwan. After the Treaty of Tianjin (1858), the first British vice-consul to Taiwan arrived here in 1861. Four years later, the official British consulate was built on the 30-meter (100ft) high hill guarding the small entrance to the harbor. Today, the British colonial-style, red-brick building houses a café (daily 11am–midnight), with a museum gallery (daily 9am–9pm; free) featuring photographs, relics, maps, and models, almost all labeled in English,

that give a fascinating insight into the city, past and present. The view from above, looking out over the harbor to the lighthouse on Qijin, is worth mentioning. The building has been fully restored, after having become an uninhabitable ruin by the 1980s after suffering a number of Taiwan's infamous devastating typhoons. Nothing remains of the fortifications that once guarded the harbor.

Harbor and Love River area

After Taipei, Kaohsiung has Taiwan's most active nightlife. The busy but pleasant **Liuhe Night Market** (Liuhe Yeshi; daily 6pm–2am; free) on Liuhe 2nd Road, some blocks south of the railway station, offers plenty of food stalls and many bargains. Here you can savor a few of the numerous local culinary specialties famous around the island.

Love River ⓙ (Aihe), which runs east from the harbor through the downtown core, has emerged as one of Kaohsiung's most popular nighttime gathering spots. The water has been cleaned and the area

Drummers perform at the 2013 Kaohsiung Lantern Festival.

A Kaohsiung Harbor Ferry to Chijin.

Liuhe Night Market.

landscaped, with attractive benches, streetlights, and scenic night lighting added. Boardwalks run along both sides, filling up with walkers, joggers, and sightseers at night, and there are cafés with outdoor seating, plus live music and busker-type fun on weekends. The 30-minute Love Boat Cruise (daily 3pm–10pm; departures every 15 minutes; narration in Chinese only) is very popular.

The young, expansive, and still growing **Pier-2 Art Center**  (Bo Er Yishu Tequ; http://pier-2.khcc.gov.tw; info center and exhibition/boutique warehouses Mon–Thu 10am–6pm, Fri–Sun 10am–8pm) is at the heart of a cultural-creative bloom underway in the city. The special zone has become one of Kaohsiung's most popular cultural attractions. The numerous old, renovated Kaohsiung Harbor warehouses here, long abandoned, were formerly used to store such treasures as fishmeal and granulated sugar. Today they are dedicated to cultural-arts treasures, including domestic and international exhibitions, festivals, live indoor and outdoor musicals, theatrical, and busker performances, and large-scale outdoor installation artworks, and graffiti-style murals.

In one warehouse is the **Kaohsiung Museum of Labor** (Gaoxiong Shi Laogong Bowuguan; Tue–Sun 10.30am–7pm; free); half of another – roof torn down to allow for under-the-sky entertainment – is now the Kaohsiung base for The Wall, a keystone in Taiwan's indie-music scene. In others are exhibition spaces and arts and crafts boutiques showcasing independent Taiwan design talent. A large tiffany and dark wood Western family-style restaurant, Pasadena's, fills one more warehouse.

Just to the north of Pier-2 is the **Takao Railway Museum** (Dagou Tiedao Gushi Guan; Tue–Sun 10am–6pm; free). This was Kaohsiung's first railway station, and long a key hub in south Taiwan's land-sea transportation. The station, Japanese in style with a Chinese hip-style roof, was targeted and severely damaged by Allied bombing in WW II. Later rebuilt, it was finally retired and became a

museum in 2010. There are exhibit rooms, a railway-document archive, and a platform and track area.

Kaohsiung's popular harbor-area bikeway rolls right by the art center and museum, the section here running where the trains that once served these facilities trundled along. There are a number of bike-rental facilities close by. The building housing the **Kaohsiung Museum of History** ⬤ (Gaoxiong Shili Lishi Bowuguan; www.khm.gov.tw; Tue–Fri 9am–5pm, Sat–Sun until 9pm) was built in 1939, during the Japanese colonial era, to serve as Kaohsiung's second City Hall. Bright and imposing, it is in the Imperial Crown Style. The facility was adapted for use as a museum after the city government relocated in the 1990s. Among the informative bilingual permanent exhibits is an exploration of the infamous February 28 Incident in 1947 (see page 40), with a focus on the city, and an intriguing photograph collection through which the visitor can time-travel around the city from the 1920s through the 1960s.

Lake attractions

A 25-minute drive northeast of downtown Kaohsiung is **Crystal Clear Lake** ⬤ (Chengqing Hu). This is the largest lake in the Kaohsiung area, and a very important source of its drinking water – Kaohsiung is prone to shortages. Similarities have been drawn between the lake and Hangzhou's renowned Xihu (West Lake), in China. A broad tree-lined esplanade leads to the Ming-style entry arch of the lake's park (daily 6am–6pm).

A leading attraction at Chengqing Hu is the tall and stately **Restoration Pagoda** (Zhongxing Ta). The winding staircase takes you to the top of the seven-story tower, which at 43 meters (141ft) is the tallest structure in sight. Lovely panoramic views of the entire district, and especially the expanse of the emerald-green lake, can be slowly taken in at the summit.

There are also islands, towers, bridges, pavilions, an orchid collection and an aquarium, along with boating, fishing, hiking, horse riding, golf, and swimming. Amble along the **Nine**-cornered Bridge (Jiuqu Qiao), which for its 230 confusing meters (755ft) meanders along in a most eccentric manner across the lake's waters – ghosts can't move at right angles, and thus fall into the waters. The aquarium facility was originally an elaborate nuclear bomb bunker, built in 1961; the 200-meter/yd tunnel now features displays on oceanic life.

Just outside the entrance gate to Chengqing Hu, a driveway leads uphill to the massive **Grand Hotel** – Cheng Ching Lake (Kaohsiung Chengqing Hu Yuanshan Dafandian), built in classical Chinese-palace style.

Twenty minutes' drive north of downtown Kaohsiung, in Zuoying, lies another lovely body of water called **Lotus Lake** ⬤ (Lianchitan; access daily 8am–6pm). The architectural attractions here include Kaohsiung's **Confucius Temple** ⬤ (Kong Miao; Tue–Sun 9am–5pm; free).

Chengqing Hu, or Crystal Clear Lake.

Traditional temple decoration.

Wuli Pagoda, on Lotus Lake.

Divided by corniced walls and 'moon gates' into various courtyards and garden grottoes, the complex is enclosed within a long wall, enameled in brilliant red and fringed with gold tiles. The temple's design was inspired by a style common during the Song dynasty, and rarely seen in Taiwan. The most interesting time to be here is September 28 each year, when solemn and majestic (and amply attended) Teacher's Day celebrations are held in honor of Confucius, the great teacher, on his birthday. Festivities begin at the crack of dawn, the same time any good teacher rises for the day.

The **Spring and Autumn Pavilions** ❶ (Chunqiu Ge; daily 8am–5.30pm; free) stand on an islet connected to the south shore of Lianchitan by a short causeway. Though the main pavilions are dedicated to Guanyin, Goddess of Mercy, a Daoist temple dedicated to

Guangong is located directly opposite the entrance to the pavilions. Legend has it that Guanyin appeared above the clouds here riding a dragon. She commanded that believers construct an image depicting the event between the 'pavilions of summer and autumn.' And so it came to be; the complex was completed and opened in 1951.

A goddess' stone's throw away stand the twin seven-tiered **Dragon and Tiger Pagodas** ❶ (Longhu Ta; daily 8.30am–5.30pm), which also sit over the water and are connected to shore by a nine-cornered bridge. Entry is down the dragon's throat, exit via the lion's, symbolizing the transformation of bad luck to good fortune. The Chinese consider filial piety a cardinal virtue, and inside are paintings of 24 scenes from traditional tales used to inspire obedience and good deeds. In one painting, a son sits on his parents' bed to allow the mosquitoes to sate themselves on him before his parents retire; another shows a son thawing a hole in a frozen lake with the heat from his body, to catch a carp for his hungry mother.

Buddha Mountain

No visitor should miss **Light of Buddha Mountain 🄡** (Foguangshan; www.fgs.org.tw; daily 7am–8pm; free), at least an hour's drive northeast of downtown Kaohsiung, off Shengdao 21 a few kilometers before it meets Shengdao 22, in lush rolling hills. Free English-language tours (donations are appreciated) are given with three days' notice. This is a key center for Buddhist scholarship in Taiwan. The complex consists of several shrine halls surrounded by cool colonnades, pavilions and pagodas, bridges and footpaths, libraries and meditation halls, ponds and grottoes, and exquisite Buddhist statuary. Near the entrance, the tallest Buddha image on the island – 32 meters (105ft) high – is surrounded by 480 life-size images of disciples that loom into view long before you reach the complex. The major shrine hall is known as the Daxiong Baodian (Precious Hall of Great Heroes). The size of a large theater, this hall has no artificial lighting. Sunlight enters through windows running the entire circumference of the hall, along the tops of the walls.

Enshrined within are three 20-meter (66ft) -tall Buddha images, seated in meditation and displaying various *mudra* (hand gestures). Every inch of wall space is neatly compartmentalized into thousands of tiny niches, each containing a small Buddha illuminated by a tiny light bulb – over 14,000 in total. Other items in this cavernous hall are a huge drum and bell hanging in the corners from wooden frames, and a pair of towering 10-meter (33ft) image-cones bearing the names of the temple's donors.

North beyond Foguangshan is an old Hakka village of deep and sturdy character called **Meinong 🄢**, known for the hand-crafting of lovely oil-paper umbrellas decorated with calligraphy and colorful paintings (see page 256). The skills needed to produce these items are increasingly rare these days, making Meinong's umbrellas collectors' items. Prices are reasonable, and the local craftsmen are proud to explain and demonstrate their skills.

TIP

In Kaohsiung's eastern rural section, Light of Buddha Mountain, one of Taiwan's key monastery complexes, offers English meditation classes and retreats. Lay people can choose from one-day weekend to five-day programs; for graduates, there is a 49-day retreat. There are also chanting and calligraphy retreats. Wake-up is at 5.40am. Rooms have TV and air-conditioning, and there is vegetarian fare.

Dragon Pagoda on Lotus Lake.

MAOLIN NATIONAL SCENIC AREA

The Maolin National Scenic Area (Maolin Guojia Fengjing Qu; www.maolin-nsa.gov.tw), in the central mountains due east of downtown Kaohsiung, is known for its strong indigenous flavor and natural treasures. The north section, in Kaohsiung, is home to Bunun and Tsou communities, the south, in Pingtung County, to Paiwan and Rukai settlements. **Sandimen** has a reputation for high-quality artisan work, notably glass-bead crafts, pottery, embroidered goods, and woven baskets. The villages of **Duona** and dramatically picturesque Wutai are home to numerous traditional stacked-slate dwellings. The **Taiwan Aboriginal Culture Park** (Taiwan Yuanzhu Minzu Yuanqu; Tue–Sun 8.30am–5pm) has first-rate reproductions of traditional architecture, song-and-dance performances, arts and crafts demonstrations, and cultural displays. The **Purple Butterfly Valley** (Zidie Yougu) is home to millions of migrating butterflies in winter – one of the world's only two known mass-wintering sites, the other in Mexico is famed for its Monarchs – and the visually stunning **Duona Suspension Bridge** (Duona Gaodiao Qiao), 103 meters/338ft above a deep-valley river, offers tremendous vistas. The region is also home to a number of quality hot-spring resorts and a network of both strenuous and easy bike routes. Note: Typhoons can severely impact this rugged region, so check weather and road conditions before your journey.

THE UMBRELLAS OF MEINONG

A remnant of last century, the paper umbrellas of Meinong provide a fascinating look at the once-again flourishing Hakka culture in southern Taiwan.

The tradition of making bamboo and paper umbrellas persists to this day in Meinong, a rural area in the northeastern section of Kaohsiung city known for its traditional Hakka community. According to local folklore, a Meinong businessman visiting Chaozhou, Guangdong (in China) discovered a small shop selling the umbrellas. Impressed by what he saw, the businessman urged the master craftsman to return to southern Taiwan with him, but he refused. Undeterred, the businessman purchased the umbrella shop, tools, and contract, giving the umbrella-maker little choice but to move to Meinong to teach his trade. Here, since 1924, the Hakka have been engaged in the crafting of bamboo and paper umbrellas, waterproofed with oil to make them both practical and decorative. Though paper umbrellas are today less popular than they once were, the tourists keep the artisans in business.

Local Hakka tradition once involved giving two paper umbrellas – seen as auspicious – to each new bride as a wedding gift. The round shape suggests a special union, as *yuan*, the Chinese word for circle, sounds like the words for 'fate' and 'satisfaction,' thereby uniting the couple in love forever. *Zhi*, meaning paper, sounds auspiciously similar to *zi* – son – wishing sons on the family. Finally, the character for umbrella, *san*, connotes the granting of blessings of abundant children and grandchildren on the couple.

A girl works on making a bamboo frame for a paper umbrella in a Meinong workshop.

A painted paper umbrella drying on the ground.

Paper umbrellas once made wedding gifts for Hakka girls. The five strings wound around the bamboo frame were said to bestow 'five fortunes' upon the new family.

Rice paddy fields around Meinong.

MEINONG'S TOBACCO CROPS

Aside from the locally made paper umbrellas and Hakka culture, Meinong was also known as the center of the most important tobacco-producing region in Taiwan. Local plantations grew about 30 percent of the nation's tobacco. Planted in late September, tobacco leaves were harvested from late January to early February. Men and women alike joined in the harvest, slinging heavy loads onto trucks for delivery to buyers.

With Taiwan accepted into the WTO in 2002, the market set tobacco production and farm-gate prices. Farmers could not compete, and the industry was shut down in 2007. Old abandoned red-brick curing sheds still dot the landscape, abandoned or used as garages or chicken pens. Learn more of this local history at the Meinong Hakka Culture Museum (Tue–Sun 9am–5pm). This young, attractive facility sits in open farm country, with views of fields and mountains in all

Meinong residents relied on paper umbrellas until commercially made ones debuted in 1963. Today, they are largely produced as souvenirs for tourists.

directions. The shape of the museum itself evokes Meinong's tobacco sheds, and there is a full-scale mock-up inside. The area has an extensive bike-route system, with one route featuring a tobacco theme. There are various rental facilities.

ghly skilled umbrella painter deftly wields a calligraphy ￼ in his right hand, while turning the umbrella with her ￼and.

A thick bamboo that grows only in the mountains of central Taiwan is used for umbrella frames. The bamboo is soaked in water to remove insect-attracting sugars.

Unusual coastline at Cat's Nose Cape.

KENDING

The attractions of this largely unspoiled, sun-kissed natural playground include exotic flora and fauna, stunning views, dramatic geographical formations, and fine beaches.

Taipei

The coastal crescent that occupies Taiwan's southern reaches is known as the Hengchun Peninsula (Hengchun Bandao). It is most often referred to simply as Kending, a vague term meant as a specific reference to Kenting National Park (Kending Guojia Gongyuan), which takes up a large part of the area's landmass. There is also the town of Kending near the middle of the peninsula in the south, adding a bit of initial confusion for those visiting the area for the first time.

The peninsula is surrounded on three sides by water; the Pacific Ocean lies off the east coast, the Bashi Channel (Bashi Haixia) is to the south, and the Taiwan Strait (Taiwan Haixia), separating Taiwan from southern China, is to the west. The merging of the waters creates a pastel tapestry of green and blue swirls. Lumbering down the middle of the peninsula is the great tail of the Central Mountain Range (Zhongyang Shanmo). Two arms reach into the sea: Goose Bell Beak (Eluanbi), longer and to the east; and Cat's Nose Cape (Maobitou), stubbier and to the west. The broad bay between the two points harbor some of the island's best swimming beaches, and many scenic attractions.

Tropical playground

The Kending area is Taiwan's tropical playground. The sun shines more here than in the north. When it does

A lone fisherman at Kending.

rain, the skies darken quickly and the clouds drop their load and move on without delay; the sun comes out again and play continues.

The peninsula is home to some of the island's best fishing. Relentless wind and water erosion has made for some spectacularly rugged coastal scenery. Offshore, coral reefs beckon snorkelers and scuba divers with schools of colorful fish. After splashing about in the surf off one of the many sand or shell-sand beaches, a leisurely stroll or hike through dense tropical forest or

Main Attractions

Kending town
Kenting National Forest Recreation Area
Mt Big Point
Longluan Lake
Eluanbi Park
National Museum of Marine Biology and Aquarium

The coastline of Kenting National Park.

open, hilly rangeland – among stately palm trees, richly flowering bougainvillea, and wide expanses of sisal plants – is just minutes away. When the sun goes down, the night heats up; the abundance of seaside bars, discos, restaurants, and resort hotels act as a honeypot for the island's nighthawks.

Wildlife spotting in the protected Kending area will bring ample reward to the nature-lover. On land there are small mammals, lizards, snakes, butterflies, and 184 species of bird. In the autumn, migratory birds, headed for warmer nesting sites in the Philippines, swarm in on their way from Korea, Japan, mainland China, and as far away as Siberia.

The town of **Hengchun** ❶ is the usual point of entry into Kending. It is situated midway between the towns of Checheng and Kending, about 9km (5 miles) from each other. It is reached by Provincial Highway No. 26 (Shengdao 26), which is the access road from Kaohsiung. The highway heads south to the coast, moves down toward the tip of Eluanbi, then snakes back up the east side of the peninsula, serving as the main route for moving around the district.

In Hengchun are the impressive Chinese clock tower and the ancient **East Gate** (Dongmen), along with remains of the town wall. This is Taiwan's only location with all four original gates intact, the East Gate being the most complete. The gates formed part of extensive fortifications raised in the late 19th century to ward off attack from foreign colonial powers and to intimidate rebellious local aborigines.

Moving about 100 meters (330ft) or so from the East Gate, you'll witness a renowned local geological phenomenon – the *chuhuo* (fire coming out). The earth here literally burns, the sprouting blue-orange flames eternally fed by a reservoir of natural gas within the earth

Kenting National Park

Beyond a few outlying areas, **Kenting National Park** ❷ (Kending Guojia Gongyuan; www.ktnp.gov.tw; free) takes up most of the southern end of the peninsula. Established in January 1982, this is Taiwan's sole tropical national park with a strong emphasis on conservation

The park encompasses both land and maritime environments, totaling 33,631 hectares (83,104 acres). A surprise to most visitors is how densely populated the park area is; many a soul was here before it came into being, new residents are permitted if moving into existing structures, and new building is allowed under strict conditions. Many locals have drifted into the tourism service trade, but there are still significant stretches of agricultural land that preserve a welcome element of traditional Taiwanese rural culture amid the fast-paced world spawned by the steady growth of the park's resort and recreational facilities. There are aboriginal farming hamlets in the northern area that are mostly hidden away.

On the beach

The resort valley of Kending, in which the town of **Kending** ❸ sits, lies between the hilly bulk of the national park in the hills to the north and the beaches fronting **Kending Bay** (Kendingwan) and **Small Bay** (Xiaowan) on the shore directly south and southeast. Xiaowan features an unspoiled white-sand beach that stretches for about 200 meters (660ft), with a boardwalk fronted by a café/bar and small snack bars. The clear azure waters at the two beaches are warm and gentle, perfect for swimming from April to October. (Note that, although swimming areas are marked at Small Bay, there are no lifeguards.) There is a wide choice of accommodations in the area, from five-star resort hotels to family-run hostels and several good campgrounds; the national park headquarters can give prices and advice on these. Close by is a nuclear power station owned and operated by the Taiwan Power Company (Taiwan Dianli Gongsi).

In Kending and Small Bay (as well as Nanwan, or South Bay, see page 264) you can rent all the toys needed for recreation in the area. Shops offer equipment and advice on snorkeling, scuba diving, and cruises of various sorts. The majority of shops also provide basic instruction for surfing, snorkeling, and diving. In Kending you'll also find outlets hiring out jeeps, scooters, and bicycles for exploring the park on land. There's no better way to search out the peninsula's countless nooks and crannies, wind blowing through your hair, than by using open-air transportation.

Exotic flora

In the low hills above the two-pronged peninsula sprawls **Kenting National Forest Recreation Area** ❹ (Kending Guojia Senlin Youlequ; daily 8am–5pm), a lovely haven for exotic flora and strange formations of coral rock exposed by tectonic activity. The Japanese established this area (the progenitor of the national park) as a preserve in 1906, and they combed the Earth to find exotic species of plants that might thrive locally. The Taiwanese have expanded the collection: today more than 1,200 species grow in the sprawling research station. Paved paths and marked scenic routes interlace the recreation area, and most trees and shrubs are identified in Latin and English. There are different areas for separate

TIP

A visit to the Kenting National Park's visitor center, on Shengdao 26 (Highway 26), a few kilometers west of the town of Kending, is by far the best way to get your bearings.

Divers emerging at sunset.

The sun and the luxurious warmth in Kending provide a favorable climate for tropical growth. The old trees and buttress roots found here are unique to the area.

Mt Big Point.

categories of plants: medicinal plants, tropical fruits, rubber trees, and so on.

Scenic points to be taken in along the paths include the 137-meter (44-ft) -long tunnel through contorted limestone called **Fairy Cave** (Xiandong). Here is an ethereal world of stalactites and stalagmites, eerily illuminated by lamp, which serves as home to bats. There is also **One Line Sky** (Yixiantian), a deep gorge that was opened up like a sandwich by an ancient earthquake.

In **Valley of Hanging Banyan Roots** (Chuironggu), visitors enter a preternatural world where thick banyan roots stretch 20 meters (66ft) through cliffs of solid stone to reach the earth, their green canopies whistling in the wind high above. Visitors can also marvel at the famous **Looking-glass Tree** (Jietong Jumu; the formal English name does not match the Chinese), estimated to be more than 400 years old. The tree's thick roots, resembling supporting buttresses, grow above the ground.

From a 27-meter (89ft) -high observation tower in the district, visitors can take in the entire breadth of the long, lazy bay that stretches from Maobitou to Eluanbi. On a clear day, if you get up to the top early enough, distant Lanyu (Orchid Island) can be spotted, as well as – some claim – the northernmost island of the Philippines.

Sheding Nature Park (Sheding Ziran Gongyuan; daily 8am–8pm; free) is located uphill and slightly eastward from the forest recreation area. Here, in contrast to the area just left, visitors find the riches of nature existing in their natural condition. It takes a little over an hour to walk through a wild jungle world of ancient trees, dark ravines, coral-rock formations, colorful birds, macaques – and old lime and charcoal kiln ruins. The walkways are punctuated with birdwatching and lookout pavilions.

To the west of the forest recreation area is **Mt Big Point** ➎ (Dajianshan), the symbol and premier landmark of the national park. Though designated a mountain, it is in fact just 318 meters (1,043ft) high.

Dajianshan provides the opportunity for good exercise and grand vistas. There are two routes to the top, both beginning at the entrance to Kending Guojia Senlin Youlequ. The first is a comparatively gentle path that meanders along the slopes to the north. The southern trail first takes the adventurous visitor past the tourist-jaded cattle, goats, and sheep of Kending Ranch (Kending Muchang; daily 8am–5pm), a large livestock research facility. Then, as the 'big' and 'point' features of the mountain's name become more self-evident, the footpath narrows and steepens, with roots, stone handholds, and ropes all lending a hand. This last section is not long, and the intrepid are rewarded with exhilarating views of green pastureland and the surf-washed coast surrounding Nanwan off to the right.

Eco-farming

Those looking for a nice change of pace can make their way to **Ever Spring Eco-Farm** ➏ (Hengchun Shengtai Nongchang; www.ecofarm.com.tw; daily 8am–10pm), between the forest recreation area and Hengchun. Access is off Shengdao 26 not far from Hengchun's grand Nanmen (South Gate). This is a large, private eco-farm engaged in natural, chemical-free farming. Incongruously, there is a rather luxurious hotel with floors of Turkish marble and saunas of aromatic Chinese cypress, but in keeping with the spirit of things, there are also rustic 'farmhouses' for rent and a good campground. Share a little quiet time with the 700 Nubian goats or forests of fireflies (from the eco-viewing platforms), ride horses, enjoy the owner's private stock of spirits distilled from honey, and both pick and dine on the farm's organically grown starfruit, mangoes, sugar apples, and other savory delights.

The Cat's Nose

Eight kilometers (5 miles) west and south of the town of Kending, **Cat's Nose Cape** ➐ (Maobitou; daily Apr–Oct 8.30am–6.30pm, Nov–Mar until 5pm; free) pokes into the sea in a jumble of contorted coral-rock formations. To get there, turn south on County Road No. 153 (Xiandao 153) where

TIP

The hotels, homestays, shops, and restaurants in Kenting National Park are privately run, and not directly supervised by park authorities, though the park authorities have a hand in controlling new building. Most are trustworthy, but check with the visitor center first. Many homestays are unlicensed, and the center will also give guidance on legal, vetted establishments.

Performing at the Spring Scream Music Festival.

SPRING SCREAM

The annual Spring Scream music festival, started in the early 1990s, has become one of the rites of spring for Taiwan's rock 'n' roll-loving expatriate crowd, who come from the far-flung corners of the island to frolic for days on end in Kending.

Held in April, the Spring Scream bash sees hundreds of bands, DJs, and other artists from Taiwan, Japan, the US, Australia, and elsewhere performing almost nonstop. Free shuttle buses take people back and forth from Kending town to the multi-stage venue, in recent years around Eluanbi Lighthouse, and charter buses also travel to and from major cities. For many, this is the party of the year. Indie rock, hip-hop, old-time rock 'n' roll, punk… whatever stimulates you, musically, is to be found here.

Rooms throughout the park are booked well in advance, and rates spike skyward, but since many of the revelers have little intention of sleeping anyway, this seems not to matter. Campsites are filled with people catching a few winks; cars and vans become temporary sleeping quarters. Many come in by chartered bus, party a day or two without break, then head back home to resume their normal lives.

Find out more about the music fest, and about booking bus and festival tickets, at www.springscream.com.

A peaceful cove.

it meets Shengdao 26, about 3km (2 miles) south of Hengchun town. This promontory is stubbier than Eluanbi, its rival across the southern bay, and does not reach out so far. Those who named it claim the massive rocks here, which have come crashing down unseen and unheard with the sea eating out the cliff sides over the years, make the cape resemble a crouching cat when seen from afar. The sea shimmers a deep sapphire-blue, and the cape provides superb views of the sun-swept peninsular crescent. A rocky path cuts through the craggy formations. This is a relaxing place for picnics, or for solitary walks along extremely rugged coastline.

Among the main points of interest are the bizarre geological formations found along what is informally called **Skirt Coast** (Qunjiao Haian Jingguan), which stretches from the peninsula's tip to Houbihu Yugang (Houbihu Fishing Harbor) on the east side. Boat tours offer the best views of the magnificent scenic tableaux, made up of flat-top bluffs, rocky cliffs, rugged coastline strewn with giant boulders, and massive coral reefs sticking

up and then sinking below the pounding waves. Be sure, as well, to search out soothing, inspirational **South Sea Cave** (Nanhaidong). A small shrine is maintained here, and elevated sea-viewing terraces make this a fruitful stop to take in the scenery and for landscape photographers.

In the corner where Maobitou meets the peninsula's main body is **South Bay 8** (Nanwan). Shengdao 26 rolls right by it. The beach here, about 1km (1,100yds) long, is just as popular as those at Kending (beach facilities daily 8.30am–5.30pm). Nanwan is actually a fishing village, and local fisherman can often be seen hauling in the day's catch.

As in Kending, quality accommodations are available, as well as a clutch of gear-rental shops that cater to enthusiasts hell-bent on water sports. In addition, matching its sister town down the coast to the east, one finds a healthy dose of restaurants, coffee shops, bars, and discos behind the beach, making this the second of the peninsula's party spots after daytime recreational activities cease, though markedly quieter. The beach has marked swimming

areas, lifeguards, and shower/changing room facilities.

Birdwatching at Longluan Lake

Above Maobitou on the western side of the peninsula, about 3km (2 miles) southwest of Hengchun, is **Longluan Lake ❾** (Longluantan), the best place in the national park – if not the entire island – to watch tropical and migratory waterbirds. Taiwan sits smack in the middle of many an Asian feathered migrant's flight path, and this protected lake is a prime spot for their seasonal recuperation. Surrounded by lush wetlands, the lake is off-limits to birdwatchers. However, a fine bird-watching center (daily 8.30am–5pm) overlooks the thriving mini eco-environment. Telescopes allow close-up observations, with a supply of onsite reference materials (in English) encouraging intelligent observation. Prime time for viewing is between October and May. Ducks, wild geese, snipes, and plover are just some of the birds to be enjoyed. The eagle-eyed might even spot the magisterial, and elusive, gray-faced buzzard.

Taiwan's tail

Opposite Maobitou, **Goose Bell Beak ❿** (Eluanbi) extends for several kilometers beyond Kending like a giant tanker plowing out to sea. Often referred to as Taiwan's tail, the promontory has Taiwan's best white sand beaches. The seascapes here are riveting. Of special note is hulking **Sail Rock** (Chuanfanshi), just off the shore on the west side of Eluanbi, near the town of Kending. This is a towering slab of coral rock that juts 18 meters (60ft) straight up from the sea's rocky bottom. With the waves rippling by, those with a historical bent and an active imagination will see what others have seen – the huge sail of a Chinese imperial war junk moving toward the horizon.

Eluanbi Park ⓫ (Eluanbi Gongyuan; daily 7am–5.30pm), covering 65 hectares (160 acres) and taking up the western part of the promontory's bottom section, features a 3km (2-mile) -long paved path that winds through ancient coral heads of fantastic shapes and through a maze of manicured lawns. It is believed that Taiwan's first aboriginal inhabitants – likely of Malayan origin, probably sailing in from the northernmost islands of the Philippines – settled in the wide bay between the two promontories. On Eluanbi and elsewhere is ample archeological evidence of the early settlers' culture.

Eluanbi Lighthouse (Eluanbi Dengta), a landmark erected in the 1880s is the park's central attraction. The lantern atop the 22-meter (72ft) tower – said to be the brightest in all of Asia – has saved countless vessels from certain peril on the notorious coral shoals that reach into the sea. A tourist complex at the foot of the lighthouse houses restaurants, a parking lot, and countless stalls selling food and souvenirs.

Most locals and visitors think that Eluanbi Park is Taiwan's southernmost point, but it is in fact **Longkeng Ecological Protection Area** (Longkeng Shengtai Baohuqu), on the peninsula's east side. Only 200 people can visit

TIP

Guided day and night walks are conducted by trained local residents, overseen by the national park. Guides may enter areas off-limits to general visitors. The visitors' center helps to set these up.

Eluanbi lighthouse, Kending.

An egret stops to rest at Longluan Lake, possibly the best area in all of Taiwan to bird-watch.

Catching a wave at South Bay.

Longkeng each day; registration is at the national park's main visitor center or on its website. There is a small information center at the gate, and from here the coast is reached on foot in about 20 minutes via a shady path lined with a dense growth of wind-defying cacti-like plants higher than one's head. Visitors emerge at the coast quite suddenly amid a bizarre moon-like world of raised coral traversed by boardwalks, along which is information signage. At the southern tip is a high-point lookout from which the Qixing Yu (Seven Stars Islands) can be seen. These small bodies of raised coral about 10km (6 miles) south of Eluanbi, considered Kending's best dive site by some, were the bane of sailors in the days of sail, and a major reason why Britain built and manned Eluanbi Lighthouse.

Eluanbi's rocky eastern side ends in dramatic cliffs. Interesting here is the sand dune at **Windblown Sand** ⑫ (Fengchuisha). This romantic, blustery spot is the site of a unique natural phenomenon. During the rainy season (May to October), sand and a type of reddish soil are carried down from a distant plateau, forming what appears to be a river of red sand running into the sea. When winter arrives powerful monsoon winds force the red-sand river – 1,500 meters/yds long and 200 meters/yds wide – back up off the shore and over the lip of the cliff side, to a height of over 70 meters (230ft).

After Kending, most people head back via Kaohsiung. On the way, past Hengchun just outside the national park at Checheng Village, a visit to the immense **National Museum of Marine Biology and Aquarium** ⑬ (Guoli Haiyang Shengwu Bowuguan; www.nmmba.gov.tw; July–Aug daily 8am–6pm, hours vary other seasons) is guaranteed to leave a powerful impression.

The shark tank has a number of varieties, the coastal and inland waterways section is well designed, and the kids enjoy the Hands-On Pond. But the big draw is the different feedings shows for the puffins, penguins, seals, reef fish (seen through an underwater tunnel), kelp forest fish, and whale sharks.

the central altar; each with its own set of carved dragon columns and a pair of guardian lions.

The **Martyrs' Shrine** (Zhonglie Zi; daily 9am–5pm; free), built into a hillside on the northern outskirts of Hualien in Zhongzheng Park (Zhongzheng Gongyuan), is an impressive architectural complex that reflects classical Chinese concepts of balance and proportion.

Local scenic areas

Qixingtan ❶, or Seven Star Lake, is a landscaped scenic area in the city's northwest near the airport. The site features a lovely arcing bay, crystalline blue-green Pacific waters, and a great view of massive Qingshui Cliff to the north, the most formidable section of the Suao-Hualien highway, many miles long and thousands of feet high. This is the north terminus of a bike path that stretches 21km (13 miles) to Nanbin Park on the city's south side. There are rental facilities at both ends. Among the many other facilities are the Stone Sculpture Park, Star Watching Plaza, Sunrise Building, a children's playground, and a seaside botanical garden. The area is dotted with signboards explaining the seaside ecology.

One of Hualien's favorite recreational resorts is **Carp Lake ❷** (Liyutan), a 20-minute drive by car southwest of the city. Taiwan's largest natural inland lake, Liyutan is a pleasant destination for a leisurely half-day excursion. Set amid tropical fruit plantations in the foothills of the towering Central Mountain Range (Zhongyang Shanmo), this fish-shaped lake resort hosts colorful dragon-boat races in June. Boating and fishing are popular here, but visitors must bring their own fishing gear. Rowboats, paddleboats, and sail craft are all available for rent. Anglers who manage to reel in one of the lake's famous carp can have it cooked at one of the numerous roadside restaurants. A 4km (2.4-mile) foot/bicycle path circles the lake (bike rentals available), and there are also a number of well-marked hiking trails that move off from the lake to the tops of the hills nearby. The hikes are not too demanding, and trailblazers are rewarded with calming vistas. Campsites and paragliding facilities are also available.

Home to the Ami

The narrow alluvial plains and foothill areas of Hualien County are home to most members of Taiwan's largest ethnic minority, the Ami, numbering about 200,000. About 90,000 live in Hualien City, giving the place a laid-back, unhurried pace; time slows down here, especially in comparison to Taiwan's other Han Chinese-dominated urban centers. During the annual Ami harvest celebration, in late August and/or early September, the city is particularly festive. A number of rural Ami communities welcome tourists to their multi-day harvest festivals; the national and county tourism authorities are the best sources of information and assistance.

Visitors being escorted around on guided tours are often taken to marble factories on the way to Tailuge, to 'look around,' with aboriginal song and dance shows sometimes put on to get you in the souvenir-buying mood.

South from Hualien

Scenery along the coastal highway heading south from Hualien grows more gentle and pastoral. On one side, the deep-blue waters of the Pacific either crash frothily against rocky capes or nuzzle the beaches of quiet coves. Inland, the Coastal Mountain Range forms a massive windscreen, sheltering the brilliant green plantations and terraced paddies that cover the East Rift Valley.

There are two routes connecting Hualien with Taitung. The foothill route, Provincial Highway No. 9 (Shengdao 9), features three rustic hotspring resorts: **Ruisui**, **Antong**, and **Hongye**. It follows the railway and

A farmer inspects a paddy field, eastern Taiwan. Rice planting remains one of the economic pillars of this region.

Dragon-boat race team saluting on Carp Lake.

runs parallel to the coast, 15km (10 miles) inland. Most people, however, prefer the coastal route of Shengdao 11 for its greater scenic attractions.

Much of the land on either side of this route falls within the boundaries of the **East Coast National Scenic Area** ❸ (Dongbuhaian Guojia Fengjingqu; www.eastcoast-nsa.gov.tw; free). Encompassing 41,500 hectares (102,500 acres), it runs from the mouth of the Hualien He (Hualien River) in the north to Xiaoyeliu (Little Wild Willows) near Taitung city. The island of Ludao (Green Island) is also within the park (see page 292). All sites described subsequently are within Dongbuhaian Guojia Fengjingqu, off Shengdao 11.

Just inside the scenic area's northern boundary, and past the visitor center, is the 51-hectare (126-acre) **Hualien Farglory Ocean Park** ❹ (www.farglory-oceanpark.com.tw; daily 9.30am–5pm). Within the eight theme areas is a whale and dolphin aquarium, sea lion habitat park, sea lion theater, Main Street, Water Fun Park, Crystal Palace, Underwater Kingdom, and more. The park is a first-class facility, facing the surf and with a superb Victorian-style hotel overlooking it. A visit could take up two full days. Shuttle buses make runs to major hotels in Hualien.

Not far south of Ocean Park is **Jiqi Seaside Resort** ❺ (Jiqi Haishui Yuchang; May–Sept daily 8.30am–6pm; free), the first good swimming beach south of Hualien. The small bay here, flanked on three sides by mountains, has clear water, and sometimes the waves break perfectly for bodysurfing. There is an impressive range of activities on offer, including paragliding and sailing. Behind the beachside resort is a recreation area where forest walks, picnic areas, and a lovely lookout over the entire area can be enjoyed.

Just south of the bay at **Jiqi**, the interested visitor can discover incredible rock formations and a tribal village. The Ami, who have been left much to themselves over the years in this isolated area, inhabit this stretch of coast. Visitors to this area can still have a glimpse of the Ami's traditional way of life.

A breathtaking view from the Suao–Hualien Highway.

AMI TRIBE SHOWCASE

The **Amis Folk Center**, by the East Coast National Scenic Area HQ, has a good visitor center plus replicas of traditional dwellings and ceremonial structures, weaving demonstrations, crafts for sale, and traditional song-and-dance performances. Visitors can inspect traditional wind and percussion instruments, generally made of bamboo (including a nose flute), and can take part in bamboo cannon, swing, and archery activities. The cannons were used to keep birds from attacking crops, to dispel evil spirits, and to send information to ancestors. Note the large tower on the grounds, a replica of the wooden watchtowers built at village edges in days of old, manned at all times, used to watch out for enemies. You'll see numerous other replicas along the highway in Taitung County.

Those seeking authentic glimpses of Ami life should visit the little coastal town of **Fengbin** ❻, a short drive south of Jiqi. The harvest festival's opening ceremonies are especially exciting here.

Thirty kilometers (19 miles) past Jiqi is the **Stone Steps** ❼ (Shitiping). This area of coastline was formed from eroded volcanic conglomerate, creating intriguing formations. In some areas the rock has been worn and polished, creating a natural staircase – hence the site's name. The rock's grayish-white color contrasts markedly with the changing blue shades of the sky and ocean. The effect is most dramatic with the deep, shifting hues and tones of daybreak and sunset.

River rafting

Not far beyond Shitiping, the **Xiuguluan River** ❽ (Xiuguluan He) offers year-round white-water rafting in a four-hour trip (Class 1–3 rapids), originating in the coastal mountain foothills next to Ruisui, one of the hot-spring areas on the inland Shengdao 9 route to Taitung. Visit the Ruisui Rafting Tourist Center (daily 9am–5pm)

at 215 Zhongshan Road, Section 3, Ruisui Township, if you are keen on this activity. Most of the rafting companies now have offices in Hualien City and arrange transportation.

The Xiuguluan is the longest river on the island's east coast, and one of the few with enough year-round water volume to allow recreational boating and rafting. The often-breathtaking scenery surrounding the gorge-pressed waters of the river is one of the primary reasons for the popularity of rafting here. The waterway begins in the inhospitable mountains of Taiwan's central reaches, making its way seaward – sometimes meandering, often roaring – along a twisting and turning concourse that snakes 108km (67 miles) before its waters push out into the Pacific. The 22km (14-mile) rafting course takes up the lower stretch of the river's route, ending just before the river mouth at the coast. The best time to test the waters is within two weeks after a typhoon, when they are at their angriest.

The highway that follows the river's course, **Ruigang Highway**

Ami harvest festival, near Hualien.

(Ruigang Gonglu), is in itself worth a trip. As well as offering dramatic views of rolling whitewater and sheer cliff faces, it takes visitors by the Ami village of Qimei.

Traces of cave life

About 40km (25 miles) south of the mouth of the Xiuguluan, near Changbin, a tall and craggy cliff borders the ocean. This cliff shelters the **Caves of the Eight Immortals**  (Baxiandong; daily 8.30am–5pm), and at the same time provides superb panoramic views of the east coast.

The caves, which form Taiwan's earliest known prehistoric site, were inhabited intermittently by different prehistoric peoples. This region is prime turf for archeologists, and artifacts are common enough that you'll see them used as markers or decorations on roadsides, in fields, and in the courtyards of local farmsteads. Many have been recovered from the caves, particularly Chaoyindong (Sound of the Tide Cave), but a number of the largest caves are now used as temples, inhibiting any appreciation of the

The Platform of the Three Immortals.

historical importance of the place. The visitor center houses some of the artifacts, plus dioramas.

Steps from the parking lot lead to where a shrine hall is built into the mouth of a large cavern facing the ocean; in an adjacent cave sit three garish pink Buddha images. The final ascent leads through bamboo thickets close to the top of the bluff. Here the trail splits. The right fork leads to the Haileidong (Sea Thunder Cave), a stone grotto where ascetics once lived and meditated. The left fork ascends to the topmost cave, containing a crude shrine with several icons. On a clear day, sharp-eyed observers can almost see the southern tip of Taiwan. After the exertion from the climb, the black sand beach at the foot of the cliffs is a refreshing place for a dip.

Immortal island

Just north of Chenggong is an island outcropping of contorted coral known as the **Platform of the Three Immortals** ⑩ (Sanxiantai; tourist centre daily 8.30am–12pm; 1–5pm). A multi-span, dragon-like bridge traverses the

knee-deep water separating the nature reserve from the mainland, and a round-island trail that takes a leisurely two hours to traverse winds through a maze of bizarre coral formations, stone-rimmed pools, exotic plants, and a cute little lighthouse, with pavilions and picnic tables set up along the way. There is good English explanatory signage.

According to legend, three of the Eight Immortals stopped here to rest while en route to Penglai, their island abode somewhere in the Pacific. Early imperial explorers sent out to find Penglai brought back descriptions of an island paradise that have led some later historians to believe that paradise was Taiwan – unknown to the Chinese at the time.

The old fishing town of **Cheng-gong** ⓫ is the largest town in the area. The east coast's largest, most intensive fish market takes places at the docks each day from 3 to 4pm. Further south, by highway-side in **Dulan** ⓬, is the sprawling, big-shouldered old Dulan Sugar Factory which makes sugar no more. The heritage complex, now protected, has been taken over by local artists from this indigenous village. There's an art workshop, café, bar, driftwood stage, homestay, and retail shop with a rich variety of hand-made arts and crafts. There's also live music Saturday nights, with local and foreign talent.

Just north of Taitung is **Little Wild Willows** ⓭ (Xiaoyeliu; daily 8.30am– 5pm), where contorted abstract sculptures have been created by the hand of nature. Countless seasons of wind and tides have turned the rock and exposed coral into otherworldly forms that compete well with the natural art carved at the place's better-known cousin, Yeliu, on the north shore near Taipei (see page 171).

Just north of Xiaoyeliu is **Shanyuan Seaside Resort** ⓮ (Shanyuan Haishui Yuchang; daily May–Sept 8.30am– 6pm). This popular destination possesses a wonderful 1.5km (1-mile) stretch of fine yellow sand. Water-sports including windsurfing are available, and the resort is the region's yachting center. The beach tapers into picturesque coral reefs at either end, making for enjoyable snorkeling.

Windsurfer at Shanyuan beach.

Spectacular Taroko Gorge, arguably
Taiwan's most famous attraction.

TAROKO GORGE

Spectacular Taroko Gorge enthralls visitors with its dramatic landscapes and is home to an abundance of wildlife, but memories of human tragedy here temper the traveler's excitement.

Taipei

Nine out of 10 people who visit Hualien tour **Taroko Gorge** (Tailuge), one of the most spectacular natural wonders of the world and Taiwan's foremost natural scenery attraction.

By car, taxi, or bus, the route from Hualien heads north for 15km (9 miles), through expansive green plantations of papaya, banana, and sugarcane. When the road reaches **Xincheng** it cuts westward, straight into the cavernous, marble-rich gorge of Tailuge (24 hours; free). *Tailuge* means 'beautiful' in the Ami language, though it is in fact the Atayal people (inhabitants of the north end of the island) who have been the most recent aboriginal residents. Visitors at once realize that the people who named the site were not exaggerating. A gorge of marble-laced cliffs, through which flows the at times torrential Liwu He (Liwu River), Taroko Gorge winds sinuously for 19km (12 miles) from Tianxiang to the coast.

During the Chinese New Year holidays only buses may enter the gorge between 7am and 4pm. At this time special shuttle buses, with guides, run from Xincheng Railway Station (charge per person).

From mountain to sea

The gorge is part of **Taroko National Park** (Tailuge Guojia Gongyuan; www.

taroko.gov.tw; 24 hours; free), which stretches 36km (22 miles) from east to west, and 42km (26 miles) north to south. Covering an expanse of 92,000 hectares (37,000 acres) in the central mountains, altitudes range from the tip of the highest mountain, Nanhutashan (Mt Nanhuta) at 3,700 meters (12,100ft), to sea level where the giant slumbering hulks drop into the pounding surf. The area is renowned for its lofty mountains, deep canyons cutting off from the main gorge, head-spinning precipices, elegant waterfalls, and raw,

Main Attractions
Eternal Spring Shrine
Buluowan Recreation Area
Swallow Grotto
Tunnel of Nine Turns
Baiyang Falls Trail
Wenshan Hot Springs

A taxi and police car driving on a mountain road in Taroko National Park.

The road through Taroko Gorge winds in and out of tunnels which splice through the thickly marbled mountains. Not surprisingly, lives were lost in its construction.

wild rapids. Wildlife is plentiful: nature-lovers paying close attention are sure to be rewarded with sightings of some of the 302 species of butterflies, 152 species of birds, 15 species of amphibians, 31 species of reptiles, and 46 species of large mammals that enjoy the run of the park, where the capture of such living beings is prohibited by law.

Over 200 million years ago, coral reefs dominated the shallow tropical waters where Taiwan now sits. As layer upon layer was built up and pressed down on layers below, limestone formed. The intense heat of powerful geotectonic movements transformed the limestone into massive deposits of marble.

The origins of the gorge lie four million years past, when the Eurasian tectonic plate began to crush against the Philippine Sea plate, pushing up the island's mighty Central Mountain

Range. The colossal pressure created by the plates as they struggled against each other threw up the huge blocks of marble lying deep beneath the surface. As time ticked slowly by, the Liwu He worked its wonders, grain by grain, etching rock away and leaving soaring cliffs with thick veins of solid marble that stand over 300 meters (984ft) high in places. It is estimated that Taiwan's heavy annual rainfall, along with the fact that the island is still being heaved higher out of the sea, is helping to deepen the gorge by about 5mm (0.2ins) a year.

Impressive but tragic road

The road that slices through the gorge, Zhongheng (Central Cross-Island Highway), is in many ways just as impressive as the gorge itself. Spanning the chasm and the high mountains to connect the east side of Taiwan to the west, the highway was hacked out by hand in sections. The road, started in 1956, was initially conceived as a military route, enabling quick troop movements should China attack and the coastal routes be cut off. Demobilized

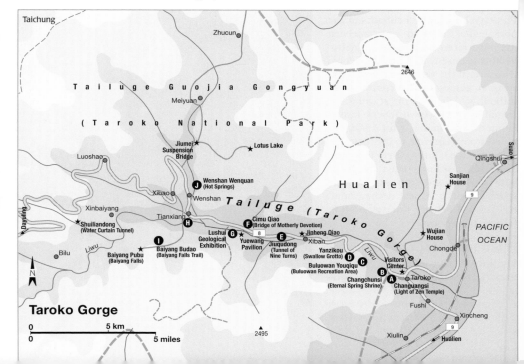

Taroko Gorge

servicemen, most of whom had grown up on the mainland, had little education, were unable to speak Taiwanese, and therefore had little prospect of civilian employment in Taiwan, were given the job of cutting out the initial one-lane highway from the mountains. More than 450 of these men lost their lives in the great engineering project, which was completed in four years. The eastern section of the highway, ending at Dayuling, 78km (48 miles) from the ocean, winds through 38 tunnels cut from solid rock.

It is a good idea to get your bearings by visiting the park's expansive visitor center at Taroko Terrace, just inside the east entrance off the highway (daily 8.30am–5pm, closed 2nd Mon of month; free). There are free brochures on various subjects, books for sale, a photo exhibit that serves as a preview of what you'll be seeing yourself, a play area that teaches children about the natural environment, and exhibits on the region's geology as well as on the history of Taroko's indigenous settlements.

The first scenic points along the highway are **Light of Zen Temple A** (Changuangsi) and **Eternal Spring Shrine B** (Changchunsi), in the first 3km (2 miles) past the visitor center at the eastern entrance to the park off Provincial Highway No. 9 (Shengdao 9). Changuangsi is a somber four-story Zen Buddhist monastery styled along classical Chinese lines. The mountainous *mise-en-scènes* here are invigorating. Nearby Changchunsi is a memorial to the retired servicemen who lost their lives constructing Zhongheng, still sometimes called the Baodao Caihong (Rainbow of Treasure Island) by members of the older generation living along the route. The shrine is perched on a cliff-bottom overlooking a boulder-strewn valley; the original, which stood immediately to its right, was wiped out in a great landslide decades ago, the slide still clearly visible. An underground spring emerges and rushes beneath the structure, floating

past a graceful moon bridge that forms part of the small complex. The spring has come to symbolize the dedication, sacrifice, and undying spirit of the rough and ready men in whose honor the shrine was erected. Appropriately, worshipers light cigarettes rather than incense in their memory.

Atayal homeland

Between Changchunsi and Yanzikuo, just off the highway to the south, is **Buluowan Recreation Area C** (Buluowan Youqiqu; daily 8.30am–4.30pm, closed 1st and 3rd Mon of month). The gorge and surrounding area were home for many generations to the Taroko tribe (commonly spelled Truku), an offshoot of the Atayal people now officially recognized as a separate tribe. The Japanese forced the tribe out onto the flatlands after a major uprising in the early 1900s. Buluowan has been designated a scenic spot by the national parks administration, and members of the tribe live and work here. The small village has a theater where traditional tribal dances are staged for visitors, a museum with

TIP

In Taroko Gorge there are three small campsites (free; first come first served), the Taroko-style huts at Buluowan, church guesthouses, and two international hotels; try to book well in advance.

The Eternal Spring Shrine, Taroko Gorge.

TIP

Taiwan is a land of earthquakes, and heavy rains cause frequent landslides and rock falls. When hiking in Taroko Gorge, stick to the marked trails, and confirm the condition of trails beforehand at the park's visitor center.

displays of Taroko arts and crafts (with an adjoining gift shop), and over 20 recreations of traditional Taroko wooden huts that visitors can rent. There is also a premium hotel in the upper area, with premium views. Food is provided at the resort; accommodations must be booked in advance. A stay of a day or two is a good opportunity to learn more of the customs and everyday life of the Taroko.

Before coming to the area, the Taroko lived further off in the mountains, away from the coast. Between 1680 and 1740, internal conflicts rented the Atayal people, and many on the losing side – the Taroko – crossed hunting trails over the Central Mountain Range, moving down the Liwu He. In the process, the aborigines already living here, from the Ami tribe, were decimated and scattered.

Swallow Grotto

At **Swallow Grotto** (Yanzikou), a series of magnificent cliffs tower so tall on either side of the road that direct sunlight hits the floor of the gorge only around noontime. A little

The Tunnel of Nine Turns.

further up the road, **Fuji Cliff** (Fuji Duanyai) sets visitors' heads reeling as they look up its sheer stone face, with the roar of the river below.

Swallows' nests once hung precariously from innumerable holes high up on the sheer gorge walls at Yanzikou. These nesting places were etched out of the limestone by natural erosion; many may, long ago, have been the exit points for powerful underground streams. With the increase in visitors in recent times, the tiny birds have left the area. Over countless years, erosion has also created grotesque formations in the immense marble outcroppings that seem to hang from the cliffs.

The half-kilometer stretch of old highway here has been made into a pedestrian trail with a lane for slow, west-only vehicles; two tunnels have been cut straight though the cliffs for regular traffic.

Walk: don't ride

Wherever possible, visitors should walk the gorge instead of riding in enclosed vehicles. From Yanzikou one can walk to **Jinheng Bridge** (Jinheng

Qiao), where the gorge's famous Yindianren (Indian) rock looms solemnly into view. Nature's mysterious forces have worked to hew the stone of the cliff face on the north bank of the river into the likeness of a native North American chief's head. The image is even crowned with a giant headdress made of vegetation that clings on top of the craggy rock.

The **Tunnel of Nine Turns** ❺ (Jiuqudong) is a remarkable feat of engineering – it cuts a twisting, crooked road of short tunnels and half tunnels through solid marble cliffs (now pedestrian-only). Located about 1km (0.6 mile) past Jinheng Qiao, one can see the exposed faces of some of the thickest deposits of marble in the area. Many of the unfortunate souls who fell to their deaths in the building of the road did so here; to get at the stone, workers would be suspended from flimsy, makeshift bamboo contraptions, dangling in mid-air above the rocks and water far below.

In this section the sheer perpendicular walls framing the slicing river's course press in to within just a few dozen feet. The effect is awesome, the vision fantastic. In some places the sky disappears from view. The **Bridge of Motherly Devotion** ❻ (Cimu Qiao), just up from the Tunnel of Nine Turns, is worth a stop to explore the rocky riverbed, a jumble of huge marble boulders tossed carelessly down the gully by some ancient convulsion. A small marble pavilion stands on a hillock.

Just beyond the bridge is the **Lushui Geological Exhibition** ❼ (daily 9am–4.30pm, closed 2nd and 4th Mon of month; free). The facility is a superb way to get your geohistoric bearings of the gorge, of Taiwan's towering mountain ranges, and the rugged east coast; a plentiful supply of information in English is offered. The first-floor exhibit expounds on fundamental geological principles and processes. The second floor explores the special landscapes and geological characteristics of Taroko National Park.

The next stop on the Tailuge tour is **Tianxiang** ❽. A suspension bridge just before Tianxiang leads across the river to an exquisite seven-story pagoda perched on a peak. The vistas here,

The Bridge of Motherly Devotion.

especially in the mornings when the slumbering mountains are wrapped in a quilt of mist, are enough to inspire religious conviction. From the pagoda a short, refreshing walk will lead you to a small temple nearby.

Not far up the road from Tianxiang, on the left side moving inland, visitors will come to the entrance of the most popular of Tailuge's many trails, **Baiyang Falls Trail** ❶ (Baiyang Budao). The trail does not demand great exertion, and is clearly marked. A 380-meter (1,247ft) tunnel begins the 3.6km (2.2-mile) round-trip trek, which opens directly onto a red-railed bridge over a small cascading river.

The goal is to reach **Water Curtain Tunnel** (Shuiliandong). To get there, six more tunnels must be navigated. The longer ones have solar-powered lamps, turned on at the entrances, which go off automatically after two-and-a-half minutes – so don't dawdle if you don't like the dark.

Along the way, the park's panoply of rich flora and fauna comes in closer than on the main highway. Try to differentiate the juniper from the dwarf

bamboo, the spruce from the pine; enjoy the Chinese photinia, the orchids, the alpine flowers, and the lithophytes (stone plants). Lucky sojourners will hear, and may even be able to spy, the now rare Formosan rock monkey (Formosan macaque), the Formosan pangolin, the Formosan long-nosed tree squirrel, the Formosan serow, and perhaps even the Formosan black bear. Wild boars, goats, hares, and snakes are also seen in the gorge. Keep your eyes peeled and cameras at the ready.

Picnic at Baiyang Falls

Upon making your way through the fourth tunnel, you will arrive at **Baiyang Falls Bridge** (Baiyang Pubu Qiao). Directly across this bridge is a suspension bridge that leads to a viewing platform on the far side. From this vantage point you can enjoy some marvellous scenery of the gushing, hurtling Baiyang Pubu and the snaking river valley. The air tends to be somewhat damp here, so an extra layer of clothing might come in handy for those prone to chills. This is a memorable spot for a light picnic and a

A suspension footbridge crossing Taroko Gorge.

session of photo-taking with the roaring of the waterfall pounding down into a deep pool.

The falls are among the better-known scenic spots in the park. Another one, Shuiliandong (Water Curtain Tunnel), is located just 300 meters (990ft) further up the trail. Leaving the falls, two more tunnels are passed through. The next, Shuiliandong, streams with a curtain of water, end to end, that gushes from the low ceiling. Unfortunately, due to the effects of the 9-21 and later earthquakes, the tunnel is currently closed indefinitely because of concern regarding its stability. The Baiyang Pubu walk should take a leisurely two hours.

Wenshan Hot Springs

Just a few minutes' drive beyond Tianxiang – approximately 3km (2 miles) – a series of steps at the mouth of the third tunnel from the town leads down to the dramatic setting of the **Wenshan Hot Springs ❿** (Wenshan Wenquan).

The magnificent walk to the bottom of the gorge is an appetizer for the hot springs themselves. After a swaying suspension bridge crosses the Dasha Xi (Dasha River), steps carved into the cliff side lead along a small tributary to a large hot pool lying in an open cave of solid marble, which is immediately adjacent to the sparkling fresh water tumbling along the rocky riverbed.

The water in the hot pool is crystal-clear, despite heavy concentrations of sulfur and other minerals that stain the rocks and whose pungent aroma wafts through the air. A bubbling spring lets the hot water seep through a crack in the cave wall, and a drain hole spills the pool into the river. Bathers can enjoy the sensation of hot spring and cold river water rushing simultaneously over their limbs; the hot waters are around 46°C to 48°C (115°F to 118°F). There are no showers or vendors to spoil the beauty of this spot, and large boulders provide the only cover for changing bathers. From here, Zhongheng continues towards Dayuling.

The Tianxiang pagoda.

Scenic Wenshan Hot Springs.

HIKING IN TAROKO

Taroko National Park has the best system of hiking trails in the country. There are almost 40 in total, all well marked, with the trailheads for numerous easy-grade trails right beside the highway in the gorge. Many of the routes are in fact the traditional paths that connected the remote and almost inaccessible Taroko settlements scattered around the gorge and the tight canyons of the Liwu He's tributaries, and a number from the gorge lead to undisturbed Taroko hamlets. The park clearly grades each trail as Scenic, Hiking, Mountaineering, or Challenging, and gives distances. Trails in the latter two categories require permits. Detailed information and advice on the trails can be obtained from the park's visitor center, and the national park website (www.taroko.gov.tw) has descriptions and reports on trail conditions.

TAITUNG

The area around Taitung city offers a soothing mix of indigenous culture, invigorating hot springs, unspoiled forests, and harmonious temples.

Because of the east coast's slower pace of economic development, the tribespeople in this region have managed to retain some of their traditional habits and customs, a solid sense of historical and cultural continuity, and a strong sense of community and solidarity. The region's weather is far less predictable, seas are rougher, hot springs are hotter, mountains higher, butterflies bigger, and the people more robust than in the tamer regions of Taiwan. Travelers here are welcomed with hospitality – and curiosity.

Reached from Hualien by both Shengdao 9 (Provincial Highway No. 9) and Shengdao 11, the sleepy seaside city of **Taitung** ⓫ is pleasant and airy. At about the same latitude as Kaohsiung on the opposite coast, Taitung is the economic hub for the lower portion of the east coast.

The city is not much of a traveler's destination in itself, but is a convenient springboard for excursions to nearby places such as Zhiben Wenquan (Zhiben Hot Springs), Ludao (Green Island), Lanyu (Orchid Island), Huadong Zonggu Guojia Fengjingqu (East Rift Valley National Scenic Area), and the Dongbuhaian Guojia Fengjingqu (East Coast National Scenic Area; www.eastcoast-nsa.gov.tw), whose south entrance lies just north along Shengdao 11. Taitung can be reached directly

by air from Taipei and Kaohsiung. There are also regular train and bus services from Kaohsiung and Hualien.

Smiling gods and native culture

Carp Hill (Liyushan), in the west section, with its **Dragon and Phoenix Temple** (Longfeng Fotang; daily 7am–10pm; free) provides fine views of city and sea. The temple, tucked into the hill's east side, has some interesting icons and a small collection of 3,000- to 5,000-year-old archeological

Main Attractions
National Museum of Prehistory
Beinan Cultural Park
Zhiben Hot Springs
Clear Awakening Temple
Zhiben National Forest Recreation Area
Guanshan/Chishang

Local fruit produce at a market near Taitung.

artifacts unearthed in the area. These stone implements include coffin slabs and hand tools, proving that people lived on Taiwan long before the dawn of written history.

On Zhonghua Road near Renai Road stands a modest Mazu temple, **Palace of the Empress of Heaven** (Tianhou Gong; daily 7am–9pm; free), with an ornately enameled and gilded facade. The Sanxingshen (Three Star Gods) of Longevity, Prosperity, and Posterity smile down from the central roof beam.

There is good seafood in the eateries along Zhengqi Road, and traditional Taiwanese snack foods can be purchased along Zhonghua Road.

On the city's outskirts, at 1 Bowuguan (Museum) Road, is one of Taitung's finest treasures, the **National Museum of Prehistory** ⑯ (Guoli Taiwan Shiqian Wenhua Bowuguan; www.nmp.gov.tw; Tue–Sun 9am–5pm). It is dedicated to increasing understanding of the island's original peoples. There are high-quality displays on both Taiwan's prehistoric cultures and present-day indigenous peoples.

Three highlights are a full-scale eight-man oceangoing canoe created by the Dao on Orchid Island for the museum, exquisite Beinan Culture jadeware unearthed in local burial sites that defined social status, and a mock-up of a dig that you descend into. There is also a regular schedule of indigenous cultural performances.

The museum is also in charge of Taitung's **Beinan Cultural Park** (Beinan Wenhua Gongyuan; Tue–Sun 9am–5pm; free), location of one of Taiwan's richest archeological finds in Taiwan, located behind the train station. There is a small museum here with an open dig site, replicas of native structures, and a hillside viewing deck.

South from Taitung

Tucked against the mountainside at the mouth of a rugged canyon, along the rocky Zhiben River, is **Zhiben Hot Springs** ⑰ (Zhiben Wenquan), one of Taiwan's oldest and most remote hot-spring resorts. Dubbed 'Zhiben' (Source of Wisdom) by the Japanese, it was developed as a resort around the beginning of the 20th century. It was,

Zhiben Hot Springs.

in fact, the Japanese who brought a love of hot-spring soaking to the Taiwanese during their 50-year uninvited stay (1895–1945) as colonial masters on the island.

The village of **Zhiben** lies on the coast 12km (7 miles) south of Taitung. The hot-springs area is another 2km (1.2 miles) inland; almost all hotels and inns are either directly beside the river's south bank or up on the hills behind. This is almost as far away as one can get from big, bustling Taipei – in spirit and in distance – and yet still be in Taiwan.

Zhiben Xiagu (Zhiben Valley), which cuts into the steep mountains beyond the first spa district, is reminiscent of the lovely wild gorges hidden deep within the remote mountain ranges of western China's Sichuan province, and is well worth exploring. Here are thick forests and clear streams, steep cliffs and waterfalls, bamboo groves and fruit orchards, robust mountain-dwellers, and exotic flora and fauna.

The resort area can be divided into three primary districts. The first district is the first reached from Taitung – a concentration primarily of older hotels, with a cluster of newer facilities, where mineral waters are piped in from the hills. The second district, inside the mouth of the valley, is home to newer hotels and downscale retail outlets. It sits directly across the Zhiben River from Zhiben National Forest Recreation Area (Zhiben Senlin Youlequ; see page 291), which is the third district. The retail establishments in the second district have sprung up, in large part, in direct response to the popularity of the forest park.

The hot-pool regimen

The Zhiben mineral water is said to be good for therapeutic bathing. Six soaks of 15 to 20 minutes each over a period of two days are said to alleviate the following ailments: skin irritations and festering sores, rheumatic inflammations, arthritis, lower spine and sciatic pain, weak limbs, poor circulation, and sluggish digestion. Non-believers

are urged to try the following regimen: soak in a hot pool for at least 15 minutes, then slide into a cool pool and swim slowly around the rim, using breaststroke or sidestroke. Freestyle swimming is too splashy here; the idea is to reach long and stretch the muscles slowly, rather than pump them full of adrenaline. Most local resort hotels also have hydrotherapy facilities; stand beneath water-jet massage spray and feel a thousand leathery palms pound your back, guaranteed to iron out the kinks from the most tightly knotted necks and to loosen the stiffest shoulders. Then drift back to the different-temperature hot pools for another soaking session, repeating the process at least twice. It makes a new person out of the weariest wayfarer.

Zhiben Valley

Zhiben Xiagu is worth a thorough exploration by foot. A few hundred meters beyond the first section of the resort village, a sign points left towards **White Jade Waterfall** (Baiyu Pubu), which lies about a kilometer up a winding paved path that echoes loudly

TIP

Zhiben's Clear Awakening Temple, located high up above the river, offers lovely waterway and forest views, notably at sunrise and sunset. A sign posted at the door asks visitors to first remove their shoes and hats before walking across the carpet for a closer look at the lovely icons at the altar.

Sleeping capsules at Zhiben Hot Springs resort.

with the chorus calls of birds and insects. The waters of the unhurried, timeless falls tumble down a jumble of strewn boulders, dense growths of fern, bamboo, and gnarled roots. Another popular Zhiben Xiagu draw is **Clear Awakening Temple** (Qingjuesi; daily 7am–9pm; free), located up a steep hill off the main road about a kilometer from the lower hot-spring area. The narrow road to the temple begins just before the second resort district (look for the red arch), moving south from the river.

A brace of big elephants in white plaster stand at the foot of the steps to the elegant shrine hall. While Daoist temples display the dragon and tiger; the elephant is strictly a Buddhist motif. Inside the hall are two of the most exquisite, tranquil and beautifully crafted Buddha images in all of Taiwan. The two statues sit together, one behind the other, gazing in meditative serenity through half-closed eyes, exuding feelings of sublime harmony, if such a thing were possible. The bronze Buddha, 3 meters (10ft) tall and weighing 1 metric ton (1.1 ton), was made in Thailand and occupies the rear of the shrine. The priceless jade Buddha, 2.5 meters (8ft) tall and weighing more than 4.5 metric tons (5 tons), is seated in the meditative lotus position in the foreground. This Buddha image was a gift from Buddhists in Burma (Myanmar), and while some say it is made of solid white jade, seeing is believing. It is, nevertheless, a movingly impressive piece of religious art.

To the left of the altar is a small, solid-gold, jewel-encrusted pagoda encased in glass. This houses two of the mysterious relics of the Buddha known as *silizi*, tiny nuggets said to have been extracted from the Buddha's ashes after his cremation over 2,500 years ago. A series of graphic color prints from India are arranged along the upper walls. Captioned in Sanskrit, these illustrate milestone events in the life of the Enlightened One.

On the ground floor is a study hall and lecture room, where the monastic community meets to study the sutras. Next to the shrine hall is a dormitory, with communal and private rooms for

Famed anthropologist Dr Jane Goodall with Taitung aboriginal children.

visitors who wish to stay a night or two, and a dining room that serves good vegetarian cuisine. Banyan trees and lush green mountains surround the monastery, and silence – despite the large and spirited resort-hotel neighbor to the left – still manages to reign supreme.

Zhiben National Forest Recreation Area

Just across the river from the second spa district is the **Zhiben National Forest Recreation Area** ⓲ (Zhiben Guojia Senlin Youlequ; http://recreation. forest.gov.tw; daily 7am–5pm, July–Sept until 6pm; free). The main entrance, across a bridge, is a 10-minute walk up the road; the suspension bridge here is meant to serve as an exit only. The suspension bridge provides quite a thrill, swaying freely when walked across. The forest recreation area is a wooded world of walking trails, greenhouses, streams and waterfalls, and ancient 'holy' trees. Thankfully, it still has comparatively few visitors, especially on weekdays: most come here to soak the days away in the hot springs, and to party the nights away in the karaokes and nightclubs.

There is also a picnic area, a designated bonfire area, and a well-marked hiking trail that is a joy to walk – you'll have a better than even chance of finding yourself completely on your own. The trail circuit takes about three hours to complete.

Perhaps no stretch of major road in Taiwan is as untrammeled as Shengdao 24, which cuts inland and westward from Zhiben to cross the mountains toward Kaohsiung. Note that the road beyond Zhiben to the aboriginal village of Wutai is narrow and often one lane only, with traffic strictly controlled due to rockfalls and other nature-induced disruptions. There is also the train, but this spends a lot of its time in tunnels.

Northwest from Taitung

With the establishment of the East Rift Valley National Scenic Area (www. erv-nsa.gov.tw; 8.30am–5.30pm), systematic development of tourism facilities has come to the bucolic, farm-carpeted region in the past decade-plus. Near the city of Taitung, **Luye** is the site of a tourist tea-plantation district in which tribespeople own most of the farms. There are numerous teahouses on the high-hill plantations, offering fine views over mountains and into the valley. The Luye Plateau, with views direct down into the valley, has a visitor center, teahouse, gift shop, and paragliding base with trained instructors. Further north, the quiet valley-base farming villages of **Guanshan** and **Chishang** have long and pleasant loop bikeways that take you through golden rice paddies, past old farmhouses, granaries, aqueducts, irrigation channels, fish ladders, tube-filling water wheels, and other facilities, and by cold streams rushing out of the hills. Each has many bike-rental outlets. Chishang is also home to the Taitung Hakka Cultural Park (Taidong Xian Kejia Wenhua Yuanqu; http://thcphakka.com.tw; Tue–Sun 8.30–11.30am, 2–5pm; free).

TIP

Adventurous types should try a soak in the Zhiben River's sandy bed instead of in the pools of the Zhiben hot-spring resort's spas. Dig a hole, let it fill with the hot mineral water that bubbles up, and slide in. The area's native people have been coming down from the hills for centuries to do just that in winter.

A field of rape in Taitung Valley.

LUDAO AND LANYU

Off the southeast coast of Taiwan are two small islands: the first is worth visiting for its stunning natural scenery, and the second for its unyieldingly traditional way of life.

Enjoying Ludao's hot springs.

For the traveler with a taste for offbeat destinations, two islands easily reached from Taitung offer worlds far removed from the mainstream of Taiwan society. Within sight of Taitung, about 30km (18 miles) due east, is **Ludao** (Green Island). Originally known as Huoshaodao (Fire-burning Island) – beacons once burned there to prevent fishing vessels from being wrecked on its coral shoals, and to help local boats find their way home – its new name was bestowed in 1949. The island was formed long ago by an enormous volcanic explosion, which pushed up the central peak. A tiny speck in a huge rolling sea, at 16 sq km (6 sq miles), Ludao has been developed for tourism over the past decade or so; during the martial-law era a holiday here likely meant sitting out a long prison sentence at poorly run government-owned lodgings. Said lodgings are now part of the **Human Rights Memorial Park** (visitor center and prison daily 8.30am–5.30pm; free).

Green Island

Ludao's human history began in 1804, when a group of fishermen from Xiao Liuqiu (Little Liuqiu), an island off the southwest coast of Taiwan, was blown off course. Liking the place where they had been washed up, one man persuaded his family and friends to move to the then uninhabited island a year after they had returned to their homes. Today, there are about 1,900 permanent residents.

The waters and reefs around Ludao are excellent for swimming, snorkeling, scuba diving, fishing, and shell collecting. Glass-bottom, semi-submersible, and submersible craft out of **Nanliao Fishing Harbor ❶** (Nanliao Yugang), on the northwest coast, offer otherworldly views of reefs – home to over 200 species of coral and more than 300 varieties of multicolored fish. Trails lead into the hills for hikers, and a paved 17km (11-mile) road circles the island's rim.

In the north, about half way to the east side, is **Gongguan Village ❷** (Gongguan), a lovely fishing village anchoring a timeless natural setting that looks as though it might be part of a movie-set tableau. Though the village cannot be recommended for its lively nightlife – there are no karaokes or nightclubs on the island – a leisurely saunter around the colorful pastel homes will cause an afternoon to float by pleasantly.

At the northeast corner of Ludao, just past Gongguan, is **Guanyin Cave ❸** (Guanyindong). According to legend, in the later 1800s an old fisherman lost his way at sea in a terrible storm. A fireball suddenly appeared in the sky and guided him safely back to shore, where he found safe haven in this underground cave, formed from eroded coral. Within it he saw a stone that resembled Guanyin, the Goddess of Mercy. Taking this as a divine sign, he prostrated himself before the stone and gave thanks for his safe return. Ever since, the cave has been sacred to the island's inhabitants, who have constructed a miniature temple inside. Visitors must first descend a tree-lined trail to the entrance. The goddess is represented by a stalagmite – possibly the very 'stone' the fisherman saw – adorned with a red cape.

Saltwater spring

Perhaps the island's main attraction is a natural phenomenon seen almost nowhere else on earth – a saltwater hot spring. **Zhaori Hot Springs ❹** (Zhaori Wenquan; pools daily 6am–10pm, trails daily 9am–4pm) is located very near the island's southeast tip. 'Zhaori' means 'facing the sun' – lucky soakers can watch the sun rise over the Pacific. The spot is also called Xu Wenquan (Rising Sun Hot Springs).

Seawater washes gently into three large, circular pools at high tide. The pools are thermal springs, and the cooler seawater acts to control the temperature, making the spot just right for soaking. As the saltwater permeates down into the earth it is heated and pressurized, then gushes back out to make soothing, bubbling mini-geysers. Only two other saltwater hot springs are known – on Japan's Kyushu and in Italy near Mt Vesuvius. On quiet

Lu Tao Lighthouse near the airport.

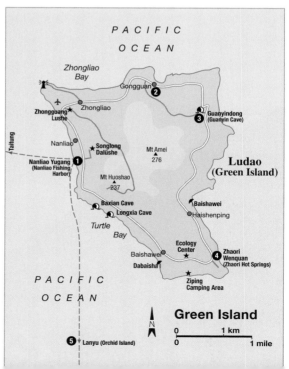

Green Island

TIP

The Dao people of Lanyu, whose traditional culture is the most intact among Taiwan's 16 recognized tribal peoples, have long been treated by visitors almost as if they are zoo exhibits on display. Some refuse to be photographed, and some demand fees if photographed. Cultural sensitivity will help avoid misunderstandings; always ask before taking pictures of people..

Lanyu's shoreline.

Ludao, there is no better fun than to head over to Zhaori Wenquan on a warm, breezy evening, slip into a steamy, slightly frothy pool, and watch the day fade slowly away. The Taiwan Tourism Bureau has built facilities around the open-air pools, and created a 'spa' pool behind the beach.

Ludao is accessible by air or sea, with regular flights, taking about 15 minutes from Taitung. Four boat companies service the island from Taitung. Visitors wishing to stay overnight on Ludao can choose from about 15 comfortable hotels, hostels, and homestays; Ziping Camping Area, near the hot springs, can accommodate 1,000 people. A tour-bus service takes visitors to ten scenic sites (Apr–Sept; NT$100, tickets valid one day, hop on/off service), with departures at one-hour intervals. Scooter rentals are also popular, available by the Nanliao visitor center, itself across from the airport.

Lanyu

Lanyu ❺ (Orchid Island) is the most unlikely jewel in the waters surrounding Taiwan. An island of steep mountains soaring high above valleys and rocky, rugged shores, this emerald isle covers an area of 45 sq km (17 sq miles). It is 60km (37 miles) east of Taiwan's southern tip, 80km (50 miles) southeast of Taitung and is home to more than 2,900 Dao (also called Yami).

With colorful costumes and a strongly matriarchal society, the Dao are often regarded as the northernmost extent of Polynesian ancestry. These people live simply from the fruits of the sea, supplementing their daily catch with taro, sweet potatoes, yams, millet, paddy rice grown using Chinese techniques, and a few fruits. Goats and pigs are also raised, with many wandering the roads.

Current government plans are to make part of Lanyu a national park. The master plan is now on hold, because, although the concentration of financial and planning resources is sure to be a boon to the island's economy, which has fallen far behind the Taiwan mainland, the Dao have put up fierce opposition. They are well aware that a surge of tourists is likely to spell the end of their culture, and want a

greater say in determining their future.

The government has constructed typhoon-proof concrete housing blocks on Lanyu island, but some of the Dao people still prefer to live in their traditional homes, adapted by centuries of use to their indigenous environment. Indigenous Dao houses are built partly below ground, with only the roof showing up against hillsides or embankments as protection from the fierce typhoons that often rip across the island. These dwellings provide rooms for weaving, ceramics-making, storage, and other practical functions, as well as for eating and sleeping. Breezy open pavilions are built on stilts outside the main house for use on sultry summer days.

The relatively pristine condition of Dao culture is a result of Japanese non-interference in the first half of the 20th century. During their occupation of Taiwan, the Japanese isolated the island as a living anthropological museum. Modern appliances were not permitted, and the ancient culture was preserved as much as possible in its original form. Since that time, however, the combination of Chinese business acumen and Christian missionary zeal has had a profound impact on the Dao. The building of a nuclear-waste disposal site on the island, foisted on the Dao under suspect circumstances, still engenders conflict today, making the islanders ever suspicious of the motivations of mainlanders.

The grand tour

The entire island can be driven around, following the 50km (31-mile) paved road, in a little over two hours. Hotels can arrange mini-bus tours, scooters can be rented, or taxis can be hired. Six villages dot the island; the traditional dwellings can now only be seen in two, on the east coast. The coastal rock formations, eroded by weather and water, are particularly impressive, with rocks shaped like lions, dragons, and turtles. One thing missing, given the island's name, are wild butterfly orchids. Almost all the plants have been dug up and sold. There are adequate accommodations and meals at a number of hotels on the island, regular flights from Taitung (about 25 minutes), and a ferry service.

Traditional Dao canoe – the pride of every Dao man who crafts it by hand and without the aid of any nails.

TRADITIONAL DAO CULTURE

The best time to visit Lanyu is in spring, a festive season when new boats are launched with much fanfare, and the favorite delicacy of the Dao – flying fish – literally leaps into their boats.

Every Dao man dreams of building at least one sacred boat in his life. The ingeniously constructed canoes are the pride of each household that can afford to make one (and a vital economic tool). Adorned with intricate decorations, they are made with traditional tools, constructed of 27 pieces of wood cut from living trees, and held together with pegs.

During the spring Feiyu Jie (Flying Fish Festival), the launch of a new boat, and a few other occasions, Dao men wear traditional loincloths and sport traditional 'armor' during ceremonies. Some still insist on wearing loincloths year-round; the armor is now merely ceremonial, consisting of a rattan vest, helmet, and perhaps a spear.

Beyond his boat, the helmet is the most prized possession of a proud Dao man, and is brought out of storage on only the most special of occasions. Conical in shape, and made of silver, it covers the head completely, with small slits left for the eyes. To make one, strips of silver are pounded from coins (previously metal from shipwrecks and raids was used, as the Dao do not smelt metal).

領角鴞穿越
OWL CROSSING

TRAVEL TIPS
TAIWAN

TRANSPORTATION

GETTING THERE AND GETTING AROUND

GETTING THERE

By air

Taiwan lies along one of the busiest air routes in Asia, and stopovers on the island may be included on any round-the-world or regional air ticket at no extra cost. Many international airlines currently provide regular air service to Taiwan. It is a good idea to make flight reservations as early as possible; this is especially true when trying to get off the island, particularly after the week-long Chinese New Year holiday period in January or February.

International airports

Most of the international air traffic to and from Taiwan goes through **Taiwan Taoyuan International Airport** (www.taoyuan-airport.com), which is in Taoyuan, a 45-minute drive from downtown Taipei.
Tourist Service Center:
Terminal 1, tel: (03) 398-2194;
Terminal 2, tel: (03) 398-3341; admin.

taiwan.net.tw/tsc.
In the south of Taiwan is **Kaohsiung International Airport**. Regular air services connect this city to numerous Asian destinations.
Tourist Service Center:
Tel: (07) 805-7888; http://khh.taiwan.net.tw.

Airport tax

Each outbound passenger must pay an airport departure tax of NT$500. This is generally included in the ticket price.

From the US

Cathay Pacific
Tel: +800 2747 3333 (toll free)
www.cathaypacific.com
China Airlines
Tel: (02) 412-9000
www.china-airlines.com
Delta Airlines
Tel: 080-665-1982
www.delta.com
EVA Airways
Tel: (02) 2501-1999
www.evaair.com

United Airlines
Tel: (02) 2325-8868
www.united.com

From Europe

KLM Royal Dutch Airlines
Tel: (02) 2711-4055
www.klm.com
Lufthansa
Tel: (02) 2325-8861
www.lufthansa.com
Singapore Airlines
Tel: (02) 2551-6655
www.singaporeair.com

GETTING AROUND

By air

Mandarin Airlines (subsidiary of China Airlines), **UNI Air** (subsidiary of EVA Airways) and two others provide scheduled domestic flights in Taiwan. Note that flights have been discontinued between urban centers on the main island's west side (Taipei, Taichung, Chiayi, Tainan, Kaohsiung, Pingtung, Hengchun), in light of competition from the High Speed Rail service.

Prices are low: for example, it costs just over NT$2,200 to fly from Taipei to Taitung (one-way). The airlines tend to have the same pricing schemes, similar schedules, and similar quality of service. To buy tickets, it is normal to show up at the domestic airline counters and simply book the first flight out (except during three-day weekends and the Chinese New Year season).

Strict security measures are enforced on all domestic flights within Taiwan, and all foreign passengers need to show their passports or ARCS (Alien Resident Certificates) prior to boarding domestic flights.

A high-speed train.

For further information on flight timetables, contact numbers, etc., visit www.caa.gov.tw/en.

Domestic Airline Offices

Taipei
Far Eastern Air Transport, 5, Alley 123, Lane 405,
Dunhua N. Road
Tel: (02) 2712 1555
Mandarin Airlines
3, Alley 123, Lane 405, Dunhua N. Road
Tel: (02) 2717 1230
UNI Airways
8 F., No. 117, Sec. 2, Changan E. Road
Tel: (02) 2508 6999

Kaohsiung

Far Eastern Air Transport
Zhongshan 2nd Road
Tel: (07) 805 7069
Mandarin Airlines
9F-2, 380 Minquan 2nd Road
Tel: (07) 802-6868
UNI Airways
2-6 Zhongshan 4th Road
Tel: (07) 791-1000

To and from airports

Taipei

Taiwan Taoyuan International Airport (www.taoyuanairport.gov.tw) is about 45km (28 miles) southwest of Taipei. The traveling time to and from downtown is 45 to 60 minutes. Major hotels offer shuttle bus services. Five major bus companies provide a frequent service as well between the airport and designated downtown spots, including major hotels: Kuo-Kuang, CitiAir, West Bus, Evergreen, and Free Go. Buses run from about 5am to midnight. The one-way fare for adults is NT$125 (Kuo-Kuang) to NT$150 (Evergreen). If you need assistance on arrival, proceed to the terminal's information center.

Beyond Taipei, bus service is also provided from the airport to Taoyuan, Banqiao, Xindian, Zhongli, Taichung, and Changhua.

There is a limo service (the cars are Mercedes and Volvos) from the international airport; the service counters can be found near the hotel service counters. A taxi from the airport to downtown Taipei will cost around NT$1,200 at current prices – the meter reading plus a 15 percent surcharge (the single NT$40 toll between the airport and Taipei not included). For the trip from Taipei to Taiwan Taoyuan International Airport the fare is supposed to be what is displayed on the meter, but few drivers will agree to the trip for a fixed fee of less than NT$1,100.

Taoyuan International Airport MRT (blue line), linking the airport with the city, opened in 2017 after many delays. It is currently the fastest way to get to the city, taking passengers from the airport downtown in 35 minutes.

Taipei Songshan Airport (www.tsa. gov.tw) is right in the city: from the bus terminal here you are only 10 to 20 minutes (depending on traffic) by cab (about NT$200) from most major downtown hotels. The bus fare to and from Taiwan Taoyuan International Airport is NT$83 (local) and NT$125 (express), both routes operate by Kuo-Kuang.

Kaohsiung

The easiest and best transport is a taxi to the downtown hotels. **Kaohsiung International Airport** (www.kia.gov. tw) is located close to the city center, on the south side. The taxi fare should be about NT$300. The city's mass rapid transit system also has services to and from the airport. Most major hotels are close to a station, though a short taxi ride station-to-hotel will still be necessary in most cases.

Taichung

Taichung's Taichung Airport (www.tca. gov.tw), at present, only operates a limited number of scheduled flights to regional destinations (China, Hong Kong, Ho Chi Minh City), along with regional charters, plus regular domestic flights. The taxi fare to downtown Taichung is about NT$180. There are three regular city bus-route services, with fares according to distance.

By long-distance bus

Fleets of private-company deluxe express buses serve Taiwan's major towns and cities. There are frequent scheduled buses to all major destinations except those on the east coast, which enjoy less frequent service and rely more on trains. By departure time, almost all buses are fully booked, especially on weekends and holidays.

The best way to purchase reserved-seat bus tickets in advance is to go directly to the appropriate bus station and buy them one or two days prior to departure. Most hotel travel desks and local travel agencies can make arrangements. Most major bus stations are located by a city's major railway station.

By train

The Taiwan Railway Administration (TRA; www.railway.gov.tw) maintains an extensive network that runs around the island and connects all major cities and towns. The trains are often full, and if you do not like to stand, a seat reservation is necessary. There is an almost unbelievable crush on long weekends and holidays, as much of the population of the north drains into the center and south to visit families. Without a travel agent, getting a seat reservation on the train can be complicated and time consuming for the uninitiated. These problems have been eased slightly with the Taiwan High Speed Rail (THSR; www.thsrc. com.tw) connecting the north and south of Taiwan along the west coast, which is operated as a separate system, not by the TRA.

The TRA offers different types of service:
Putong (Ordinary) – slowest, most basic, and very cheap; many with no air-conditioning
Local Train – short- to medium-distance commuter train; cheap, slow, no reserved seats or air-conditioning
Juguang Express – assigned seating, air-conditioned (second-fastest)
Ziqiang Express – assigned seating, air-conditioned (fastest)

Reservations for express trains in Taiwan can be made up to seven days before your travel date; tickets can be collected up to three days in advance – have your passport with you. Although you may purchase round-trip tickets in advance, the booking for the return trip must be confirmed upon arrival at your destination. It is highly advisable to purchase tickets at least several hours in advance, and preferably a full day prior to departure. In all cities and towns, advance train tickets may be purchased directly at the main railway station by lining up at the appropriate counter. Most hotels and travel agencies can arrange advance train reservations.

If you are planning to travel around Taiwan by train, go to counter No. 1 at **the Taipei Railway Station** West Service Desk (Service Hotline 0800-765-888). Show them your itinerary. The staff will provide a quote for the total fare, which will be quite cheap compared with buying tickets individually. Tickets must be purchased three days before departure. For details, call (02) 2371-3558 (English spoken).

By car

It's best to rely on public transport such as the subways (Taipei and Kaohsiung), buses, taxis, and tour buses to get around Taiwan cities and towns. Trying to drive yourself around a congested city is a needless risk. However, if you plan an extended tour through the countryside, renting a car is a good way to go, as you'll see many more sights and enjoy the freedom to stop whenever and wherever you wish.

Car-rental agencies that place ads in the English-language dailies are reputable and have representatives who speak English. You can also call an Avis, Budget, or Hertz reservation center before your trip to Taiwan, which have associations with local companies.

If you would like to splurge a bit and see the island in true comfort and convenience, the best way is to hire an air-conditioned limousine, driven by a chauffeur who also acts as a personal guide and interpreter. Any hotel travel desk or local travel agency can arrange this. The cost varies according to the type of car and, of course, the length of the trip.

Motoring tips

No matter how well you drive, Taiwan traffic demands considerable attention. There is often great congestion, and though most drivers nowadays obey the rules of the road, there are still too many who do not, taking startlingly illogical risks and making constant vigilance necessary. The roads themselves are well maintained, however, and give relatively easy access to all of Taiwan's major sights.

Following are some helpful points worth bearing in mind:

There are millions of motor scooters on the roads, and they constitute the single greatest hazard to car drivers.

Also steer clear of all military vehicles. Military drivers are notorious for their careless and/or aggressive

Taipei bus signage.

driving. Regardless of the law, drivers of military vehicles almost always claim the right of way. This same rule applies to buses, gravel trucks, and all other oversized vehicles. The 'system' used is the larger the vehicle, the more 'rights' are assumed; pedestrians are at the bottom of the ladder, though most drivers now give way at pedestrian crossings, too many grudgingly.

Major roads have clear English signage, but local roads, especially in rural areas, may have Chinese-only signage. It is best to look both at route numbers and the English place names, and match them with those on your maps. Route numbers are also inscribed on the stone mileage indicators set along the roadsides.

Taiwan's 'freeways' are in fact tolled. Lanes at toll stations are marked in Chinese and English (for cars with toll tickets, cars paying cash/buying toll tickets, trucks, etc.), with lane violations strictly punished with hefty fines. If renting a car, ask the agency for a familiarization drive before setting out. You can buy sets of toll vouchers at the toll stations (have your money ready), which brings a 20 percent discount.

Keep your gas tank at least a third full at all times. In the more remote mountainous and coastal regions, gas (fuel) stations are rare.

Rules of the road

Seat belts are mandatory on all roads for drivers and all passengers; all fines will be given to the driver or owner of the vehicle.

Safety seats are obligatory for children four years and under, or under 18kg (39.5lbs); they are also obligatory for back-seat passengers aged 4 to 12 or weighing 18 to 36kg (39.5 to 79.5lbs).

There is no right turn on a red light. Motorcycle/scooter riders must wear a helmet; drivers cannot turn left at an intersection, but must instead proceed to the waiting section on the right hand of the intersection for the road they wish to travel on.

Speed limits on freeways and provincial highways are generally 90 or 100kmh (60 or 62mph).

Yield signs are frequently ignored; the rule-of-thumb is whoever gets the nose of his vehicle in a space first owns that space.

Signal lights are often not used, so beware.

Parking

Double-parking is permitted if emergency flashers are on and the

engine is left running; most local drivers forget about the flashers and engine parts of this law. Sidewalk curbs have been painted different colors in Taipei. If red, no parking is allowed, day or night. If yellow, parking is only allowed for five minutes during the day (though the time limit is frequently ignored). If left unpainted or a white line, parking is permitted any time.

Taipei city transport

Taxis

Taxi fares are calculated according to meter. If you wish to retain a taxi for a full day, or for a long, round-trip excursion, ask a hotel concierge to negotiate either a set fee or a discount on the meter fare.

Taiwan taxi meters calculate both time and distance to determine the fare. The meters have three windows. The top-left window shows the time consumed, when not moving, in minutes and seconds. The top-right indicator is the distance in kilometers. The largest window meter shows the fare in NT dollars. The rate in Taipei (closely followed elsewhere) is NT$70 for the first 1.25km (0.75 mile), an additional NT$5 for each 250 meters/yds, and NT$5 for each 100 seconds the taxi is moving under 5kmh (3mph). From 11pm to 6am there is an NT$20 surcharge, calculated from time of boarding, and from two days before Chinese New Year Eve until the end of the holidays nighttime fares plus an NT$20 gratuity is charged. Give an NT$10 tip for cabs dispatched by phone, and for luggage placed in the trunk (boot).

Small towns and villages have fixed rates for the use of a taxi within a certain area, generally ranging

Evening rush hour in Taipei.

from NT$50 to NT$70. It is best to ask locals for the correct rate; even Taiwanese travelers have to do this to avoid being overcharged.

Note: Although Taiwan's taxi drivers are almost uniformly friendly and polite, too many tend to drive recklessly. Especially outside Taipei, tourists are sometimes scared out of their wits as their taxi drivers weave carelessly between speeding buses and trucks, narrowly miss pedestrians, run through red lights, careen through swarms of buzzing motorcycles, and screech blindly around corners.

Very few taxi drivers in Taiwan speak or read English sufficiently well to follow directions given in English. Have your destination written out in Chinese before venturing out by cab. Hotel name cards, local advertisements, even restaurant matchboxes will prove useful in getting you around town by taxi.

Mass Rapid Transit

The construction of Taipei's Mass Rapid Transit (MRT) system, also called the Taipei Metro, began in 1988. Seven lines are now operational, making

travel to most areas of the city fast and convenient. In any station, you can buy individual tokens or buy a day pass for NT$150 (includes NT$50 deposit). The latter allows you to use the system as you please for that one day. You may transfer to different lines, and there are also same-day transfers that can be used on the city bus routes. There are also 24-, 48- and 72-hour passes (NT$180, 280 and 380), convenient if you are planning to stay in Taipei for a few days. The system runs from 6am to midnight.

There are charts with clear English on the ticket machines. Check the amount indicated for the station you want to go to (your own station is marked in yellow, others in white). Fares range from NT$20 to NT$65, depending on distance. The Taipei Metro Service Hotline number is (02) 2181-2345 (24 hours).

Bicycles are permitted on the end carriages of trains on weekends and holidays at NT$80 per trip (no access during 4 to 7pm heavy travel period). Access to the stations when with a bike is via the street-level elevators at each station designed for use by

the disabled. Access is permitted at a steadily increasing number of stations; designated stations are clearly marked on boards within the system, as well as online (www.metro.taipei).

The Kaohsiung metro system became operational in 2008, with two lines running through the city north-south and east-west. The north-south line connects Kaohsiung's international airport, main train station, and its high-speed rail station with downtown. For more info, go to www.krtco.com.tw. The Kaohsiung version of Taipei's EasyCard (see box) is the I-Pass Card.

City buses

For budget travelers in Taipei, buses provide a frequent and inexpensive means of transport to points within or outside the city limits. Bus service in other cities is poor.

It is advisable to avoid the buses in Taipei during the 7.30 to 9.30am and 5 to 7pm rush hours. All buses are air-conditioned. The fare is NT$15 (adults) for each leg of a route (some long routes are broken up into separate legs; most journeys that do not cross into suburban areas involve just one leg). Fares can be paid in cash by dropping correct change in a box beside the driver; no change is given if too much is paid. Most locals nowadays use the EasyCard (see box), swiping the card against a digital sensor pad beside the driver.

City bus services run continuously from about 6am until 11.30pm. To tell the driver to stop at the next stop, push one of the large colored buttons mounted on the sides. There are so many buses and bus routes within metropolitan Taipei that it is best to ask a hotel clerk or local acquaintance for directions before venturing out. All buses are designated by code numbers, which indicate their routes; starting and ending points are written in Chinese at either side of the number. Most buses now also have start and end points written in English. More information on the bus system, including downloadable maps, can be found at www.taipeibus.taipei.gov.tw.

Taipei Pass

The Taipei Pass (available at Taipei Metro station info counters) allows unlimited use of the metro system as well as Taipei/New Taipei City buses. There is a one-day pass (NT$180), two-day pass (NT$310), three-day pass (NT$440), and five-day pass (NT$700), plus a special one-day pass that also gives you three rides on the Maokong Gondola (NT$350). Visit www.easycard.com.tw.

Taiwan Tourist Shuttle Service

The Taiwan Tourist Shuttle service was launched by the Taiwan Tourism Bureau, (in cooperation with local governments) to provide independent travelers with a convenient, inexpensive, eco-friendly mode of travel to visit key tourist attractions outside major cities. There are currently over 20 coach routes, all launched from High Speed Rail and regular railway stations. All buses are standardized and of high quality, and there are departures every half hour on weekends (9am–4pm) and every

hour on weekdays (9am–5pm). Day passes are around NT$400, and riders can get on and off buses as often as desired at designated stops along a route. You can also buy a one-way ticket. Special packages are also available on many routes; for example, the Sun Moon Lake package brings steep discounts on the Sun Moon Lake Ropeway, Shuili Snake Kiln, and other area attractions.

For more information, visit the Tourism Bureau's www.taiwantrip.com.tw website.

A – Z

A HANDY SUMMARY
OF PRACTICAL INFORMATION

A

Accommodations

Hotels

Luxury hotels in Taiwan are renowned for their attentive, gracious service rendered with a spirit of pride and a genuine desire to please. Visitors are treated as personal guests rather than anonymous patrons, and hospitality is approached more as an art than as an industry.

However, Western travelers will occasionally encounter frustrations. One reason is the language barrier. Although trained in English, many local hotel staff understand little, and may avoid losing face by pretending to understand.

Another reason is cultural: Taiwanese priorities often differ from Westerners', and what seems of vital importance to you, such as punctuality, may seem trivial to the locals.

Tourist hotels in Taiwan are generally ranked into two categories: International Tourist and Regular Tourist hotels. The former will offer greater luxury and more varied facilities, while the latter provide more basic accommodations. Ranked below these are budget hotels, homestays, and guesthouses/hostels.

Hotels in Taipei are quite expensive. Singles or twin rooms will cost, in international tourist hotels, anything between NT$6,500 and $10,000. In Kaohsiung, the cost per room drops to between NT$4,500 and $6,500. Other quality places with some business, recreational, and dining facilities are considerably cheaper and you can expect to pay between NT$2,500 and $4,000 per

Temples are free to visit.

night. Taiwan's hotels accept all major credit cards.

Almost all International Tourist and Regular Tourist hotels offer significant room-rate reductions and other deals by booking via their websites. Room rates are reduced even further if an online reservation service is used:

Hotel chains

The country's two largest chains are Howard Hotels (tel: 0800-011-068; www.howard-hotels.com.tw) and Chinatrust Hotels (tel: 02-2998-6788; www.chinatrusthotel.com). These are not cookie-cutter chains – each high-quality facility has its own distinctive look and personality.

Homestays

Almost unheard of two decades ago, there has been a homestay explosion in the past decade. The term homestay is used rather than B & B because many do not provide breakfast, and if they do, it may not

be a full hot meal, instead something simple and hearty like a pot of tea and simple local breakfast foods, such as steamed buns with meat fillings, etc. The category is wide open: you may be staying in rooms in someone's house, or may be staying in a custom-built residence that might better be described as a small inn. There are few homestays in the cities; most are in the countryside in scenic locations. Official oversight is still not comprehensive; to assure quality, it is best to choose from among recommendations provided by the Taiwan Tourism Bureau, which has published a guidebook listing 115 of the best options entitled *Taiwan Homestay Accommodation for International Youth Travelers*, and also has information online (http://info.taiwan.net.tw/homestay/english/index.html and www.welcome2taiwan.net). Prices run from NT$500 to $2,000 per person per night.

Youth hostels and guesthouses

The China Youth Corps (CYC) operates a series of youth activity centers and youth hostels. Reservations may be arranged online or by writing or calling CYC headquarters at 219 Songjiang Road, Taipei, tel: (02) 2502-5858; limited English beyond website. Facilities may also be contacted directly. For an address list, go to the CYC website or contact tourism bureau offices overseas or in Taiwan.

Due to their popularity, groups and individuals from overseas should make reservations at CYC and other facilities well in advance. They are usually fully booked from July to September, and from January to February (holiday time for local students). If you haven't booked,

TRANSPORTATION

call ahead to make sure there is room. Rates vary, but on average three meals a day can be had for about NT$500. The average price is NT$1,000 to NT$1,500 per person a night. Most places have private rooms at higher rates, and some have large bungalows.

Other non-CYC guesthouses and hostels provide inexpensive accommodations, clean rooms with basic furnishings, shared shower facilities, and simple cooking facilities. Many are members of Hosteling International (www.yh.org.tw), and accommodate people of all ages.

Addresses

Taipei's address system may at first appear a bit complicated, but once you get the knack of it you'll find it is quite logical, and it negates the need to memorize countless names in this densely populated metropolis.

All addresses have a building number, alley or lane number, street name, and section. Here is an example: No. 15, Lane 25, Zhongxiao East Road, Section 3. The city is broken down into a grid, north-south Zhongshan Road and east-west Zhongxiao Road serving as axes. All city-stretching arteries are broken down into sections; for Zhongxiao East Road, Section 1 is that closest to Zhongshan Road, Section 2 further away, and so on. The pattern is repeated, headed west, for Zhongxiao West Road.

On each section building numbers start counting at '1' closest to the grid axis. Thus, there can be a No. 1 Zhongxiao E. Rd, Sec. 1, a No. 1 Zhongxiao E. Rd, Sec. 2, and so on. Referring to our sample address again, the 'lane' in the address means you go to Sec. 3 of Zhongxiao East Road and find building No. 25; right beside that building will be a lane – Lane 25. Go down that lane and find building No. 15.

If you see something like 'No. 15, Alley 6, Lane 25,' go to Lane 25 and find building No. 6. Alley 6 will be beside that building. Then go down the alley to building No. 15. The key is that 'lanes' are bigger, leading off major arteries, and alleys lead off lanes. Once you get the hang of it you can quickly guess what area any address is in – much different from facing such addresses as No. 12896 Interminable Boulevard in other places.

This same system is used throughout the island. But since Taipei is the only place divided into a grid, you won't see the 'north/south/east/west' designations used elsewhere.

Admission charges

Temples and shrines are free, and welcome visitors. Public museums are often free or have a nominal entrance fee, though larger facilities like the National Palace Museum will have fees over NT$100. More and more public museums are offering extended evening hours with free entry, almost always on Saturday, a few on Friday as well.

Privately run museums will usually have entrance fees of a few hundred NT$. National parks and scenic areas are either free or have a nominal entry fee, usually per vehicle, but may have entry fees for special designated areas; these will be nominal.

The Taipei EasyCard can now be used at the Taipei Zoo and a limited number of museums. This brings a discount of 10 percent. The range of such uses for the card is expanding, though extremely slowly.

The arts

The three English-language papers each carry weekend culture and entertainment supplements, which come out on Friday or Saturday. The bimonthly *Travel in Taiwan* and monthly *This Month in Taiwan* magazines have sections on the upcoming month's cultural activities, arts and entertainment events. For the most part, tickets must be purchased from the venue staging an event; this can often be frustrating because of language problems, so it is always best to have a local friend handle the purchase, either by phone or by accompanying you in advance to the ticket office. Tickets to events at many major venues are available via ERA Ticket (www.ticket.com.tw), though again it is best to have a Chinese speaker help you navigate the system.

Classical music and dance

Taiwan has produced numerous world-class musicians. The National Taiwan Symphony Orchestra and the Taipei Symphony Orchestra regularly perform western music at various venues in Taipei. The favorite venue for most Taipei-based expats is the National Concert Hall (www.ntch.edu.tw), on the grounds of the Chiang Kai-shek Memorial Hall; many top musicians from around the world come to the island for special performances. Traditional Chinese music has its roots in temple ritual, court traditions, and village music. Try catching temple music at the elaborate rituals held annually, on September 28, to celebrate the birthday of Confucius at Taipei Confucius Temple.

There is no traditional Han Chinese traditional dance. Most traditional dance is performed by local indigenous groups at various indigenous theme parks around the island, during harvest festival celebrations, and at a few native-theme hotels. On the other hand, modern dance has gained popularity in Taiwan over the last few decades.

The National Concert Hall.

The Cloud Gate Dance Theatre (www.cloudgate.org.tw), led by Lin Hwai-min, spearheaded the movement. It combines both Chinese and Western techniques and ideas, choreographed to the music of contemporary Chinese musicians. The internationally acclaimed group holds regular performances in Taipei.

The Taipei Dance Circle (http://td circle.org.tw), a breakaway from the Cloud Gate Dance Theatre, also regularly performs its own unique style of modern dance.

Chinese Opera

Taiwan is one of the best places in the world to attend Chinese-style opera. From the melodies sung by magnificently costumed performers and the orchestral accompaniment, to the astounding acrobatics and martial-arts displays of the performers, a night at the Beijing or Taiwanese opera is both an entertaining and educational experience.

Taipei EYE stages special performances of opera, puppetry, and other traditional folk arts especially tailored for international tourists, introducing numerous forms in an exciting 90-minute program each Friday and Saturday night, and on some Monday and Wednesday nights. Intros are given, subtitles are shown, and visitors can visit backstage to see how makeup is applied. Located in the heritage site Taiwan Cement Hall, 113 Zhongshan N. Road, Sec. 2; tel: (02) 2568-2677; www.taipeieye.com.

For another taste of Beijing or Taiwanese opera, try the television set – performances are broadcast almost every day. In the back alleys of Taipei and outside the capital city, keep your eyes open for traveling opera companies that set up and stage performances, lasting several days, in temple courtyards and other public places. These performances are generally sponsored by the government in an attempt to keep traditional culture alive, or by a rich local, who will gain merit in the eyes of the gods (to whom the show is actually presented, not the local mortals) by sponsoring a benevolent act.

Crafts

The Taiwanese take great pride in the things they can make with their hands: from lanterns and toys, handbags and baskets, bamboo and rattan crafts, rugs and carpets, to knitwear and embroidery.

In Taipei, an excellent selection of local handicrafts (including those of the aborigine tribes) is on display for sale at the Taiwan Handicraft Promotion Center, at 1 Xuzhou Road; tel: (02) 2393-3655; www.handicraft. org.tw. This is a good place to do souvenir and gift shopping, with reasonable prices. Prices are set, rising progressively as one moves from the first to the fourth level. Overseas shipping for purchased items can be handled by the center. Other similar display centers, many linked to various government units and thus with good reputations, dot the island.

Cinema

Residents of Taiwan are enthusiastic moviegoers, mostly watching Hong Kong and Western films. Taiwan is one of Hollywood's most lucrative markets, and all major Hollywood studios have permanent representatives here.

Most of the foreign films that come to Taiwan are from the United States, and they are always shown in English, with Chinese subtitles. This means that traveling movie fans need not fear a shortage of Western film entertainment when in Taiwan. The local cable-TV services, carried in all hotels, also have numerous dedicated movie channels.

The daily English-language newspapers carry information on English-language films currently playing in Taipei. There are usually three to five performances per day, with the last show beginning around midnight. By far the most popular movie-viewing venue for foreigners in Taipei is the VieShow Cinemas, in the city's posh Xinyi District. Clean, neon-bright and comfortable, the 24-hour complex also houses international-brand sit-down restaurants such as California Pizza Kitchen and street performers, making for the ideal night out.

B

Budgeting for your trip

The Tourism Bureau has the best information on budget travel, contained in the free booklet *Taiwan Homestay Accommodation for International Youth Travelers*. The booklet details 115 of the best homestay facilities (there are now thousands) and nearby attractions, in English and Japanese. The guidebook is available at overseas

bureau offices, international and domestic airports in Taiwan, as well as visitor-information centers around the island. The facilities listed are not exclusive to young travelers.

The cost for a domestic beer at a bar or restaurant will be about NT$100, about NT$130 for an imported brand. A glass of wine will be about NT$200. A main course at a budget restaurant will be just NT$100 to NT$150, about NT$350 or so at a moderate restaurant, and NT$600 or so at an expensive restaurant. A cheap hotel will be NT$1,500 to NT$2,000, a room in a moderate hotel starts around NT$3,000, and a room in a de luxe hotel starts at NT$6,000 or more. A taxi from Taiwan Taoyuan International Airport into Taipei costs about NT$1,200, and from Kaohsiung International Airport into downtown Kaohsiung about NT$300.

Business travelers

Work and play are convenient for those traveling on business to major urban centers. All international tourist hotels have internet connections in rooms, and almost all now have business centers.

Taxis are ubiquitous and almost always clean, and fares are low compared to other countries. Get your hotel to write out your destination in Chinese to show to drivers, who almost never speak English. In Taipei some drivers have received English training; look for the plum-blossom logos on their cars, neon-lit at night, or call (02) 2799-7997. In cities, drivers are obliged to give receipts, though most store them away; ask for a *shouju* (receipt). Many will just hand you the receipt, which already has the company name stamped on, and tell you to fill in the amount yourself.

Traffic is often a headache in Taiwan's cities, especially during rush hours, which last about two hours morning and evening, so give yourself plenty of extra time when going to meetings. If late, a grace period of about 20 to 25 minutes is given by locals (who fight the traffic every day) before mild irritation sets in. Be sure to apologize anyway, and phone ahead to explain if at all possible.

C

Children

Though Taiwanese take their children to places that would be thought of as 'adult' in the West, such as certain cafés, upscale restaurants, and so on, there are still few facilities set up for special needs – especially for those with babies. All international tourist hotels will go out of their way to help, and many family-oriented resorts have special facilities and programs for children. Only a limited number of hotels have babysitting services, but this number is steadily growing, especially at top international hotels and family resorts. Some public facilities now have diaper-changing and breast-feeding facilities, notably the international airports and metro systems, but finding one is a hit-and-miss endeavor. Ask at a venue's visitor center or ticket counter. Most quality restaurants now have high chairs available.

Outside Taipei, Taiwan is not a place especially friendly to pedestrians. Taipei has worked hard to widen main-artery sidewalks and get scooters off them, but few parents use strollers (pushchairs). Local mothers prefer papooses, with baby in front rather than back. To find out about child-friendly places to visit, there is no better source than Taipei's Community Services Center (see page 314); its *Centered on Taipei* magazine always has new info on where you can go with children.

The island has come a long way in the past decade and more with child-friendly recreation facilities, including quality theme parks, tourist farms, and supervised beaches with proper facilities. The Tourism Bureau website (www.taiwan.net.tw) has a wealth of information on specific locations in all these categories.

All metro trains have special dark-blue seats in each car, available for children.

Climate

Taiwan has a humid subtropical climate, with long hot summers and moderate winters. In the north and east of the island and in the mountains, the months from December to March are often damp and chilly, with strong winds and frequent rain. The Taipei area is notorious for this, and snow occasionally falls on the summits of the Central Mountain Range (Zhongshan Shanmo). Further south and west, winters are noticeably sunnier and warmer.

Temperatures begin to rise in March, and by early May everywhere is hot and humid. The heat lasts until October. Most of Taiwan's rain falls

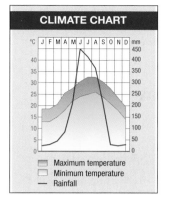

CLIMATE CHART

- ▨ Maximum temperature
- ☐ Minimum temperature
- — Rainfall

from May to September, mostly in intense but short-lived showers and thunderstorms. Mean annual rainfall ranges from 2,500 to 5,000mm (100 to 200ins).

Taiwan's location also subjects it to annual typhoons, which pass through between July and October. Most of these cause little more than strong winds and heavy rains over the island, but there are occasional powerful winds and severe storms.

When to visit

The most pleasant time of the year to visit is mid-September through November, especially in Taipei and the mountains. The southwest is usually very pleasant from October until March.

Crime and safety

Taiwan, though not without crime, is a safe place to visit, with little in the way of violent crime. When going out, especially to crowded places, the main fear of locals is pickpocketing. As elsewhere, avoid making showy displays of wealth, leaving valuables lying around hotel rooms or unattended, even momentarily, in public places, etc.

Drivers in areas outside Taipei may be aggressive, and not wish to give way to pedestrians even when legally obliged to do so, so be alert when crossing the street.

If you run into any serious difficulty, contact the Foreign Affairs Police Corps, National Police Administration at (02) 2394-0238, which is supposed to have English-speaking personnel available at all times.

Customs regulations

All inbound passengers must fill in a customs declaration form upon

arrival. The following items are strictly prohibited from entry into Taiwan: gambling apparatus or foreign lottery tickets; pornographic materials; publications promoting communism or originating in communist countries; firearms; toy guns; all drugs or narcotics of a non-prescription and non-medical nature.

All personal belongings such as clothing, jewelry, cosmetics, food, and similar items may be brought into Taiwan free of duty. Items such as computers, stereo equipment, TV sets and video recorders, though also duty-free, must be declared on arrival. Each passenger 20 years of age or older is also permitted to bring in duty-free alcoholic beverages (1,000cc or less without limitation on number of bottles) and tobacco products (200 cigarettes, 25 cigars, or 450 grams/1lb of pipe tobacco). Gold exceeding a total value of US$20,000 is not permitted.

Passengers must declare the amount of foreign currencies they carry upon arrival. If not declared, the portion of foreign currencies in excess of US$10,000 (or its equivalent in other foreign currency) shall, upon arrival, be subject to confiscation. The unused balance may then be declared on the Outbound Passenger Declaration Form upon departure.

Otherwise, outbound passengers are limited to taking US$10,000 or the equivalent in other currencies out of Taiwan. Up to NT$60,000 in cash may be carried. Visitors who want to bring in more than NT$60,000 in cash must apply for a permit from the Central Bank of China before entering Taiwan.

For more detail, visit the **Directorate General of Customs** website at: http://eweb.customs. gov.tw.

Outbound declaration

An outbound passenger declaration form must be completed when carrying any of the following items:

Foreign currency, local currency, gold and silver ornaments in excess of allowed amounts.

Any unused foreign currency declared upon arrival.

Commercial samples and personal effects such as cameras, calculators, recorders, etc., which you wish to bring back to Taiwan duty-free in the future.

Computer media, discs, tapes, etc. Passengers who have not declared gold, silver, and foreign currencies on arrival and are then discovered to be carrying these items in excess of the legally designated quantities will have the excess amount confiscated by customs, and may be subject to punishment by law. The designated legal limits are as follows:

Foreign currency – US$10,000, or equivalent, in cash (excluding unused portion of currency declared upon arrival).

Republic of China currency – NT$60,000 in bank notes.

Gold/silver ornaments or coins – US$10,000.

Articles that may not be taken out of the country include unauthorized reprints or copies of books, records, videotapes, and so on; genuine Chinese antiques (over 100 years old), ancient coins and paintings.

D

Disabled travelers

Unfortunately, Taiwan is not an especially friendly place for travelers with disabilities. The international airports have facilities for the physically challenged. Each metro station provides elevator access from street level; there is also a reserved spot for wheelchairs in the first and last car of each train, and each car has special dark-blue seats for the disabled. The sidewalks on most major Taipei City streets have now been specially outfitted with tiles that help the visually impaired, and there is a special audio signal at crosswalks. Over 25 percent of Taipei public buses are now low-floor buses.

Top-class hotels and resorts, theme parks, and a few museums have special access ramps installed at entrances, and most public washrooms now have specially fitted cubicles, and, for males, urinals. More hotels are now offering rooms and other facilities for the disabled, but it is best to confirm this beforehand.

E

Eating out

Eating is one of the greatest pleasures Taiwan holds in store for the traveler, and you are almost guaranteed a great snack or meal, whatever your price range.

Selecting a restaurant

If you are a novice to Chinese food, the best places to try local

cuisine are the restaurants in the international tourist hotels throughout the country, which serve probably the best (and most expensive) Chinese food available in Taiwan.

An alternative is to visit one of the many eateries in the food courts of the main department stores. Everything is freshly cooked, and the prices are quite low. If you see one eatery with no customers waiting, chances are that the food is not very good. It is better to go to another where you have to wait in line.

The third suggestion is to go to an ordinary restaurant. Remember that large hall-like Chinese restaurants most often cater to groups rather than individuals. Four people at a table should be the minimum, and don't expect the food to be cheap.

Don't be afraid to experiment because of the language barrier; there are so many items on a Chinese menu that most foreigners become daunted and hesitate to order unusual dishes, thereby missing out on local specialties and delicacies. The first few times you dine locally, if possible, bring along a local friend who will show you how you've been led miserably astray when eating Chinese cuisine back home; after this, each meal becomes a pleasant adventure.

Types of cuisine

The majority of Taiwanese can trace their origins to Fujian province, across the strait in China, yet there are people from every corner of the mainland. All have distinctive culinary traditions, making Taiwan perhaps the best spot in the world to explore the many different types of Chinese cuisine.

Northern style (Beijing, Inner Mongolia). Recommended dishes: Beijing duck, lamb and leek, hot and sour soup, celery in mustard sauce, cold shredded chicken with sauce, sweet and sour yellow fish, steamed vegetable dumplings.

Electricity

Taiwan uses electric current of 110 volts at 60 cycles; appliances from Europe, Australia, and Southeast Asia will need an adaptor or transformer. Many buildings have sockets with 220 volts especially for the use of air-conditioners.

Southern style (Cantonese). Recommended dishes: roast duck, poached chicken with onions and oil, greens with oyster sauce, steamed whole fish, dim sum, roast pigeon, cabbage with cream.

Western/central style (Hunan, Sichuan). Recommended dishes: (Sichuan) steamed pomfret, chicken 'Duke of Bao,' 'pockmarked grandma's bean curd,' fragrant egg sauce, duck smoked in camphor and tea, twice-cooked pork; (Hunan) frog legs in chili sauce, honeyed ham, beggar's chicken, minced pigeon in bamboo cup, steamed whole fish.

Eastern/coastal style (Shanghai). Recommended dishes: West Lake vinegar fish, river eel sautéed with leek, braised pork haunch, sautéed sweet pea shoots, 'drunken chicken,' 'lion-head meatballs,' braised beef loin.

Taiwanese food. Recommended dishes: steamed crab, poached squid, fresh poached shrimp, shrimp rolls, grilled eel, sashimi, grilled clams, turtle soup.

Chinese vegetarian cuisine. Recommended dishes: try the various types of 'beef,' 'pork,' and 'chicken,' made entirely from various forms of soybean curd and different types of mushrooms, as well as fresh and crispy vegetables.

Street snacks

Some of the best-loved local foods are the *xiaochi*, or 'small eats.' Throughout Taiwan, devoted foodies will be found in neighborhood night markets eating meals made up of hot snacks sourced from a number of different vendors. The food is invariably freshly cooked because the turnover is high.

Embassies and consulates

The Republic of China (Taiwan) has formal diplomatic relations with 24 sovereign political entities. Countries outside this group set up trade and commerce offices, quasi-embassies that handle all the responsibilities that a full embassy does.

Australia: Australian Office Taipei
27-28F, President International Tower, 9-11 Songgao Road, Taipei
Tel: (02) 8725-4100
www.australia.org.tw

Canada: Canadian Trade Office in Taipei
6F, Hua-Hsin Building, 1 Songzhi Road, Taipei
Tel: (02) 8723-3000
www.canada.org.tw

It is essential for hosts to entertain guests generously.

New Zealand: New Zealand Commerce and Industry Office Taipei
9F, 1 Songzhi Road, Taipei
Tel: (02) 2720-5228
www.nzcio.com

South Africa: Liaison Office of South Africa
Suite 1301, 13F, 205 Dunhua N. Road, Taipei
Tel: (02) 8175-8588
www.southafrica.org.tw

UK: British Trade & Cultural Office
26F, President International Tower, 9-11 Songgao Road, Taipei
Tel: (02) 8758-2088
http://ukintaiwan.fco.gov.uk

US: American Institute in Taiwan
7, Lane 134, Xinyi Road, Sec. 3, Taipei
Tel: (02) 2162 2000
www.ait.org.tw

Taiwan Representative Offices Overseas

Australia: Taipei Economic and Cultural Office in Australia
Unit 8, 40 Blackall Street, Barton, Canberra
Tel: (02) 6120-2000
www.teco.org.au

Canada: Taipei Economic and Cultural Office in Canada
Suite 1960, 45 O'Connor Street, World Exchange Plaza, Ottawa
Tel: (613) 231-5080
www.taiwan-canada.org

Ireland: Taipei Representative Office in Ireland
8 Lower Hatch Street, Dublin
Tel: (353) 678-5580
www.taiwan-roc.org/IE

New Zealand: Taipei Economic and Cultural Office in New Zealand
Level 21, 105 The Terrace, Wellington
Tel: (04) 473-6474
www.roc-taiwan.org/NZ

South Africa: Taipei Liaison Office in the Republic of South Africa
1147 Schoeman Street, Hatfield, Pretoria
Tel: (012) 430-6071
www.roc-taiwan.org/ZA

UK: Taipei Representative Office in the UK
50 Grosvenor Gardens, London
Tel: (020) 7881-2650
www.roc-taiwan.org/UK

US: Taipei Economic and Cultural Office in the US
4201 Wisconsin Avenue NW, Washington D.C.
Tel: (202) 895-1800
www.roc-taiwan.org/US

Emergencies

When traveling in Taiwan, have your passport with you. In case something untoward happens and you cannot identify yourself, have a note in Chinese attached to the passport; this will identify your hotel or a Chinese-speaking person to contact in case of emergency.
Fire: 119
Ambulance: 119
Police: 110
The Women and Children Protection Hotline 113 is a 24-hour emergency, legal information, and psychological service for victims of domestic violence and/or sexual abuse; run by World Vision Taiwan (www.world

vision.org.tw), commissioned by Ministry of the Interior.

Entry requirements

Visas and passports

Citizens of the following countries, with passports valid for at least six months and confirmed onward or return tickets, are allowed visa-free entry to Taiwan for a period of 90 days: Austria, Belgium, Bulgaria, Canada, Croatia, Cyprus, Czech Republic, Denmark, Estonia, Finland, France, Germany, Greece, Hungary, Iceland, Ireland, Israel, Italy, Japan, South Korea, Latvia, Liechtenstein, Lithuania, Luxembourg, Malta, Monaco, the Netherlands, New Zealand, Norway, Poland, Portugal, Romania, Slovakia, Slovenia, Spain, Sweden, Switzerland, the UK, USA, and Vatican City State.

Citizens of Australia, Malaysia, and Singapore are allowed visa-free entry for a period of 30 days.

Visa-exempt entry, under normal conditions, cannot be converted to a visitor or resident visa.

More detailed information regarding roc visitor visas can be obtained from the **Bureau of Consular Affairs**, Ministry of Foreign Affairs, 3-5F, 2−2 Jinan Road, Sec. 1, Taipei, Taiwan; tel: (02) 2343-2888; e-mail: post@boca.gov.tw; www.boca. gov.tw. Visa application forms can now be downloaded.

Visa extensions

Apply for extensions at least 15 days before your regular visa expires. To extend a regular tourist visa in Taipei, visit the **National Immigration Agency (NIA)**, 15 Guangzhou St, Taipei; tel: (02) 2388-9393 or the 24-hour service hotline 0800-024-111.

Etiquette

Greetings

The Taiwanese, like the Koreans and Japanese, used to bow and clasp their hands together when being introduced to someone new, but today the Western handshake has displaced the ancient custom. Nevertheless, locals still shy away from boisterous greetings in public, such as hugs, kisses, and resounding slaps on the back. A firm handshake, friendly smile, and slight nod of the head are appropriate gestures of greeting.

TRANSPORTATION

A − Z

LANGUAGE

Names

In Chinese, a person's family surname precedes both given name and formal title. For example, in the name Li Wuping, Li is the surname and Wuping is the given name. In the expression 'Li *Jingli*,' Li is the surname and *jingli* (manager) is the title. Chinese-language names generally consist of three names – one surname and two given names – but many people use only two. The majority of Chinese family names come from the *Lao Bai Xing* (Old Hundred Names), first formulated over 3,000 years ago in feudal China. Among the most common are Li, Wang, Chen, Huang, Zhang, Yang, Liang, and Sun. Locals prefer to be addressed by their family name and title, as above, rather than by their full name.

Business cards

During formal introductions between working professionals, locals usually exchange business cards, which has become the tradition throughout Asia. In fact, many people don't even listen to oral introductions, but wait instead to read the person's card. It is a good idea to have some personal cards printed before traveling anywhere in East Asia, even if not traveling on business. Always hand and take a card with both hands, and be sure to take a close look at the card given, to show you take the other person and his/her position and authority seriously. Place the card on the table in front of you during meetings. Do not toss it in your briefcase or wallet when getting ready to leave; slide it into a place that shows you value the person and the relationship that has been established. These things will be noticed, and if handled improperly will create negative feelings.

Entertaining

The Chinese term *qingke* literally means 'inviting guests,' and refers to the grand Chinese tradition of entertaining friends and associates with lavish generosity, usually with a banquet-style meal. In Taiwan, locals are often perplexed when they see Westerners call for their bill at restaurants, then pull out their phone calculators and proceed to figure out precisely how much each person at the table must contribute. The Chinese tradition, on the contrary, is to compete for the privilege of paying the bill for the whole table – though it is understood that in the end the

person who has done the inviting will almost always be 'allowed' to pay.

To the Taiwanese, inviting guests out for dinner and drinks is a delightful way to repay favors or to cultivate new business relationships, and they do so often, for this is a gift that the giver always shares with the recipients. And the very moment you've paid a hefty dinner bill, everyone at the table is immediately obliged to invite you out as their guest sometime in the not-too-distant future. This way, although the bill is high when it's your turn to *qingke*, you only end up paying for one out of, say, 10 banquets. In the final analysis, it all balances out, and everyone takes turns earning the 'big face' that comes with being a generous host. If in Taiwan for a limited time, do try if possible to entertain anyone who has entertained you before heading home. Not doing so is bad form.

Toasts

When toasted at dinner parties, it is good manners to raise your wine glass with both hands: one holding it and the other with the fingertips touching the base. The host will take his seat opposite (not beside) the guest of honor, and it is fitting to have the host's back to the door and the guest of honor facing it. It is said this is because, in feudal times, the host gave you a wall to sit in front of to show you would not be attacked from behind; both hands raised when toasting kept any hands from going for weapons under the table.

Tea

Tea served at the end of a meal is your host's polite way of indicating that the party is over and that it is time for you to leave. So don't overstay your welcome, even though your host may insist. Do not let the host leave before you, and thank him heartily for his hospitality when departing.

Polite courtesy

Chinese-style courtesy may be confusing to Westerners. For example, even though it is late and the host would love to call it a day, he will gently persuade his guest to stay longer. In this case, it is up to the guest to detect from the host's tone what is the best thing to do. This requires skill and cultural sensitivity. An experienced traveler once ventured, 'The rule of thumb is to do the exact opposite that your Chinese friend suggests.' Try this if you must, but with discretion.

Titles

Some of the most common titles used in Chinese during introductions are as follows.
Xiansheng/Mister (as in Li *Xiansheng*)
Taitai/Mrs (Li *Taitai*)
Xiaojie/Miss (Li *Xiaojie*)
Furen/Madame (Li *Furen*)
Laoban/Boss (Li *Laoban*)
Jingli/Manager (Li *Jingli*)

F

Festivals

In addition to ancient festivals such as the Lunar New Year and the Mid-Autumn (Moon) Festival, national holidays such as Double Tenth National Day and 228 Peace Memorial Day, and commemorative days, there are scores of other local Taiwanese festivals known as *baibai*, which are colorful celebrations held in honor of local deities. There are over 100 popular gods in Taiwan, and not only are their birthdays commemorated, each of their 'death days' and 'deification days' are also occasions for celebration.

The celebration of *baibai* days begins with the faithful offering the best food and wine to the respective deities, and ends with the devotees themselves gorging on the offerings – but not before they are sure that the deities have had their fill by consuming their 'essence.' This is usually the time taken for a joss stick (incense stick) to burn out. Few Taiwanese remain entirely sober on these occasions, and everyone spends a lot of money to *qingke*, or 'invite friends out.'

National holidays and commemorative days, of more recent origin, follow the Western solar calendar, but most festival dates still follow the lunar calendar. Thus, they vary from year to year and can fall any time within a two-month period. Check exact dates at the time of planning for your trip.

January/February

Foundation Day of the Republic of China: Celebrated every January 1, this day commemorates the founding of the republic on January 1, 1912. On that day, Dr Sun Yat-sen was inaugurated as the first president of the newly founded Republic of China. Also on that day, China officially switched from the lunar to the Gregorian calendar. This occasion is celebrated annually in

Taipei with parades, dragon and lion dances, traditional music, patriotic speeches, and, of course, lots of firecrackers.

Chinese Lunar New Year: Most important time of year in the Chinese calendar, beginning the first day of the first lunar month. This is a time for families to be together. Some private companies will give holidays longer than the official holiday period.

Traditionally called the Spring Festival, the Lunar New Year remains the biggest celebration of the year in Taiwan, as it has for millennia in all Chinese communities. The festival is observed in various stages for a full month, from the 16th day of the 12th lunar month, although offices and shops generally close for only a week or so around New Year's Day.

Many ancient customs are associated with the Lunar New Year. For example, all outstanding debts must be paid off before New Year's Eve; failure to do so is a grave affront and an omen of bad luck for the coming year. Many wealthy businessmen in Taiwan keep running accounts in their favorite restaurants and clubs, paying their bills only once a year, just before Lunar New Year's Eve. Another custom is exchanging gifts, especially little red envelopes (*hongbao*) stuffed with 'lucky money,' the amount depending on the closeness of the relationship between the giver and recipient.

Festival foods

Traditional foods are associated with specific festivals, and visitors should try them where possible. During Chinese New Year people eat *fagao* and *jiaozi*; radishes and pineapples are both eaten and used as decorations. The characters for *fagao*, which are little cupcakes, are homonyms for 'go up,' as in to rise to a better social position. *Jiaozi*, meat- and vegetable-filled dumplings, are shaped like ingots, and denote prosperity. The characters for 'radish' and 'pineapple' are homonyms for, respectively, 'good fortune' and 'prosperity.' *Yuanxiao* are enjoyed during the Lantern Festival; the round balls represent the 'unity' of the family in the New Year season. *Yuebing*, or moon cakes, eaten during the Mid-Autumn Festival, are also symbols of family unity.

Everyone dresses up in new clothes at New Year, from hats down to shoes; this symbolizes renewal and a fresh start in life for the coming year. People visit family and friends and spend a lot of money on entertainment. Indeed, local banks are sometimes plagued with cash shortages at this time of year. The dominant color is red, which is universally regarded as auspicious among the Chinese; red flowers, red clothing, red streamers, red cakes and candies, and the ubiquitous red envelopes appear everywhere.

At the stroke of midnight on New Year's Eve, the entire island suddenly reverberates to the staccato explosions of millions of firecrackers and skyrockets, as every temple and household in Taiwan lights the fuses that will frighten evil spirits from their thresholds, ensuring an auspicious start to the Chinese Lunar New Year. The Chinese invented gunpowder for this very purpose over 1,000 years ago. In recent years the government has been encouraging the use of quieter, more eco-friendly firecrackers that leave less debris behind.

The stock phrase to offer all your friends and acquaintances whenever and wherever you encounter them during the period is '*gongxi facai*,' which means 'I wish you happiness and prosperity' (literally, 'Congratulations! Get rich!'). The good-humored rhyming retort to this greeting is '*hongbao nalai*,' or 'hand over a red envelope.'

2-28 Peace Day: Held on February 28, this national holiday commemorates the 2-28 Incident, a seminal event in the island's modern history. It is marked by memorial services for the victims and with such other public activities as music concerts, art exhibitions, and group runs. Taiwan's president attends the main ceremony at Taipei's 2-28 Peace Memorial Park, during which he rings a ceremonial bell, bows to the victims' families, and presents certificates declaring the victims were guilty of no crimes.

February/March

Lantern Festival: This festival, which falls on the first full moon of the Lunar New Year, marks the traditional end of the Spring Festival. Celebrants appear at night in the streets, parks, and temples of Taiwan carrying colorful lanterns with auspicious phrases inscribed on them in elegant calligraphy. This tradition is supposed to

insure against evil and illness in the coming year. The festival food associated with this event is a sweet dumpling of glutinous rice stuffed with bean- or date-paste and called *yuanxiao*. Major temples are excellent places to observe the Lantern Festival. Prizes are awarded for the most beautiful and original lantern designs.

The largest celebrations on this day are the Taipei Lantern Festival, which is held in the area around Taipei City Hall and Sun Yat-sen Memorial Hall, Kaohsiung Lantern Festival, held along the Love River, and the official national event, rotated among cities. Over 100,000 people cram into each venue to watch the respective giant theme floats, see the thousands of lanterns and live pop-music shows, enjoy the traditional snacks, and take part in the many demonstrations and activities.

Yanshui Beehive Rockets Festival: One of the world's most bizarre celebrations takes place in Yanshui is a fishing town now officially part of sprawling Tainan City. On Lantern Festival eve, thousands of danger-seekers crowd into the narrow streets where the infamous 'rocket hive' fireworks are set off one after another.

Pingxi Sky Lantern Festival: Pingxi, a small town southeast of Taipei now part of New Taipei City, sits in a narrow valley on the upper Keelung River. Over 10,000 revelers crowd in and around town on the 15th lunar night of the new year, Lantern Festival eve, and the night before, to watch 'sky lanterns' journey upwards into the night. Upwards of 3,000 rising, flickering, slow-shooting stars may fill the darkness at any moment. The effect is one of surreal and sensual beauty.

The largest sky lantern to date was 18 meters (59ft) tall. Each, even the smallest, contains at least one prayer/wish, written on the outside, the mini unmanned hot-air balloons delivering them to the gods. Buy your own small and simple wish-deliverer on-site for as little as NT$250. The origin of sky lanterns is ancient and military in nature, used for communications. It is said the isolated Han Chinese settlers in this valley used them to signal each either when bandits and aborigine warriors were about.

Birthday of Guanyin: Guanyin, Goddess of Mercy, is one of the most popular Buddhist deities in Taiwan, Korea, and Japan. Known for her compassion and love for people, she is one of Taiwan's patron protective deities. Her birthday is celebrated with colorful *baibai* ceremonies in major temples throughout Taiwan.

April/May

Tomb Sweeping Day: Traditionally calculated as the 105th day after the Winter Solstice and called the Qingming (Clear and Bright) Festival, Tomb-Sweeping Day in Taiwan is now celebrated annually on April 5, which coincides with the date of President Chiang Kai-shek's death, in 1975. Though April 5 remains the date of the traditional Chinese festival it is no longer a national holiday in Taiwan.

During this festival, entire families travel to their ancestral burial grounds to clear accumulated dirt, debris, and plant growth from the tombs, place fresh flowers before the entrances, and perhaps plant some new trees, flowers, and bushes in the area.

Birthday of Mazu: One of the biggest *baibai* of the year in Taiwan, this festival is dedicated to Mazu, Goddess of the Sea, guardian deity of Taiwan's fishermen and one of the island's patron saints. It is celebrated with great fanfare in the over 900 temples where Mazu is enshrined. The biggest festival takes place in central Taiwan, at the elaborate Mazu temple in Beigang, near Chiayi City. But you can also get an eye- and earful at the famous Longshan (Dragon Mountain) Temple in the oldest section of Taipei. The festivities include sacrificial offerings of roast pig and boiled chickens, billows of smoke from incense and burning paper money, undulating lion and dragon dances, colorful parades, and lavish feasting.

Cleansing of the Buddha Festival: This day commemorates the birth of Sakyamuni (the historical Buddha) some 2,500 years ago. The festival is marked in temples throughout the island with cleansing-of-Buddha ceremonies, during which all statues of Buddha are ritually washed while monks recite appropriate sutras. Many of the icons are then paraded through the streets to the sound of gongs and drums.

May/June

Dragon Boat Festival: One of the Chinese culture's most ancient festivals, this event commemorates the death of Qu Yuan. An accomplished poet and upright minister, he plunged to his death in a river about 2,500 years ago to protest the corruption and misrule of his king, who had banished him from the court. According to legend, on hearing of his tragic death the local people rowed their boats out on the river and dropped stuffed rice dumplings tightly wrapped in bamboo leaves into the water, to both supplicate and nourish his spirit and to distract the fishes from eating him. These dumplings, called *zongzi*, remain this festival's major food item.

The Dragon Boat Festival is celebrated with colorful dragon-boat races, commemorating the boats that raced out to look for Qu Yuan, which in recent times have become a major sporting event in Taiwan. Teams from around Taiwan and around the world compete for top honors in various divisions. The Taipei event is the biggest. The bows of the boats are carved into elaborate dragon heads, and the crews row vigorously to the resounding beat of a large drum placed at the stern of each boat.

June/July

Birthday of Chenghuang: This *baibai* festival is celebrated with great pomp and ceremony at Taipei's Xiahai Chenghuang (Xiahai City God) Temple at 61 Dihua Street, Sec. 1. The worship of city gods is a practice that has been recorded in China as far back as the early Xia dynasty (2200–1524 BC), and remains one of Taiwan's liveliest celebrations. City gods are said to have the power to protect a city's inhabitants from both natural disasters and enemy intruders, and they also advise the Lord of Heaven and the King of Hell regarding appropriate rewards and punishments for the city's residents after death. No wonder locals pay them such lavish homage!

Among the colorful festivities of this *baibai* are parades with icons of the City God held high

upon pedestals, offerings of whole pigs stretched on bamboo racks, processions of celebrants wearing stilts and colorful costumes, lion and dragon dances, and lavish feasts.

July/August

Chinese Valentine's Day: Chinese Valentine's Day is derived from the legend of the herd boy and the spinning girl. The herd boy (a star formation in the constellation Aquila, west of the Milky Way) and the spinning girl (the star Vega in the constellation Lyra, east of the Milky Way) appear closest together in the sky on this night, and all the magpies on Earth are said to ascend to the sky to form a bridge across the Milky Way so that the lovers may cross over for their brief once-a-year tryst. This is a festival for young unmarried girls and for young lovers, who observe the romantic occasion by exchanging gifts, strolling in moonlit parks, and praying in temples for future matrimonial bliss.

August/September

Ghost Month: The Chinese believe that on the first day of the seventh lunar month (usually in August) the ghosts of deceased relatives return to their earthly homes for a visit. Trays of succulent foods are set out before each home as an offering to them, and Buddhist priests are invited to every neighborhood and alley to bless these offerings and supplicate the spirits with prayer. Incense is burned and bundles of paper 'clothing,' spirit money, and other offerings are set alight for use by the spirits in the other world. These offerings are also meant to prevent the ghosts of criminals and spirits whose living descendants neglect to honor them, (called 'good brethren') from entering one's home and causing trouble. It is not an auspicious time for marriage or commencing important new ventures. Rites are held daily in all Buddhist temples during Ghost Month, which formally ends on the last day of the seventh month, when the spirits return to the underworld and the gates slam shut for another year. The north coast city of Keelung hosts major Ghost Month celebrations.

Birthday of Confucius: Celebrated as Teacher's Day on September 28, this day commemorates the birth of the sage Confucius in 551 BC. Known as China's greatest teacher, Confucius continues to exert profound influence on culture and society in Taiwan. Elaborate

---

Additional festivals background

A superb and wonderfully informative booklet, *Festivals in Taiwan*, is available from the tourism bureau, providing detailed, accurate and consistent information (often frustratingly difficult to get) on Taiwan's major festivals.

traditional ceremonies are held every year on this day, the most extensive at 6am at Taipei Confucius Temple (275 Dalong Street), complete with ancient musical instruments, formal court attire, ritual dances, and other Confucian rites as old as the sage himself.

Tickets to attend this ceremony must be reserved in advance. Reservations can be made through local tourism authorities. Three hundred tickets are handed out on a first-come, first-served basis at the temple gate on the day itself, but note that many people come the night before to line up.

September/October

Mid-Autumn (Moon) Festival: The Chinese believe that the harvest moon is the fullest, brightest moon of the year, and they celebrate its annual appearance by proceeding en masse to parks, hillsides, riverbanks, and seashores to gaze at 'The Lady in the Moon,' and to enjoy barbecues, nibble on tasty snacks, and drink wine.

The festival is celebrated by exchanging gifts of *yuebing*, or mooncakes, which traditionally have been large, round pastries stuffed with sweet-bean paste, mashed dates, chopped nuts, minced dried fruits, and other fillings. Exchanging *yuebing* also has patriotic overtones, because during the successful overthrow of the Mongol Yuan dynasty by the Chinese Ming, secret plans for the insurrection are said to have been concealed in moon cakes, which the Mongols did not eat, and distributed to patriots.

Double Tenth National Day: 'Double Tenth,' or *shuangshi*, refers to the tenth day of the tenth month in the Western calendar, and commemorates the overthrow of the Manchu Qing dynasty, China's last, by revolutionaries starting on October 10, 1911. It is celebrated with a grand parade of lion and dragon dance troupes, drum troupes, sword-fighting and martial arts troupes, and cultural troupes in splendid variety. Most of the action takes place in the huge plaza in front of the Presidential Office Building in Taipei. In some years there is a demonstration of the nation's military prowess, including skydiving demonstrations. This is followed by nighttime fireworks shows in all major cities.

Hotels and restaurants in Taipei are full throughout the week prior to Double Tenth day, as tens of

Giving gifts

Some don'ts: No knives or scissors; sharp objects are not auspicious, and suggest you wish to cut off the friendship. No clocks or watches; also inauspicious, these suggest 'deliverance' of the receiver to their final end. No handkerchiefs; connotations of the crying done at funerals. No towels – as they are traditionally given as gifts to those attending funerals. Always present gifts formally, with two hands, palms up.

thousands of overseas Chinese from all over the world pour into town for the festivities. Tourists who intend to visit Taipei at this time should make early reservations for hotels and flight space.

G

Gay and lesbian travelers

Taiwan is one of Asia's most progressive countries in terms of LGBT rights. Homosexuality is legal, but same-sex marriage and the right to adopt for same-sex couples has not yet been recognized; legislation has been proposed, but has stalled. The Taiwanese have a strange fascination with cross-dressers and transvestites in a performance context – men have traditionally played female roles in Beijing opera – yet gay men and women generally hide their same-gender preferences from relatives and colleagues. There are clubs and bars in Taipei that cater to gay men and women, but these are less common in the smaller towns and cities. Much greater tolerance is being shown in the city of Taipei now, and the city even publishes its own free guide for the gay community. There is also an annual Taiwan Pride parade and festival held in the city, the largest LGBT event in Asia. Good information can be found online at www.utopia-asia.com and www.stickyrice.ws.

H

Health and medical care

Tap water is not recommended for drinking. Ice in drinks is generally safe; most establishments save for the smallest in the countryside now use filtered or purified water. Most

people boil tap water, and many hotels provide boiled drinking water. Boil for at least five minutes. Bottled water is available at convenience stores and supermarkets, but make sure the seal is intact, and inspect the contents. If it is not 100 percent clear, do not buy it; some inspections have shown some bottled water not up to standard.

In Kaohsiung people do not drink boiled tap water, because of trace levels of arsenic. Residents get their water from pumps that look like gas pumps located throughout neighborhoods.

Effective cholera inoculation certificates are required for passengers coming from certain countries or who have stayed more than five days in infected areas. Visitors staying over three months are required to have an hiv test. Otherwise, health certificates are not normally required. It is recommended to have inoculations against tetanus, Hepatitis A, and, in some cases, Hepatitis B well in advance if traveling to remote areas. If you are visiting rural areas in summer, the Japanese encephalitis vaccine is recommended. Malaria is not a problem in Taiwan. Contact the **National Quarantine Service**, Department of Health, 6 Linsen N. Road, Taipei; tel: (02) 2395-9825. In case of emergency, dial 119 (note that the operators speak limited English). Detailed health advice for visits anywhere in the world is available from masta (Medical Advice for Travelers Abroad), at www.masta-travel-health.com. The number for the MASTA Travel Health Line (in UK) is tel: 0330 100 4200 (standard rate).

Medical treatment

The quality of medical facilities and services is excellent in the major cities, and medical treatment and dental work generally cost far less than in any Western country or Japan. The official online window for Taiwan medical travel is www.medicaltravel. org (tel: 02-2885-1528); packages are available in which you are met at and taken to the airport, have an English-speaker available at all times, and also travel to scenic sites. Hospitals have pharmacy facilities open at all hours to fill doctor prescriptions.

It is advisable to inform your country's representative office where you are staying when in Taiwan. In the event of a medical emergency, they should be able to help. Avoid using the services of small clinics and the smaller hospitals, whose doctors and nurses are often overworked and speak limited English. Following is a list of major hospitals:

Taipei
Chang Gung Memorial Hospital
199 Dunhua N. Road
Tel: (02) 2713-5211
Mackay Memorial Hospital
92 Zhongshan N. Road, Sec. 2
Tel: (02) 2543-3535
National Taiwan University Hospital
7 Zhongshan S. Road
Tel: (02) 2312-3456
Taiwan Adventist Hospital
424 Bade Road, Sec. 2
Tel: (02) 2771-8151

Hualien
Buddhist Tzu Chi General Hospital
707 Zhongyang Road, Sec. 3
Tel: (03) 856-1825

Kaohsiung
Chang Gung Memorial Hospital
123 Dapi Road
Tel: (07) 731-7123

Taichung
Taichung Veterans General Hospital
160 Zhonggang Road, Sec. 3
Tel: (04) 2359-2525

Tainan
Chi Mei Medical Center
901 Zhonghua Road, Yongkang District
Tel: (06) 252-1176
National Cheng Kung University Hospital
138 Shengli Road
Tel: (06) 235-3535

Drinking games

A popular method of downing liquor or beer other than toasting is the 'rock, paper, scissors' finger game, in which the loser must drain his glass dry. Also popular are various forms of a 'fingers-guessing game.' The basic form: two contestants each shoot out a number of fingers, at the same time. As this is done, one guesses how many fingers in total will be exposed. If wrong, the other gets a chance to guess next round. If right, the other must down his full glass.

Locals can be seen engaging in these spirited contests in restaurants and pubs throughout Taiwan. One who walks away sober is positively considered, by friends, a man with the 'capacity of an ocean.'

Tainan Hospital
125 Zhongshan Road
Tel: (06) 220-0055

Traditional medicines

Beyond popular and well-known medicines such as tiger balm, foreigners can take the opportunity to learn about other traditional medicines while in Taiwan. Many of these are extremely effective. However, be sure you do not purchase items made in China, which are common despite prohibitions on direct trade; such items are not subject to the same high testing and quality-control production standards as in Taiwan, and there is a constant stream of health-related warnings.

I

Internet

All international tourist hotels provide internet access in private rooms, and many regular tourist hotels now do as well. All the international tourist hotels provide Internet access for guests in business centers, charging in the area of NT$200 per hour. Libraries often have free internet access. There are a internet cafés in the major cities, both stand-alone and chain outlets, but be advised that most cater to teen aficionados of video games. These places aren't quiet. Fees are calculated by the minute, and because of heavy competition are most often NT$1 per minute or less. This same competition means locations open and close with impressive speed. Be aware that staff will have some trouble communicating with you in English, save techno-jargon. Look for true cafés and coffee shops that have wireless internet access as a bonus for customers. In Taipei numerous pubs and bars also now offer wireless access.

Taipei City is also engaged in a large-scale program to bring wireless access to the entire metropolis. Called Taipei Free, there are now over 4,500 public-area hotspots. For more information, visit www.tpe-free. taipei.gov.tw.

L

Lost property

Local folk will most likely turn in any found property at the local police

The number of death

In the West we often see elevators without a 13th floor. In Taiwan, in hospitals and many public buildings, you will be whisked directly from the third to the fifth floor. This is because the words for 'death' and 'four' are pronounced the same. No need for tempting ill fortune by sending people to the 'floor of death' in a building.

precinct, especially if they discover any non-Chinese documents. Staff at the precinct may not be able to speak English, so contact the Foreign Affairs Police, who do, and who can help you trace the valuables. Local embassies and consulates do not concern themselves with the lost property of their nationals, unless a major crime is involved.

In the Taipei MRT system, fill out a lost-property form at the information counter (in all stations), at the Lost and Found Service Center at Taipei Main Station, B3 level, next to Information Counter No. 1. Service hours are noon to 8pm, Tuesday through Saturday, or by calling the 24-hour customer service at (02)-218 12345.

For lost passports, contact the National Immigration Agency (nia), 15 Guangzhou Street, Taipei, tel: (02) 2388-9393 or 24-hour service hotline for foreigners at 0800-024-111.

M

Maps

Extremely detailed maps are found in all major bookstores – but in Chinese. You'll find little if anything in English. Your best bet are the free maps available at the tourist-service counters at the country's major entry points, in the major cities, and at entry points to major tourist areas such as national scenic areas and national parks. Staff at all these places, save perhaps some scenic areas and national parks, should be able to converse with you in English.

Media

Print

Three English-language newspapers, all of less than international quality but useful for local news, are published daily in Taiwan. They are the China Post (www.chinapost.com.

Taiwanese currency.

tw), *Taiwan News* (www.etaiwannews. com) and *Taipei Times* (www.taipei times.com). The Taipei Times is by far the best; it has a liberal, pro-democracy editorial position, and in general supports the Democratic Progressive Party. All are morning papers. In addition to international and regional news, these newspapers carry financial news, entertainment sections, features, sports reports, and guides to English-language programs on TV and radio. Most hotel newsstands carry all three, and convenience stores will carry one or two.

The Xinwenju (Government Information Office) publishes an illustrated monthly magazine in English, *Taiwan Review* (http://taiwanreview.nat.gov. tw), which features articles on local politics and culture, travel in Taiwan, and other aspects of local life. Over the past decade or more its journalistic integrity has unfortunately slipped, the result of political pressures from the powers that be. The *Review* now more obediently follows the agenda set on high, notably for articles affecting Taiwan's overseas image. *Taiwan Panorama* (www.taiwanpanorama. com.tw), a glossy bilingual monthly, covers Taiwan society and culture. The Tourism Bureau sponsors an illustrated bimonthly, *Travel in Taiwan* (https://issuu.com/ travelintaiwan) that explores local travel and cultural subjects; it is available free from Tourism Bureau offices and at major hotels.

The American Chamber of Commerce puts out a quality monthly

entitled *Topics* (www.amcham.com. tw) that provides good overview articles on the workings of Taiwan's economy, as well as pieces on specific firms.

The Taipei City Government publishes *Discover Taipei Bimonthly* ('Publications' section at http://english.gov.taipei) exploring travel and culture topics related to the capital-city region. This Month in Taiwan (www.tmit-media.com), most easily sourced in print form in major hotels and travel information desks, is filled with practical information on Taiwan travel, nightlife, entertainment, recreation, and other topics. Centered on Taipei, published 10 times a year by the Community Services Center (www.communitycenter.org.tw), is a lifestyle magazine for the international community, with info on shopping, food, culture, art, and more.

Many major international newspapers and periodicals are available in Taiwan, including the International Herald Tribune, Wall Street Journal, *Time*, *Newsweek*, *Life*, and *The Economist*; these are sold at large bookstores and hotel newsstands.

Television and radio

Cable is now ubiquitous in Taiwan. Private homes enjoy 80 or more channels. Quality hotels will carry (free) international mainstays such as HBO, CNN, Star TV, ESPN, and more. Program schedules for the international networks are carried in the English dailies. ICRT (International Community Radio Taipei) is the only English-language radio station available. It can be received in the

north and south at FM 100.7/AM 576, in Hsinchu and the Taichung area at 100.1. Local radio stations broadcast a wide variety of Chinese, Taiwanese, and Western music. Almost all radio and TV stations broadcast 24 hours a day.

Money

The Taiwanese currency is the New Taiwan Dollar, written as NT$. There are 100 cents to one dollar. At the time of writing the exchange rate was NT$31 to US$1.

Major foreign currencies can be easily exchanged for NT$ at major local and foreign banks, international tourist hotels, and the two international airports. Banks offer the most favourable rates. In smaller towns or in the countryside, however, it is practically impossible to change foreign currency into NT$. In smaller towns usually only the Bank of Taiwan changes foreign currency; the procedure is complicated and time-consuming.

Important: Be sure to obtain receipts of all such transactions. You'll find they save you a lot of hassle when you try to reconvert unused New Taiwan dollars at the bank on departure. The banks at Taiwan Taoyuan International Airport outside Taipei are best. There is also a bank at Kaohsiung International Airport.

Traveler's checks are widely accepted at most hotels, foreign-tourist-oriented restaurants and souvenir shops, major department stores, and local branches of the issuing banks. Major credit cards such as American Express, Visa, MasterCard, and Diners Club are now accepted at almost all urban establishments.

N

Nightlife

Nightlife options in Taipei, Kaohsiung, Taichung, and Tainan are varied and plentiful. A night on the town usually begins with a meal; beer, wine, and spirits are ordered along with dinner, and the liquid refreshment rarely stops flowing (see page 107). 'When drinking among intimate friends, even a thousand rounds are not enough,' proclaims an ancient Chinese proverb, and many of the people of Taiwan take that advice to heart. Light inebriation is a form of convivial communication here, an opportunity to drop the formal mask

Orientation

For anyone planning to be in Taiwan for any significant length of time, a visit to the Community Services Center in Taipei can be invaluable. A non-profit foundation run by expatriates, the center can help answer most questions on Taiwan.
Community Services Center
25, Lane 290, Zhongshan N. Road, Sec. 6
Tianmu, Taipei
Tel: (02) 2836-8134
www.communitycenter.org.tw

of business and reveal the 'inner person.' Since the people of Taiwan are food fanatics who appreciate good cuisine of all kinds, Taipei also has a range of Western restaurants, many operated by accomplished European chefs.

KTV

A familiar part of the Taipei night scene is the KTV (karaoke TV) club. Venues are decorated in a variety of themes, from Versailles palaces to high-tech chrome-and-neon space stations. After selecting the appropriate-size private room, customers can order drinks, snacks, and even light meals while leafing through a catalog of traditional, pop, Western, and Asian songs. Desired selections are keyed in via a small terminal in the room. Songs can be selected any time and are queued in line. Wall outlets allow for plenty of microphones. A note of caution: in the late 1990s there were a series of disastrous fires at KTVs around the island; safety standards are now enforced much more strictly, but it is still best to get local acquaintances to confirm the safety of a place.

Bottle clubs

A popular form of Taiwan nightlife is the so-called bottle club. Customers buy liquor by the bottle; it is later stored in special racks for future use. These clubs are generally upscale, with expensive furnishings, tasteful decor, low lights, and 'atmosphere.' Some provide live entertainment. Wealthy local patrons commonly keep bottles of good French cognac. The island's businessmen often choose bottle clubs for entertaining friends and associates on corporate expense accounts.

Taipei pubs and bars

Taipei abounds with pubs and bars. One of the easiest places to go bar-hopping is the so-called Sugar Daddy Row area around Shuangcheng Street, off Linsen N. Road near the Imperial Hotel. There are lots of establishments within easy walking distance of one another. Also called 'the Zone' or 'the Combat Zone' by expats, this area used to be a favorite place for R & R for US servicemen in the 1960s and 1970s. Now much toned down, the Zone is still a popular haunt for those who just can't sit down in one spot for very long, and think more action is always waiting in the next watering hole. Hostess bars catering to male professionals now predominate.

Winehouses

One of the quintessential forms of post-dinner activity for groups of Taiwan's men is the *jiujia*, or winehouse (quite different to beerhouses). People begin to arrive at about 9pm. Most serve food and expect guests to order several dishes, but the main meal is usually taken elsewhere. Winehouse specialties usually include a variety of 'potency foods' like snake-bile soup, turtle-bile stew, sauteed eel, or black-fleshed chicken. All are alleged to be aphrodisiacs.

At least four persons should participate in a winehouse party and at least one should be a local man who is familiar with the routine. Without enough guests, the party cannot reach that vital stage of excitement the Chinese call *renao*, literally 'hot and noisy.' A Chinese-speaking guest helps translate the nuances of the conversation and activity. Beyond the cultural experience, this type of establishment may not be to the taste of foreigners; they are very expensive, and in many cases you must pay for the drinks, and the time, of the 'hostesses' who entertain guests with conversation.

O

Opening hours

Official government business hours in Taiwan are 8.30am to 12.30pm and 1.30 to 5.30pm, Monday through Friday. Banks are open 9am to 3.30pm Monday through Friday. Business and government hours are 9am to 5.30pm Monday through Friday; government offices will

generally keep some staff available to handle visitors during the lunch hour, but companies will not.

Retailers are generally open from 10 or 11am until 9 or 10pm Monday through Saturday; most now keep the same hours on Sunday, or close a little earlier. Many smaller shops and stalls keep longer hours and remain open all week, from about 10am until 10pm or later. Museums are usually closed on Mondays; many are also closed the day after national holidays. More are now offering extended hours on Saturday, and sometimes Friday, nights. While offices and banks close on public holidays, many retail outlets remain open at least part of the day.

P

Photography

Beyond common sense and universal rules regarding invasion of privacy, there are few restrictions in terms of etiquette here. The natives of Orchid Island, after decades of being treated as something akin to zoo specimens, are sensitive to close-up shots, so it is best to keep your distance and, if a close-up is desired, to use a long lens and a circumspect approach. Photographing military bases is not permitted.

The island is a good place to shop for equipment, especially in Taipei. The city's well-known Camera Street, which has a history of over 40 years, is in the west end, stretching from the head of Boai Road to the end of Wuchang Street. Over 40 shops sell the latest in cameras and other related equipment. Many also still supply traditional equipment, mostly of professional calibre. Prices are not as low as in Hong Kong, but are generally 20 to 30 percent lower than those found in the West. This is also true of the next-best Taipei location for photographic equipment, Guang Hua Digital Plaza.

Postal services

Taiwan has one of the fastest, most efficient, and most inexpensive postal services in the world. Post offices are open from 8am to 6pm Monday to Friday; selected major offices are open 8am to 4pm on Saturday. Letters mailed to the US from Taiwan usually arrive at their destinations within five to seven days of posting; the postage rate for a letter under 2 grams (0.07oz) to the

Public holidays

Traditional holidays correspond to dates in the lunar calendar and thus change from year to year. Taiwan comes to a virtual standstill during the minimum four-day holiday at Chinese New Year; depending on the days of the week on which these fall, the government may grant a full work week off.

Foundation Day of the Republic of China: January 1
Chinese Lunar New Year: January/February
Peace Memorial Day: February 28
Women's Day/Children's Day: April 4
Tomb Sweeping Day (Qingming Festival): April 5
Dragon Boat Festival: May/June
Mid-Autumn Festival/Moon Festival: September/October
National Day (Double Tenth): October 10

US is NT$15. Local mail is delivered within 24 to 48 hours.

Taipei's **Central Post Office** is located at the North Gate intersection, close to the Taipei Railway Station. This is the best place to collect and post mail in Taipei; some clerks speak passable English at the international counters. This office also provides inexpensive cartons and packing services for parcel posting.

Stamps may be purchased at the mail counter of any hotel in Taiwan, and at all convenience stores. Letters may be dropped in any hotel or public mailbox. Local mail goes into the

Prayers at Longshan Temple.

green boxes (right-hand slot for mail within the city, left for outside), and international mail goes into the red boxes (right-hand slot for prompt delivery, left for airmail).

For more information, call 0800-700-365 or visit the Chunghwa Post website at www.post.gov.tw.

R

Religious services

The majority of the population follows a mix of Buddhism, Daoism, and Confucianism. A minority follow Islam and Christianity. Taiwan is recognized as one of the world's most religiously tolerant countries; there is no religious discrimination.

The country's main mosque is **Taipei Grand Mosque** (tel: (02) 2321-9445) on Xinsheng S. Road across from Daan Park. There are guided visits, but non-Muslims may not enter the main prayer hall or the second-floor prayer hall for women.

Approximately 4.5 percent of the population is Christian, the aboriginal peoples predominantly. Protestants, mostly Presbyterian, take up about 80 percent, Roman Catholics the remainder.

The following Taipei churches provide services in English:

Anglican/Episcopalian
Church of the Good Shepherd
509 Zhongzheng Road. (Shilin District)
Tel: (02) 2873-8104
www.goodshepherd.com.tw
Sunday services at 9.30am, normally combined English/Chinese service 10.30am on fourth Sunday each month.

Roman Catholic
Mother of God Church
171 Zhongshan N. Road, Sec. 7 (Tianmu District)
Tel: (02) 2871-5168
www.motherofgodcatholic.org
Sunday services at 10am and 7pm. For more details on English services, the best source is the weekend editions of the English daily papers.

S

Smoking

Smoking is banned in all indoor public places in the country. Between 20 and 25 percent of the population

smoke, and about 15 percent in Taipei, with numbers slowly but steadily decreasing as a result of anti-smoking campaigns.

Sport

In recent times, organized sports and strenuous outdoor activities have gained popularity in Taiwan. Local health experts inform people that traditional Chinese approaches to health and longevity are not enough; rigorous physical exercise is also required. The island frequently hosts international sports events, and regularly sends teams and individuals to compete abroad. (To avoid confrontation with China, Taiwan is officially named 'Chinese Taipei' in many international competitions.) The sports most easily accessible to the tourist in Taiwan are bicycling, golf, tennis, and swimming.

Golf

Golf is the oldest organized sport in Taiwan, and all of Taiwan's golf clubs are open to foreign visitors for guest memberships. The clubs are open year-round. Many are private, but others are open to all, although they offer preferential rates and tee-off times to members on weekends and holidays.

Arrangements for guest privileges in Taiwan's golf clubs may be made through hotel travel desks and local travel agencies, who will also arrange for regular club members to accompany or sponsor temporary guests in those clubs whose rules require it. Clubs, shoes, caddies, and food and beverage facilities are available at all clubs.

Further inquiries regarding golf in Taiwan, and especially north Taiwan, may be directed to the International Golf Society of Taipei, run by expats; www.taiwan-golf.com. The Tourism

Diving guide

The Taiwan Visitors Association publishes the best available English-language source of information on diving in Taiwan; a free booklet entitled *Diving in Taiwan: Guide to Scuba Diving in Taiwan*. It is chock-full of detailed information on dive sites, diving associations, gear rental shops, and more. Solid English information can also be found online at http://diveadvisor.com/taiwan.

Bureau has a good introduction to the country's courses on its website; visit www.taiwan.net.tw, then visit the Travel Suggestions, Special Interests and LOHAS sections in turn.

Tennis

There are hundreds of courts around the island, some at tourist hotels, most at public sports clubs and sports-park facilities, and some at private clubs that accommodate non-members. Ask your hotel for help with bookings at the nearest available courts.

More information is available at the **Chinese Taipei Tennis Association**, Room 705, 7F, 20 Zhulun Street Taipei; www.tennis.org.tw; tel: (02) 2772-0298.

Martial arts

The Chinese have traditionally kept themselves in shape by practicing various ancient forms of martial arts and related breathing and meditation exercises.

In Taiwan, every morning at dawn thousands of people pour into parks, temple courtyards, and other public places around the island to practice *taiji quan*, martial arts, yoga, sword dances, or simple aerobics. Visitors may also get a good workout each morning by simply joining whatever group interests them and mimicking their gentle movements. The most popular places in Taipei for early-morning exercise sessions are 2-28 Memorial Peace Park, the grand plazas at Chiang Kai-shek Memorial Hall and Sun Yat-sen Memorial Hall, and Daan Park.

Even if you don't participate, you should try to catch this scene at least once while in Taipei. If you are interested in serious study, information is available from the **National Tai Chi Chuan Association of Taiwan**, Room 608, 20 Zhulun Street, Taipei; tel: (02) 2778-3887; www.cttaichi.org. The association also runs its own classes, from beginner to advanced, in different disciplines.

Swimming

In addition to public beaches, there are numerous swimming pools at various upscale hotels, clubs, and resorts around the island. If your hotel does not have swimming facilities, ask the concierge for assistance.

The number of public facilities is also increasing. The Taipei City Government has now introduced a low-fee, state-of-the-art

sports center in each of its 12 administrative districts, all with swimming pools.

Scuba Diving and Snorkeling

The coral reefs off Kenting National Park, at the southern tip of Taiwan, offer very good diving. The rocky, shallow shoreline here also permits excellent snorkeling. In the north, divers can explore underwater coral kingdoms off the coast of Yeliu, which is famous for the strange formations of coral protruding from its seaside promontory. The islands of Lanyu, Ludao, and Penghu are other first-rate diving locales, with the possibility of sighting larger marine life off the latter.

Several local diving clubs organize regular excursions to popular diving areas. For further information, contact the following organization: **Chinese Taipei Diving Development Association** 509 Zhongyang Road, Nangang District Tel: (02) 2786-2451

Shopping

Where to shop

The Taiwanese flock to upscale shopping venues. Large-scale department stores and massive malls are the very definition of what is perceived as sophisticated, cosmopolitan living.

Many malls make a shopping trip a full-day outing, attracting visitors by almost always having a department store, scores of fashion boutiques, and upscale outlets selling everything a consumer could possibly desire – DVDs, CDs, gift items, books, jewelry, watches, electronic goods, cameras, and of course, clothing and accessories.

A wide selection of restaurants and eateries, as well as a food court, are de rigueur, and big-city malls will most likely have a cinema complex and a number of nightlife venues such as pubs, bars, and perhaps dance establishments. Almost all are open daily from about 10am or 11am, closing around 9.30pm or 10pm. Cinemas and nightlife venues located within shopping malls are open till late.

Antiques stores

Taipei is one of the better places in the region to search for Chinese antiques: items designated as anything over 100 years old. The best outlets, and those most

experienced in dealing with foreigners, are located in Tianmu, the expat enclave in northern Taipei; check the English-language papers for ads. Most items are of wood and are sourced in mainland China, Taiwan having already been scoured almost dry. Tianmu-area outlets are reputable, staff speak English, and they can arrange shipping. Items run the gamut, as do prices.

Student travelers

The government of Taiwan has introduced various programs specifically targeted at attracting student/youth travelers. Both study and work travel are possible, special rail passes and accommodations are available, and a Tour Buddy program has been set up so students can tour with knowledgeable local youths. Visit the Tourism Bureau website (www.taiwan.net.tw) or a special website targeted at the youth traveler (https://youthtravel.tw). The latter site gives details on the Youth Travel Card, available for individuals aged 15 to 30, which brings deals on accommodations, food and shopping, etc.

T

Tax

There is a value-added tax of 5 percent on goods and services in Taiwan. Foreign tourists who spend more than NT$3,000 (approximately US$90) in the same TRS (Tax Refund Shopping) outlet in a single day and take the goods out of the country within 30 days will be eligible for a refund of the 5 percent value-added tax, providing they fill in an application form at the Foreign Passenger VAT Refund Service Counter at the airport or harbor before departure, and present the goods in question along with the original invoice/s.

Over 200 businesses around the country, including many department stores, now sport the TRS logo. For more details, visit www.taiwan.net.tw.

Telephones

Long-distance calls

Long-distance calls within Taiwan can be made from private or public pay phones. Just punch in the correct area code and number.

TRANSPORTATION

Telephone codes

Country code: 886
Area codes:
Taipei City/New Taipei City/
Keelung 02
Changhua County 04
Chiayi 05
Hsinchu 03
Hualien County 038
Kaohsiung 07
Miaoli County 037
Nantou County 049
Penghu County 06
Pingtung County 08
Taichung 04
Tainan 06
Taitung County 089
Yilan County 039
Yunlin County 05

Local calls

Local city calls may be dialed from any public pay telephone. Public phones in Taiwan are divided primarily into two types: coin and card. Coin-operated phones accept coins in denominations of NT$1, NT$5, and NT$10. For local calls, NT$1 buys one minute of phone time. Phone cards are divided into magnetic-strip stored-value cards and IC stored-value cards, and can be used all over Taiwan. Magnetic-strip cards sell for NT$100 each, and IC cards are available in NT$200 and NT$300 versions. The cards are sold in railway stations, bus stations, scenic spots, and convenience stores. You need to dial the area code first if calling from one county/city to another; if calling within the same county/city, there is no need to dial the area code.

International calls

IDD calls can be made by dialing the international dialing code 002 + country code + city code + local number. International reverse-charge (call collect) and credit calls can be made through dedicated phones at airports and major hotels.

Calls to the USA can be made through AT&T Direct, and to over 220 other countries through AT&T World Connect. For detail, visit www.att.com/global.

For reverse charges or credit calls, dial 00801, then the access number for the country being called, as follows:
Australia: 00801-610-061
Canada: 00801-120-012
UK: 00801-440-044
US (AT&T): 00801-102-880
On private phones, the overseas

operator may be reached by dialing 100. For directory assistance in English dial 106 or (02) 2311-6796. For international information, call this free number: 0800-080-100. International direct dialing is available from many public phones, marked in English as idd-capable, especially in hotels. Visa, MasterCard and jcb cards can be used, as well as IC cards that can be purchased at 7-Elevens. Calls can also be made on public facilities at Chunghwa Telecom offices.

Country Codes

Australia 61
Canada 1
Ireland 353
New Zealand 64
South Africa 27
Taiwan 886
UK 44
United States 1

Tipping

Generally speaking, tipping is not expected in Taiwan, although token gratuities are always appreciated. Hotels and restaurants automatically add a 10 percent service charge to bills, but this money rarely gets distributed in full among the staff, so a small cash tip of 5 to 10 percent is always welcome in restaurants. An NT$50 tip per piece of luggage tip is usual for hotel and airport porters, and for assistants providing special services in hair salons.

Tipping is not necessary for taxi drivers, unless they load luggage for you (NT$10). Taxis still cost far less in Taiwan than most places of similar economic development, but the cost of gas (petrol) and maintenance here is quite high, so drivers appreciate even the smallest tips. Oversupply, fierce competition, and low fares mean that most taxi drivers nowadays spend 12 or more hours on the road a day, many of them seven days a week, often transferring their vehicle to another driver when they go off-shift.

Time zone

Taipei and all Taiwan is +8 hours from Greenwich Mean Time (GMT). It is +13 from Eastern Standard Time (EST) in the eastern US and Canada, +12 during EST daylight savings time. The time difference with Sydney is -3 hours in summer, -2 in winter.

The only places in Taiwan where heavy tips are routinely expected are in winehouses and bottle clubs, where big tipping wins you 'big face.'

Toilets

Around Taiwan, public-use washrooms are provided at most major tourist sites and at major parks. However, the sheer numbers of visitors often overwhelm the facilities on weekends and holidays, and cleanliness falls by the wayside. Some do not provide toilet paper, or the supply is quickly used up, so always have your own handy. Unlike some other Asian destinations, there are no charges for the use of public washrooms in Taiwan. If nature calls and you are away from a tourist site, your best bets are temples, fast-food outlets, shopping malls, and the larger hotels. The mass rapid-transit systems in Taipei and Kaohsiung have clean washrooms and toilet paper, but this may not be true during the heavy-use rush hours. Around the island, more and more 7-Elevens in scenic areas are providing clean washroom facilities, generally with paper. Note that parks, temples, and major tourist sites will most likely solely have squat toilets.

Tourist information

Service and information centers, run by the Taiwan Tourism Bureau, are located at both international airports. The staff speak English, and can help with transport, accommodation, and other travel requirements.

There are two national organizations in Taiwan that oversee and promote the tourism industry. The Tourism Bureau is the official government organ responsible for tourism in Taiwan. The Taiwan Visitors Association is a private organization that promotes Taiwan tourism abroad and provides travel assistance to visitors in Taiwan. The two work closely together, and divide the running of Taiwan tourism promotion offices overseas, with the former running significantly more. The TVA does not operate tourist-information centers in Taiwan itself.

The Tourism Bureau operates tourist information centers in all major urban centers. It also operates centers in all national scenic areas, for which it is responsible. Major cities also now run their own local tourist assistance centers. The Ministry of the Interior operates

A – Z

LANGUAGE

tourist information centers in all national parks, for which it is responsible. All such information centers provide materials in English, and have staff on hand who can function in English.

Taipei

Tourism Bureau (Main Office), Ministry of Transportation and Communications
9F, 290 Zhongxiao E. Road, Sec. 4
Tel: (02) 2349 1500
www.taiwan.net.tw
Taiwan Visitors Association
5F, 9, Minquan E. Road, Sec. 2
Tel: (02)2594-3261
www.tva.org.tw
Travel Information Service Center (TISC)
240 Dunhua N. Road (just south of Taipei Songshan Airport)
Tel: (02) 2717-3737
Email: tisc@tbroc.gov.tw

Kaohsiung

Tourist Service Center
5F-1, 235 Zhongzheng 4th Road
Tel: (07) 281-1513/0800-711-765
e-mail: trainkhh@ms48.hinet.net
Tourist Service Center, Tourism Bureau
Taiwan Taoyuan International Airport
Terminal I
Tel: (03) 398-2194
Terminal II
Tel: (03) 398-3341
Kaohsiung International Airport
Tel: (07) 805-7888
The Tourism Bureau provides a toll-free number (0800-011-765) for visitors in Taiwan with travel inquiries. Service is 24 hours, in Chinese, English, and Japanese.

Taichung

Tourist Service Center
1F, 95 Gancheng Street
Tel: (04) 2254-0809/0800-422-022
e-mail: tisctch@ms39.hinet.net

Tainan

Tourist Service Center
10F, 243 Minquan Road, Sec. 1
Tel: (06) 226-5681/0800-611-011
e-mail: traintna@ms48.hinet.net

Useful numbers
Tourist Information Hotline: (02) 2717-3737 (8am–8pm) 0800-011-765 (24hr, toll-free)
International Community Service Hotline (National Police Administration): 0800-024-111
Foreign Affairs Police:
Taipei: (02) 2381-7494
Hsinchu: (03) 555-7953
Kaohsiung: (07) 221-5796

Keelung: (02) 24271857
Taichung: (04) 2327-3875
Bureau of Consular Affairs, Ministry of Foreign Affairs:
Taipei: (02) 2343-2888
Kaohsiung: (07) 211-0605
Taichung: (04) 2222-2799
National Immigration Agency, Taipei: (02) 2389-9983
English Speaking Taxi (Taipei): (02) 2799-7997

W

Websites

www.taiwan.net.tw
The government tourism bureau site is good on general information, and offers a good deal of practical info that is kept up-to-date.
http://iff.immigration.gov.tw
A wide range of practical info specifically for foreigners living/traveling in Taiwan, from the National Immigration Agency.
www.booking.com
Discounts on accommodation, guest reviews.
www.agoda.com
Reviews, discount deals, reward points, wide coverage.
www.taiwan.gov.tw
Government Information Office site; very informative on all aspects of Chinese/Taiwanese culture from architecture to philosophy, and useful links.
www.romanization.com
A wealth of information on Taiwan's numerous Romanization systems, Taipei street names, and more practical material, plus links to numerous digital versions of important out-of-print book titles on Taiwan's politics, culture, and history.
www.taiwandc.org
A portal to organizations and student groups dedicated to Taiwan democracy, with information on Taiwan's history, people, society, culture, and political system.
www.taiwannights.com
Good info on clubbing, restaurants, bars, and other sources of nighttime fun on the island.

What to wear

During the hot season, appropriate clothing should include light and loose cotton clothing and comfortable walking shoes. Many Chinese businessmen prefer to wear leisure suits with open collars to beat the heat, although if

Weights and measures

Metric system in most instances. However, in both traditional public markets and small local shops throughout Taiwan, vendors still often weigh and measure using traditional Chinese units. If on your own without an interpreter, the following conversion table will help you figure out the unit price of items.
Length: The Chinese 'foot' is called a chi: 1 chi = 11.9ins or 0.99ft (0.32 meters).
1 zhang = 10 chi
Weight: The Chinese 'pound' is called a catty or jin: 1 jin = 1.32lbs/21.2oz (0.6kg).
The Chinese 'ounce' is called a liang: 1 liang = 1.32oz (37.5 grams).
Area: The Chinese measure area in units of ping and jia: 1 ping = 36 sq. feet (3.3 sq. meters)
1 jia = 2.40 acres (0.9 hectare)

you come for business, it is better to be overdressed. Hotels, restaurants and offices are air-conditioned.

During the winter months, be sure to bring some comfortable woolens to help protect you from the chilly, moisture-laden winter air. Sweaters, woolen jackets and dresses, warm trousers and socks will all come in handy during Taiwanese winters, especially in Taipei. People in Taiwan tend to dress a bit more formally on winter evenings than in summer.

During both seasons, it is advisable to bring along some sort of rain gear; thunderstorms can occur at any time. Most local people use umbrellas, which can be purchased at convenience stores, drugstores, supermarkets, and department stores.

Women travelers

Taiwan is a safe travel destination for women, though as with anywhere else it is not advisable to walk alone or take taxis alone late at night. For any specific medical needs, doctors at major hospitals will be able to communicate in English, though most other staff will not. Among others, Taipei's Community Services Center specifically recommends the Priority Care Center, tel: (02) 2776-2654, ext. 2670–2672, at the Taiwan Adventist Hospital in Taipei (www.tahsda.org.tw).

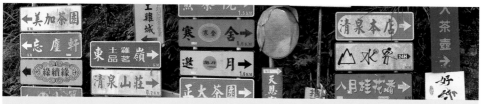

LANGUAGE

UNDERSTANDING THE LANGUAGE

WRITTEN SCRIPT

Chinese writing is based on ideograms, or 'idea-pictures,' which graphically depict ideas and objects with written characters derived directly from actual diagrams of the subject. The oldest recorded Chinese characters appeared on oracle bones excavated in the 19th century in China and dating from the ancient Shang dynasty (1523–1028 BC). At that time, questions of vital interest to the emperor were inscribed upon the dried shells of giant tortoises and ox scapulae, which were then subjected to heat. The heat caused the shells to crack, and diviners then interpreted Heaven's answers to the emperor's questions by 'reading' the cracks. The answers were then inscribed on the shells, which were then stored in the imperial archives. Based on the number and complexity of the characters inscribed on these oracle bones, Chinese historians concluded that Chinese written language was invented during the reign of the Yellow Emperor, around 2700 BC.

The written characters reached their current stage of development about 2,000 years ago during the Han dynasty, and they have changed very little since then, which makes Chinese the oldest ongoing writing system in the world. The importance of China's written language cannot be overstated: it held together a vast and complex empire composed of many different ethnic groups, and due to its non-phonetic nature, it formed a written common denominator among China's various dialects. Once the symbols were learned, they gave the reader access to an enormous wealth of historical and literary writings accumulated in China over a long period of continuous cultural development – now thought to be more than five millennia. Written Chinese has evolved continuously from generation to generation, transmitting with it the accumulated treasures of Chinese culture right down to the present era. The simple act of writing one's own surname in Chinese immediately recalls and identifies one with a host of historical and literary heroes, spanning five millennia, who shared the same name.

There are about 50,000 Chinese characters listed in Chinese dictionaries, but the vast majority are either obsolete or used in highly specialized branches of learning. About 3,000 characters are required for basic literacy, such as reading newspapers and business documents, and about 5,000 are required for advanced literary studies. About 2,000 Chinese characters are still used in the written languages of Korea and Japan. Few scholars, however, are capable of using over 6,000 characters without resorting to dictionaries.

SPOKEN LANGUAGE

There are only several hundred monosyllabic vocal sounds in the Chinese spoken language, which means that many written characters share the same pronunciation. To somewhat clarify matters, the Chinese developed a tonal system that uses four distinctive tones in Mandarin Chinese to pronounce each syllable. Even so, many characters share both common syllables and tones, and the only way to be really sure which words are meant when spoken is to consider the entire context of a statement, or demand a written explanation.

Grammatically, spoken Chinese is simple and direct. There are no conjugations, declensions, gender distinctions, tense changes, or other complicated grammatical rules to memorize. The spoken language consists of simple sounds strung together in the 'subject/verb/ object' construction common to most Western languages. Tones, while foreign to Western tongues, come naturally with usage and are not difficult to master. Even within China, the various provinces often give different tonal inflections to the various sounds. Proper word order and correct context are by far the most important elements to know about spoken Chinese grammar.

In Taiwan, the Mandarin dialect (known as *guoyu*, or the 'national language') was declared the official lingua franca by the government in the late 1940s. Mandarin is based upon the pronunciations that prevailed in the old imperial capital of Beijing. In addition to Mandarin, the local 'Taiwanese' dialect is derived from China's Fujian province, ancestral home of the vast majority of Taiwan's populace of Han Chinese descent. Taiwanese is commonly spoken among locals, especially in the rural regions, and many local television stations broadcast programs in the dialect. The Hakka minority, also of Han Chinese descent, has its own dialect, but many of the younger generation lack fluency. The country's indigenous peoples, each of which has its own language, face this same problem. Since the 2000s, there has been a conscious effort by both the Hakka and the native groups, with some government support, to increase fluency, and there is now both Hakka and indigenous television programming.

The older generation still speaks some Japanese – a remnant of Japan's colonial occupation – and younger people tend to understand at least basic English. Though English is a required subject for all students in Taiwan throughout high school, it is spoken fluently by very few.

TRANSLITERATION

The transliteration system used in Taiwan is Hanyu Pinyin, the same system used in China. Non-Hanyu spellings are used when more familiar (Taipei, Kaohsiung, Chiang Kai-shek, etc.); invariably, these forms were in use long before the Hanyu Pinyin was adopted.

USEFUL PHRASES

Greetings

Hello, how are you? *Ni hao ma?*
Fine; very good *Hen hao*
Not so good *Bu hao*
Goodbye *Zai jian*
See you tomorrow *Mingtian jian*
Good morning *Zao an*
Good evening *Wan an*
You; you (plural) *Ni; nimen*
I; we *Wo; women*
He, she, it; they *Ta; tamen*
Who? *Shei?*
Mr Li *Li Xiansheng*
Miss Li *Li Xiaojie*
Mrs Li *Li Taitai*
Thank you *Xie-xie*
You're welcome *Bu keqi*

Time and place

Where? *Nali?*
What time? *Jidian zhong?*
What day? *Libai ji?*
Today *Jintian*
Tomorrow *Mingtian*
Yesterday *Zuotian*
One o'clock *Yi dian zhong*
Two o'clock *Liang dian zhong*
Very far *Hen yuan*
Very close *Hen jin*

Food and drink

Restaurant *Canting*
Bar *Jiuba*
Let's eat; to eat *Chifan*
Let's drink; to drink *Hejiu*

Ice; ice-cubes *Bing; bingkuai*
Water; cold water *Shui; bing shui*
Soup *Tang*
Fruit *Shuiguo*
Tea *Cha*
Coffee *Kafei*
Hot *Re*
Cold *Leng*
Sugar *Tang*
A little bit *Yidian, Yidiandian*
A little more *Duo yidian*
A little bit less *Shao yidian*
Bottoms up! *Ganbei!*
Settle the bill *Suanzhang*
Let me pay *Wo (lai) qingke*

Numbers

One *Yi*
Two *Er (liang)*
Three *San*
Four *Si*
Five *Wu*
Six *Liu*
Seven *Qi*
Eight *Ba*
Nine *Jiu*
Ten *Shi*
Eleven *Shiyi*
Twelve, etc. *Shier, etc.*
Twenty *Ershi*
Thirty *Sanshi*
Forty, etc. *Sishi*
Fifty-five *Wushi wu*
Seventy-six *Qishi liu*
One hundred *Yibai*
One hundred and twenty-five *Yibai ershi wu*
Two hundred, etc. *Liangbai*
One thousand *Yiqian*
Ten thousand *Yiwan*
Fifty thousand *Wuwan*

Transportation

Hotel *Fandian*
Room *Fangjian*
Airport *Feijichang*
International airport *Guoji jichang*
Bus/coach *Bashi*
Bus (public) *Gonggong qiche*
Taxi *Jichengche*
Telephone *Dianhua*
International call *Guoji dianhua*
Telegram *Dianbao*
Airplane *Feiji*
Train *Huoche*
Reservation *Dingwei*
Key *Yaoshi*
Clothing *Yifu*
Luggage *Xingli*

Shopping

How much? *Duoshao?*
Too expensive *Tai gui*
Make it a bit cheaper *Suan pianyi dian*

Body language

The Taiwanese do not engage in much casual contact, except between good friends. What is seen as friendly touching by Westerners is seen as advances by members of the opposite sex. So be careful. Many a Western expat, especially in office situations, has been surprised to find he is perceived as a *selang* – a 'color wolf,' or playboy – by local colleagues.

When pointing to themselves, locals point to their nose with their index finger. To beckon a person over, extend your arm, palm down, and make a gentle scooping motion toward yourself; a common way Westerners beckon, making a hooking motion with the index finger, palm up, means someone/something is dead. Touching the index finger to the cheek, scratching it up and down, indicates a person has *diulian*, or 'lost face'; the motion simulates a red face and embarrassment. Pressing the index and middle finger together, then tapping them gently against the temple a few times rapidly, means a person is crazy or unstable; the term *shodo* is often uttered, from the Japanese pronunciation of 'short,' as in an electrical short in the brain.

Money *Qian*
Credit card *Xinyong ka*
Old *Lao*
New *Xin*
Big *Da*
Small *Xiao*
Antique *Gudong*
Red *Hong*
Green *Lu*
Yellow *Huang*
Black *Hei*
White *Bai*
Blue *Lan*
Gold *Jin, huangjin*
Jade *Yu*
Wood *Mu*
Proprietor, shop owner *Laoban*
Wrap it up *Bao qilai*

Basic sentence patterns

I want... *Wo yao...*
I don't want... *Wo buyao...*
Where is...? *...zai nali?*
Do you have...? *Ni you meiyou...?*
We don't have... *Women meiyou...*
I like... *Wo xihuan...*
I don't like... *Wo bu xihuan...*
I like you *Wo xihuan ni*
I wish to go... *Wo yao qu...*

FURTHER READING

HISTORY AND POLITICS

From Far Formosa: The Island, Its People and Missions by George Leslie Mackay, D.D. Reprint of 1896 edition; a look at Formosa by a respected figure whose name is still familiar in Taiwan, with a hospital and other organizations named after him.
Islands in the Stream: A Quick Case Study of Taiwan's Complex History by April Lin and Jerome Keating. An easy-read primer, focused on political history, which will bring you up to the present in just a few hours.
Japanese Rule in Formosa by Yosaburo Takekoshi. Reprint of the 1907 edition; a demanding and detailed anthropological look at Taiwan's people from the imperial Japanese perspective.
Sketches from Formosa by Rev. W. Campbell. Reprint of the 1915 edition; an intriguing look at late-19th and early-20th century Taiwan through a contemporary's eyes.
Statecraft and Political Economy on the Taiwan Frontier, 1600–1800 by John Robert Shepherd. A dense, scholarly book, this is the best single English source for the period in question.
Taiwan: Nation-State or Province by John F. Copper. Perhaps the best primer on the island, with eminently readable sections on geography, economy, history, and more.
Why Taiwan Matters: Small Island, Global Powerhouse by Shelly Rigger. An exploration of why Taiwan, despite its small size, has so much economic and political weight on the world stage.

BUSINESS READING

Directory of Taiwan by The Taiwan News. An indispensable annual that bills itself, correctly, as 'the most authoritative bilingual directory of government, business and cultural organizations in Taiwan.'

Taipei Living by Taipei Community Services Center. Updated biannually by the center, which helps expats settle in, this handy reference book expands six fold on the type of information found in this guide's Travel Tips.

CULTURE AND FOOD

Birdwatcher's Guide to the Taipei Region by Rick Charette. Colorful illustrated guide to birdwatching trails in and around the city, with maps.
Culture Shock! Taiwan: A Guide to Customs and Etiquette by Chris and Ling-li Bates. A concise and lighthearted primer for confused foreigners on the ins and outs, dos and don'ts of getting along with the locals.

Send Us Your Thoughts

We do our best to ensure the information in our books is as accurate and up-to-date as possible. The books are updated on a regular basis using local contacts, who painstakingly add, amend and correct as required. However, some details (such as telephone numbers and opening times) are liable to change, and we are ultimately reliant on our readers to put us in the picture.
We welcome your feedback, especially your experience of using the book "on the road". Maybe we recommended a hotel that you liked (or another that you didn't), or you came across a great bar or new attraction we missed.
We will acknowledge all contributions, and we'll offer an Insight Guide to the best letters received.

Please write to us at:
**Insight Guides
PO Box 7910
London SE1 1WE**
Or email us at:
hello@insightguides.com

Formosan Odyssey: Taiwan, Past and Present by John Ross. A lighthearted, highly entertaining, and insightful account of a New Zealander's north-south trek down the island.
Private Prayers and Public Parades by Mark Caltonhill. Answers all your questions on Taiwan's religious life – which gods you're looking at, origins of festivals, explanations of practices such as tomb sweeping, throwing of oracle blocks, and more.
Reflections on Taipei by Rick Charette. A look at Taipei's people, their culture, and the city's development in modern times via discussions with long-term expatriate residents.
Taiwan: A Political History by Denny Roy. Detailed, reliable, easy-reading travel down Taiwan's road to democracy.
Taiwan A to Z: The Essential Cultural Guide by Amy Liu. Gives insight on Taiwanese traditions, festival, peoples, etiquette, etc., along with guidance to working with locals.
The Ugly Chinaman by Bo Yang, translated by Don J. Cohn and Jing Qing. For centuries the Chinese have been navel-gazing, wondering how their culture has become so petrified; this modern classic, by a famous dissident, caused great controversy in the 1980s.
Window on Taiwan by Mark de Fraeye. An expensive and beautifully illustrated work by photographer de Fraeye, with accompanying essays by a range of experts.

FICTION

Crystal Boys by Pai Hsien-yung. Explores the difficulties of growing up gay in conservative Taipei, with the main setting old Taipei New Park, today's 2-28 Memorial Peace Park.
Wild Kids: Two Novels about Growing Up by Chang Ta-chun. A journey into the disillusionment and cynicism of modern Taiwan youth, depicting dysfunctional families and the generation gap with searing satire.

CREDITS

Insight Guide Credits

Distribution
UK, Ireland and Europe
Apa Publications (UK) Ltd;
sales@insightguides.com
United States and Canada
Ingram Publisher Services;
ips@ingramcontent.com
Australia and New Zealand
Woodslane; info@woodslane.com.au
Southeast Asia
Apa Publications (SN) Pte;
singaporeoffice@insightguides.com
Worldwide
Apa Publications (UK) Ltd;
sales@insightguides.com
Special Sales, Content Licensing and CoPublishing
Insight Guides can be purchased in bulk quantities at discounted prices. We can create special editions, personalised jackets and corporate imprints tailored to your needs.
sales@insightguides.com
www.insightguides.biz

Printed in Poland by Pozkal

First Edition 1983
Sixth Edition 2017

www.insightguides.com

Editor: Sarah Clark
Author: Justyna Kosecka, Rick Charette
Head of Production: Rebeka Davies
Update Production: Apa Digital
Picture Editor: Tom Smyth
Cartography: original cartography Colourmap Scanning Ltd, updated by Carte

Contributors

This new edition of *Insight Guide Taiwan* was managed by **Sarah Clark**. The book was thoroughly updated by **Justyna Kosecka**, building on the substantial work of Canadian-born, Taipei-based writer, **Rick Charette**, who has lived in Taiwan since 1988 and knows the city intimately. His many writings on the island, as well as on China and all things Asian have been published by newspaper, magazine, and book publishers in Taiwan and abroad.

Other previous contributors include **Brent Hannon**, **Chris Taylor**, **Julie Gaw**, **Scott Rutherford**, **Daniel Reid**, **Bernd Hans-Gerd Helms**, **Linda Chih-Ling Hsu**, **John Gottberg Anderson**, **Paul Zach**, **Keith Stevens**, **Andy Unger**, and **Jon-Claire Lee**.
Much of the vibrant photography in the book is the result of a specially commissioned shoot by **Chris Stowers**.
Insight Guide Taiwan was indexed by **Penny Phenix**.

About Insight Guides

Insight Guides have more than 45 years' experience of publishing high-quality, visual travel guides. We produce 400 full-colour titles, in both print and digital form, covering more than 200 destinations across the globe, in a variety of formats to meet your different needs.
    Insight Guides are written by local authors, whose expertise is evident in the extensive historical and cultural background features.

Each destination is carefully researched by regional experts to ensure our guides provide the very latest information. All the reviews in **Insight Guides** are independent; we strive to maintain an impartial view. Our reviews are carefully selected to guide you to the best places to eat, go out and shop, so you can be confident that when we say a place is special, we really mean it.

Legend

City maps

- Freeway/Highway/Motorway
- Divided Highway
- Main Roads
- Minor Roads
- Pedestrian Roads
- Steps
- Footpath
- Railway
- Funicular Railway
- Cable Car
- Tunnel
- City Wall
- Important Building
- Built Up Area
- Other Land
- Transport Hub
- Park
- Pedestrian Area
- Bus Station
- Tourist Information
- Main Post Office
- Cathedral/Church
- Mosque
- Synagogue
- Statue/Monument
- Beach
- Airport

Regional maps

- Freeway/Highway/Motorway (with junction)
- Freeway/Highway/Motorway (under construction)
- Divided Highway
- Main Road
- Secondary Road
- Minor Road
- Track
- Footpath
- International Boundary
- State/Province Boundary
- National Park/Reserve
- Marine Park
- Ferry Route
- Marshland/Swamp
- Glacier   Salt Lake
- Airport/Airfield
- Ancient Site
- Border Control
- Cable Car
- Castle/Castle Ruins
- Cave
- Chateau/Stately Home
- Church/Church Ruins
- Crater
- Lighthouse
- Mountain Peak
- Place of Interest
- Viewpoint

INDEX

INSIGHT ◉ GUIDES

OFF THE SHELF

Since 1970, INSIGHT GUIDES has provided a unique perspective on the world's best travel destinations by using specially commissioned photography and illuminating text written by local authors.

Whether you're planning a city break, a walking tour or the journey of a lifetime, our superb range of guidebooks and phrasebooks will inspire you to discover more about your chosen destination.

INSIGHT GUIDES

offer a unique combination of stunning photos, absorbing narrative and detailed maps, providing all the inspiration and information you need.

PHRASEBOOKS & DICTIONARIES

help users to feel at home, when away. Pocket-sized with a free app to download, they go where you do.

CITY GUIDES

pack hundreds of great photos into a smaller format with detailed practical information, so you can navigate the world's top cities with confidence.

EXPLORE GUIDES

feature easy-to-follow walks and itineraries in the world's most exciting destinations, with our choice of the best places to eat and drink along the way.

POCKET GUIDES

combine concise information on where to go and what to do in a handy compact format, ideal on the ground. Includes a full-colour, fold-out map.

EXPERIENCE GUIDES

feature offbeat perspectives and secret gems for experienced travellers, with a collection of over 100 ideas for a memorable stay in a city.

www.insightguides.com

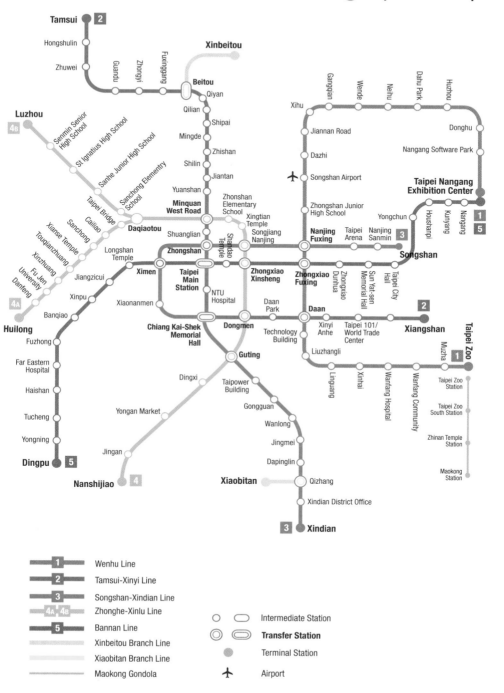

Taipei Metro Map

Tamsui 2
Hongshulin
Zhuwei
Guandu
Zhongyi
Fuxinggang
Xinbeitou
Beitou
Qiyan
Qilian
Shipai
Mingde
Zhishan
Shilin
Jiantan
Yuanshan
Zhonshan Elementary School

Gangqian
Wende
Neihu
Dahu Park
Huzhou
Xihu
Jiannan Road
Dazhi
Songshan Airport
Donghu
Nangang Software Park
Taipei Nangang Exhibition Center

Luzhou
4B
Senmin Senior High School
St Ignatius High School
Sanhe Junior High School
Sanchong Elementry School
Taipei Bridge
Cailiao
Sanchong
Xianse Temple
Touqianzhuang
Xinzhuang
Fu Jen University
Danfeng
4A
Xinpu
Banqiao
Huilong

Minquan West Road
Xingtian Temple
Songjiang Nanjing
Zhongshan Junior High School
Yongchun
Houshanpi
Kunyang
Nangang
1
5

Daqiaotou
Shuanglian
Longshan Temple
Jiangzicui
Zhongshan
Shandao Temple
Nanjing Fuxing
Taipei Arena
Nanjing Sanmin
3
Songshan

Ximen
Taipei Main Station
NTU Hospital
Zhongxiao Xinsheng
Zhongxiao Fuxing
Zhongxiao Dunhua
Sun Yat-sen Memorial Hall
Taipei City Hall

Xiaonanmen
Daan Park
Daan
2
Xiangshan

Chiang Kai-Shek Memorial Hall
Dongmen
Technology Building
Xinyi Anhe
Taipei 101/World Trade Center
Muzha
Taipei Zoo
1

Guting
Liuzhangli
Linguang
Xinhai
Wanfang Hospital
Wanfang Community
Taipei Zoo Station

Fuzhong
Far Eastern Hospital
Haishan
Dingxi
Taipower Building
Taipei Zoo South Station

Tucheng
Yongan Market
Gongguan
Zhinan Temple Station

Yongning
Wanlong
Jingmei
Maokong Station

Jingan
Dingpu 5
Dapinglin
Xiaobitan
Qizhang
Xindian District Office
Nanshijiao 4
Xindian
3

Legend

▬ 1 ▬	Wenhu Line
▬ 2 ▬	Tamsui-Xinyi Line
▬ 3 ▬	Songshan-Xindian Line
▬ 4A 4B ▬	Zhonghe-Xinlu Line
▬ 5 ▬	Bannan Line
▬▬▬	Xinbeitou Branch Line
▬▬▬	Xiaobitan Branch Line
▬▬▬	Maokong Gondola

○ ⬭ Intermediate Station
◎ ⬒ **Transfer Station**
● Terminal Station
✈ Airport

Zhijiang Rd
Henyi Street
Wuhua Street
Zhongqing Rd
Shilin Yeshi
(Shilin Night Market)
Yuanshan Dafandian
(Grand Hotel)
Zh
(National Reve
Martyr

Sun Yat-sen Freeway
Belan Road

Sun Yat-sen Freeway
→ Taiwan Taoyuan International Airport,
Taoyuan →

Renxian Street
Hebei North Road
Lanzhou Rd
Dunhuang Rd
Baoan Gong
(Baoan Temple)
Kong Miao
(Confucius Temple)
Ertong Yule Zhongxin
(Children's Entertainment Center)
Huabo Gongyuan
(Taipei Expo
Park)
Lin A
Guzu
(Lin
Home

Zhengyi North Rd
Sanhe Road
Renai Street
Sanchong Elementary School
Yanping North Road
Kulun St
Taibei Gushi Guan
(Taipei Story House)
Mengxiang Weilai
Tianshi Sheng
(Pavilion of D
Pavilion of Fut
Pavilion of An

Yuanshan
Minzu
West Road
Chongqing North Road Sec. 3
Dalong Street
Chengde Road
Taibei Shili Meishuguan
(Taipei Fine Arts Museum)
Minzu East Road
Xinsheng Expy
Jilin Road

Zhiqiang Road
Changji St
Dehui St
Nongan
Zongshan Elementary School
Taiwan Visit
Association

SANCHONG
Zhengyi S. Road
Taipei Bridge
Daqiaotou
Minquan West Road
Nongan St
Minquan West Road
Jinzhou
Zhongshan N. Rd Sec. 2
Xintian
(Xingtian T

Zhongzheng Rd
Datong S. Road
Cailiao
Zhengyi S. Road
Taipei Bridge
Dihua Street
Yanping N. Rd
Nangang N. Rd
Jinxi Street
DATONG
Linsen N.
Xingtian
Street
Minshe

Chongqan St
Huanhe South Road
Gu Xianrong Guzhai
(Koo Xian-rong Residence)
Minquan West Road
Jinzhou
Zhongshan N. Rd Sec. 2
Xinsheng Expy
Jilin Road

New Taipei Expressway
Dadaocheng Matou
(Dadaocheng Wharf)
Minsheng West Road
Shuanglian
Nanjing E. Rd Sec. 2

Lin Liuxin Jinian Ouxi Bowuguan
(Lin Liu-hsin Puppet Theatre Museum)
Dihua
Guide St
Xiahai Chenghuang Miao
(Xiahai City God Temple)
Nanjing
W.
Zhongshan Road

Tamsui
Zhongxiao Bridge
Changan West Road
Taibei Dangdai Yishu Guan
(Museum of Contemporary Art)
Changan E. Rd Sec. 1

Zhongxing Bridge
Beimen
Civic Blvd
Civic Boulevard

Huanhe Expressway
Zhongxiao
West
Rd
Beimen
(North Gate)
Taibei Huochezhan
(Taipei Main Train Station)
Beiping E Rd
Shandao Si
(Shandao Temple)
Zhongxiao E. Rd
Stiandao
Temple

Xining S. Rd
Boai Rd
Taipei Main Station
Xinguang Motian Dalou
(Shin Kong Life Tower)
Zhongxiao E. Rd
Xinsheng Expy

XIMENDING
Chengdu Rd
Ximen Honglou
(The Red House)
Ximen
Guoli Taiwan Bowuguan
(National Taiwan Museum)
ER-ERBA HEPING GONGYUAN
(2-28 MEMORIAL PEACE PARK)
NTU Hospital
Jinan
Linsen N. Rd
Hangzhou N. Rd Sec. 1
Jina

Huajiang Yanya Ziran Gongyuan
(Huajiang Waterfowl Nature Park)
Kangding Road
Kunming Street
ZHONGZHENG
Zhonghua Road
Yanping S. Rd
Chongqing S. Road Sec. 1
Zhongshan North Road Sec. 1
Renai Rd Sec. 1
Renai Rd Sec. 1

Banqiao, Lin Ben Yuan Yuandi
(Lin Family Mansion and Garden)
Guilin
Huaxi Jie Yeshi
(Snake Alley)
Longshan Si
(Longshan Temple)
Guangzhou
Boai
Zongtong Fu
(Presidential Office Building)
Ketagalan Blvd
Guojia Yinyueting
(National Concert Hall)

Longshan Temple
Aiguo W. Rd
Guojia Xiju Yuan
(National Theater)
Zhongzheng Jiniantang
(Chiang Kai-shek Memorial Hall)
Dongme
Xinyi

Heping W. Rd
Sec. 3
Guangzhou
Street
Xiaonanmen
CKS Memorial Hall
Aiguo E. Road
Roosevelt Rd Sec. 1
Lishue St
Qin
(Tai

Huanhe S. Rd Sec. 2
Guoli Lishi Bowuguan
(National Museum of History)
Heping W. Rd Sec. 2
Nanchang Rd Sec. 1
Hangzhou S. Rd Sec. 1
Jinhua
Jinshan S. Rd Sec. 2
Chaozhou St

WANHUA
Juguang Road
Mengjia Boulevard
Xichang
Wanda Rd
ZHIWU YUAN
Nanhai Road
Guting
Heping E. Rd Sec. 1

Huanhe S. Rd Sec. 2
Xiyuan Road Sec. 2
Dongyuan St
Baoxing Street
Tingzhou Road Sec. 1
Guoxing Rd
Tingzhou Road Sec. 2
Roosevelt Rd Sec. 3

Huanhemanan Expressway
Wanda Road
Dinghan Rd
Zhonghua Road
YOUTH PARK
Xindian
Shuiyuan Expressway
Zhongzheng Bridge
Shuiyuan Expy
Taipower Building
Jian